Nikolaj Malchow-Møller and
Allan H. Würtz

An insight into

statistics

for the social sciences

Hans Reitzels Forlag

An Insight into Statistics
– for the Social Sciences
1st edition, 1st printrun
© the authors and Hans Reitzels Forlag 2014

Publishing editor: Martin Laurberg
Translation: Tam McTurk
Copy editor: Dorte Steiness
Cover design: Imperiet
Typesetting: Odd Design
Printing: Ednas Print
Printed in Slovenia 2014
ISBN: 978-87-412-5691-7

hansreitzel.dk

An insight into
statistics
for the social sciences

Contents

Preface

This book is designed for an introductory course (10 ECTS credits) in statistics for students in bachelor programmes within social science. It is relevant to subjects such as economics, business economics, psychology, political science and sociology.

Chapters 2–7 cover probability theory (populations, probability measures, stochastic variables, distributions, descriptive measures and stochastic processes), while chapters 9–18 cover statistical methods (estimators, hypothesis tests and confidence intervals for estimators, hypothesis testing of relationships and linear regression).

Throughout the book, focus is on explaining the relationship between probability theory and statistical methods. As such, chapters 1 and 8 explain that a common task in social science is to use a sample to obtain knowledge about an unknown population – e.g. the average income of the citizens of a country, or their attitudes towards a political issue. However, in order to deal with the uncertainty that a sample entails, we must be familiar with probability theory.

The book also focuses on understanding relationships between different variables, which are all affected by uncertainty. This could be the relationship between people's income and their consumption of certain goods, which is a typical subject for an empirical study in the social sciences. Within social science we typically do not have the option of conducting laboratory experiments, where it is possible to explore what happens to one variable (consumption) when you change another variable (income). The statistical methods employed must instead take into account that both values are stochastic. As a result, we focus on explaining concepts such as conditional probability and conditional expectation, as well as methods for testing relationships between stochastic variables.

Chapters 17–18 also apply this approach to linear regression – unlike many other textbooks, in which it is assumed that the explanatory variables are not stochastic. Although this may seem to result in more cumbersome notation, it does ensure greater consistency with the rest of the book. It also represents a more realistic approach, reflecting the typical situations that we encounter in practice within social science.

The authors would like to thank Viggo Høst and Lars Skipper for their input and comments. We would also like to thank editor Torben Bystrup Jacobsen for his thorough review of the manuscript to the previous edition of this book. We are also extremely grateful to editor Martin Laurberg of Hans Reitzels Forlag for all his work and patience in bringing this current edition to fruition.

Nikolaj Malchow-Møller and Allan H. Würtz
July 2014

1 Statistics and knowledge

When is something pure chance, and when is there an underlying relationship? This is the key question around which the whole of this book revolves. Statistics provide the answer by helping us gain insight into situations characterised by uncertainty.

Statistics help us to examine relationships and make predictions. Indeed, statistical analysis will often include elements of both. In order to predict the demand for laptops, for example, it is important to be aware of consumer income levels and the relationship between income and consumption. *Statistics* help us with this.

Statistical analyses help us to connect our ideas (theories) to the real world via observations of the latter. In the case of the laptops, we may have a theory about the relationship between income and demand for computers. Using observations about consumer income and purchasing patterns for computers, statistics will help us either quantify the relationship or prove that none exists. Analyses of this kind have to take into account multiple forms of *uncertainty*. One source of uncertainty is that we are only observing a limited number of consumers. However, uncertainty also exists due to circumstances that it may not be possible to observe but that also affect the demand for computers, such as consumers' socio-economic backgrounds and lifestyles. As a result, tools are needed to handle uncertainty. *Probability theory* provides these tools.

This book is therefore about both statistics and probability theory. Section 1.1 looks at a number of real-life problems for which we will develop tools for analysis in this book. Section 1.2 puts the methods for achieving insight via the use of statistics into a more scientific/theoretical (methodological) context, and Section 1.3 provides a brief overview of the contents of the rest of the book.

1.1   Examples

In the example above, the aim was to predict the demand for laptops by determining a relationship between income and demand. This section contains some further examples of problems for which statistical analysis helps to provide an answer.

Example 1.1: A lottery draw

In a lottery draw, 36 balls numbered from 1 to 36 are placed in a large bowl. Seven balls are pulled from the bowl. It costs DKK 4.00 per lottery ticket (i.e. to pick seven numbers). John would very much like to know the probability of winning the DKK 5 million jackpot if he buys two tickets. He is also curious to know how much he can "expect" to win.

Example 1.2: Packing screws

A company produces 35 mm screws on a newly purchased machine. The screws are automatically packaged in boxes of 500. However, even if the packing machine is set to 500, the boxes do not always contain exactly 500 screws. This results in complaints from customers. Management demands that a maximum of 1% of boxes contain fewer than 500 screws. The packaging machine has to be reset to comply with this requirement. The question is, therefore, how many screws per box the machine should be set to.

Example 1.3: Defective cars

In a car factory, experience shows that 0.8% of finished vehicles suffer from serious defects. A leading dealer places an order for 1,000 cars. Management is concerned that the dealer will terminate the contract if too many of the vehicles have serious defects, and wishes to know the risk of more than 10 of them being in that category. The factory has also just launched a new production line for its latest model. To improve production processes, management wishes to know what proportion of cars from this line will be defective. More precisely, will the proportion be the same as for the existing production line?

A Danish ice-cream maker is considering entering the Swedish market, and has asked the strategy department to analyse the potential. The department needs to know the level of demand for ice-cream in Sweden in order to assess whether it would be worthwhile commencing sales and marketing activities. It commissions market research. However, it is unsure of how many people to include in the study and how to choose them so that the survey is not too expensive but is sufficiently accurate. The cheapest option would be to interview people on the streets of Malmö, but the strategy department has doubts about the usefulness of data obtained by that method.

In the run-up to another EU referendum in Denmark, public interest in the outcome of the vote is huge. A polling company attempts to predict the outcome. It polls a sample of 1,000 people, and wants to ascertain the margin of error, or uncertainty, both for the percentages of yes and no voters and for the overall result. The company would also like to know how many people it would need to poll to reduce the margin of error to 1%.

In all of these examples, the problems are rooted in some form of uncertainty. In Example 1.1, it is uncertain which lottery balls will be drawn. In Example 1.5, it is uncertain what proportion of Danes will vote yes. In both situations, statistical methods help us to manage the uncertainty. However, different kinds of analysis are required to answer the questions in these two examples. The next section elaborates on this methodological difference and outlines the structure of the rest of the book.

1.2   Deduction and induction

All of the problems and analyses in this book share the same basic set-up – that is, there is a population of elements from which a sample is extracted. The population might, for example, consist of Danish voters. By conducting an opinion poll, we take a sample of the voters. The population might also, for example, be the 36 lottery balls in the machine, in which case the sample consists of the seven balls that are drawn.

Figure 1.1:
Basic set-up

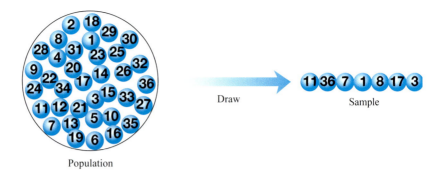

Population

Draw

Sample

Two general types of analyses are possible in this kind of set-up: *inductive* analyses and *deductive* analyses (Figure 1.1).

Deduction is used in cases where we know about the population and want to learn about the sample. The lottery draw in Example 1.1 is an analysis of this type. In this case, we know the population down to the smallest detail. We know that it consists of 36 balls of equal size, and we know what is written on every single one of them. However, we do not know what the sample will look like. The question is therefore how we can use our knowledge of the population and the method of selection to predict something about the sample, i.e. the seven balls that will be drawn. What is the probability, for example, of drawing the seven balls with the numbers 1, 2, 3, 4, 5, 6 and 7?

Induction is used in cases where we know about the sample and want to learn about the population, for example, in the opinion poll in Example 1.5. In this case, nobody knows the proportions of yes and no voters in the population, so an opinion poll is conducted to find out. This involves taking a sample of all those eligible to vote (the population) and observing its content. The yes proportion of the sample is then used to estimate the proportion of the population (i.e. the total electorate) who will vote yes.

In other words: deduction utilises our knowledge of the general (the population) to learn about the specific (the sample). Induction, on the other hand, uses our knowledge of the specific (the sample) to learn about the general (the population).

Figure 1.2:
Deduction and induction

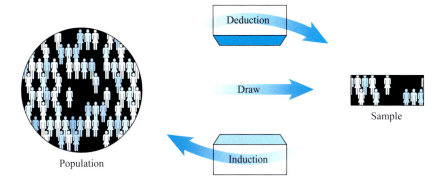

All of the problems in this book fall into one of these two categories. Making a deduction consists of applying probability theory (e.g. if we want to calculate the probability of throwing a three at dice or winning the lottery). Induction uses statistics (e.g. when determining voting patterns based on a sample). As we will see, there is a very close correlation between the two types of analysis, but it is important to be aware of the conceptual difference.

The difference between inductive and deductive analyses has, however, perplexed even the purported master of deduction: *"I have a turn both for observation and deduction,"* Sherlock Holmes tells Dr Watson.[1] This is somewhat surprising, as detective work is a prime example of induction rather than deduction. Sherlock Holmes uses the few clues that he finds (the sample) to gain knowledge about what lies behind them (the crime).

The interaction between the two types of analysis arises because the statistical methods are based on probability theory. We use the sample to infer about the population, but in order to do so we must first know something about how, and with what probability, the sample was obtained. For this, we use probability theory. We must therefore first learn about probability theory before we turn to the statistical methods.

Chapters 2 to 7 cover the tools from *probability theory* used in deductive analyses. Equipped with these tools, we look at situations commonly encountered in practice, where we lack knowledge about the population and try to remedy this by means of analysing a sample. Chapters 8 to 18 thus cover the *statistical methods* used for inductive analyses.

---

1   A Study in Scarlet, Chapter 2, in: Arthur Conan Doyle, *The Penguin Complete Sherlock Holmes*, Penguin Books Ltd, London, 1981. Ironically, the chapter from which the above quotation is taken is called "The Science of Deduction".

1.3   A brief summary of the chapters

Chapter 2 provides a detailed introduction to the population concept, including how to describe a population and its elements. Chapter 3 shows how to formalise the uncertainty associated with populations and samples. To allow for more complex analyses of uncertainty, Chapter 4 shows how to model uncertainty using stochastic variables and their probability distributions. By modelling uncertainty in this way, we can actually analyse complex problems involving uncertainties using well-known, simple mathematical techniques such as addition and multiplication. Chapters 3 and 4 are absolutely key to an understanding of the other chapters in the book.

Uncertainty is represented by means of a probability distribution. However, just as a detailed Ordnance Survey map does not provide a particularly good view of the main roads in the area, a probability distribution can be confusing if what you really require is an overview of the most important aspects of the uncertainty in question. In Chapter 5, therefore, we introduce descriptive measures for probability distributions, which provide summaries of the uncertainty expressed in single numbers. In Chapter 6, we describe various selected probability distributions that have proved very useful for solving practical problems. In Chapter 7, we go a step further and introduce stochastic processes, which are useful in practical problems where time is involved. This chapter is more technical than the others, and can be skipped without negatively affecting your understanding of the other chapters.

Chapter 8 serves as an introduction to inductive analysis, which forms the subject matter of the remaining chapters. The purpose of inductive analysis is to learn about the characteristics of a given population. The first important step in this process is to choose a sample. In Chapter 9, therefore, we discuss different ways of selecting samples.

Chapters 10–14 deal with inductive analysis in cases where we wish to learn about a single characteristic in the population. We show how to construct an estimator, i.e. an estimate of a descriptive measure calculated on the basis of a sample. How an estimator is constructed depends on the manner in which the sample is drawn. In Chapter 10, we look at an estimator for a mean value in the case of a random sample, while Chapter 11 looks at cases in which the sample is selected in other, often more cost-effective ways. Chapter 12 deals with estimators for descriptive measures other than the mean value.

In Chapter 13 we demonstrate how to establish a confidence interval for an unknown population size. Confidence intervals are a way of describing the uncertainty associated with an estimator, since it is based on a sample.

Before you prepare a statistical analysis, you will often have a (more or less tangible) theory regarding the population. To test such a theory, you must first devise hypotheses to test by use of a sample. This is discussed in Chapter 14.

From Chapter 15 onwards, we focus on methods of studying relationships between the characteristics of a population. Social scientists are often interested in analysing such relationships, for example, between income and consumption, or how a person's behaviour relates to his/her experiences. In Chapters 15 and 16, we introduce methods to test hypotheses about relationships using both quantitative data (Chapter 15) and qualitative data (Chapter 16).

Chapters 17 and 18 go a step further and formulate specific relationships. In Chapter 17 we look at the most commonly used specification of such a relationship: the simple linear regression model. Chapter 18 extends this to the multiple linear regression model.

2 Populations

In a statistical context, a population consists of a collection of elements (e.g. individuals, companies, countries, customers or more abstract objects). From a population, we can draw a sample. Understanding the interaction between a population and the extraction of a sample is crucial in statistical analyses, and is therefore a key element of this book. Before we examine this in greater depth in the following chapters, let us first introduce the concepts of populations and their elements.

This chapter will only deal with real populations. In Section 2.1 we explain precisely what is meant by a real population and its elements. In Section 2.2, we show how to represent and compare the qualitative and quantitative characteristics of the individual elements in a population.

Since a population may contain many elements, it is often useful to summarise them in an orderly fashion. Section 2.3 shows how to do this with graphical tools (e.g. a histogram) or single numbers (e.g. a mean value). The section also concentrates on summarising a single characteristic of the elements in a population (e.g. age or income). Section 2.4 looks at how to describe relationships between such characteristics in a population.

2.1 Real populations

A *population* is a collection of elements, each of which can have a number of characteristics. For example, a population may consist of all Danish citizens, each of whom has individual characteristics such as age, gender, education, residence, job and income. Although the elements in a population may have many different characteristics, our focus is usually only on those that are of interest to the study concerned, such as age and/or income.

When both the elements of a population and their characteristics actually exist, we call this a *real population*. A real population is, in principle, observable. In later chapters, we will argue in favour of the usefulness of also defining the more abstract type of population referred to as a *super-population*.

2.2   Measurement scales

In order to conduct statistical analyses, you must first be able to measure the elements' characteristics. Measurements are calculated according to different scales. The type of scale has implications for the methods of analysis that are applicable. In this section, we look more closely at different types of scales.

This book works exclusively with characteristics that can be represented with a numerical value. This is not as restrictive as it may sound. Think, for example, of a person for whom the relevant characteristic is that she is for or against a proposed piece of legislation. On the face of it, this may not seem to have much to do with numbers, but we can represent "for" with the numerical value 0 and "against" with the numerical value 1.

Different characteristics are measured according to different scales. For example, a person's marital status (single, married, divorced, widowed) is measured against a different scale than their weight in kilograms. Since the type of scale is of great significance to the choice of analysis method, measurements are divided into qualitative and quantitative. Whenever the four basic arithmetical operations (addition, subtraction, multiplication and division) cannot be applied meaningfully to the values obtained by a measurement, then that measurement is said to be *qualitative*. If they can be used meaningfully, then the measurement is said to be *quantitative*.

A distinction is also made between two types of qualitative measurement scales: *nominal* and *ordinal*. Similarly, we distinguish between two kinds of scales in quantitative measurements: *interval scales* and *ratio scales*. These subdivisions are illustrated in Table 2.1, along with the mathematical operations that can be applied within each of the four measurement scales. The four scales will be explained in greater depth in the following sections.

Table 2.1:
Measurements, measurement scales and mathematical operations

Measurement	Measurement scale	Meaningful mathematical operations
Qualitative	Nominal	$=, \neq$
	Ordinal	$=, \neq, >, <$
Quantitative	Interval	$=, \neq, >, <, +, -$
	Ratio	$=, \neq, >, <, +, -, \cdot, /$

2.2.1 Nominal scale

Hair colour is an example of a characteristic with a nominal scale of measurement. Assume, for the purposes of illustration, that hair can only be white, black or red, and that white is represented by the value 1, black by the value 2 and red by 3. It makes no sense to use the four arithmetical operations in this instance (e.g. multiplying the white by the red). Nor does it make any sense to talk about red being greater than black, even though red is represented by the numerical value 3, while black "only" has the numerical value 2. In fact, all you can say in this example is that a person's hair colour is equal to or different from the colour of someone else's. In other words, you can differentiate the various values on the scale: 1 = white, 2 = black, 3 = red. A nominal scale of measurement is therefore characterised by the fact that there is no structure or link between the values on the scale.

2.2.2 Ordinal scale

Unlike a nominal scale, with an ordinal scale it is meaningful to talk about some values being greater or less than others. If, for example, you want to measure students' views about the quality of the coffee in their canteen by offering three possible responses on a questionnaire – "dissatisfied", "satisfied" or "highly satisfied" – these can be represented by the numerical values 1, 2 and 3. In this case, it makes sense to say that "dissatisfied" (= 1) is less than "satisfied" (= 2), which in turn is less than "highly satisfied" (= 3). An ordinal scale is thus characterised by the values of the scale being ranked in order. On an ordinal scale, however, it does not make sense to evaluate the size of the difference between two values. For example, it cannot be concluded that the difference between "satisfied" and "very satisfied" is the same as between "dissatisfied" and "satisfied". In other words, the numeric values cannot be subtracted from each other in a meaningful way.

2.2.3   Interval scale

On an interval scale, it makes sense to talk about the difference between two values. For example, the difference in body temperature between two individuals with temperatures of +37° and +38° Celsius is 1° Celsius, which is the same as the difference between two other people with temperatures of +38° and +39°, respectively. On the other hand, it is not meaningful to talk about a relative relationship between the two temperatures measured in Celsius. Although it might appear to make sense to say that +40° Celsius is twice as hot as +20°, the problem with this becomes clear when we try to compare +30° Celsius with –10° Celsius. In order to make relative comparisons meaningful, a natural (i.e. non-arbitrary) zero point is needed. A natural zero point is defined by the absence of the characteristics in question. A temperature of 0° Celsius does not indicate an absence of heat.

2.2.4   Ratio scale

A ratio scale is an interval scale with a natural zero point. For example, a person's weight has a natural zero point – the point at which s/he weighs nothing (and is therefore not present). In this context it does makes sense to talk about the relative ratio between two values. For example, one man weighs 210.4 kg, which is twice as much as another man weighing 105.2 kg. The values on a ratio scale can also be integers, for example the number of times a person has been married. The natural zero point for the number of marriages is zero (i.e. never having been married).

2.2.5   Choice of scale

It is worth noting that it is often possible to measure the same characteristic on different scales. Sometimes the measurement scale is dictated by the physical parameters of that which is being measured. However, an element of subjectivity often comes into play too. For example, the measurement of temperatures in Celsius belongs on an interval scale, whereas the measurement of temperatures in Kelvin belongs on a ratio scale.

In the social sciences, it is often the case that the object of measurement cannot be precisely defined in physical terms – for example, a person's intelligence or a person's attitude towards the quality of the coffee in the canteen. This means that it is not always obvious how the measurement scale should be designed and interpreted. There is, therefore, close interaction between the measurement of a characteristic and the analyst performing the measurement.

2.3 Summarising a single characteristic

To provide an overview of a population's interesting aspects, it is useful to employ methods that summarise certain characteristics of the population concerned. This is particularly important when the population has many elements. Even with a population of just 50 people, it can be difficult to establish an overview of, for example, their income or age based solely on observing the 50 different values for these. In this section, we will therefore look at a range of graphical and numerical methods of summarising and illustrating selected characteristics of the elements of a real population.

For this purpose, it is relevant to introduce a little notation. Therefore, let N_{pop} be the number of elements in the population, let a_j be the jth element's value of the characteristic a (e.g. income) and let b_j be the jth element's value of another characteristic b (e.g. consumption), where j is an integer between 1 and N_{pop}.

Example 2.1: Income and consumption – part 1

In a population consisting of five individuals, $N_{pop} = 5$, each individual has a monthly income in thousands of DKK (characteristic a) and a monthly consumption of groceries (characteristic b). The values for these characteristics are shown in Table 2.2.

Table 2.2: The population's elements

j (individual)	a_j (income in tDKK)	b_j (consumption in tDKK)
1	36	9
2	28	5
3	25	6
4	32	8
5	28	6

Income for individual number 3 is thus $a_3 = 25$ (tDKK), while individuals 2 and 5 have the same income $a_2 = a_5 = 28$ (tDKK). Consumption for individual number 5 is $b_5 = 6$ (tDKK).

2.3.1   Frequencies and histograms

One way to summarise a characteristic of a population is to calculate the proportion of elements in the population that have a particular value of the characteristic. To this end, we define the *relative frequency function,* which provides these proportions. Let z be a value of a characteristic. The relative frequency function, $g(z)$, is then defined as follows:

> **The relative frequency function**, $g(z)$, for a characteristic in a real population, is defined by:
>
> $$g(z) = \frac{no.\ of\ elements\ with\ the\ value\ z}{no.\ of\ elements\ in\ the\ population}$$

The number of elements in the population is equal to N_{pop}. The numerator in the fraction above is also called the *frequency,* and $g(z)$ is therefore the *relative frequency* of elements with the value z. The relative frequency function can be visualised by depicting it in a *bar chart,* as shown in the following example.

Example 2.2: Income and consumption – part 2

In Example 2.1, the proportion of elements with an income of 28 is equal to $2/5 = 0.4$. The relative frequency function calculated for all of the different levels of income in the population is:

$$g(z) = \begin{cases} 0.2 & if \quad z = 25 \\ 0.4 & if \quad z = 28 \\ 0.2 & if \quad z = 32 \\ 0.2 & is \quad z = 36 \end{cases}$$

For all other values of z, $g(z) = 0$. The relative frequency of income 28 is thus 0.4. The bar chart in Figure 2.1 represents relative frequencies by the height of the different bars.

Figure 2.1:

Bar chart

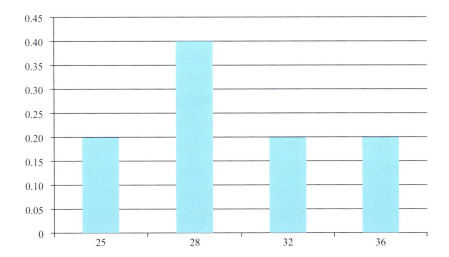

When illustrating many different values of a characteristic, a bar chart quickly becomes unmanageable. Instead, it is often useful to create a *histogram*. A histogram is similar to a bar chart, but differs in that it merges values that are close together. As a result, histograms are particularly useful for quantitative measurements. In a bar chart, the height of a bar indicates the relative frequency of a given value, whereas in a histogram the area of a bar indicates the relative frequency of a group.

A histogram is constructed as follows. First, the values of a characteristic are divided into intervals. For example, if the values are between 0 and 100, you can have 10 intervals of width 10, where the first interval contains all values greater than or equal to 0 and less than or equal to 10. The second interval contains values greater than 10 and less than or equal to 20, and so on. Note that a value must belong to one, and only one, group. In this example, the first interval is called the 5-interval because 5 is the midpoint.

The next step is to construct a bar, the area of which corresponds to the relative frequency of the elements in the group. If a group contains 25% of the elements and has a width of 10, the height of the bar must therefore be: $0.25/10 = 0.025$ (or 2.5 if you use percentages). Example 2.3 illustrates the difference between a bar chart and a histogram.

A football team's goals in a given season were scored by 12 different players. These players therefore form a population in which the elements have the following values: 1, 2, 3, 4, 5, 6, 7, 8, 13, 13, 13 and 17, representing the number of goals scored by each player. A bar chart of the relative frequency is shown in Figure 2.2:

Figure 2.2:

Bar chart

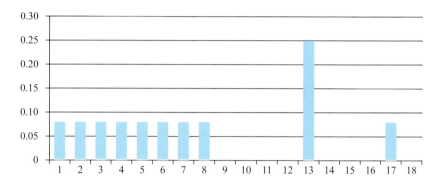

As the bar chart shows, the value 13 accounts for 25% of the values. You can now construct a histogram for the values by dividing them into intervals of width 5. The first interval consists of the values 0 to 5, referred to as the 2.5-interval. The next consists of the values 5 to 10, referred to as the 7.5-interval. Third, the values 10 through 15, referred to as the 12.5-interval. Finally, the last group of values, from 15 to 20, is called the 17.5-interval. Figure 2.3 shows the histogram.

Figure 2.3:

Histogram – version 1

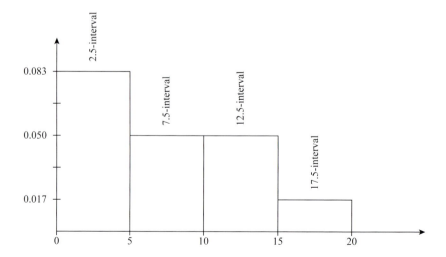

Since each interval is of width 5, and since the 12.5-interval contains 25% of the elements in the population (3 out of 12), the height of this bar is $0.25/5 = 0.05$. Correspondingly, the 2.5-interval comprises a total of 5 elements, so the height of this column is $(5/12)/5 = 0.083$.

When drawing a histogram, it is not necessary for all of the groups to have the same width. For example, the last two intervals could be merged together into a single interval. This group would then have width 10, and since it contains 4 out of 12 elements, the height of the bar would be $(4/12)/10 = 0.033$, as shown in Figure 2.4.

Figure 2.4:

Histogram –
version 2

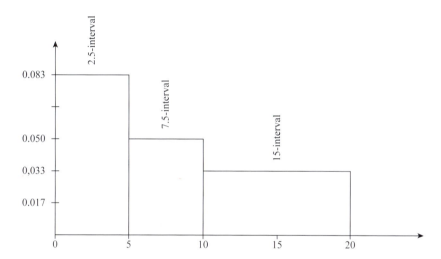

Another type of diagram that illustrates the relative frequency function is a *pie chart*. In a pie chart, the pie represents the whole population, and the various slices represent different values (or groups of values) in the population. A slice's share of the pie then corresponds to its value's relative frequency in the population. If the area of the whole pie equals 1, the area of a slice is therefore given by the relative frequency function. Pie charts are useful for both qualitative and quantitative measurements.

Figure 2.5 shows a pie chart of the incomes in the population from Example 2.1.

Figure 2.5:
Pie chart

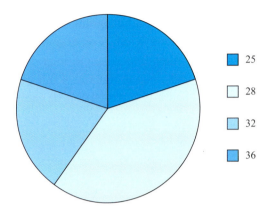

It is sometimes interesting to identify the proportion of the population that has an income less than or equal to a given value – for instance, the proportion of people living below the poverty line. Such proportions are also referred to as cumulative shares or cumulative relative frequencies. Formally, the *cumulative relative frequency function*, $G(z)$, can be defined as follows:

The cumulative relative frequency function, $G(z)$, for a characteristic in a real population is defined by:

$$G(z) = \frac{no. \ of \ elements \ with \ value \ \leq z}{no. \ of \ elements \ in \ the \ population}$$

Frequencies, relative frequencies and cumulative relative frequencies for the population in Example 2.1 are calculated in Table 2.3.

Table 2.3:
Cumulative
relative
frequencies

Values	Frequency	Relative frequency	Relative cumulative frequency
25	1	0.2	0.2
28	2	0.4	0.6
32	1	0.2	0.8
36	1	0.2	1.0

The cumulative relative frequency function of this population is then:

$$G(z) = \begin{cases} 0 & if & z < 25 \\ 0.2 & if & 25 \leq z < 28 \\ 0.6 & if & 28 \leq z < 32 \\ 0.8 & if & 32 \leq z < 36 \\ 1 & if & 36 \leq z \end{cases}$$

From the cumulative relative frequency function, it can be directly deduced that the proportion of the population with an income of no more than 28 is $G(28) = 0.6$. Note that it is also possible to calculate the cumulative relative frequency function of an income value that does not exist in the population. For example, the proportion of the population with an income of a maximum of 33 is equal to 0.8, as $G(33) = 0.8$.

2.3.2   Median and quantiles

Often, it is useful to describe a population by means of just a few pieces of key data. One such key figure is the *median*. A median value divides the elements of the population into two equal sized groups, one of which has values greater than the median, the other of which has values less than the median. Calculating the median is mainly useful in quantitative measurement.

One way of finding the median is to rank all of the values from smallest to largest. The smallest value is defined as $a_{(1)}$. The parentheses around the subscript indicate that these are ranked values. It is therefore not the case that $a_{(1)} = a_1$, where a_1 is the value of the first element. Only if the first element is also the smallest element does $a_{(1)} = a_1$. The second-smallest value in the population is represented by $a_{(2)}$ and the maximum value by $a_{(N_{pop})}$.

The median is the middle-ranked value. For example, if there are 25 elements in a population, then the median is the value of the 13th-smallest element, $a_{(13)}$ – i.e. there are 12 values $a_{(14)}, ..., a_{(25)}$ that are at least as large as $a_{(13)}$, and 12 values, $a_{(1)}, ..., a_{(12)}$ that are at least as small as $a_{(13)}$.

If the population has an even number of elements, then no single element divides the population into two equal parts. In a population of 10 elements, the median is instead the average of the fifth- and sixth-smallest elements, namely: $0.5 \cdot (a_{(5)} + a_{(6)})$.

From this, we can extrapolate a general rule for calculating the median value of a real population:

The median of a characteristic a in a real population is given by:

$$median = \begin{cases} a_{(0.5 \cdot N_{pop} + 0,5)} & \text{if } N_{pop} \text{ is } \text{uneven} \\ 0.5 \cdot \left(a_{(0.5 \cdot N_{pop})} + a_{(0.5 \cdot N_{pop} + 1)} \right) & \text{if } N_{pop} \text{ is } \text{even} \end{cases}$$

where N_{pop} is the number of elements in the population and $a_{(j)}$ is the jth-lowest ranked element of the population.

Example 2.6: Income and consumption – part 5

Table 2.4 shows ranked income values for the elements in the population from Example 2.1.

Table 2.4:
Ranked values

Ranking, j	Ranked value $a_{(j)}$
1	25
2	28
3	28
4	32
5	36

Since N_{pop} is an odd number in this example, the median is $a_{(0.5 \cdot 5 + 0.5)} = a_{(3)} = 28$

The median is an example of a *quantile*. In general, a *p-quantile* is a value such that the share p of the elements in the population have a value less than (or equal to) the value of the p-quantile. p is therefore always between 0 and 1. For example, if you study the age of individuals in a population, then the 0.1-quantile marks the age at which 10% are younger and 90% are older. The median is therefore also a 0.5-quantile.

As for the median, we can posit an arithmetical rule for the calculation of a p-quantile in a real population. For this purpose, it is practical to define $[x]$ to mean the integer value of a number, x. For example, $[5.5] = 5$ and $[831.97] = 831$. Then you can compute the p-quantile as follows:

The p-quantile of a characteristic a in a real population is given by:

$$p - quantile = \begin{cases} a_{\left(\left[p \cdot N_{pop} + 1\right]\right)} & \text{if } p \cdot N_{pop} \text{ is } not \text{ a integer} \\ \frac{1}{2}\left(a_{\left(p \cdot N_{pop}\right)} + a_{\left(p \cdot N_{pop} + 1\right)}\right) & \text{if } p \cdot N_{pop} \text{ is a integer} \end{cases}$$

where N_{pop} is the number of elements in the population, $a_{(j)}$ is the jth-lowest ranked element in the population, and "[ ]" indicates the integer value of a number.

Example 2.7: Income and consumption – part 6

For the population in Example 2.1, the 0.75-quantile is: $a_{\left(\left[0.75 \cdot 5 + 1\right]\right)} = a_{\left(\left[4.75\right]\right)} = a_{(4)} = 32$, as $0.75 \cdot N_{pop} = 0.75 \cdot 5 = 3.75$ is not an integer.

The 0.1-, 0.25-, 0.75- and 0.9-quantiles are often utilised when summarising a population using quantiles. Along with the median, these figures provide a good picture of the distribution of the values in the population.

There are some five million people in Denmark. Table 2.5 is based on Statistics Denmark's figures for January 2008, and shows selected quantiles for the age in years of Danish men and women.

Table 2.5:
Quantiles for women's and men's ages in Denmark

Quantiles	0.1	0.25	0.5	0.75	0.9
Women	8	20	40	58	72
Men	7	19	38	56	68

The table shows that a higher proportion of men are young, compared with women. In other words, half of the men are aged 38 or under, while half of the women are aged 40 or over.

2.3.3   Box plot

In a box plot (also called a "box-and-whisker plot"), you plot the minimum value, the 0.25-quantile, the median, the 0.75-quantile and the highest value in the population, as shown in Figure 2.6. Graphically, lines are drawn to connect the minimum value with the 0.25-quantile and the 0.75-quantile with the maximum value. A rectangle is then drawn, with the 0.25-quantile and the 0.75-quantile at either end. Finally, the median is marked by a vertical line through the rectangle. A box plot is useful, for example, for comparing different populations.

Figure 2.6:
Box plot

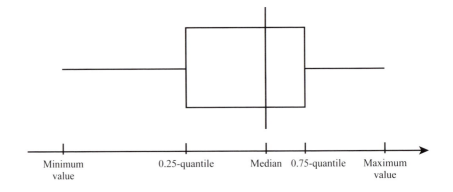

2.3.4   Mean value and variance

For quantitative measurements, it is possible to calculate additional key figures to describe main characteristics of the population. One such figure is the *mean value*. The mean value of a characteristic a in a real population is defined as follows:

> **The mean value** of a characteristic a in a real population is given by:
>
> $$\mu_a = \frac{1}{N_{pop}} \cdot \left(a_1 + a_2 + \ldots + a_{N_{pop}}\right) = \frac{1}{N_{pop}} \sum_{j=1}^{N_{pop}} a_j$$
>
> Where N_{pop} is the number of elements in the population and $a_1, a_2, \ldots, a_{N_{pop}}$ are the different values of the characteristic a in the population.

The sum symbol $\sum_{j=1}^{N_{pop}} a_j$ means that you add up all of the values of a in the population. The mean value is thus the average value of a characteristic in the population. This is the value one should give to each element in the population if the sum in the population was to be equally divided among the elements.

Example 2.9: Income and consumption – part 7

In the population in Example 2.1, the mean value of the income is equal to:

$$\mu_{income} = \frac{1}{5} \cdot \left(36 + 28 + 25 + 32 + 28\right) = 29.8 \ (tDKK)$$

Note that none of the individuals actually has an income equal to the mean value. Similarly, you can show that the mean value of consumption in the population is $\mu_{consumption} = 6.8$ (tDKK).

Two populations can have the same mean value, but still be very different. For example, if a population contains two elements with the values 15 and 13, then its mean value is 14. However, the mean value is also 14 in a population with two elements with the values 26 and 2. However, in the latter population, the values are more spread out than in the former. The mean value is therefore not a complete description of a population.

One key figure that provides an overview of the spread in a population is the *variance*. The variance gives an impression of how the values in the population are distributed around the mean value. The variance for a real population is defined as follows:

> **The variance** of the characteristic a in a real population is given by:
>
> $$\sigma_a^2 = \frac{1}{N_{pop}}\left((a_1 - \mu_a)^2 + (a_2 - \mu_a)^2 + \ldots + (a_{N_{pop}} - \mu_a)^2\right)$$
>
> $$= \frac{1}{N_{pop}}\sum_{j=1}^{N_{pop}}(a_j - \mu_a)^2$$
>
> where N_{pop} is the number of elements in the population, $a_1, a_2, \ldots, a_{N_{pop}}$ are the different values of the characteristic a in the population, and μ_a is the mean value of the characteristic a.

In extreme cases where all of the elements in a population have the same value, $a_1 = a_2 = \ldots = a_{N_{pop}}$, the variance is 0. In all other cases, the variance will be greater than 0. The square root of the variance is often also calculated because it has the same unit of measurement as the values themselves. This is called the *standard deviation* and is defined as follows:

> **The standard deviation** of a characteristic a in a real population is given by:
>
> $$\sigma_a = \sqrt{\sigma_a^2},$$
>
> where σ_a^2 is the variance of the characteristic a in the population.

The standard deviation is a measurement of the average deviation from the mean value in the population.

In the population in Example 2.1, the variance of income is equal to:

$$\sigma^2_{income} = \tfrac{1}{5} \cdot \left(\left(36 - 29.8\right)^2 + \left(28 - 29.8\right)^2 + \left(25 - 29.8\right)^2 \right.$$
$$\left. + \left(32 - 29.8\right)^2 + \left(28 - 29.8\right)^2 \right) = 14.56$$

In this case, the variance is measured in $(tDKK)^2$. The standard deviation is, however, $\sigma_{income} = 3.82$ (tDKK).

The variance or standard deviation can be used to compare two populations, for example, incomes in Denmark and incomes in the USA. We might expect the variance to be somewhat higher in the latter case. In Chapter 5, we will look more closely at both the mean value and the variance.

2.4 Summarising multiple characteristics

Social scientists are often interested in exploring the relationships between different characteristics. For example, many social scientists have studied whether there is a relationship between gender and income, for example, whether men have a tendency to earn more than women. In this section, we will therefore look at a variety of methods, graphical as well as numerical, to summarise and illustrate relationships between two (or more) characteristics in a real population.

2.4.1 Cross-tables and scatter plots

To describe relationships between two characteristics in a population, you can draw up a *cross-table*. A cross-table tabulates the frequencies or relative frequencies of various combinations of the two characteristics in a population.

Consider the following population of 12 elements, in which each element is an individual with two characteristics: (1) the person's gender (female or male) and (2) the person's favourite sport out of three options offered (football, handball or figure skating). The 12 elements in the population are as follows: (man, figure skating), (woman, handball), (woman, figure skating), (woman, figure skating), (man, football), (woman, handball), (man, football), (woman, handball), (man, football), (man, handball), (woman, handball) and (woman, football).

A clearer picture of this population can be obtained by cross-tabulating the frequency of each possible combination of the two characteristics, as shown in Table 2.6.

Table 2.6:
Cross-tabulation of frequencies

	Football	Handball	Figure skating
Woman	1	4	2
Man	3	1	1

You can also cross-tabulate relative frequencies, as shown in Table 2.7.

Table 2.7:
Cross-tabulation of relative frequencies

	Football	Handball	Figure skating
Woman	1/12	4/12	2/12
Man	3/12	1/12	1/12

The differences between men and women are due both to differences in preference and to the different numbers of men and women in the population. In order meaningfully to evaluate the difference between the favourite sports of men and women, it may be more useful to calculate the relative frequencies for each gender separately. This is done in Table 2.8, which shows that the proportion of women who prefer handball is much greater than the proportion of men who prefer handball.

Table 2.8:
Cross-tabulation of relative frequencies by gender

	Football	Handball	Figure skating
Woman	1/7	4/7	2/7
Man	3/5	1/5	1/5

A good visual image of the correlation between two characteristics is provided by a *scatter plot*. In a scatter plot, the values of the two characteristics for each element are indicated by plotting them as a point in a two-dimensional co-ordinate system.

In Figure 2.7, the values of the two characteristics (income and consumption) are plotted for the five elements in the population from Example 2.1. Income (characteristic *a*) is shown on the horizontal axis, while consumption (characteristic *b*) is shown on the vertical axis. Thus, the point on the far right represents the first element in the population, which has income equal to 36 (tDKK) and consumption of 9 (tDKK) (see Table 2.2). From the plot, there seems to be a positive relationship between income and consumption in the population.

Figure 2.7:

Scatter plot

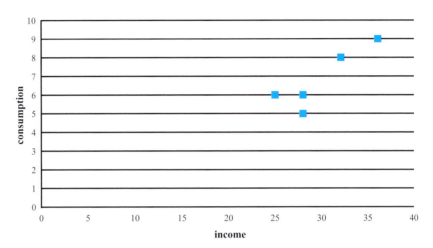

2.4.2   Covariance and correlation

Relationships between characteristics in a population can be summarised using simple key figures. As above, let a_j be the *j*th element's value of the characteristic *a*, while b_j is the *j*th element's value of the characteristic *b*. The *covariance*, $\sigma_{a,b}$, between the two characteristics of a real population is defined as follows:

> **The covariance** between the two characteristics, a and b, in a real population is:
>
> $$\sigma_{a,b} = \frac{1}{N_{pop}}\big((a_1 - \mu_a) \cdot (b_1 - \mu_b) + (a_2 - \mu_a) \cdot (b_2 - \mu_b) + \ldots$$
>
> $$+ \big(a_{N_{pop}} - \mu_a\big) \cdot \big(b_{N_{pop}} - \mu_b\big)\big) = \frac{1}{N_{pop}}\sum_{j=1}^{N_{pop}} (a_j - \mu_a) \cdot (b_j - \mu_b)$$
>
> where $a_1, a_2, \ldots, a_{N_{pop}}$ and $b_1, b_2, \ldots, b_{N_{pop}}$ are the values of the two characteristics for the N_{pop} elements in the population and μ_a and μ_b are the mean values of the two characteristics in the population.

A positive covariance means that there is a tendency for an element with a high value of one characteristic also to have a high value of the second characteristic. If the covariance is negative, it means that there is a tendency for an element with a high value of one characteristic to have a low value of the other characteristic. Here, "high" and "low" values are relative to the mean values of the characteristics concerned.

This can also be seen from the definition of the covariance in the box above. If a_1 and b_1 are both higher (or both lower) than their means, μ_a and μ_b, then the term $(a_1 - \mu_a) \cdot (b_1 - \mu_b)$ will be positive and the first element will therefore add a positive number to the covariance. If, on the other hand, $a_1 > \mu_a$ and $b_1 < \mu_b$ then the term $(a_1 - \mu_a) \cdot (b_1 - \mu_b)$ will be negative and the first element will therefore tend to make the covariance negative.

It is often more informative to look at the correlation coefficient, $\rho_{a,b}$, which is a number between -1 and 1:

> **The correlation coefficient** between two characteristics, a and b, in a real population is:
>
> $$\rho_{a,b} = \frac{\sigma_{a,b}}{\sigma_a \cdot \sigma_b}$$
>
> where $\sigma_{a,b}$ is the covariance between the two characteristics and σ_a and σ_b are the standard deviations of the two characteristics.

The correlation coefficient has the same sign as the covariance. If the correlation coefficient is positive, this indicates a positive relationship between the two characteristics. If the correlation coefficient is negative, there is a negative relationship between the two characteristics.

In the population in Example 2.1, the covariance between income and consumption is:

$$\sigma_{income,consumption} = \tfrac{1}{5} \cdot \big((36 - 29.8) \cdot (9 - 6.8) + (28 - 29.8) \cdot (5 - 6.8)$$
$$+ (25 - 29.8) \cdot (6 - 6.8) + (32 - 29.8) \cdot (8 - 6.8)$$
$$+ (28 - 29.8) \cdot (6 - 6.8) \big) = 4.96$$

The correlation coefficient is:

$$\rho_{income,consumption} = \frac{4.96}{\sqrt{14.56} \cdot \sqrt{2.16}} = 0.88$$

There is thus a positive relationship between income and consumption. Consequently, there is a tendency for individuals with a relatively high level of consumption also to have a relatively high income. This confirms the impression created by the scatter plot in Figure 2.7.

Note that we cannot conclude anything definitive about causality based solely on correlation. In Example 2.13, there is a positive correlation between income and consumption. The reason for this may be that a high income allows you to consume more, and therefore that the income is the reason for the higher consumption. However, it may also be the case that people aspire to a high level of consumption, which necessitates a high income. In this case, the consumption becomes the reason for the higher income. Finally, there may be completely different factors, such as lifestyle choice or social class, that determine both consumption and income. We will return to the discussion of causality later in the book.

2.5   Exercises

1. Review questions:
   a) What is a real population?
   b) Account for the four types of measurement scale.
   c) Explain what is shown by the relative frequency function and the cumulative relative frequency function.
   d) Explain the difference between a bar chart and a histogram.
   e) How do you find the median and a p-quantile in a real population?

f) Explain how to calculate the mean value, variance and standard deviation in a real population.

g) What do a cross-table and a scatter plot show?

h) Explain how to calculate a covariance and a correlation coefficient, and how to interpret them.

2. After a freshers' night out at the university, the age and the "number of units of alcohol imbibed" per student are recorded. The population size is 21 individuals with the following characteristics (age, number of units): (18, 5), (22, 0), (18, 21), (22, 7), (24, 2), (20, 10), (20, 7), (27, 0), (19, 32), (20, 5), (20, 10), (22, 12), (24, 2), (24, 4), (22, 10), (20, 14), (24, 6), (27, 0), (22, 0), (20, 10), (20, 21) and (24, 2).

   a) Show the relative frequency function and the cumulative relative frequency function for the "number of units of alcohol imbibed" in the population.

   b) Draw a bar chart showing the relative frequencies of the "number of units of alcohol imbibed".

   c) Draw a histogram of interval width 5 for the "number of units of alcohol imbibed".

   d) Construct a pie chart for the "number of units of alcohol imbibed".

   e) Find the median of the "number of units of alcohol imbibed" and the 0.25- and 0.75-quantiles.

   f) Draw a box plot for the "number of units of alcohol imbibed".

   g) Calculate the mean value, the variance and the standard deviation for the "number of units of alcohol imbibed" in the population.

3. Consider the population in exercise 2.

   a) Cross-tabulate the relative frequencies of "age" and "number of units of alcohol imbibed".

   b) Draw a scatter plot for "age" and "number of units of alcohol imbibed".

   c) Calculate the covariance between "age" and "number of units of alcohol imbibed". What does it tell you?

   d) Also, calculate the correlation coefficient.

3 Uncertainty and probability

Most social science problems involve an element of uncertainty. In order to analyse these problems, we need to have a deeper understanding of the concept of uncertainty and of the tools used to deal with it. The main tools here consist of mathematical models that quantify the uncertainty. This chapter begins by discussing precisely what is meant by uncertainty. Section 3.2 then looks at uncertainty in relation to the selection of a sample from a population. The probability model introduced in Section 3.3 formalises this uncertainty, making it possible to assign probabilities to various events. In Section 3.4, we learn how to calculate these probabilities. Section 3.5 then looks at the concept of conditional probability, that is, the probability of an event taking place given that some other event has already occurred. Section 3.6 explains what is meant by independence and dependence between two distinct events, and how dependence is often confused with a causal relationship.

3.1 Uncertainty

We consider a situation to be uncertain when we do not know what will happen. Often, all of the possible events are in fact known, but we just do not know which one of them will actually occur.

Example 3.1: The weather tomorrow

It is June, and we do not know what the weather will be like tomorrow. However, we do know that there will be sun, clouds, rain, snow or a combination of some or all of these. No other possibilities exist.

The price of a 30-year mortgage bond at 12 noon is relevant to many companies in the financial sector, and particularly to homeowners considering restructuring mortgages. In theory, tomorrow's price could be any value between 0 and infinity, but we can exclude some values (e.g. a price of 3.21 billion) as highly unlikely.

Bicycle manufacturers have an interest in predicting the level of demand (consumption) for bikes in Denmark during the next financial year. All they know with certainty in advance is that the demand will be an integer that is greater than or equal to zero.

All three of the above examples involve uncertainty. However, the uncertainty can arise for a variety of reasons. In Example 3.3, people may not actually know how many bikes they will want to buy because they do not know how much they will earn next year or how much their household expenses will be. Alternatively, the individual consumer may know exactly how many bikes he or she will want to buy next year, but this information is not available to the manufacturers. In both cases, demand will be uncertain from the manufacturers' point of view.

Irrespective of the reason for the uncertainty, we are interested in being able to quantify it. The bicycle manufacturers in Example 3.3 may wish to calculate the probability that demand will be lower than 300,000 next year. They might also like to know how the price of petrol will affect this probability. Similarly, the homeowners in Example 3.2 might want to know the probability of the price being less than 100, as mortgages are only available as long as the price remains below this level.

To deal with uncertainty and make these kinds of calculations, we can construct a mathematical probability model. However, before we are able to do that, we will need to take a closer look at the concepts of population, selection mechanism and sample, which provide the framework for a basic understanding of the concept of uncertainty.

3.2   Experiment: From population to sample

This section looks at the relationship between a population and a sample. As mentioned in Chapter 2, a *population* is the statistical term for a collection of individuals, physical objects or abstract constructions. For example, in a study of incomes in Denmark, the population might consist of everybody in Denmark. If we were studying a roll of a dice, then the six sides would make up the relevant population. A *sample* is a set of values from the population, such as 1,000 incomes or a series of rolls of a dice.

The sample is the result of a *selection mechanism,* which is used to select the sample from the population. For example, if a dice is rolled three times, the selection mechanism could be described as follows: "Put the dice in the cup, shake it, roll the dice and read the result. Repeat until you have the results of three rolls." In this case, the sample consists of the results of the rolls of the dice. A sample is associated with uncertainty. This uncertainty arises because the cup is shaken, so it is impossible to know the outcome in advance.

The selection mechanism used to obtain a sample of, for example, 1,000 incomes in Denmark, is different. It could take the following form: "Write the civil registration (social security) numbers of everybody in Denmark on pieces of paper and put them in a (very) big hat. Shake the hat thoroughly and pull out one of the pieces of paper while keeping your eyes closed. Find the income of the person whose number you have pulled out and note the result. Repeat this 1,000 times." This would give you a sample of 1,000 incomes. In this case, the uncertainty arises because the big hat is shaken and you pick out pieces of paper with your eyes closed. In practice, the big hat could be replaced by a computer, which in principle would perform the same function. The selection mechanism describes both how the uncertainty arises and the number of elements of the population you want to study.

Taken together, a population, a selection mechanism and a sample are called an *experiment*. The word experiment may have connotations of laboratories, but in the world of statistics the concept covers far more ground. The example of a sample of Danish incomes is, therefore, an experiment in a statistical sense. Figure 3.1 illustrates the three components of an experiment.

Figure 3.1:
An experiment

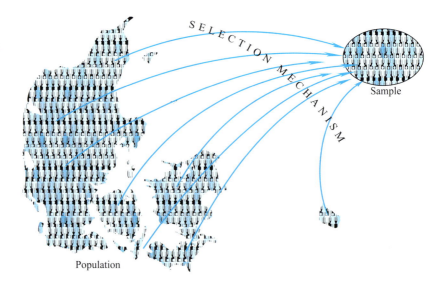

SELECTION MECHANISM

Sample

Population

We are interested in samples for two reasons. Firstly, they constitute microcosms of the population. They can therefore be used to infer things about the whole population. For example, the sample of incomes can be used to obtain an estimate of the Danes' (the population's) average income. Secondly, samples may be of interest in themselves. This is the case, for example, if you have made a bet about the number that will be rolled on a dice. Irrespective of the nature of your interest in the sample, there is uncertainty involved because you do not know what the outcome will be in advance.

All of the problems contained in this book can essentially be described as the experiment illustrated in Figure 3.1, provided that we broaden our interpretation of what a population is. We will therefore explain what we mean by populations, and then distinguish between two types: *real populations* and *super-populations*.

3.2.1   Real populations

We have already looked at real populations in Chapter 2. A real population is one that exists in the real world. It has a finite number of elements, which allows you to count the elements and define a cumulative relative frequency function, as we did in Chapter 2. The selection mechanism from a real population typically consists of a physical act. When we select a person or roll a dice, we perform an action, and we thus exercise a certain amount of control over the selection mechanism. As we will see in Section 3.3, the selection mechanism has direct consequences for how probabilities are calculated. In Chapter 9, we will discuss various selection mechanisms and sources of error that may arise in practice when selecting a sample from a real population.

3.2.2   Super-populations

We can also work with abstract, non-existent populations when describing uncertainty. The following examples illustrate this.

Example 3.4: A super-population of bond prices

The price of the 30-year mortgage bond at 12 noon the next day is uncertain. At noon the next day we will know the price, but how does it emerge? In theory, the price could be any value between zero and infinity, but only one of these values will be realised. You could consider all of the possible values as a population of prices, but you will not find this population anywhere. However, by imagining this non-existent population of possible prices, you could say that the price at 12 noon tomorrow is a sample from this population.

Example 3.5: A super-population of financial results

A company's performance in the next financial year is uncertain. However, when the accounts are drawn up at the end of the year, there is only one number on the bottom line. In order to formalise our uncertainty about financial performance next year, it is again useful to think of a population consisting of all possible outcomes. One of these possible outcomes will end up being the actual result. In this experiment, the sample comprises the company's actual reported performance.

Example 3.6: A super-population of weather

In Example 3.1, we can imagine tomorrow's weather being selected from a population consisting of sun, clouds, rain, snow and mixed weather.

The examples above illustrate how we can apply our way of thinking about experiments with real populations to experiments with non-existent populations. In order to distinguish between a real and a non-existent population, we refer to the latter as a *super-population.* Unlike a real population, a super-population can have an infinite number of elements.

In an experiment that utilises a super-population, the selection mechanism is abstract. The analogy of pulling the result out of a hat does not really work with the price of a bond, a company's financial performance or tomorrow's weather because the super-population does not exist in reality. As a result, it makes no sense to talk about relative frequency functions in relation to super-populations.

3.2.3   Selection mechanism and sample

When analysing the characteristics of a population based on a sample, which we referred to as *induction* in Chapter 1, knowledge of the selection mechanism is essential.

The following may sound paradoxical but it is nevertheless correct: the more "randomly" the selection mechanism picks elements from the population, the easier it is to make a credible inference. Example 3.7 illustrates this.

Example 3.7: An unusual dice

Imagine that one of your friends writes new numbers on the six sides of a dice. You do not yet know which numbers they are – you have to watch your friend roll the dice (thereby producing your sample) to find out. The six numbers on the sides of the dice are the unknown values in the population.

First, consider the usual selection mechanism for a dice game; that is, that your friend puts the dice into a cup and shakes it before rolling the dice and revealing the number. If he keeps going for a sufficiently long time, and you therefore have a big enough sample, there is a very good chance that you will be able to work out which six numbers are on the sides of the dice. In this case, the selection mechanism is characterised as random because the cup is shaken.

Now consider the following selection mechanism. Your friend "cheats" so that the same number comes up every time. Based on this sample, you would have to conclude that the same number appears on all six sides, or that the dice is rigged. In this case, the selection mechanism is entirely deterministic and contains no element of randomness.

In the example above, the random selection mechanism is better than the deterministic one because the former will always reveal at least as much about the sides of the dice as the latter, which will only tell us about one of the sides.

A selection based on random occurrence, which is clearly described (e.g. shaking the dice repeatedly), is termed *probabilistic*. The opposite of probabilistic selection is *systematic* selection.

The above example is a bit of a caricature. It might rightly be argued that a systematic selection mechanism that shows us the six sides of the dice, one after the other, would be preferable in this case. However, a probabilistic selection, which shows us the six sides in random order, would be just as good. As we will see later in this book, a probabilistic sample is clearly preferable in situations where the population is much larger than the selected sample. An important ingredient of a good empirical study is, therefore, a selection mechanism that incorporates a random mechanism for the selection of elements from a population.

In the next section, we introduce the probability model, which is used to formalise the uncertainty.

3.3   The probability model

When we add two numbers together, nobody will doubt that the result will be a number. But should we doubt it? Numbers do not grow in the wild; they are abstract constructions. There is, however, no doubt about the benefits of numbers and of being able to add and subtract them to and from one another. The reason that we do not fear these kinds of calculations is that they have a mathematical foundation, which guarantees that we are able to add two numbers together without sleeplessly worrying whether the result of this exercise will also be a number.

When working with uncertainty, we face a similar situation. We must formalise the uncertainty in order to perform calculations on it. As an example, we may wish to calculate the probability that there will be neither rain nor snow tomorrow, or that the bond price will be between DKK 100 and DKK 105. The mathematical foundation that ensures we are able to do this is the *probability model*.

The probability model contains the mathematical interpretation of the experiment in Figure 3.1, and it allows us to perform calculations on the uncertainty involved. We will now look at the three components of the probability model: *sample space, event space* and *probability measure*. The sample space is the direct mathematical translation of the experiment. The event space consists of the events of the experiment for which we wish to calculate the probabilities. The probabilities are described by the third part of the model, the probability measure.

3.3.1   Sample space

As described above, an experiment results in a sample. An *outcome* is a value of a sample. In the experiment "rolling a dice", a "three" is one possible outcome. The sample can therefore assume the value "three". To keep track of all the possible outcomes, one define a *sample space*:

> **The sample space**, Ω, for an experiment is the collection of all of the possible outcomes of the experiment (values of the sample).

We use the Greek symbol Ω (Omega) to denote the sample space. In "rolling a dice", the sample space is: $\Omega = \{$one, two, three, four, five, six$\}$. Curly brackets are used to indicate a collection of elements (outcomes), also referred to as a set. The result of an experiment is one, and only one, of these elements, e.g. a "three".

Example 3.8: Heads or tails

The experiment "toss a coin" can result in two possible outcomes: "heads" or "tails". The sample space is therefore $\Omega = \{H, T\}$, where H is "heads" and T is "tails". A more complicated experiment might be to "toss a coin twice". In this experiment, an outcome consists of the results of both tosses of the coin. If the first toss of the coin is heads and the second tails, the outcome is written (H, T). Note that even if the experiment is composed of two tosses of the coin, (H, T) is considered as one outcome, rather than two. The parentheses around H and T indicate that it is a single composite outcome. The sample space for this experiment is: $\Omega = \{(H, H), (H, T), (T, H), (T, T)\}$. Either the coin will come up heads twice, (H, H), or heads then tails, (H, T), and so on.

A sample space consists of outcomes that are combinations of the elements in a population. In Example 3.8, where the coin is tossed twice, the population is $\{H, T\}$, and the outcome is a combination of these two population elements, for example, (H, H) or (T, H).

While it is fun to toss coins and roll dice, the real-life uncertainties that people face tend to be more complex. However, we can still use the same techniques to describe them as we used in the experiments with coins and dice.

An umbrella shop is interested in how many umbrellas customers buy. The next customer who comes into the store may or may not buy one. She may even buy two, so she has a spare. The sample space for this experiment is therefore: Ω = {0 umbrellas, 1 umbrella, 2 umbrellas}. This choice of sample space precludes the possibility of someone buying more than two umbrellas. However, if that it is a possible outcome of the experiment, then the sample space has to be expanded.

It does not take much of a stretch of the imagination to work out that the shop in Example 3.9 is also interested in the relationship between rain and umbrella sales. This could also be formalised as an experiment "to observe whether it is raining at the time the customer enters the shop, and the number of umbrellas that the customer buys". The sample space for this experiment is:

$$\Omega = \{(\text{rain, 0 umbrellas}), (\text{rain, 1 umbrella}),$$
$$(\text{rain, 2 umbrellas}), (\text{dry weather, 0 umbrellas}),$$
$$(\text{dry weather, 1 umbrella}), (\text{dry weather, 2 umbrellas})\}$$

This is a sample space because all possible outcomes are contained within Ω. Only one of them can become the result of the experiment.

3.3.2   Event space

When analysing an experiment, a collection of outcomes is often more interesting than individual outcomes. In Example 3.9, for instance, you may be interested in whether a customer buys or does not buy umbrellas. In this case, the most interesting outcome is "0 umbrellas" rather than the outcomes "1 umbrella" and "2 umbrellas". A collection of outcomes is referred to as an *event:*

An **event** is a collection of outcomes. An event is said to have occurred when one of its outcomes happens.

Formally, an event is A, a subset of the sample space, Ω. We write this as: $A \subset \Omega$.

Figure 3.2 illustrates the relationship between the sample space, outcomes and events. The sample space is "the square", which consists of all the individual outcomes, "the balls". An event is then a set of balls, illustrated by "the circles" in the figure.

Figure 3.2:

Sample space, outcomes and events (A og B)

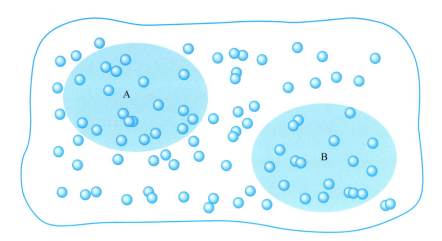

Example 3.11: A roll of a dice

In the experiment "rolling a dice" we can define an event, A, as: "the dice shows an odd number". This event occurs if the dice lands on a one, a three or a five. Formally, this can be written as: $A = \{one, three, five\}$.

Column one in Table 3.1 shows the sample space for the umbrella experiment in Example 3.9. Column two shows a series of events for this experiment. Note that curly brackets are used to indicate a set of outcomes. The third event in the table is therefore "buy at most one umbrella". This event consists of the outcomes "0 umbrellas" and "1 umbrella". The collection of events is called the *event space*.[2]

Many of the events have a natural interpretation, such as the "buy" event in Table 3.1. Other events do not have quite such a natural interpretation, for example, the event that consists of the outcomes "0 umbrellas" and "2 umbrellas". This event could be called the "don't buy one umbrella" event. Note that an individual outcome may also constitute an event in the event space. For example, the event "no purchase" consists of the single outcome "0 umbrellas".

Table 3.1:
Sample space
and event
space

Sample space, Ω	Event space
0 umbrellas	{0 umbrellas}, i.e. "no purchase"
1 umbrella	{1 umbrella, 2 umbrellas}, i.e. "buy"
2 umbrellas	{0 umbrellas, 1 umbrella}, i.e. "buy at most one umbrella"
	{2 umbrellas}, i.e. "buy two umbrellas"
	{1 umbrella}, i.e. "buy one umbrella"
	{0 umbrellas, 2 umbrellas}, i.e. "don't buy one umbrella"
	{0 umbrellas, 1 umbrella, 2 umbrellas}, i.e. "the sure event"
	$\varnothing$, i.e. "the impossible event"

Among the events in Table 3.1 are two notable sets. The first is the set of all outcomes, namely: {0 umbrellas, 1 umbrella, 2 umbrellas}. No matter what outcome occurs, this event always occurs. Hence the term *the sure event*. We use the symbol Ω for the sure event, because it contains all of the outcomes in the sample space. The opposite of the sure event is *the impossible event*, which is characterised by the fact that no outcome satisfies it. It is denoted by the special symbol $\varnothing$.

In order to describe whether two events occur simultaneously, or whether at least one of two events occurs, we define what are known as *intersections of events* and *unions of events*. These are defined in the box below and illustrated in Example 3.12.

---

2   The event space is also called a sigma-algebra. Formally, the event space has to meet particular conditions before the term sigma-algebra can be applied. However, it would be beyond the scope of this book to go into the details of those conditions.

Intersections of events and unions of events:

Let A and B be two events.

$A \cap B$ is called the intersection of events A and B and comprises the outcomes that are included in both A and B.

$A \cup B$ is called the union of events A and B and comprises the outcomes that are included in either A or B (or both).

Venn diagram:

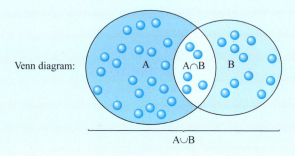

Example 3.12: Sale of umbrellas – part 3

Consider the events "buy" and "buy at most one umbrella" in the example from Table 3.1. The intersection of these two events is the outcome "1 umbrella", which is the only outcome found in both sets:

$$\text{"buy"} \cap \text{"buy at most one umbrella"} = \{1 \text{ umbrella}\}$$

However, the union of the two events is given by:

$$\text{"buy"} \cap \text{"buy at most one umbrella"}$$
$$= \{0 \text{ umbrellas, 1 umbrella, 2 umbrellas}\}$$

and is found by taking all the outcomes contained in the two events. Note that the outcome "1 umbrella" is found in both events. However, it only appears once in the union of the events.

If they have outcomes in common, various events can therefore occur at the same time, whereas two events are mutually exclusive (or disjoint) – they cannot both occur at the same time – if they share no outcomes.

For every event, there is an opposite event. The opposite event of A is defined as the set of all the outcomes not in A. This is also called the *complementary event* and is indicated here by the superscript c (for "complementary"). The opposite event of A is therefore designated A^c. The two events are not just mutually exclusive – it is also the case that either one event will occur or the other event will occur. Formally, the following therefore applies:

$$A \cap A^c = \varnothing \text{ and } A \cup A^c = \Omega$$

3.3.3   Probability measure

In order to measure uncertainty, you can assign probabilities to the various events. The probability is the likelihood of the event occurring. We will now look at some different interpretations of the concept of probability and the ways in which you can assign probabilities to events.

One way of interpreting the probability of an event is as the proportion of instances in which a given event will occur if you repeat the experiment an infinite number of times. Of course, this is an abstraction – unless you are extremely optimistic about your own longevity, it is clearly impossible to repeat an experiment an infinite number of times. Nevertheless, the abstraction still works. Consider the experiment "tossing a coin". If we toss the coin many times, we expect that about half of the outcomes will be heads. Why? Try to reverse the argument: why not? It is difficult to argue that the result will not be heads about half of the time. If that were to happen, then there would have to be something making the coin land on heads more often (or less often) than tails. The coin could be bent, it might not be tossed high enough and with enough spin, or perhaps one side meets more air resistance than the other. However, if we can refute these conditions as irrelevant to the outcome of the experiment, then we are left with no arguments as to why we should not get heads approximately half of the time.

Key to this is symmetry: all things being equal, all outcomes have the same chance of occurring. Therefore, we assign the probability "1 divided by the number of possible outcomes" to each outcome. This simple principle can solve many complex problems associated with assigning probabilities to events. It is summed up in the box below. Note that the letter P is used to indicate the probability.

Using symmetry to assign probabilities:

If a sample space consists of K outcomes, $\Omega = \{\omega_1,\ldots,\omega_K\}$, all of which have the same chance of selection, then the probability of an event that only has a single outcome is equal to $\frac{1}{K}$:

$$P(\omega_1) = \cdots = P(\omega_K) = \frac{1}{K}$$

The probability of an event, A, which consists of k outcomes, is:

$$P(A) = \frac{k}{K}$$

This symmetry argument can be expanded slightly when the experiment involves a real population. Imagine that we have a real population consisting of N_{pop} elements, of which k elements all have the value z of a characteristic. This could, for example, be the population of Denmark, which has approximately 2.5 million elements with the value z = "*man*", i.e. k = 2.5 million and N_{pop} = 5.0 million. The k elements with the value z constitute the proportion k/N_{pop} of the population. The relative frequency function is therefore equal to k/N_{pop} at the point z: $g(z) = k/N_{pop}$. If all of the elements in the population have the same chance of selection, and the outcome of the experiment is given by the value of the element selected, then the probability of the experiment resulting in the outcome z is equal to the proportion k/N_{pop}. In other words, the probability is 2.5 mill./5.0 mill. = 0.5 of selecting a man from the Danish population. This principle is summed up in the box below.

Using the relative frequency function to assign probability

Experiment: Selecting an element from a real population with N_{pop} elements. The outcome of the experiment is equal to the value of the selected element.

If all of the elements in the population have an equal chance of selection, then the probability of the outcome z is equal to the value of the relative frequency function evaluated in z:

$$P(z) = g(z)$$
$$= \frac{\text{number of elements with the value } z \text{ in the population}}{N_{pop}}$$

Note the difference between the two boxes above. The first is relevant in a situation in which all K outcomes of the experiment are equally likely. This is used to assign each outcome the probability $\frac{1}{K}$. For example, when rolling a dice, each of the six sides has the probability $\frac{1}{6}$. In the second box, the various outcomes of the experiment do not need to be equally likely. Here, instead, we go back to the population and say that if all of the elements have an equal chance of selection, then we can use the proportion of elements with the value z as the probability for the outcome z. For example, if all of the individuals in a population consisting of 1,000 men and 500 women have the same chance of being selected, then the probability that the one individual we select will be a man is $\frac{1,000}{1,000+500} = \frac{2}{3}$.

There is a 50% chance that it will rain tomorrow. In this instance, we cannot appeal to symmetry or repeat the experiment "the weather tomorrow" an infinite number of times. Indeed, we cannot even repeat it twice. But experience can be helpful here. On previous days with approximately the same temperature, wind direction, humidity and cloud cover, it rained on the next day about half of the time. We can also use knowledge from laboratory experiments to predict the chances of clouds and therefore rain. This knowledge is often fed into mathematical models that are used, for example, to simulate weather patterns on computers. Later in the book, in the chapters on regression analysis, we will look at mathematical models that can be extremely useful for making predictions. The idea is that scientific models use observations of the past to predict future situations and probabilities.

Experience can also be used for predictions that are not based on clear mathematical models, as illustrated by Example 3.13.

Example 3.13: Sale of umbrellas – part 4

The umbrella shop knows from experience that the proportion of customers who do not buy is $\frac{1}{4}$, while half of all customers buy one umbrella, and a quarter of them buy two. If we observe a random customer who comes into the shop, we can use this previous experience as a measure of the likelihood that the customer will buy an umbrella. The probability of the customer not buying anything is therefore $\frac{1}{4}$. Similarly, the probability that the customer will buy one umbrella is equal to $\frac{1}{2}$, and the probability of her buying two umbrellas is equal to $\frac{1}{4}$.

How likely is it that the horse Ibrahim will win its race on Sunday? Some people may invoke the jockey's star sign and singing voice when evaluating the chances – and, mathematically speaking, ascribing probability on whatever basis you choose is not a problem. Often, intuition is all you have to go on, although we know that intuition is partly informed by experience. In circumstances such as these, the probabilities are said to have been arrived at subjectively.

Formally, *the probability measure* is a function of an event. This applies regardless of whether the probability is ascribed using symmetry arguments, experience or subjectiveness.

For this mathematical system to work, probabilities must be ascribed to all of the events in the event space in a manner that complies with certain requirements. These requirements are as follows:

A probability measure, $P(\ )$, must comply with:

(i) $0 \leq P(A) \leq 1$ where A is an event.

(ii) $P(\Omega) = 1$ where Ω is the sure event.

(iii) $P(A \cup B) = P(A) + P(B)$ if the events A and B are mutually exclusive (disjoint), i.e. $A \cap B = \varnothing$.

These three requirements help to ensure that the system of probabilities is consistent, i.e. it does not contain any contradictions.[3] Firstly, outcomes must not have negative probabilities or probabilities greater than 1. Secondly, the probability of the sure event is equal to 1, because this event always occurs, since it consists of all of the outcomes in the sample space, Ω. Finally, it follows that if two events are mutually exclusive (i.e. they have no outcomes in common), then the probability of the union of the events is equal to the sum of the probabilities of the two events. That A and B do not have outcomes in common means that the intersection of the events, $A \cap B$, is empty. As illustrated in Example 3.14, the assigned probabilities in Table 3.2 satisfy the three conditions above.

---

3   Formally, $P(A_1 \cup A_2 \cup A_3 \cup ...) = P(A_1) + P(A_2) + P(A_3) + ...$ is also required if none of the events have outcomes in common. However, this condition will typically be met if the conditions (i)–(iii) from the box above are met.

In Example 3.13, the probabilities of the customer purchasing 0, 1 and 2 umbrellas, respectively, were $\frac{1}{4}$, $\frac{1}{2}$ and $\frac{1}{4}$. We can now use these probabilities to calculate the probabilities for the remaining events. For example, the event "purchase" consists of the two outcomes: "1 umbrella" and "2 umbrellas", which have the probabilities $\frac{1}{2}$ and $\frac{1}{4}$. The probability of the event "purchase" can then be calculated as the sum of these probabilities: $\frac{1}{2} + \frac{1}{4} = \frac{3}{4}$. Table 3.2 shows the probabilities for the other events in the umbrella experiment.

Table 3.2:
Sample space, event space and probability measures

Sample space, Ω	Event space	Probability measure
0 umbrellas	{0 umbrellas}, i.e. "no purchase"	1/4
1 umbrella	{1 umbrella, 2 umbrellas}, i.e. "buy"	3/4
2 umbrellas	{0 umbrellas, 1 umbrella}, i.e. "buy at most one umbrella"	3/4
	{2 umbrellas}, i.e. "buy two umbrellas"	1/4
	{1 umbrella}, i.e. "buy one umbrella"	1/2
	{0 umbrellas, 2 umbrellas}, i.e. "don't buy one umbrella"	1/2
	{0 umbrellas, 1 umbrella, 2 umbrellas}, i.e. "the sure event"	1
	$\emptyset$, i.e. "the impossible event"	0

3.4 Rules for probability calculations

One implication of the three properties of probabilities outlined in the box above is *the addition rule*, which expresses the relationship between the probability of a union of events and the probability of the intersection of the events:

The addition rule for probabilities:

The following applies for events A and B:

$$P(A \cup B) = P(A) + P(B) - P(A \cap B)$$

The addition rule tells us that the probability of a union of events is equal to the sum of the probabilities of the individual events involved minus the probability of the intersection of the events. The latter has to be deducted because the probabilities of the outcomes that are part of both A and B, are included in both $P(A)$ and $P(B)$. In order not to include the probabilities of these outcomes twice, we subtract them via $P(A \cap B)$.

Example 3.15: Sale of umbrellas – part 6

In the umbrella experiment from Table 3.2, the events "buy" and "buy at most one umbrella" both have the probability $\frac{3}{4}$. To work out the probability of the union of the two events, "buy" $\cup$ "buy at most one umbrella", we add together their individual probabilities and subtract the probability of the intersection of the two events. The intersection of the events consists of the outcome "1 umbrella", which has the probability $\frac{1}{2}$. The probability of the union of events "buy" $\cup$ "buy at most one umbrella" is therefore: $\frac{3}{4} + \frac{3}{4} - \frac{1}{2} = 1$. This also fits well with the finding from Example 3.12 that:

$$\text{"buy"} \cap \text{"buy at most one umbrella"}$$
$$= \left\{ 0 \text{ umbrellas, 1 umbrella, 2 umbrellas} \right\}$$

which is the entire sample space, Ω, and $P(\Omega)$ is, of course, precisely 1.

For an event A and its opposite event A^c, the probability of at least one of them occurring is equal to 1. This is because the union of these two events is the certain event. Formally:

$$P\left(A \cup A^c\right) = P(\Omega) = 1$$

In addition, since A and A^c are mutually exclusive:

$$P\left(A \cap A^c\right) = P(\varnothing) = 0$$

As a consequence of this, and with the help of the addition rule for probabilities, we get:

$$P(A) = 1 - P\left(A^c\right)$$

We can also work out the probability of an event, A, if we know the probability of the intersection of the events A and B (where B is any event) and the probability of the intersection of the events A and B^c. In this case, we get:

$$P(A) = P(A \cap B) + P(A \cap B^c)$$

Example 3.16: Sale of umbrellas – part 7

In the experiment from Example 3.10, let A be the event that a customer buys one umbrella, and let B be the event that it rains. Assume that the probability that a customer buys one umbrella is $P(A) = 0.15$ and that the probability that it rains is $P(B) = 0.25$. We can then work out the probabilities of the opposite events, A^c and B^c. If we also know that the probability that a customer will buy one umbrella, and that it will rain at the same time, is $P(A \cap B) = 0.1$, we can then also work out the probabilities of the other intersections of events involving A, B, A^c and B^c. This is done in Table 3.3.

For example, the probability that the customer will buy one umbrella and it will not rain is given by:

$$P(A \cap B^c) = P(A) - P(A \cap B) = 0.15 - 0.1 = 0.05$$

Table 3.3:
Events, opposite events, intersections of events and probabilities

Events	B: (rain)	B^c: (no rain)	
A: (1 umbrella)	$P(A \cap B) = 0.1$	$P(A \cap B^c) = 0.05$	$P(A) = 0.15$
A^c: (not 1 umbrella)	$P(A^c \cap B) = 0.15$	$P(A^c \cap B^c) = 0.7$	$P(A^c) = 0.85$
	$P(B) = 0.25$	$P(B^c) = 0.75$	$P(\Omega) = 1$

Often, it is possible to use information about an event that has already occurred in order to improve your predictions about whether another event will occur in the future. If we use information about how much it has rained this year, for example, we will be better able to predict crop yield than if we do not use this information. Another example is the risk of hereditary illness. If we know the medical history of a given individual's parents, this can be used to better predict the individual's own risk of contracting a hereditary illness. The theory of conditional probabilities concerns how information about one event can be used to evaluate the probability of another event.

In some cases, information about whether an event will occur will completely remove the uncertainty regarding whether another event will occur. This is the case when two events, A and B, have no outcomes in common (A and B are mutually exclusive). If we know that event B has occurred, i.e. that one of the outcomes in B has occurred, then the probability of event A occurring is equal to zero.

We call the probability of event A occurring, given that we know that event B will occur (or has occurred), *the conditional probability of event A given event B*. This probability is symbolised by $P(A|B)$, where the vertical line means "given" or "conditional on".

The conditional probability, $P(A|B)$, is calculated as follows: when event B occurs, we are able to focus on the outcomes that are included in event B. Of these outcomes, some are in A, while others are not in A. To calculate the conditional probability, we need the probability of the outcomes that are included in both A and B. This probability is $P(A \cap B)$. Since we know that the event B will occur (or has already occurred), the probability $P(A \cap B)$ must be seen in relation to the probability of the event B, i.e. $P(B)$. This is the intuition underlying the principle of conditional probability, which is presented in the following box:

The conditional probability of event A given event B is defined as:

$$P(A|B) = \frac{P(A \cap B)}{P(B)}$$

provided that the probability of event B is strictly greater than 0, i.e. $P(B) > 0$.

When we know that event B has occurred, then we can think of the outcomes in B as a sample space, within which we will find the probability of the outcomes that also belong to A.

In Example 3.16, the probability of event A (that a customer will buy one umbrella) is $P(A) = 0.15$, while the probability of event B (that it rains) is $P(B) = 0.25$. Finally, the probability of the intersection of the events (that a customer buys one umbrella and it rains) is given by $P(A \cap B) = 0.1$. Given that it rains, the probability that a customer will buy one umbrella is therefore:

$$P(A|B) = \frac{P(A \cap B)}{P(B)} = \frac{0.1}{0.25} = 0.4$$

Here, we can see the value of the information about event B. If we do not know whether it will rain, our best estimate of the probability that a customer will buy one umbrella is equal to 0.15. However, if it rains (in other words, if event B has occurred), then the probability of a purchase is actually considerably higher, namely 0.4.

We can extend the concept of conditional probability to a situation where we have knowledge of several events. In this case, we define the conditional probability as the probability of an event given that several other events will occur (or have occurred). $P(A|B,C)$ is thus the probability of event A, given that both event B and event C occur. Formally, this probability is given by:

$$P(A|B,C) = P(A|(B \cap C))$$

In other words, this is the probability of event A given the intersection of events B and C. If we think of this intersection as a new event, D, where $D = B \cap C$, then $P(A|B,C) = P(A|D)$, which is a probability that is conditional on only one event, just as in the original definition of the conditional probability. Therefore, $P(A|B,C)$ can be calculated as:

$$P(A|B,C) = P(A|D) = \frac{P(A \cap D)}{P(D)} = \frac{P(A \cap B \cap C)}{P(B \cap C)}$$

3.6   Independence and spurious relationships

One of the biggest empirical challenges in the social sciences is to examine relationships between different phenomena and decide whether the relationships are *causal.* A causal relationship between two phenomena means that one causes the other. An understanding of whether a relationship is causal or not is essential if we want to use the results of a study to formulate new policy in a particular area. For example, if we wish to prevent young people becoming criminals, it is important to understand the causes of crime.

It is worth drawing attention to the fact that the concept of causality has never been precisely and unambiguously defined – in fact, it has been the subject of discussion among philosophers for at least the last 2,500 years. We will therefore refrain from providing a precise definition of causality in this book. Broadly speaking, we have in mind that an event A causes an event B, if A occurs first and affects the probability that B will occur. An essential element of causality is therefore that, in terms of time, the causative event occurs before the event that is caused.

We will now show how to use the tools from the first section in this chapter to build a framework within which to explore relationships between different phenomena in the presence of uncertainty. In this section, we therefore define what is meant by independent and dependent events. We will also show why dependency between two events is not necessarily the same as a causal relationship. This will help us to determine whether or not a given relationship is causal.

3.6.1   Independence

A central probabilistic concept when evaluating relationships between two or more events is *independence.* If the information that an event, B, has occurred does not change the probability that another event, A, will occur, then we say that the two events are independent. Formally, this is expressed as: $P(A|B) = P(A)$. The probability of event A is therefore the same whether or not we include information about whether B has occurred.

The formal (and slightly more general) definition of independence is that the probability of the intersection of two events A, and B, is given by the product of the probabilities of the two individual events:

$$P(A \cap B) = P(A|B) \cdot P(B) = P(A) \cdot P(B)$$

To see how this definition implies $P(A|B)=P(A)$, just divide by $P(B)$ on both sides of the equality sign (assuming that $P(B)>0$), and use the definition of conditional probability from the box in Section 3.5. Note that if $P(B)=0$, then the two events are always independent – as implied by the general definition of independence above – but in this case, the conditional probability, $P(A|B)$, is not defined.

The following box summarises the definition of independence:

Independence: Two events, A and B, are independent if and only if:

$$P(A \cap B) = P(A) \cdot P(B)$$

which implies:

$$P(A|B) = P(A) \text{ whenever } P(B)>0$$

and

$$P(B|A) = P(B) \text{ whenever } P(A)>0$$

If the above conditions are not met, then the events are said to be dependent. However, the fact that two events are statistically dependent does *not* mean that they are directly connected. For example, several countries have discovered a statistical dependence between the number of storks and the number of childbirths. However, this does not mean that the stork brings the babies. Conversely, if two events are independent, then we can usually confidently conclude that they have nothing to do with each other.

When two events have nothing to do with each other, yet are dependent in statistical terms, this is due to other events that have not been included in the analysis. For example, the relationship between storks and childbirth could be due to the wider social trend from an agrarian to an industrial and then a service society, which has destroyed part of the stork's original habitat and at the same time reduced the number of children being born. In other words, if we take social developments into account, then the relationship between the number of storks and the number of births disappears.

We use the concept of *conditional independence* to denote that a third event, C, can explain an apparent relationship between two events, A and B.

> **Conditional independence:** The events A and B are independent conditional on event C (where $P(C) > 0$), if and only if:
>
> $$P(A \cap B|C) = P(A|C) \cdot P(B|C)$$
>
> which implies:
>
> $$P(A|B,C) = P(A|C) \text{ whenever } P(B)>0$$
>
> and
>
> $$P(B|A,C) = P(B|C) \text{ whenever } P(A)>0$$

The conditional independence between A and B means that the probability of event A is not influenced by whether event B occurs, if you already know whether event C has occurred or not.

3.6.2   Direct, indirect and spurious relationships

Countless empirical studies have concluded that, in statistical terms, there is a relationship between two entities. Later in this book we will look at how to conduct such studies. Whenever you hear that there is a relationship between two entities, you should always consider whether the study has been adjusted to take account of the fact that other entities may be the underlying cause of the relationship.

In statistical terms, there are essentially three situations in which the events A and B exhibit dependence. The three situations are:

1. A and B *depend directly* on each other: $A \rightarrow B$ or $B \rightarrow A$.
2. A and B *depend indirectly* on each other through an event C: $A \rightarrow C \rightarrow B$ or $B \rightarrow C \rightarrow A$.
3. A and B *do not depend* on each other but both depend on a third event C: $A \leftarrow C \rightarrow B$.

In all three situations $P(A|B) \neq P(A)$. When we say that A and B depend on each other, then it is usually implicitly understood that it is situation 1 that is correct. It is also usually implicit that one of the events causes the other. However, where there is statistical dependence between A and B, it could just as well be situation 3 that applies. In this case, there is effectively no dependence between A and B, in the sense that one event causes the other. We call an apparent relationship such as this a *spurious* relationship.

You can find out whether you are in situation 1 or one of the other two situations by studying whether there is an event C in relation to which it can be said that A and B are independent conditional on C: $P(A|B,C) = P(A|C)$. In this case, one of the last two situations applies. However, in order to determine whether this is the case, we need to have a good idea of what C could be.

In practice, the purpose of a study will usually indicate what the events A and B represent. However, event C is less clear. This is where you have to use your common sense and knowledge of the problem being studied to identify event C. The following example illustrates this.

Example 3.18: Quality of schools

Imagine an experiment where you select a school at random and observe whether it is privately owned (B) or not (B^c), and whether the grade-point average for the school is high (A) or not (A^c). It turns out that $P(A|B) = 0.7$ while $P(A|B^c) = 0.4$. We can therefore conclude that the events A and B are not independent in statistical terms. You can then ask yourself what the cause of this relationship is. Is it due to the different quality of the teaching in the two types of schools?

Research suggests that a student's performance in school depends, among other things, on how much time parents have devoted to stimulating the pupil linguistically during their first six years of life. Let the event C denote whether the pupils have received sufficient language stimulation in their first six years of life. The probability that a grade-point average in school is high, given that the pupils have received sufficient linguistic stimulation, is assumed to be: $P(A|C) = 0.8$.

You can then find the probability that the grade-point average is high is conditional on both the type of school and the amount of linguistic stimulation. If we find here that $P(A|B,C) = 0.8$, then $P(A|B,C) = P(A|C)$ and A and B are then independent conditional on C. This means that there is no direct relationship between A and B. Instead, the relationship between the type of school and the grade-point average can be spurious. This can be due to well-stimulated children increasingly being sent to private schools, which in turn may be related to well-stimulated children coming from families with relatively high incomes, that better can afford private schools.

As the example shows, you can sometimes show that an apparent dependence between two events, A and B, does not apply if you take into account a third event, C. Often, it can be difficult to identify this third event, and you may need to experiment with different ideas of C. Even if you do not find a third event that explains the relationship between A and B, this does not mean, of course, that such an event does not exist.

If you find that C explains the relationship between A and B, you still cannot conclude that there is a direct dependence between C and A and between C and B. It may be that a fourth event, D, explains both relationships. As mentioned in the example, it could be the family's socio-economic status that determines the language stimulation, the choice of school and the grade-point average. This also illustrates how difficult it can be to identify direct, and ultimately causal, relationships in the social sciences.

3.7   Exercises

1. Review questions
   a) What does an experiment consist of?
   b) Give examples of real populations and super-populations
   c) Explain in brief the three elements of the probability model: sample space, events and probabilities
   d) Explain the relationship between sample space and sample
   e) Explain in brief the different ways of assigning probabilities
   f) Which three properties must probabilities fulfil?
   g) Explain the addition rule for probabilities
   h) Explain what we understand by conditional probability
   i) What does it mean that two events are, respectively, independent and conditionally independent?

2. A football expert estimates that the home team has a 40% chance of winning and a 70% chance of not losing an impending match.
   a) Identify the population, the sample and the sample space in this experiment.
   b) Explain, on the basis of the properties of probabilities, the probability of a draw.
   c) What is the probability that one of the teams will win?

3. In a night school class for organ players, three students are under the age of 40, four are between 40 and 65 and two are aged 65 and over. A prize draw is held for a free ticket to a concert. The names of

all nine people are put in a hat, which is shaken thoroughly, and one name is selected at random.

a) What is the population and what does the relative frequency function look like?

b) What is the probability of the event that the winner is a student aged 40–65?

c) What is the probability of the event that a student aged 40+ is selected?

4. Falkirk United (FU) is competing in the district championships. The preliminary round consists of three games. The probability of FU losing a match is 0.9, and the outcomes of the three matches are independent.

a) What is the probability of FU not losing their second match?

b) What is the probability of FU losing all three matches?

c) What is the probability of FU losing two matches?

d) What is the probability of FU not having lost the second match, given that we know that they lost two matches in the preliminary round? Compare the answer with your answer to question a), above.

4 Random variables

In Chapter 3 we showed how to assign probabilities to various events associated with an experiment. In practice, an experiment will often involve many different events to which we will want to assign probabilities. Even in the relatively simple experiment in Table 3.1, there were eight different events, all of which had different designations. If we had to find names and symbols for all of the various events related to an experiment, the notation would soon become excessively cumbersome.

Fortunately, it is possible to define a function, called a *random variable* or a *random variable*, which makes it much easier to work with events and their probabilities. In Chapter 3 we needed a different symbol for each event. A random variable can represent many different events with a single symbol. Random variables build on the probability model from Chapter 3 and are particularly useful when we have to analyse relationships characterised by uncertainty.

In Section 4.1, we define a random variable. There are two kinds of random variable – discrete and continuous. We start by considering discrete random variables in Section 4.2, and in Section 4.3 we look at relationships between discrete random variables. Similarly, Sections 4.4 and 4.5 examine continuous random variables and relationships between these.

4.1   Definition of a random variable

A random variable is a function that assigns a numerical value to any outcome of an experiment:

$$X\left(outcome\right) = number$$

Example 4.1: Rolling a dice

In the experiment "rolling a dice", the sample space is: Ω = {one, two, three, four, five, six}. Here, we can define a random variable, X, which counts the number of dots on the dice:

$$X(\text{one}) = 1, X(\text{two}) = 2, X(\text{three}) = 3,$$
$$X(\text{four}) = 4, X(\text{five}) = 5, X(\text{six}) = 6$$

If the outcome of the experiment is a "one", then the random variable, X, assumes the value 1. In the same way, it assumes the value 6 if we throw a six.

Example 4.2: Sale of umbrellas – part 1

In the example of the umbrella shop from Chapter 3, we can define a random variable, X, which assumes a value equal to the number of umbrellas that a customer buys. In other words:

$$X(0 \text{ umbrellas}) = 0, \quad X(1 \text{ umbrella}) = 1, \quad X(2 \text{ umbrellas}) = 2$$

Note that we use capital letters like X and Y to denote a random variable. On the other hand, we use lower case, x and y, to indicate the specific values assumed by the random variable. For example, if you throw a dice, as in Example 4.1, then it will result in the random variable, X, assuming a certain value, x, which may be 1, 2, 3, 4, 5 or 6.

Often, the definition of a random variable is self-evident, as in the examples given above. However, if the outcomes of the experiment are measured qualitatively, the definition may not be quite as obvious. In these cases, we can "code" the outcomes, as Example 4.3 illustrates.

Example 4.3: Heads or tails

In the experiment "tossing a coin", there are two possible outcomes: heads and tails. In this case, we can define a random variable, X, by coding heads to 0 and tails to 1. Thus, the random variable, X, is given by:

$$X(\text{heads}) = 0, \quad X(\text{tails}) = 1$$

We are at liberty to choose the numerical values that the random variable can assume. In Example 4.3, we could just as well have defined X as assuming the value 4 in the case of heads, and the value 13.2 for tails. However, if a random variable is to be useful, the values must be chosen with some care, so that they suit the problem being studied.

For a given experiment, we can define many different random variables, each of which represents a different aspect or property of the outcome of the experiment. This is illustrated in Example 4.4.

Example 4.4: Two random variables

An experiment consists of selecting a person at random from the Danish population and then observing the gender and age of the individual concerned. One possible outcome of this experiment is as follows: (male, 43 years old). In this case, we can define a random variable, X, that assumes the value 0 if the individual selected is a man, and the value 1 if it is a woman. Similarly, we can define a random variable, Y, that assumes a value corresponding to the age (in years) of the person selected. This means that if we select a man aged 43, then $X = 0$ and $Y = 43$.

In Example 4.4, two random variables are linked to the outcome (age and gender) of the experiment. Experiments like this are particularly relevant within the social sciences. For example, an experiment could consist of selecting a person at random and observing his or her income and consumption of a given product. Such experiments can be used to determine the demand for a product. We will look at this in greater detail later in the book.

4.1.1   Two types of random variables

Random variables are either *discrete* or *continuous*, and this affects the way in which we assign probabilities to their values. What determines whether a random variable is discrete or continuous is whether or not it is possible to count the number of possible outcomes.

The random variable, X, in Example 4.3, which indicated the outcomes heads and tails with the values 0 and 1 respectively, is a *discrete random variable.* It can only assume a countable number of values (0 and 1). When an experiment has a finite number of outcomes, then the random variable defined by the experiment will always be discrete.

A random variable, Z, that specifies the water level in a harbour at a given time, is a *continuous random variable.* Assuming that the water level may be between 0 and 12 metres, the outcome could, for example, be 10.344211... metres. The exact water level has an infinite number of decimal places (although in practice it is impossible to measure it with that degree of accuracy). Therefore, in principle, any of the infinitely many values between 0 and 12 metres is a possible outcome. In fact, there are so many values between 0 and 12 that they cannot possibly be counted. Therefore, the random variable is said to be continuous.[4]

The same experiment can easily lead to both a discrete and a continuous random variable. In Example 4.4, Y is a discrete random variable, because it indicates the age of a person measured in whole years. If, instead, we measure age with infinite accuracy and define a random variable, Z, for this measurement, then Z is a continuous random variable. In a given situation, your choice of random variable – if, indeed, you have a choice – will depend partly on the precision you want or need in the measurement, and the methods you subsequently wish to employ to analyse the problem at hand. As will become apparent later in the book, the methods at your disposal vary depending on whether you use discrete or continuous random variables.

The probability of a continuous random variable is more difficult to describe than that of a discrete random variable. We have therefore divided the following discussion into two parts. In Sections 4.2 and 4.3, we deal with the more tangible discrete random variables, and then we move on to continuous random variables in Sections 4.4 and 4.5.

4.2   Discrete random variables

One of the advantages of random variables is that their values correspond to different events in the probability model. We can therefore use the probability measure for the events from Chapter 3 to assign a probability to any value of a random variable. In this section, this is done for discrete random variables.

---

4   Note that there is a difference between "infinite" and "uncountable". A random variable may assume an infinite number of different values without this meaning that they are uncountable. For example, if the random variable, X, can assume the values 1, 2, 3, etc., then there are an infinite number of values it can assume. However, they can be counted systematically starting from 1. Therefore, X is a discrete random variable. A random variable that indicates the water level, on the other hand, has an uncountable number of values, since they cannot be set up and counted in a systematic manner.

In Example 4.2, the random variable, X, indicated the number of umbrellas bought. We can derive the probabilities for its values directly from the probability measure in column 3 of Table 3.2. Thus, the probability that X is equal to 0 is 1/4. This is written: $P(X = 0) = \frac{1}{4}$. Similarly, $P(X = 1) = \frac{1}{2}$ and $P(X = 2) = \frac{1}{4}$. Note that, in this example, the random variable, X, can only assume three values: 0, 1 and 2. The overall probability of these outcomes is $P(X = 0) + P(X = 1) + P(X = 2) = \frac{1}{4} + \frac{1}{2} + \frac{1}{4} = 1$. The probabilities add up to one because the values 0, 1 and 2 represent all of the possible values of X.

It is worth emphasising that the values of a random variable correspond to particular events in an experiment. Once we know the probabilities for the different values that a random variable can assume, we no longer have to worry about the probabilities of the different events of the underlying experiment that lead to a specific value for the random variable. The experiment – and therefore the probability model – are replaced by the random variable and its distribution.

4.2.1 The probability function

The probabilities for the different values that a discrete random variable can assume are summed up by its probability function:

> **The probability function**, $f(x)$, for a discrete random variable, X, is defined as:
>
> $$f(x) = P(X = x)$$

When working with several random variables, it can be an advantage to use subscripts on the probability functions, so we know which probability function belongs to which random variable. For example, $f_Y(y)$ can be the probability function of the random variable, Y.

The random variable, X, from Example 4.5 has the following probability function:

$$f_X(0) = \tfrac{1}{4}, \; f_X(1) = \tfrac{1}{2}, \; f_X(2) = \tfrac{1}{4} \text{ and } f_X(x) = 0 \text{ for } x \neq 0,1,2$$

A probability function, f, has the following properties: firstly, it assumes only values between 0 and 1. Probabilities can neither be negative nor exceed 1. Secondly, the sum of the probabilities of all of the values of the random variable must be equal to *1*:

> **Properties of the probability function, $f(x)$, for a discrete random variable, X:**
>
> i) $\quad 0 \leq f(x) \leq 1$
>
> ii) $\quad \displaystyle\sum_{i=1}^{N} f(x_i) = f(x_1) + f(x_2) + \ldots + f(x_N) = 1$
>
> where $x_1, x_2, \ldots, x_N$ are the N different values of X.

The summation sign, $\sum_{i=1}^{N} f(x_i)$, means that you have to add together $f(x_i)$ over all the N different possible values of x_i. Therefore, $\sum_{i=1}^{N} f(x_i)$ is equal to $f(x_1) + f(x_2) + \ldots + f(x_N)$, where $x_1, x_2, \ldots, x_N$ are the N different possible values of X.[5]

The probability function enables us to calculate the probability of various composite events. It is just a matter of adding up the probabilities for the values of X that correspond to the event in question.

Let X be defined as in Example 4.5 and 4.6. Using the probability function for X, we can calculate the probabilities of the various events from the umbrella example in Chapter 3:

---

5   If X can assume infinitely many (countable) values, then we write $N=\infty$.

$$P(\text{"buy one umbrella"}) = f(1) = \tfrac{1}{2}$$
$$P(\text{"buy two umbrellas"}) = f(2) = \tfrac{1}{4}$$
$$P(\text{"no purchase"}) = f(0) = \tfrac{1}{4}$$
$$P(\text{"buy"}) = f(1) + f(2) = \tfrac{1}{2} + \tfrac{1}{4} = \tfrac{3}{4}$$
$$P(\text{"buy at most one umbrella"}) = f(0) + f(1) = \tfrac{1}{4} + \tfrac{1}{2} = \tfrac{3}{4}$$

where, for example, the probability of the last event is found by adding up the probabilities of $X = 0$ and $X = 1$, as these values correspond to the event "buy at most one umbrella".

4.2.2 The cumulative distribution function

The probability of a random variable assuming a value less than or equal to a certain value, x, is known as a cumulative probability. The cumulative probabilities are given by the cumulative distribution function, which is often denoted with a capital letter, e.g. $F(x)$:

> **The cumulative distribution function, $F(x)$, for a discrete random variable, X, is defined as:**
>
> $$F(x) = P(X \leq x) = \sum_{x_i \leq x} f(x_i)$$

The cumulative probability is calculated by summing up the probability function, $f(x)$, for all the values, x_i, which are less than or equal to x. This is exactly what is implied by the summation sign, $\sum_{x_i \leq x} f(x_i)$.

Example 4.8: Sale of umbrellas – part 5

For the random variable, X, in Example 4.6, $F(1) = f(0) + f(1) = \tfrac{1}{4} + \tfrac{1}{2} = \tfrac{3}{4}$. The probability that X will assume a value less than or equal to 1 is equal to the probability of $X = 1$ plus the probability of $X = 0$. We have plotted the graph of the cumulative distribution function for X in Figure 4.1.

It shows that F is equal to 0 for values of x less than 0, as X in this example cannot assume negative values. At the point $x = 0$, F "jumps" to the value $\tfrac{1}{4}$, because at this point we add the probability $P(X = 0)$

to the cumulative probability. The probability of getting a value less than or equal to zero is therefore $\frac{1}{4}$. Similarly, F increases from $\frac{1}{4}$ to $\frac{3}{4}$ at the point $x = 1$, because here we add $P(X = 1) = \frac{1}{2}$ to the cumulative probability. Between 0 and 1 there are no increases in the cumulative probability because the probability of X assuming a value in this range is zero.

Figure 4.1:
The cumulative distribution function for X

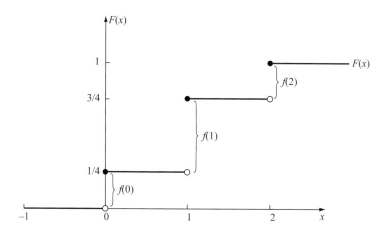

As the example illustrates, the cumulative distribution function, $F(X)$, for a discrete random variable is a step function. The vertical distance between two steps is equal to the value of the probability function, $f(x)$, at the point between the two steps.

The cumulative distribution function can also be used to find the probability that X will assume a value in a given range, for example between a and b. This probability can expressed as:

$$P(a < X \leq b) = F(b) - F(a)$$

The probability that X will be greater than a but less than or equal to b is equal to the probability that X will be less than or equal to b, which is $F(b)$, minus the probability that X will be less than or equal to a, which is $F(a)$. This is illustrated in Figure 4.2. When we get to continuous random variables later in this chapter, we will show how useful this formula is for calculating probabilities.

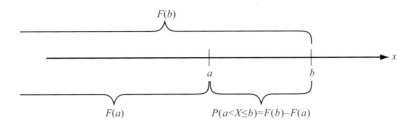

The formula above does not include the probability of $X = a$. If, instead, you want to calculate the probability $P(a \le X \le b)$, this is given by:

$$P(a \le X \le b) = F(b) - F(a) + f(a)$$

4.2.3 Probability functions and relative frequency functions

In Chapter 3, we argued that the relative frequency function can be used to assign probabilities to the outcomes of an experiment in certain situations. This is the case when the experiment consists of selecting an element from a real population with N_{pop} elements, and where the outcome of the experiment is equal to the value of the selected element. If all elements in the population have an equal chance of selection, then the probability of the outcome z is given by the proportion of elements in the population with the value z. The probability is therefore equal to $g(z)$, where g is the relative frequency function.

This principle can be applied to random variables as well. Let Z be a random variable, the value of which is given by the value of the element selected. If the selection mechanism is such that all elements in the population have the same chance of being selected, then the probability function for Z is equal to the relative frequency function for the population, i.e. $f(z) = g(z)$. This is summarised in the box below.

Connection between the relative frequency function and the probability function:

Let a real population have the relative frequency function $g(z)$, where the property z is a numerical value.

Let Z be a discrete random variable, the value of which is given by the value of the element selected.

If all elements in the population have an equal chance of selection, then the probability function, $f(z)$, is given by:

$$f(z) = g(z)$$

and the cumulative distribution function, $F(z)$, is given by:

$$F(z) = G(z)$$

where $G(z)$ is the cumulative relative frequency function.

Example 4.9: Men and women

In Example 4.4, we selected an individual from a population comprising both men and women. The random variable, X, assumed the value 0 if the result of the selection was a man, and the value 1 if it was a woman. If the population consists of 49% men and 51% women, then the relative frequency function for this population is given by:

$$g(0) = 0.49$$

$$g(1) = 0.51$$

If all individuals have an equal chance of being selected, then there is a 49% probability that the result will be a man, i.e. that X will assume the value 0. Therefore, the probability function for X is:

$$f(0) = 0.49$$

$$f(1) = 0.51$$

In other words, it is exactly the same as the relative frequency function.

The relationship between probability functions and relative frequency functions is very useful when we have to specify a probability function for a random variable that represents the possible values in a real population. It also means that we often talk about the relative frequency function as if it were a probability function. Conversely, we often speak of the probability function as if it were a relative frequency function. We do this when the random variable is defined on the basis of a real population, such that its value is equal to the value of the element selected, and the selection mechanism means that all elements in the population have the same chance of selection.

4.3   Relationships between discrete random variables

We are often interested in studying relationships, for example, between a child's upbringing and his or her education, or between the price of a product and its consumption. Random variables make it easier to handle more complex problems than the ones we considered in Chapter 3.

To describe relationships characterised by uncertainty, we use two or more random variables. In this section, we present some important tools with which to describe the relationships between random variables.

4.3.1   Joint probability

Let us imagine a situation where a bank has to evaluate the creditworthiness of a company. To make the example as simple as possible, we assume that the evaluation includes the following two aspects: (1) the risk of bankruptcy and (2) market conditions. Both of these aspects are subject to uncertainty. We therefore have a statistical experiment that can be modelled with two random variables: X, which will assume the value 0 if the company goes bankrupt, and the value 1 if it does not; and Y, which is equal to 1 if the market conditions are favourable, and 0 if they are not. The bank knows from experience with similar companies that the probabilities of the different outcomes are as shown in Table 4.1.

Table 4.1:
Joint probabilities

	$X = 0$ (bankruptcy)	$X = 1$ (not bankruptcy)
$Y = 0$ (unfavourable market)	0.2	0.2
$Y = 1$ (favourable market)	0.1	0.5

The lower-right corner of Table 4.1 represents the probability that both the market conditions are favourable and the company does not go bankrupt. This is known as a *joint probability,* because it is a "both ... and" probability. The probability function that gives the probability of the different combinations of the values of X and Y is called the *joint probability function.* It is defined as follows:

The joint probability function, $f(x,y)$, for two discrete random variables, X and Y, is defined as:

$$f(x,y) = P(X = x \text{ and } Y = y)$$

The probability of unfavourable market conditions and bankruptcy is $f(0,0) = 0.2$. We note that the four joint probabilities in Table 4.1 add up to 1, because there are a total of four possible outcomes, and the sum of the probabilities must equal 1, as in the case with one random variable.

When you add up the probabilities of the joint probability function for all the possible combinations of the values of the random variables involved, the result will always be equal to 1.

Properties of the joint probability function, $f(x,y)$, for two discrete random variables, X and Y:

i) $0 \leq f(x,y) \leq 1$

ii) $\displaystyle\sum_{i=1}^{N_X}\sum_{j=1}^{N_Y} f(x_i,y_j) = f(x_1,y_1) + f(x_1,y_2) + \dots + f(x_{N_X},y_{N_Y}) = 1$

where $y_1, y_2, ..., y_{N_Y}$ are the N_Y possible values that Y can assume, and $x_1, x_2, ..., x_{N_X}$ are the N_X possible values that X can assume.

4.3.2   Marginal probability

If you are interested in the probability of the company not going bankrupt, no matter how the market develops, this can be calculated by adding up the probabilities for all of the outcomes in Table 4.1 where the company does not go bankrupt. The company can avoid bankruptcy under both favourable and unfavourable market conditions. Thus, the overall probability of avoiding bankruptcy is given by

$f(1,0) + f(1,1) = 0.2 + 0.5 = 0.7$. In purely mechanical terms, this number is arrived at by a summation of the probabilities in the column headed "not bankruptcy", as shown in Table 4.2.

In cases where, as in the bank example, there is more than one random variable, then the probabilities of each random variable are called the *marginal probabilities*. The marginal probability function for X is denoted $f_X(x)$ and is defined as follows:

The marginal probability function, $f_X(x)$, for a discrete random variable, X, is defined by:

$$f_X(x) = \sum_{i=1}^{N_Y} f(x, y_i) = f(x, y_1) + f(x, y_2) + ... + f(x, y_{N_Y})$$

where $y_1, y_2, ..., y_{N_Y}$ are the N_Y possible values that Y can assume.

Put simply, by adding together the joint probability of all possible y values for a given value of x, we arrive at the marginal probability of x. Similarly, the marginal probability function for Y is defined by a summation of all possible values of x:

$$f_Y(y) = \sum_{i=1}^{N_X} f(x_i, y) = f(x_1, y) + f(x_2, y) + ... + f(x_{N_X}, y)$$

In table 4.2 we find the marginal probability of Y by summing up horizontally. For example, the probability of an unfavourable market (whether the company goes bankrupt or not) is given by: $f_Y(0) = f(1,0) + f(0,0) = 0.2 + 0.2 = 0.4$. Similarly, the marginal probability of a favourable market is equal to $f_Y(1) = f(1,1) + f(0,1) = 0.5 + 0.1 = 0.6$. The marginal probabilities also add up to 1, as they are equal to the probabilities you would have in a situation with just a single random variable. Thus, when you include a second random variable in the analysis, you effectively split the marginal probabilities into smaller "chunks" (the joint probabilities).

Table 4.2: Joint and marginal probabilities

	$X = 0$ (bankruptcy)	$X = 1$ (not bankruptcy)	Marginal probability of $Y: f_Y(y)$
$Y = 0$ (unfavourable market)	0.2	0.2	0.4
$Y = 1$ (favourable market)	0.1	0.5	0.6
Marginal probability of $X: f_X(x)$	0.3	0.7	

4.3.3   Conditional probability

The definition of the conditional probability between two events in Section 3.5 can also be directly applied to the conditional probability between two random variables. As we shall see, the basic idea and interpretation are essentially the same. The difference is that random variables allow for easier handling of the more complicated situations that we will often encounter in practice.

Using the example from Section 4.3.2, we can imagine that, for some reason or another, the bank knows (or believes) that market conditions will be favourable. The question then is how to use this information better to predict the probability that the company will not go bankrupt. As the bank knows that the market is favourable ($Y = 1$), only uncertainty about the outcome of X remains. Table 4.2 shows that the joint probability of a "favourable market" and "not bankrupt" is 0.5, whereas the joint probability of a "favourable market" and "bankrupt" is 0.1. In a favourable market, the probability of not going bankrupt is five times greater than that of going bankrupt.

By dividing these numbers by the marginal probability of a favourable market, we are able not only to retain the relationship between these probabilities but also to adjust them so that they add up to 1. These adjusted probabilities (in this case, because we know that the market will be favourable) are called conditional probabilities:

$$P\big(X = 0 \big| Y = 1\big) = \frac{P\big(X = 0, Y = 1\big)}{P\big(Y = 1\big)} = \frac{0.1}{0.6} = 0.167$$

$$P\big(X = 1 \big| Y = 1\big) = \frac{P\big(X = 1, Y = 1\big)}{P\big(Y = 1\big)} = \frac{0.5}{0.6} = 0.833$$

Here, the vertical line "|", just as in Chapter 3, means "given" or "conditional on". The two conditional probabilities add up to 1, and the difference between them is still a factor of 5. In other words, the probability of the company being successful, given that we know that the market is favourable, is 0.833. Thus, our knowledge that the market is favourable has changed our evaluation of the probability of the company being a success. Without the information that Y is equal to 1, we would have used the marginal probability for $X = 1$, which is 0.7 according to Table 4.2. In this example, it is therefore more probable that the company will avoid bankruptcy when we know that the market is favourable.

Another way to interpret the formula for conditional probability is to say that our knowledge of Y means that we no longer have to use the whole of the joint distribution for X and Y. Some of the outcomes in the joint distribution have become irrelevant, namely those where $Y = 0$. This leaves only the outcomes where $Y = 1$, and it is the relative probabilities of these outcomes that are now relevant. We therefore divide them by their sum, so that they sum to 1. This is similar to the way in which we assigned conditional probabilities in Chapter 3.

Formally, the conditional probability function for X given $Y = y$ is defined as follows:

> **The conditional probability function**, $f_{X|Y}(x|y)$, for a discrete random variable, X, given that $Y = y$, is defined as:
>
> $$f_{X|Y}(x|y) = \frac{f(x,y)}{f_Y(y)}, \text{ if } f_Y(y) > 0$$

Note that the conditional probability of X given $Y = y$ is only defined for values of y with a positive marginal probability. In the example above, Y can only assume the values 0 and 1. It therefore makes no sense to talk about the conditional probability of X given $Y = 3$, as this is an impossible situation.

In contrast to the definition of conditional probability for two events in Section 3.5, the definition of conditional probability for two random variables applies to many different events because each random variable can assume many different values, and each value corresponds to an event. However, the interpretation of conditional probability is exactly the same as in Section 3.5.

In practice, it might be that we know the conditional probability of Y given X, but we would like to know the conditional probability of X given Y. Put simply, we have to "reverse" the condition.

For example, consider a new storm warning system. In a laboratory, simulations can be used to calculate the probability of how the warning system will function in flood conditions, and also how it will function when there is no flood. In other words, we can calculate the probabilities for a warning being issued in the event of a flood. Outside the laboratory, however, we are more interested in whether our feet will get wet. Expressed as probabilities, we therefore want to know what the probability is of a flood, given that a warning is issued, but also the probability of flooding given that no warning is issued. We must therefore reverse the probabilities worked out in the laboratory.

To reverse a conditional probability, we can use the following rules.

Rules for calculating conditional probabilities:

$$f_{X|Y}\left(x|y\right) = f_{Y|X}\left(y|x\right) \cdot \frac{f_X\left(x\right)}{f_Y\left(y\right)}$$

and:

$$f_{X|Y}\left(x|y\right) = f_{Y|X}\left(y|x\right) \cdot \frac{f_X\left(x\right)}{\sum_{i=1}^{N_X} f_{Y|X}\left(y|x_i\right) \cdot f_X\left(x_i\right)}$$

(Bayes' theorem)

A brief technical explanation of the formulas: the first formula is a result of the fact that the joint probability, $f(x,y)$, is equal to both $f_{Y|X}(y|x) \cdot f_X(x)$ and $f_{X|Y}(x|y) \cdot f_Y(y)$. This follows from the definition of the conditional probability in Section 4.3.3. If we set $f_{Y|X}(y|x) \cdot f_X(x)$ equal to $f_{X|Y}(x|y) \cdot f_Y(y)$ and divide by $f_Y(y)$ on both sides of the equality sign, we arrive at the first formula in the box above. The second formula (Bayes' theorem) then follows from the fact that the marginal probability of Y, $f_Y(y)$, can be calculated by adding together the joint probabilities of all possible values of x for a given value of y, i.e.:

$$f_Y(y) = \sum_{i=1}^{N_X} f(x_i, y) = \sum_{i=1}^{N_X} f_{Y|X}(y, x_i) \cdot f_X(x_i)$$

$$= f_{Y|X}(y|x_1) \cdot f_X(x_1) + f_{Y|X}(y|x_2) \cdot f_X(x_2)$$

$$+ ... + f_{Y|X}(y|x_{N_X}) \cdot f_X(x_{N_X})$$

where $x_1, x_2, ..., x_{N_X}$ are the values that X can assume.

Example 4.10: A warning system

Let the random variable, X, indicate whether a flood is present, i.e. $X = 1$ if it is, and $X = 0$ if it is not. Similarly, let the random variable, Y, state whether the alarm system issues a warning, i.e. $Y = 1$ if it does, and $Y = 0$ if it does not. Assume that warnings are issued in 90% of the cases where there is flooding. Similarly, false warnings are issued in 2% of the cases, where there is no flood. The conditional probabilities are therefore:

$$f_{Y|X}(1|1) = 0.90, \ f_{Y|X}(0|1) = 0.10,$$

$$f_{Y|X}(1|0) = 0.02, \ f_{Y|X}(0|0) = 0.98$$

Finally, we know from historical experience of floods that there is a 5% chance of flooding. The marginal probability of a flood is thus:

$$f_X(1) = 0.05, \ f_X(0) = 0.95$$

The conditional probability that there will be a flood, given that a warning is issued, can now be calculated by inserting into the formula of Bayes' theorem:

$$f_{X|Y}(1|1) = f_{Y|X}(1|1) \cdot \frac{f_X(1)}{f_{Y|X}(1|0) \cdot f_X(0) + f_{Y|X}(1|1) \cdot f_X(1)}$$

$$= 0.9 \cdot \frac{0.05}{0.02 \cdot 0.95 + 0.90 \cdot 0.05} = 0.703$$

There is, therefore, approximately a 70% chance that there will be a flood if the system issues a warning. Similarly, the probability of a flood when no warning is issued is:

$$f_{X|Y}(1,0) = f_{Y|X}(0|1) \cdot \frac{f_X(1)}{f_{Y|X}(0|1) \cdot f_X(1) + f_{Y|X}(0|0) \cdot f_X(0)}$$

$$= 0.1 \cdot \frac{0.05}{0.1 \cdot 0.05 + 0.98 \cdot 0.95} = 0.005$$

A warning system like this means that the probability of a flood arriving without warning is ten times smaller than the overall risk of a flood. However, there is also a 30% chance of a false warning.

Note that the conditional probability for X given Y is only equal to the conditional probability of Y given X in exceptional cases.

4.3.5 Independence

In Section 3.6, we discussed statistical independence between two events. Now we want to extend this to statistical independence among many different events. This is relatively easy to do with the help of random variables.

In the example above, about the bank, we can compare the marginal probability for X, $f_X(x)$, with the conditional probability for X, $f_{X|Y}(x|y)$, when we know that Y assumes a specific value, y. If the two probabilities are different, then the information about Y has changed our knowledge of X. This does not mean that we now know the outcome of X. Rather, some values of X have become more or less probable than they were when we did not know the outcome of Y. Our predictions about X change because we now know the outcome of Y.

If information about Y does not change the distribution of X, then X and Y are said to be *independent*. Formally, this can be written as follows:

Independence:

Two discrete random variables, X and Y, are independent if and only if:

$f(x,y) = f_X(x) \cdot f_Y(y)$ for all values of x and y.

Which implies that

$f_X(x) = f_{X|Y}(x|y)$ for all values af x and y where $f_Y(y) > 0$,

and

$f_Y(y) = f_{Y|X}(y|x)$ for all values of y and x where $f_X(x) > 0$.

When X and Y are independent, then the marginal distribution of X, $f_X(x)$, is equal to the conditional distribution of X given Y, $f_{X|Y}(x|y)$. In other words, the information about Y does not change our perception of the probabilities for the various values of X. You cannot, therefore, use Y to predict anything about X.

The formal definition of independence between X and Y is that the joint probability can be written as the product of the marginal probabilities: $f(x,y) = f_X(x) \cdot f_Y(y)$. Inserting this into the definition of the conditional probability function above gives us $f_X(x) = f_{X|Y}(x|y)$.

Example 4.11: Tossing a coin twice

Suppose we toss a coin twice and define the random variable, X, as being equal to 1 if the first toss is tails, and 0 if it is heads. Let Y be defined similarly for the second toss. There are four possible combinations of the values of X and Y. Since we cannot argue that one combination is more likely than another, then the probability of each combination is equal to 0.25 according to the symmetry argument from Section 3.3.3. We can derive the same result by working on the premise that there is no relationship between X and Y. Therefore, X and Y must be independent. The probability function for X is $f_X(0) = 0.5$ and $f_X(1) = 0.5$. Similarly, the probability function for Y is $f_Y(0) = 0.5$ and $f_Y(1) = 0.5$. Since X and Y are independent, then $f(x,y) = f_X(x) \cdot f_Y(y) - 0.5 \cdot 0.5 = 0.25$ for $x = 0$ or 1 and $y = 0$ or 1.

Table 4.2 clearly shows that X and Y are not independent in the bank example. Take, for example, the joint probability of an unfavourable market and bankruptcy: $f(0,0) = 0.2$. This probability is not equal to the product of the two marginal probabilities: $f_X(0) \cdot f_Y(0) = 0.3 \cdot 0.4 = 0.12$.

4.4   Continuous random variables

To deal with probabilities for random variables that have an uncountable number of outcomes, it is necessary to use slightly different mathematical tools than those used in Sections 4.2 and 4.3. The difference compared to discrete random variables is that we need to replace the probability function with what is referred to as a probability density function. However, the concepts of joint and conditional probabilities follow exactly the same recipe as for discrete random variables. Let us start by illustrating the problems involved in assigning probabilities to a continuous random variable with an example:

Example 4.12: Production of goods – part 1

A company is trying to predict its output (measured in tons) next year. However, it does not have particularly reliable information on which to base this prediction, because the output depends on the weather and prices for raw materials. It therefore assumes that there is an equal probability of all quantities between 10 and 20 tons being produced. However, it also assumes that a minimum of 10 and a maximum of 20 tons will be produced. Therefore, the probability that the output is between 10 and 20 tons is equal to 1. But what is the probability that exactly 14.55325 tons will be produced? The answer is 0. Perhaps even more surprising, the probability is also 0 for any other quantity between 10 and 20 tons.

The probability of a continuous random variable assuming a specific value is zero because there are an uncountable (and hence infinite) number of values it can assume. If the probability of each of these values is greater than 0, then the overall probability will be infinitely large. But we do know that the total probability must be equal to 1. Therefore, it is necessary to find a new way to describe the uncertainty when random variables are continuous. This is done with the help of the cumulative distribution function.

4.4.1 The cumulative distribution function

The cumulative distribution function (or just the distribution function) is defined exactly as in Section 4.2.2:

> **The cumulative distribution function**, $F(x)$, for a continuous random variable, X, is defined as:
>
> $$F(x) = P(X \leq x)$$

We can use this definition both when X is discrete and when X is continuous. Example 4.13 shows how to employ the cumulative distribution function.

Example 4.13: Production of goods – part 2

In Example 4.12, X was the quantity of goods produced. It was assumed that this was at least 10 tons. Therefore, $F(x) = 0$ for all values of x less than 10 tons, as there is no probability of an output less than 10 tons. On the other hand, $F(x) = 1$ for $x \geq 20$ tons, since we assumed that no more than 20 tons would be produced. Now we have two reference points: $F(10) = 0$ and $F(20) = 1$. The question, then, is what values $F(x)$ assumes when x is between 10 and 20 tons.

The company assumed that all values between 10 and 20 tons were equally likely, but this did not allow us to say to anything meaningful about the probability of a particular value, since the probability of any given value occurring was 0. In order to capture the idea behind all of the values having equal probability, we can instead try to say something about an interval of values. It is thus possible to divide the range between 10 and 20 into a countable number of intervals. If we focus on intervals of values, instead of a particular value of the continuous random variable, we are able to use the approach adopted for a discrete random variable. When the starting point is that all values are equally probable, this assumption can be transferred to intervals of equal length, which must then also have the same probability. For example, the probability of obtaining a value in the interval 10 to 11 tons must be the same as the probability of obtaining a value in the interval 11 to 12 tons. Since the possible values lie between 10 and 20 tons, this interval can be divided into 10 smaller intervals of 1 ton each. Since all of these intervals must be equally probable, the probability of a value in each interval must be 0.1. This implies, for example, that $P(10 < X \leq 11) = 0.1$. From Section 4.2.2, we also know that this probability can be written with the help of the cumulative distribution function:

$$P\big(10 < X \le 11\big) = 0.1 = F\big(11\big) - F\big(10\big) = 0.1$$

Since $F(10) = 0$, then $F(11)$ must necessarily be equal to 0.1:

$$F\big(11\big) = P\big(10 < X \le 11\big) + F\big(10\big) = 0.1 + 0 = 0.1$$

This approach allows us to calculate the cumulative distribution function, $F(x)$, for this specific example. The result is shown in Figure 4.3.

The graph of a cumulative distribution function for a continuous random variable can take on many different shapes. Common to them all, however, is that they are continuous (unbroken).

4.4.2 The probability density function

In section 4.2.2 we showed that the cumulative distribution function for a discrete random variable was a step function, where the distance between two steps corresponds to the probability of the value in the point between the steps. The cumulative distribution function, F, for a continuous random variable on the other hand, is a continuous function with no jumps. However, we can use the slope of the graph of F to say something about how the cumulative probability changes when x is increased. The slope of the graph of $F(x)$ is denoted by $f(x)$ and is called the probability density function. It may be a little bit confusing that we also used $f(x)$ to denote the probability function for a discrete random variable. However, tradition prescribes this notation, and it is not usually a problem because when the situation arises we typically know whether a random variable is discrete or continuous, and therefore whether $f(x)$ is a probability function or a probability density function.

Example 4.14: Production of goods – part 3

In Figure 4.3, we have also plotted the probability density function for the production example. Since the probability density function is given by the slope of $F(x)$, and since this is a constant equal to 0.1, the probability density function remains flat between 10 and 20. This is because we assumed that all intervals of the same length would be equally probable. Note that the area under the density function is equal to $0.1 \cdot 10 = 1$. This is no coincidence. The area under a probability density function is always equal to 1, just as the sum of the probabilities for a discrete random variable must be 1.

Figure 4.3:
Probabili-
ty density
function and
cumulative
distribution
function

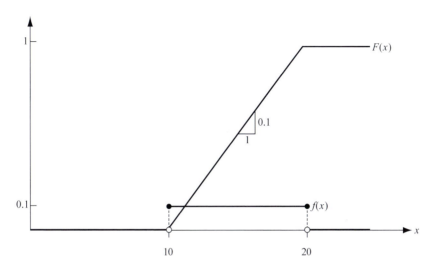

Formally, the probability density function is defined as the first derivative of the cumulative distribution function:

> **The probability density function**, $f(x)$, for a continuous random variable, X, is defined as:
> $$f(x) = \frac{dF(x)}{dx}$$

Similarly, if we know the probability density function, $f(x)$, we can find $F(x)$ by means of integration:

$$F(x) = \int_{-\infty}^{x} f(z)\, dz$$

The cumulative probability, $F(x_1)$, is therefore given by the area under the probability density function, $f(x)$, to the left of x_1, as illustrated in Figure 4.4.

Figure 4.4:
The cumulative
probability as
the area under
the proba-
bility density
function

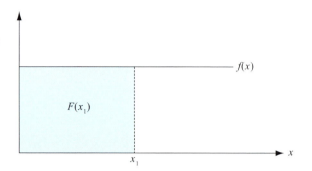

Example 4.15: Production of goods – part 4

From Figure 4.3, we can see that the cumulative distribution function
from the product example is given by:

$$F(x) = \begin{cases} 0 & if & x < 10 \\ 0.1 \cdot (x - 10) & if & 10 \leq x \leq 20 \\ 0 & if & 21 < x \end{cases}$$

We are therefore able to infer that the probability density function must
be given by:

$$f(x) = \begin{cases} 0 & if & x < 10 \\ 0.1 & if & 10 \leq x \leq 20 \\ 0 & if & 20 < x \end{cases}$$

as the derivative of $0.1 \cdot (x-10)$ is 0.1, while the derivatives of 0 and
1 are 0.

The continuous distribution for X from the production example is only
one of (infinitely) many different continuous distributions. The assumption of equal probability for equally large intervals meant that the probability density function was constant. If all intervals of the same length
do not have the same probability, then the probability density function
and the cumulative distribution function will take on different forms, as
we shall see in the following chapters.

4.5　Relationships between continuous random variables

The principles outlined in Section 4.3 about relationships between discrete random variables can be directly transferred to continuous random variables, the difference being that here, $f(x)$ is a probability density function. The box below summarises the formulas for the joint, marginal and conditional probability density functions. The summation sign from Section 4.3 has now been replaced by an integration sign (the continuous version of the summation sign).

The joint probability density function for two continuous random variables, X and Y, is written:

$$f(x,y)$$

The marginal probability density function, $f_X(x)$, for a continuous random variable, X, is defined as:

$$f_X(x) = \int_{-\infty}^{\infty} f(x,y)\,dy$$

The conditional probability density function, $f_{X|Y}(x|y)$, for a continuous random variable, X, given that $Y = y$, is defined as:

$$f_{X|Y}(x|y) = \frac{f(x,y)}{f_Y(y)} \quad \text{if } f_Y(y) > 0$$

The condition for independence between two continuous random variables also takes the same form as for discrete random variables:

Independence:

Two continuous random variables, X and Y, are independent if and only if:

$f(x,y) = f_X(x) \cdot f_Y(y)$ for all values of x and y

This implies

$f_X(x) = f_{X|Y}(x|y)$ for all values of x and y where $f_Y(y) > 0$,

and

$f_Y(y) = f_{Y|X}(y|x)$ for all values of y and x where $f_X(x) > 0$.

Two continuous random variables, X and Y, can assume values between 0 and 2. The marginal probability density functions are given by:

$$f_X(x) = \begin{cases} \frac{x}{2} & \text{if } 0 \leq x < 2 \\ 0 & \text{otherwise} \end{cases} \quad \text{and} \quad f_Y(y) = \begin{cases} \frac{y}{2} & \text{if } 0 \leq y < 2 \\ 0 & \text{otherwise} \end{cases}$$

If we assume that X and Y are independent, then the joint probability density function, $f(x,y)$, is given by:

$$f(x,y) = f_X(x) \cdot f_Y(y) = \begin{cases} 0.25 \cdot x \cdot y & \text{if } 0 \leq x < 2 \text{ and } 0 \leq y < 2 \\ 0 & \text{otherwise} \end{cases}$$

since $\left(\frac{x}{2}\right) \cdot \left(\frac{y}{2}\right) = 0.25 \cdot x \cdot y$. The conditional probability density function for X given $Y = y$ is then:

$$f_{X|Y}(x|y) = \frac{f(x,y)}{f_Y(y)} = \frac{0.25 \cdot x \cdot y}{0.5 \cdot y} = \frac{x}{2}$$

for $0 \leq y < 2$ and $0 \leq x < 2$. As a result of the assumed independence, the conditional probability density function is exactly the same as the marginal probability density function.

The rules for calculating conditional probabilities also look the same as before, with the summation sign replaced by an integration sign:

Rules for calculating conditional probabilities:

$$f_{X|Y}(x|y) = f_{Y|X}(y|x) \cdot \frac{f_X(x)}{f_Y(y)}$$

and:

$$f_{X|Y}(x|y) = f_{Y|X}(y|x) \cdot \frac{f_X(x)}{\int_{-\infty}^{\infty} f_{Y|X}(y|x) \cdot f_X(x) dx}$$

(Bayes' theorem)

4.6   Exercises

1. Review questions:
   a) What is the relationship between a random variable and an outcome of an experiment?
   b) Explain briefly the difference between discrete and continuous random variables.
   c) What are the properties of the probability function for a discrete random variable?
   d) How is the cumulative distribution function defined?
   e) Briefly explain the circumstances under which the relative frequency function of a population is equal to the probability function for a discrete random variable.
   f) How is the joint probability function for two discrete random variables defined?
   g) Explain the difference between marginal and conditional probabilities.
   h) What are the conditions for independence between two random variables?

2. Let X be a discrete random variable, the probability function of which is given in the table below.
   a) Determine the following probabilities: $P(X \le 3)$, $P(1 < X \le 3)$ and $P(X \ge 3)$.
   b) Find the cumulative distribution function, $F(x)$.
   c) Use the cumulative distribution function to calculate the probabilities in a).
   d) Plot the cumulative distribution function in a diagram with x on the horizontal axis.

x	$f(x) = P(X = x)$
1	0.12
3	0.43
4	0.07
5	0.30
0	0.08

3. Let Y be a discrete random variable that can assume seven different values. The cumulative distribution function for Y is given in the table below:

a) Plot the cumulative distribution function in a diagram with y on the horizontal axis.
b) Determine $P(Y < 3)$.
c) Determine $f(3) = P(Y = 3)$.
d) Determine the probability of $2 \le Y < 5$.
e) Find the probability function, f, for Y.

y	$F(y) = P(Y \le y)$
0	0.0083
1	0.0692
2	0.2553
3	0.5585
4	0.8364
5	0.9723
6	1

4. Consider the following experiment: Choose a person at random from the Danish workforce. Let the random variable, X, indicate the individual's gender, while Y indicates whether the person has changed jobs within the past year ($Y = 1$) or not ($Y = 0$). Assume that X and Y have the following joint probability function:

	$Y = 1$	$Y = 0$
$X = 1$ (man)	0.35	0.23
$X = 0$ (woman)	0.15	0.27

a) Calculate the marginal probability functions, $f_X(x)$ and $f_Y(y)$.
b) What is the probability of a change of jobs if the respondent is a man? And if it is a woman?
c) Are the two random variables independent?

5. Fill in the blank fields in the following probability table for the two discrete random variables, X and Y:

	$Y = 3$	$Y = 10$	$f_X(x)$
$X = 1$	0.3525	0.0572	
$X = 2$			
$f_Y(y)$	0.8600		

a) Are X and Y independent?
b) Determine the conditional probability functions, $f_{X|Y}(x|y)$ and $f_{Y|X}(y|x)$.

6. Let X and Y be two discrete independent random variables with the following marginal probability functions:

x	$f_X(x)$
1	0.24
2	0.47
3	0.29

and

y	$f_Y(y)$
2	0.67
0	0.33

a) Determine the conditional probability functions for X and Y.
b) Find the joint probability function for X and Y.

7. Let X be a continuous random variable with the following cumulative distribution function:

$$F(x) = \begin{cases} 0 & if & x \leq 0 \\ \frac{x}{3} & if & 0 < x \leq 3 \\ 1 & if & x > 3 \end{cases}$$

a) Plot the cumulative distribution function.
b) Calculate the probability that X is less than 2.4.

c) Calculate $P(1.5 < X \leq 2.5)$ and $P(X > 1.25)$.

d) Find $P(X = 2)$.

e) Can you find the probability density function?

8. In a car factory, 1.5% of the vehicles have a defect in the injection system that threatens to destroy the engine after only a short drive. As a result, all cars are tested when they leave the assembly line. However, the test is not entirely foolproof. The factory owner knows that if a car has a fault in the injection system, then there is a 90% chance that it will fail the test. However, he also knows that there is a 1% chance that a flawless car will fail the test.

   Let X be the random variable that takes the value 1 if a car has the defect, and 0 if not. Let Y be another random variable that takes the value 1 if the vehicle fails the test, and the value 0 if it does not.

   a) Derive the conditional probability function for Y given X, and then the marginal probability function for X, $f_X(x)$.

   b) Are X and Y independent?

   c) What is the probability that a vehicle that fails the test actually has a faulty injection system? (Use Bayes' theorem.) What is the probability of it not having the problem?

9. Let Y be a continuous random variable with the following probability density function:

$$f(y) = \begin{cases} 0 & if & y < 0 \\ \frac{1}{4} & if & 0 \leq y \leq 4 \\ 0 & if & y > 4 \end{cases}$$

   a) Plot the probability density function in a diagram with y out of the first axis.

   b) What is the probability that Y is less than 2? Illustrate this with the help of the figure from a).

   c) What is the probability at $1 \leq Y \leq 2.5$? Illustrate this probability.

   d) Can you work out the cumulative distribution function for Y?

5 Descriptive measures

Total income in Denmark is divided among more than 5.5 million people. With a letter height of 3 mm and a line spacing of 2 mm (i.e. a normal typographic layout), a complete list of 5.5 million incomes would be approximately 27.5 km long. Even the quickest reader with a photographic memory would be unable to glean much of an overview of the income distribution in Denmark by looking at such a list. In order to achieve some kind of understanding, we can instead define a number of descriptive measures that reveal interesting aspects of the overall income distribution in the country. One such descriptive measurement could be the average income. Another might be the income that separates the poorest 10% from the rest of the population. Of course, a single descriptive measure cannot describe an entire distribution – the average income is just one piece of data against the more than five million numbers that make up the overall income distribution – so care must be taken to avoid misinterpretation.

In Chapter 2, we introduced various descriptive measures, including the mean value and the variance, which could be used to obtain an overview of a real population. In this chapter, we will extend the use of these descriptive measures to random variables. This enables us to describe many additional situations that also involve uncertainty, for example, selections from super-populations.

Descriptive measures for random variables are divided into two classes. One class is based on observations of averages. The average income is an example. We can also construct descriptive measures for the spread of a distribution, which are based on averages. Overall, this class of descriptive measures is referred to as *moments*. The second class of descriptive measures is based on subdivisions of a distribution. An example is the income that separates the poorest 10% from the rest of the population. Overall, this class of descriptive measures is referred to as *quantiles*.

Moments are discussed in Section 5.2 and quantiles in Section 5.3. In Section 5.4, we will discuss how to use (and abuse) descriptive measures. We will look at descriptive measures for relationships between random variables in Section 5.5. Throughout the chapter, descriptive measures are defined for the distribution of a random variable instead of as descriptive measures for a real population, as was the case in Chapter 2. In Section 5.1, we explain why we chose this more general approach, and we explain the relationship between descriptive measures for a distribution of a random variable and for a real population.

5.1   Descriptive measures and random variables

In Chapter 2, we introduced a series of descriptive measures for a real population. These measures included the mean value, the variance and the median, and they described aspects of an existing real population. We now wish to take the idea behind this group of descriptive measures and transfer it to random variables, which can be used to deal with more general situations in which there is an element of uncertainty, and where the population involved can be a super-population.

In Chapter 2, we defined the relative frequency function, $g(z)$, for a real population. This tells us how the elements in the population are distributed, i.e. how big a proportion of the elements in the population have the incomes z_1, z_2, z_3, etc. The mean value for a real population can therefore be considered as a summary description of the relative frequency function.

In Chapter 4, we introduced random variables, which are used to handle complicated situations involving uncertainty. The probabilities for the range of values that a discrete random variable can assume are expressed by its *distribution*. A descriptive measure for a distribution of a random variable is therefore a summary description of the probability function (or probability density function if the random variable is continuous).

The connection between a real population and the distribution of a random variable was explained in Chapter 4. When the value of a random variable is given by the value of the element selected from a real population, and when all elements in the population have the same chance of selection, then the probability function, f, is equal to the relative frequency function, g. When this is the case, we can think of the distribution of the random variable as the distribution of the underlying population. In such cases, we often talk about the probability distribution for the random variable as *the population distribution,* and the descriptive measures for the population distribution are then called *population measures.*

The advantage of defining descriptive measures based on the distribution of random variables is that we can then also use the descriptive measures in situations where the random variable does not correspond to a selection from a real population. This applies, for example, to selections from super-populations or from real populations in which all of the elements do not have the same chance of selection. Let us illustrate this with some examples.

Example 5.1: A real population

In connection with the income distribution mentioned at the start of this chapter, we can define the following experiment: "Select a person and let the random variable, X, state his or her income." If all individuals have the same chance of selection, then the probability function for X will be equal to the relative frequency function for the population. Thus, X has the same "distribution" as the population. If a share of 0.1 of the population earns more than DKK 300,000, then the probability that X will assume a value greater than 300,000 is also 0.1. In this case, it makes no difference whether we describe the distribution of the population or the distribution of X.

Example 5.2: A super-population

In the example from Chapter 3 of a 30-year bond, the price at noon is a random variable, Y, with a given probability distribution. For example, the probability of the price being below 100 is 0.3. However, the probability distribution for this variable cannot be interpreted in terms of proportions of the super-population of prices. However, we are still able to describe the probability distribution for Y using different descriptive measures.

Many of the examples in this chapter will feature the relationship mentioned in Example 5.1 between the distribution of the random variable and the distribution of a real population. However, it is important to remember that descriptive measures also apply in many other situations in which the distribution of the random variable does not correspond to the distribution of an underlying real population, as is the case in Example 5.2.

5.2　Moments

The most commonly used moment for a random variable, X, is the *mean value,* also referred to as the *expected value.* The mean value is typically denoted by the letter μ or $E(X)$, where the E stands for expectation. Another frequently used moment is the *variance*, which describes how much the possible values of X, on average, are spread around the mean value. The variance is typically denoted with σ^2 or $V(X)$.

The interpretation of a moment is the same, regardless of whether the random variable is discrete or continuous. Technically, there is a difference in the method of calculation, so we will consider the two cases separately. As the concept can be grasped more intuitively in the case of discrete random variables, we shall focus on these. The sections on continuous random variables will therefore mainly contain the required formulas for calculating the moments.

5.2.1　Expected value of a discrete random variable

Intuitively, the expected value of a random variable, X, is equal to the average of all of the values of X, which you would get if you could repeat the realisation of X an infinite number of times. Formally, the expected value of a discrete random variable is defined as follows:

The expected value (mean value), $E(X)$, of a discrete random variable, X, with the probability function, $f(x)$, is given by:

$$E(X) = \sum_{i=1}^{N} x_i \cdot f(x_i) = x_1 \cdot f(x_1) + x_2 \cdot f(x_2) + \ldots + x_N \cdot f(x_N)$$

where $x_1, x_2, \ldots, x_N$ are the different values X can assume.

The expected value is a weighted average of all of the possible values that X can assume, where the weights used are the probabilities of the different values. The expected value of a random variable, X, is also referred to as the mean value, and is denoted by the Greek letter μ.

Example 5.3: A game of dice – part 1

Make X a random variable that indicates the number rolled on a dice. Since the probability of achieving the result 1 is one in six, etc., the expected value of X is given by:

$$E(X) = 1 \cdot \frac{1}{6} + 2 \cdot \frac{1}{6} + 3 \cdot \frac{1}{6} + 4 \cdot \frac{1}{6} + 5 \cdot \frac{1}{6} + 6 \cdot \frac{1}{6} = 3.5$$

The mean value of a roll of the dice is therefore 3.5. However, this is a value that it is not actually possible to roll with dice. The interpretation of the expected value is that if we throw the dice (i.e. repeat the experiment) many times, then the average of the realised values of X will approximate 3.5. Notice how this is similar to the interpretation of the concept of probability from Chapter 3 as the proportion of times an event occurs when you repeat an experiment infinitely.

Physically, we can interpret the mean value as a balance point. If you imagine that a probability is a counterweight, and that the probability distribution is all of the counterweights placed on a see-saw, then the mean value is the point at which you support the see-saw so that it is in balance. Figure 5.1 illustrates this for Example 5.3.

Figure 5.1:
Mean value as
a balance point

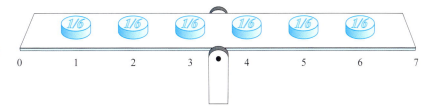

If a distribution is symmetrical around a point, then the mean value is equal to this point of symmetry. In Example 5.3, the probability distribution is symmetrical around the point 3.5, as seen in Figure 5.1. Each side of the distribution is a reflection of the other, with 3.5 at the centre.

Example 5.3 is an example of a random variable that assumes the same values as the elements of the real population from which it is selected – namely, 1, 2, 3, 4, 5 and 6. Since all of the elements in the population have the same chance of selection, the probability function, f, is equal to the relative frequency function, g. The population therefore also has the mean $\mu = 3.5$.

As we saw in Chapter 2, this mean value of the population can be calculated as the average of the N elements that comprise the real population. This is done by finding the sum of the elements and dividing by the number of elements, N_{pop}:

$$\text{Mean value of population} = \frac{z_1 + z_2 + \ldots + z_N}{N_{pop}}$$

where $z_1, z_2, \ldots, z_N$ are all of the elements in the population. In Example 5.3, the mean value of the population is: $\frac{1+2+3+4+5+6}{6} = 3.5$. Let us take another example:

Let us assume that all of the students in a class of 10 have the same chance of selection, and let the random variable, Y, indicate the height of the individual selected. The heights in centimetres for the 10 students are as follows: 134, 128, 164, 143, 144, 137, 122, 134, 140, 129. The height 134 cm occurs twice. Thus, this height has the relative frequency $\frac{2}{10}$, whereas the other heights in the population each have a relative frequency of $\frac{1}{10}$. The height 134 cm must therefore be ascribed the probability $\frac{2}{10}$, while the remaining 8 heights are each ascribed the probability $\frac{1}{10}$. Thus, the expected value of Y is equal to:

$$E(Y) = 122 \cdot \tfrac{1}{10} + 128 \cdot \tfrac{1}{10} + 129 \cdot \tfrac{1}{10} + 134 \cdot \tfrac{2}{10} + 140 \cdot \tfrac{1}{10} +$$
$$143 \cdot \tfrac{1}{10} + 144 \cdot \tfrac{1}{10} + 164 \cdot \tfrac{1}{10} = 137.5$$

Thus, the mean value of Y is 137.5 cm, which is also the population's mean value.

We may also be interested in the expectation associated with a function of a random variable. If $h(X)$ is a function of the random variable, X, then $h(X)$ itself is a random variable, and we can therefore calculate its expected value.

Let X be the random variable from Example 5.3, which indicates the numbers rolled on a dice. Assume that you take part in a game where you receive twice the value of the numbers rolled on the dice in DKK. Suppose also that it costs DKK 5 to join the game. We can then define a new random variable, Y, which indicates what you win from the game. This variable is given by: $Y = -5 + 2 \cdot X = h(X)$. If you throw a one, then X assumes the value 1, and Y therefore assumes the value $-5 + 2 \cdot 1 = -3$. Since X can assume the values 1, 2, 3, 4, 5 and 6, then Y can assume the values –3, –1, 1, 3, 5 and 7. In other words, if you are lucky and throw a six, then your net gain is DKK 7.

You can calculate the expected value of a function of X with the help of the probability distribution for X:

> **The expected value of a function**, $h(x)$, of a discrete random variable, X, with the probability function, $f(x)$, is given by:
>
> $$E\big(h(X)\big) = \sum_{i=1}^{N} h(x_i) \cdot f(x_i) =$$
> $$h(x_1) \cdot f(x_1) + h(x_2) \cdot f(x_2) + \dots + h(x_N) \cdot f(x_N)$$
>
> where $x_1, x_2, \dots, x_N$ are the different values X can assume.

The only difference compared to the expression for the expected value of X is that the value $h(x)$ has replaced x.

Example 5.6: A game of dice – part 3

In Example 5.5, you can calculate the expected value of Y as:

$$E(Y) = E(-5 + 2 \cdot X) = -3 \cdot \tfrac{1}{6} + (-1) \cdot \tfrac{1}{6} + 1 \cdot \tfrac{1}{6} + 3 \cdot \tfrac{1}{6} + 5 \cdot \tfrac{1}{6} + 7 \cdot \tfrac{1}{6} = 2$$

The expected value of the game – which costs DKK 5 to enter but where you win twice the number rolled on the dice – is therefore DKK 2. This can be interpreted as the average win per game if you played the game an infinite number of times.

If you have already calculated the expected value of X, then there are some special cases in which you can calculate the expected value of $h(X)$ without having to resort to lengthy calculations. These cases occur when $Y = a + b \cdot X$, where a and b are constants. For example, if you want to change the unit of measurement of a random variable, X, then the random variable with the new unit of measurement can be written as $Y = b \cdot X$. In these cases, we can express the expected value of Y directly as a function of the expected value of X. The following rules show exactly how this is done.

The expectation associated with a sum, $E(a + b \cdot X)$, is equal to the sum of the expectations associated with the parts in the sum, $E(a)$ and $E(b \cdot X)$. In addition, the expectation associated with a constant, $E(a)$, is equal to the constant itself. Finally, the expectation associated with a constant multiplied by a random variable, $E(b \cdot X)$, is equal to the constant multiplied by the expectation associated with the random variable, $b \cdot E(X)$.

Example 5.7: A school class – part 2

Following on from Example 5.4, we decide to measure the students' height in metres instead of centimetres. In other words, we define a new random variable $Z = 0.01 \cdot Y$, in which Y is the variable from Example 5.4. If Y indicates the height of the selected individual in centimetres, Z will therefore give us the height in metres. The mean value of Z is then:
$E(Z) = 0.01 \cdot E(Y) = 0.01 \cdot 137.5 = 1.375$ metres.

Example 5.8: A game of dice – part 4

In Example 5.5, Y is a function of X, which satisfies the third rule for the calculation of expected values in the box above. When we know the mean value of X, we can skip the somewhat cumbersome calculation in Example 5.6 and instead compute the mean value of Y as:
$E(Y) = E(-5 + 2 \cdot X) = -5 + 2 \cdot E(X) = -5 + 2 \cdot 3.5 = 2$

It is worth emphasising that the expected value of a function of X, $E(h(X))$, is not in general equal to the function of the expected value, $h(E(X))$. Example 5.9 illustrates this.

The random variable, X, can assume the values 3 and 5, with the probability 0.5 for each. Thus $E(X) = 3 \cdot 0.5 + 5 \cdot 0.5 = 4$. Let $Y = X^2$. As X equals 3 with probability 0.5, then Y equals 9 with probability 0.5. Similarly, $X = 5$ with probability 0.5, and thus $Y = 25$ with probability 0.5. The expected value of Y is therefore $E(Y) = 9 \cdot 0.5 + 25 \cdot 0.5 = 17$. So $E(Y) = E(X^2) = 17$, while $(E(X))^2 = 4^2 = 16$.

5.2.2 Expected value of a continuous random variable

We use integral calculus to calculate the expected value of a continuous random variable. Consider examples 4.12 and 4.13 from the previous chapter, where a company had to predict next year's production. The probabilities for each individual outcome were zero, because there were infinitely many potential outcomes. On the other hand, there was a positive probability of production between 10 and 11 tons. As in the case with discrete random variables, we have to match probabilities and values of outcomes. Since the probability of a particular outcome is 0 for a continuous random variable, we have to use the density function instead. The weighing is done by integrating the density function multiplied by the values of the outcomes. The formula for this is as follows:

> **The expected value (the mean value)**, $E(X)$, of a continuous random variable, X, with density function, $f(x)$, is given by:
>
> $$E(X) = \int_{-\infty}^{\infty} x \cdot f(x)dx$$

We will not use integral calculus much in this book. Yet we can still work comfortably with expected values of continuous random variables, as the calculation rules for continuous random variables are the same as for discrete random variables. These rules are:

> **Calculation rules: Expected values**
>
> i) $E(a) = a$
>
> ii) $E(b \cdot X) = b \cdot E(X)$
>
> iii) $E(a + b \cdot X) = E(a) + E(b \cdot X) = a + b \cdot E(X)$
>
> where X is a continuous random variable, and a and b are constants.

Example 5.10: Production of goods – part 1

Let X be the continuous random variable from examples 4.12–4.14, which indicated the company's production next year. We assumed that all outcomes between 10 and 20 tons were equally probable. Thus, the distribution is symmetrical around 15 tons, and the mean value of X is therefore equal to 15 tons. With the help of integral calculus, you can show that this is indeed the case:

$$E(X) = \int_{-\infty}^{\infty} x \cdot f(x) dx = \int_{10}^{20} x \cdot 0{,}1 \, dx = 0.1 \cdot \left(0.5 \cdot 20^2 - 0.5 \cdot 10^2\right) = 15$$

Now assume that 250 kg is wasted during the production process. Let Y be the random variable that indicates the net quantity in kilos: $Y = 1000 \cdot X - 250$, as X is measured in tons and Y is measured in kilos. The mean value of Y is found by using the third calculation rule from above:

$$E(Y) = E(1{,}000 \cdot X - 250) = 1{,}000 \cdot E(X) - 250 = 1{,}000 \cdot 15 - 250$$
$$= 14{,}750 \text{ kg}$$

5.2.3   Variance of a discrete random variable

After having calculated the mean value, you might be interested in knowing how the values are spread around the mean value. Suppose that we have a random variable, X, which assumes the values 40 and 60 with equal probability. The mean value is then $E(X) = 50$. Suppose that we have another random variable, Y, which assumes the values 0 and

100, again with equal probability. The mean value is again $E(Y) = 50$, but the two variables clearly have different distributions. The distribution for Y is more spread out than the distribution for X.

To obtain a descriptive measure for this spread, we can examine the expected squared spread around the mean value. This measure is called *the variance* and is denoted by $V(X)$ or σ^2.

The variance, $V(X)$, of a random variable, X, is defined as:

$$V(X) = E\left(\left[X - E(X)\right]^2\right) = \sigma^2$$

The variance can also be calculated as:

$$V(X) = E(X^2) - (E(X))^2 = E(X^2) - \mu^2$$

where $\mu = E(X)$.

This definition applies regardless of whether the random variable is discrete or continuous. It is the calculation of the expected values, $E(X^2)$ and $E(X)$, that distinguishes discrete and continuous random variables. For a discrete random variable, the variance can be computed as follows:

The variance of a discrete random variable, X, with the probability function, $f(x)$, is calculated as:

$$V(X) = \sum_{i=1}^{N}(x_i - \mu)^2 \cdot f(x_i)$$

$$= (x_1 - \mu)^2 \cdot f(x_1) + ... + (x_N - \mu)^2 \cdot f(x_N)$$

where $\mu = E(X)$ and $x_1,...,x_N$ are the values that X can assume.

The calculation of $V(X)$ is the same as if we were to calculate the expected value of the random variable, Y, given by $Y = h(X) = (X - E(X))^2 = (X - \mu)^2$. The variance is thus a weighted average of the different values of $(X-\mu)^2$, where the weights used are the probabilities of the different values, i.e. the probabilities of the different values of X.

Let us calculate the variance in some of the examples from earlier:

In the dice game from Example 5.3, the variance is:

$$V(X) = (1 - 3.5)^2 \cdot \tfrac{1}{6} + (2 - 3.5)^2 \cdot \tfrac{1}{6} + (3 - 3.5)^2 \cdot \tfrac{1}{6} + (4 - 3.5)^2 \cdot \tfrac{1}{6}$$
$$+ (5 - 3.5)^2 \cdot \tfrac{1}{6} + (6 - 3.5)^2 \cdot \tfrac{1}{6} = 2.9167$$

Alternatively, we can first find $E(X^2)$:

$$E(X^2) = 1^2 \cdot \tfrac{1}{6} + 2^2 \cdot \tfrac{1}{6} + 3^2 \cdot \tfrac{1}{6} + 4^2 \cdot \tfrac{1}{6} + 5^2 \cdot \tfrac{1}{6} + 6^2 \cdot \tfrac{1}{6} = 15.167$$

and calculate the variance as:

$$V(X) = E(X^2) - \mu = 15.167 - 3.5^2 = 2.9167$$

For the random variable, Y, from example 5.4, the variance is given by:

$$V(Y) = (122 - 137.5)^2 \cdot \tfrac{1}{10} + (128 - 137.5)^2 \cdot \tfrac{1}{10} + (129 - 137.5)^2 \cdot \tfrac{1}{10} +$$
$$(134 - 137.5) \cdot \tfrac{2}{10} + (137 - 137.5) \cdot \tfrac{1}{10} + (140 - 137.5)^2 \cdot \tfrac{1}{10} +$$
$$(143 - 137.5)^2 \cdot \tfrac{1}{10} + (144 - 137.5)^2 \cdot \tfrac{1}{10} + (164 - 137.5) \cdot \tfrac{1}{10} = 120.85$$

We can also use the square root of the variance: $\sigma(X) = \sqrt{V(X)}$ as a measure of the spread. This measure is called *the standard deviation*, and it is measured in the same units of measurement as the random variable, X, for which it is calculated.

> **The standard deviation**, $\sigma(X)$, of a random variable, X, with variance, $V(X)$, is given by:
>
> $$\sigma(X) = \sqrt{V(X)}$$

The standard deviation of the random variable, X, from Example 11.5 is given by:

$$\sigma(X) = \sqrt{V(X)} = \sqrt{2.9167} = 1.708$$

As in the case of the mean value, we also have some rules that we can apply when working with variances and standard deviations:[6]

Calculation rules: Variance and standard deviation

i) $V(a) = 0$ $\qquad\qquad\qquad \Rightarrow \sigma(a) = 0$

ii) $V(b \cdot X) = b^2 \cdot V(X) = b^2 \cdot \sigma^2 \quad \Rightarrow \sigma(b \cdot X) = |b| \cdot \sigma(X)$

iii) $V(a + b \cdot X) = V(b \cdot X) = b^2 \cdot \sigma^2 \Rightarrow \sigma(a + b \cdot X) = |b| \cdot \sigma(X)$

where X is a discrete random variable, a and b are constants, and $\sigma^2 = V(X)$.

The variance of a random variable is thus unaffected by the fact that a constant, a, is added to the random variable. Intuitively, an additive constant does not alter the distance between the possible values that the random variable may assume. As a consequence, the constant does not change the distance between the individual values and the mean value. However, a constant, b, matters when it is used to multiply the values of X. If b is greater than 1, it will spread the values more, and thereby increase the overall variance.

Note that the rules for standard deviations are obtained by taking the square root of the expressions for the variance.

The variable Y in Example 5.5 is given by: $Y = -5 + 2 \cdot X$. From Example 5.11, we know that the variance of X is 2.9167. Thus, we can compute the variance of Y by using the rules above:

---

6   We can derive these rules from the ones for expected values in Section 5.2.1 because the variance, as mentioned above, is formally an expectation of a function, $h(X)$.

$$V(Y) = V(-5 + 2 \cdot X) = 2^2 \cdot V(X) = 4 \cdot 2.9167 = 11.67$$

The standard deviation of Y consequently becomes:

$$\sigma(Y) = \sqrt{V(Y)} = 3.416$$

5.2.4   Variance of a continuous random variable

The variance of a continuous random variable is defined in exactly the same way as for a discrete random variable. The only difference is the way in which it is calculated. As for the mean value of a continuous random variable, the calculation of the variance involves integral calculus.

The variance of a continuous random variable, X, with density function, $f(x)$, is calculated as:

$$V(X) = \int_{-\infty}^{\infty} (x - \mu)^2 \cdot f(x)dx$$

where $\mu = E(X)$.

The rules for working with variances and standard deviations are the same as for a discrete random variable:

Calculation rules: Variance and standard deviation

i) $V(a) = 0$ $\qquad\qquad\qquad\qquad \Rightarrow \sigma(a) = 0$

ii) $V(b \cdot X) = b^2 \cdot V(X) = b^2 \cdot \sigma^2 \quad \Rightarrow \sigma(b \cdot X) = |b| \cdot \sigma(X)$

iii) $V(a + b \cdot X) = V(b \cdot X) = b^2 \cdot \sigma^2 \Rightarrow \sigma(a + b \cdot X) = |b| \cdot \sigma(X)$

where X is a continuous random variable, a and b are constants, and $\sigma^2 = V(X)$.

5.2.5 Moments of higher order

The variance of a random variable, X, is defined as the expected value of one particular function of this random variable, namely $\left[X - E(X)\right]^2$. Thus, the variance is the expected squared deviation of the random variable from its mean value. However, we could also raise $X - E(X)$ to the third or fourth power rather than the second before calculating the expectation. All of these different possibilities are collectively referred to as moments, and are defined as follows:

> **The kth moment**, m_k, of a random variable, X, is: $m_k = E\left(X^k\right)$
>
> **The kth central moment**, m_k^*, of a random variable, X, is:
>
> $$m_k^* = E\left(\left[X - E(X)\right]^k\right)$$

The mean value is equal to the first moment: $m_1 = E\left(X^1\right) = E(X)$, and the variance is equal to the second central moment: $m_2^* = E\left(\left[X - E(X)\right]^2\right)$.

The third central moment, $m_3^* = E\left(\left[X - E(X)\right]^3\right)$, describes how skewed the distribution of X is. If the distribution of X is symmetric, then the third central moment is 0. Finally, we are also sometimes interested in the fourth central moment: $m_4^* = E\left(\left[X - E(X)\right]^4\right)$. This moment is sensitive to values of X that are far from the mean value. As a result, this descriptive measure is often used to describe the probability for extreme values compared to the mean value.

There are also distributions for which no moments exist. This can happen if there is a high probability of extreme (i.e. large negative or positive) values of the random variable. To understand this, we can use the picture of the mean value as the point at which we have to support a see-saw with counterweights to keep it in balance (see Figure 5.1). If counterweights are placed too far towards the ends, and they are too heavy, the see-saw will break. Example 5.15 illustrates a situation in which the mean value of a random variable does not exist.

Example 5.15: No mean value

Assume that the discrete random variable, X, can take the following values: $x = 2, 4, 8, 16,...$, with the probabilities $f(x) = \frac{1}{x}$. In other words: X can assume arbitrarily high values, albeit with less and less probability.

First we check that $f(x)$ actually is a probability function. According to Section 4.2.1, the sum of the probabilities must be 1. Here it can be shown that the sum of the following infinite sequence actually is equal to one (try to check it yourself):

$$f(2) + f(4) + f(8) + f(16) + \cdots = \tfrac{1}{2} + \tfrac{1}{4} + \tfrac{1}{8} + \tfrac{1}{16} + \cdots$$

Furthermore, as $f(x) \geq 0$ then it follows from Section 4.2.1 that $f(x)$ is indeed a probability function.

The mean value of a discrete random variable is defined as the sum of all the possible values of the random variable, multiplied by their respective probabilities. If you undertake this calculation, you get the following:

$$E(X) = 2 \cdot f(2) + 4 \cdot f(4) + 8 \cdot f(8) + 16 \cdot f(16) + \cdots$$
$$= 2 \cdot \tfrac{1}{2} + 4 \cdot \tfrac{1}{4} + 8 \cdot \tfrac{1}{8} + 16 \cdot \tfrac{1}{16} + \cdots = 1 + 1 + 1 + 1 + \cdots$$

In other words, you get an infinite sum of ones and therefore an infinitely big number. Thus, the mean value of X does not exist.

For virtually all of the distributions that we present later in this book, both the mean value and the variance exist.

5.3 Quantiles

Quantiles provide an alternative way of summarising a distribution. Whereas moments are based on averages, quantiles are based on partitions of the distribution. The most commonly used quantile is the *median*. In brief, the median of a random variable, X, is a value such that X is greater than or equal to this value with probability 0.5 and less than or equal to this value with probability 0.5. Visually speaking, the median therefore divides the probability distribution for X in the middle. This is illustrated in Figure 5.2, which depicts the probability density function of a continuous random variable, X.

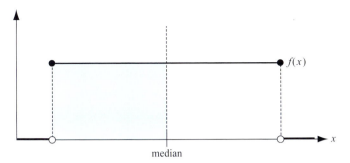

median

We can also find values of X that divide the distribution in a different way. These values are referred to as p-quantiles, where p denotes the part of the distribution to the left of the p-quantile. The median is thus the 0.5-quantile. The general definition of a p-quantile, applicable to both continuous and discrete random variables, is a little convoluted. Let us therefore start with the easiest case, which – for once – occurs when the random variable is continuous. For a continuous random variable, X, the p-quantile is that value of (or those values of) x that, when inserted into the cumulative distribution function, gives us p.

> The p-**quantilefor a continuous random variable**, X, with cumulative distribution function, $F(x)$, is a value, q_p, such that:
> $$F(q_p) = p$$

The continuous random variable, X, from Example 5.10, which indicated a company's output, had the following cumulative distribution function, cf. Example 4.14:

$$F(x) = \begin{cases} 0 & \text{if } x < 10 \\ 0.1 \cdot (x - 10) & \text{if } 10 \le x \le 20 \\ 1 & \text{if } 20 < x \end{cases}$$

The median (0.5-quantile), $q_{0.5}$, for X is determined as a solution to $F(q_{0.5}) = 0.5$, i.e. $0.1 \cdot (q_{0.5} - 10) = 0.5$, which gives us $q_{0.5} = 15$. The median is therefore the same as the mean value in this case (cf. Example 5.10). The 0.05-quantile is found in the same manner:

$$F(q_{0.05}) = 0.05 \Leftrightarrow 0.1 \cdot (q_{0.05} - 10) = 0.05 \Leftrightarrow q_{0.05} = 10.5$$

A random variable can have multiple median values (and p-quantiles), however, as illustrated in Example 5.17.

Example 5.17: Multiple median values

Suppose that the continuous random variable, X, has the density function illustrated in Figure 5.3; that is, there is a 0.5 probability of values between 1 and 2, and similarly a 0.5 probability of values between 3 and 4. Hence, there is a probability of 0 that X will assume a value between 2 and 3. But at the same time, all values between 2 and 3 split the probability mass into two equal parts. Therefore, all values between 2 and 3 meet the requirement for a 0.5-quantile according to the definition in the box above. Thus, these values are all median values.

Figure 5.3:
Probability
density
function
with multiple
medians

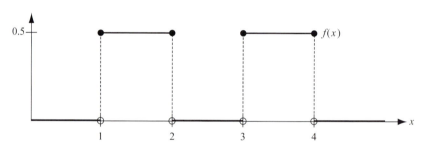

When, as in Example 5.17, there is an interval of values where all of the values meet the requirement to be a p-quantile, then we typically choose the midpoint in the interval. In Example 5.17, 2.5 will therefore become the median. We face a similar problem when dealing with discrete random variables, which we will now look at more closely.

Example 5.18: A game of dice – part 8

Let X be the discrete random variable that indicates the number rolled on a dice. As we established earlier, the probability distribution for X is as follows:

$$f(1) = \tfrac{1}{6}, \ \ f(2) = \tfrac{1}{6}, \ \ f(3) = \tfrac{1}{6}, \ \ f(4) = \tfrac{1}{6}, \ \ f(5) = \tfrac{1}{6}, \ \ f(6) = \tfrac{1}{6}$$

There is, therefore, a probability of 0.5 of getting a value of X less than 3.1, but there is also a probability of 0.5 of getting a value less than 3.5. So which of these values is the median? As in the case of continuous random variables, we typically choose the midpoint of the interval of values, all of which divide the probability mass into two equal parts. In this case, the value 3.5 therefore becomes the median.

The main problem when formulating the condition for a p-quantile for a discrete random variable stems from the fact that the cumulative distribution function, F, for a discrete random variable is a step function (see, for example, Figure 4.1). Therefore, it is typically not possible to solve the equation $F(q_p) = p$, which is the definition of a p-quantile for a continuous random variable. Below, we provide a general and somewhat cumbersome definition of a p-quantile that applies to both continuous and discrete random variables. However, for continuous random variables, the general definition is equivalent to the simpler definition shown in the box above.

> **Definition of p-quantile**
> For a random variable, X, with cumulative distribution function, $F(x)$, the value , q_p, is a p-quantile if and only if:
>
> i) $P(X < q_p) \le p$
>
> ii) $P(X > q_p) \le 1 - p$

The first condition says that an outcome that is less than the p-quantile must have maximum probability of p, while the second condition says that the probability of an outcome greater than the p-quantile must be less than or equal to $1 - p$. This convoluted definition is necessary because the cumulative distribution function for a discrete random variable is a step function and is therefore not continuous. However, the "spirit" of a p-quantile is exactly the same as in the case of a continuous random variable.

Example 5.19: Heads or tails

The discrete random variable, Y, which takes the value 1 if a coin lands on heads, and the value 2 if it lands on tails, has the following cumulative distribution function:

$$F(y) = \begin{cases} 0 & if & y < 1 \\ 0.5 & if & 1 \le y < 2 \\ 1 & if & y \ge 2 \end{cases}$$

Let us try to find the 0.25-quantile. We cannot use the definition of a
p-quantile for a continuous random variable here because it is impossible to find a value of $q_{0.25}$ that solves $F(q_{0.25}) = 0.25$ (see Figure 5.4.).
However, since Y is a discrete random variable, we have to use the
general definition of a p-quantile. The value 1 is a potential candidate
for the 0.25-quantile. We therefore check the conditions i) and ii) from
the box above. For i) we get $P(Y < 1) = 0$ which is less than 0.25. For
ii) we get $P(Y > 1) = 1 - P(Y \le 1) = 1 - 0.5 = 0.5$, which is less than
$1 - 0.25 = 0.75$. As such, both conditions are satisfied, and therefore 1
is a 0.25-quantile. Graphically, the 0.25-quantile is the value of y, where
$F(y)$ "jumps" above 0.25.

Figure 5.4:
Cumulative
distribution
function and
0.25-quantile

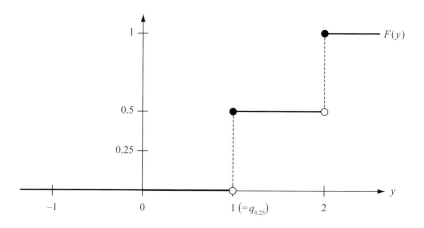

Finally, we note that quantiles, unlike moments, always exist. A number
of quantiles also have special names, as shown in the box below.

> **Special names for quantiles:**
>
> $q_{0.5}$ is called the median
>
> $q_{0.25}$ and $q_{0.75}$ are called quartiles
>
> $q_{0.1}, q_{0.2}, \ldots q_{0.9}$ are called deciles
>
> $q_{0.01}, q_{0.02}, \ldots q_{0.99}$ are called percentiles.

5.4   Choice of descriptive measures

The average resident of Dublin has fewer than two legs. You might infer from this that a major environmental disaster has struck the Irish capital, but even if there is just one resident of the city with only one leg (and none of them have more than two!) then this statement is actually correct. We must therefore be careful with the interpretation of descriptive measures such as the mean value, even though the calculations are performed correctly. It is also important to choose descriptive measures that provide a relevant picture of the distribution. Regarding the number of legs Dubliners have, it might be more useful to know the probability of a randomly selected inhabitant of the city having two legs.

Another example is the choice of descriptive measures for the income distribution in Ireland. Suppose that the random variable, X, indicates the income of a single, random Irish citizen. If the expected value of X is high, does this mean you can conclude that the whole Irish population is rich? No, it means that *on average* they are rich. If the majority of the population is poor, but a small number are extremely rich, then the mean value of the income will be high. The median income will be low, however, because the median is not particularly affected by the existence of a small group of rich people. It makes no difference to the median whether the richest 49% are just slightly richer than the median or incredibly rich. Both the mean value and the median are valid descriptive measures, but they tell two very different stories about the same inhabitants.

What the mean value and the median have in common is that they both provide a measure of the *central tendency* of a distribution. The median stems from a partition of the possible outcomes, whereas the mean value also uses information about the values of the different outcomes. Which of these two measures gives the best description of the distribution's middle, or the "typical" observation, depends on what we want to study.

In a symmetrical distribution, the median and the mean value are equal to each other. In practice, however, measurement errors often occur. For example, in the case of an income distribution, it may be that an extra 0 is added to some of the high incomes. Errors of this type will typically affect the calculation of the mean value more than the calculation of the median. Therefore, the median is said to be more *robust*.

5.4.1   The mode

The mode of a random variable is a commonly used (perhaps too commonly used) descriptive measure. This mode (which is also called the modal value) is the most likely value in a distribution. If the random variable is given by a simple random selection from a real population, the mode of the random variable will be the most frequently occurring value in the population.

Example 5.20: Mode

Suppose that the random variable X is defined as the outcome of a simple random selection from the following population: $\{1, 2, 3, 4, 5, 6, 7, 8, 9, 10, 1\}$. In this case, the mode is 1. For comparison, the mean value of X is equal to 5.09 and the median is 5.

The above example shows that you should not consider the mode as an alternative to the mean value or the median.

We use the terms *unimodal* and *bimodal* to describe the shape of a distribution. In a unimodal distribution, the probabilities are concentrated around the mode, with decreasing probabilities as the value moves further away from the mode (see Figure 5.5). Thus, for a continuous random variable, a unimodal distribution has only one peak. A bimodal distribution, by contrast, has two peaks, as seen in Figure 5.5.

Figure 5.5:
Unimodal
and bimodal
distribution

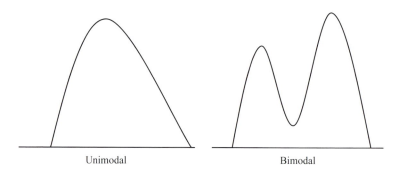

Unimodal   Bimodal

5.5   Descriptive measure for relationships between random variables

In order to spread the risk, trust funds invest in many different types of shares. Some shares tend to increase in value when others go down, and vice versa. Holding different types of shares ameliorates the effects of large and potentially bankruptcy-inducing fluctuations in individual share prices.

To describe relationships between random variables, for example share prices, we can look at their joint distribution. We already did this in Chapter 4, but because the joint probability function contains the full information about the variables' distribution, it is difficult to use it to gain an overview. Below, we therefore look at some descriptive measures that will be extremely useful when we seek to describe, for example, the relationship between the prices of various shares.

5.5.1   Expected value of a sum of random variables

The return on a share can be described as a random variable, X. Suppose that there is also another share with a return given by the random variable, Y. We can now put together a portfolio of shares where a is the number of shares of the first type, and b is the number of shares of the second type. Our total return will then be given by the random variable Z:

$$Z = a \cdot X + b \cdot Y$$

What is the expected return from this portfolio? This can be determined by using the following general formula for the expected value of a sum of random variables, which applies to both discrete and continuous variables:

> **The expected value of a sum of random variables** (discrete or continuous) is given by:
>
> $$E(a \cdot X + b \cdot Y) = E(a \cdot X) + E(b \cdot Y) = a \cdot E(X) + b \cdot E(Y)$$
>
> where a and b are constants.

The expected value of the sum of two random variables does not depend on how the two random variables move together. It depends solely on their individual expected values.

The expected return from the portfolio, Z, is therefore equal to the expected return of a X-shares and b Y-shares:

$$E(Z) = a \cdot E(X) + b \cdot E(Y)$$

5.5.2 Covariance

A portfolio's variance, $V(Z) = V(a \cdot X + b \cdot Y)$, is one measure of its risk. The variance of a sum of random variables, irrespective of whether they are discrete or continuous, depends on the variance of each individual random variable, but also on the *covariance*. In Chapter 2, we calculated the covariance between two characteristics in a real population. The covariance between two random variables is defined in a similar way:

> **The covariance**, $Cov(X,Y)$, between two random variables, X and Y, is defined by:
>
> $$Cov(X,Y) = E\left[(X - \mu_X) \cdot (Y - \mu_Y) \right]$$
>
> where $\mu_X = E(X)$ and $\mu_Y = E(Y)$. An alternative formula for calculating the covariance is:
>
> $$Cov(X,Y) = E(X \cdot Y) - \mu_X \cdot \mu_Y$$

The calculation of the expected values depends on whether the random variables are discrete or continuous. For two discrete random variables, we can compute the covariance as follows:

> **The covariance between two discrete random variables**, X and Y, is calculated as:
>
> $$Cov(X,Y) = \sum_{x_i}\sum_{y_j}(x_i - \mu_x) \cdot (y_j - \mu_Y) \cdot f(x_i, y_j)$$
>
> or:
>
> $$Cov(X,Y) = \left(\sum_{x_i}\sum_{y_j} x_i \cdot y_j \cdot f(x_i, y_j)\right) - \mu_X \cdot \mu_Y$$
>
> where $\mu_X = E(X)$, $\mu_Y = E(Y)$ and $f(x,y)$ is the joint probability function.

The summation signs $\sum_{x_i}\sum_{y_j}$ mean that we are summing over all the possible combinations of values of X and Y.

The covariance expresses something about how the two variables are related. A positive covariance means that high values of Y are most likely to occur when we observe high values of X, and correspondingly that low values of Y are most likely to occur together with low values of X. Conversely, a negative covariance means that low values of X are most likely to occur together with high values of Y and vice versa.

Example 5.21 illustrates the calculation of the covariance between two discrete random variables.

Example 5.21: Market trend and company bankruptcy

Consider the random variables X and Y, from Section 4.3, which indicated, respectively, whether a company went bankrupt ($X = 0$) or not ($X = 1$), and whether the market conditions would be unfavourable ($Y = 0$) or favourable ($Y = 1$). Their joint probability function was given in Table 4.2. To find the covariance between these two variables, we first calculate their expected values:

$$\mu_X = E(X) = 0 \cdot f_X(0) + 1 \cdot f_X(1) = 0 \cdot 0.3 + 1 \cdot 0.7 = 0.7$$

$$\mu_Y = E(Y) = 0 \cdot f_Y(0) + 1 \cdot f_Y(1) = 0 \cdot 0.4 + 1 \cdot 0.6 = 0.6$$

Here, we must remember to use the marginal probabilities. Then $E(X \cdot Y)$ is calculated:

$$E(X \cdot Y) = \sum_{x_i} \sum_{y_j} x_i \cdot y_j \cdot f(x_i, y_j)$$

$$= 0 \cdot 0 \cdot f(0,0) + 1 \cdot 0 \cdot f(1,0) + 0 \cdot 1 \cdot f(0,1) + 1 \cdot 1 \cdot f(1,1)$$

$$= 0 \cdot 0 \cdot 0.2 + 1 \cdot 0 \cdot 0.2 + 0 \cdot 1 \cdot 0.1 + 1 \cdot 1 \cdot 0.5 = 0.5$$

The covariance is therefore given by:

$$Cov(X,Y) = E(X \cdot Y) - \mu_X \cdot \mu_Y = 0.5 - 0.7 \cdot 0.6 = 0.08$$

In Example 5.21, the covariance is equal to 0.08. This tells us that there is the greatest chance of bankruptcy ($X = 0$) when the market is unfavourable ($Y = 0$), and the greatest chance of avoiding bankruptcy ($X = 1$) when the market is favourable ($Y = 1$).

In calculating the covariance between two continuous random variables, we have to use integral calculus. In the formula for the covariance between two discrete random variables, the sum signs must be replaced with integral signs, and the joint probability function replaced with the joint density function. However, the interpretation remains exactly the same as before:

The covariance between two continuous random variables, X and Y, is calculated as:

$$Cov(X,Y) = \iint_{x,y} (x - \mu_x) \cdot (y - \mu_Y) \cdot f(x,y) \, dy \, dx$$

or:

$$Cov(X,Y) = \left(\iint_{x,y} x \cdot y \cdot f(x,y) \, dy \, dx \right) - \mu_X \cdot \mu_Y$$

where $\mu_X = E(X)$, $\mu_Y = E(Y)$ and $f(x,y)$ is the joint probability density function.

There are also some rules for calculating covariances that apply regardless of whether the random variables are continuous or discrete. These are:

Calculation rules: Covariance

i) $Cov(X,Y) = Cov(Y,X)$

ii) $Cov(a \cdot X, b \cdot Y) = a \cdot b \cdot Cov(X,Y)$

iii) $Cov(a + X, b + Y) = Cov(X,Y)$

iv) $Cov(X + Z, Y) = Cov(X,Y) + Cov(Z,Y)$

where X, Y and Z are (discrete or continuous) random variables, and a and b are constants.

We are now ready to present the expression for the variance of a sum of random variables, and hence the variance of our share portfolio: $V(Z) = V(a \cdot X + b \cdot Y)$:

The variance of a sum of random variables:

$$V(a \cdot X + b \cdot Y) = V(a \cdot X) + V(b \cdot Y) + 2 \cdot Cov(a \cdot X, b \cdot Y)$$
$$= a^2 \cdot V(X) + b^2 \cdot V(Y) + 2 \cdot a \cdot b \cdot Cov(X,Y)$$

Here, we have used rule ii) from the box above in the final step. The variance of a sum of random variables is thus equal to the sum of the individual variances plus two times the covariance.

Example 5.22: Risk diversification – part 1

Let X and Y be two continuous random variables that indicate the future return on two different shares: share$_X$ and share$_Y$. We assume that the mean values of X and Y are both equal to 4, and the variances, $V(X)$ and $V(Y)$, are both equal to 2. This is the easiest way to illustrate the effect of the covariance. Assume that the covariance between X and Y is equal to -1. If you choose to buy two of share$_X$, you get an expected return of:

$$E(2 \cdot X) = 2 \cdot E(X) = 2 \cdot 4 = 8$$

with a variance of:

$$V(2 \cdot X) = 4 \cdot V(X) = 4 \cdot 2 = 8$$

You get the same expected return and variance if, instead, you buy two of share$_Y$, because it has the same mean value and variance as share$_X$. If, on the other hand, you buy one of each share, you get an expected return of:

$$E(X + Y) = E(X) + E(Y) = 4 + 4 = 8$$

which is the same as if you had either two shares of type X or two of type Y. The variance in the portfolio, on the other hand, is:

$$V(X + Y) = V(X) + V(Y) + 2 \cdot Cov(X,Y) = 2 + 2 + 2 \cdot (-1) = 2$$

which is four times less than if you had either two shares of type X or two shares of type Y. By spreading the investment across two shares, you are able to reduce the total variance without compromising the expected return! The reason is that when X gives a low return, Y typically gives a high return. In this way, you reduce the probability of major fluctuations in the overall performance of the portfolio.

5.5.3 Correlation coefficient

One problem with the covariance as a measure of how two variables are related is that its size depends on the random variables' unit of measurement. If we multiply the random variables, X and Y, by two constants, a and b, then we also multiply the covariance by these:

$$Cov(a \cdot X, b \cdot Y) = a \cdot b \cdot Cov(X,Y)$$

This is a consequence of rule ii) from the box above. Therefore, if we redefine X, e.g. from centimetres to metres, then we also change the covariance between X and Y. In order to obtain a measure of the relationship between two random variables that is independent of such irrelevant transformations of the random variables, *the correlation coefficient* is often used. The correlation coefficient is obtained by dividing the covariance by the square root of the product of the variances:

> **The correlation coefficient,** $\rho\left(X,Y\right)$ for two random variables, X and Y, is given by:
>
> $$\rho\left(X,Y\right) = \frac{Cov\left(X,Y\right)}{\sqrt{V\left(X\right)\cdot V\left(Y\right)}}$$

The correlation coefficient has the same sign as the covariance, but it always lies between –1 and 1. If the correlation coefficient is equal to 1 or –1, then the two variables are said to have a perfect positive and a perfect negative correlation, respectively.

Example 5.23: Risk diversification – part 2

The correlation coefficient for between X and Y from Example 5.22 can be calculated as:

$$\rho\left(X,Y\right) = \frac{Cov\left(X,Y\right)}{\sqrt{V\left(X\right)\cdot V\left(Y\right)}} = \frac{-1}{\sqrt{2\cdot 2}} = -\frac{1}{2}$$

In section 4.3.5, we introduced the concepts of dependence and independence between two random variables as a means of analysing the relationship between them. Independence is a stronger concept than covariance, as independence between two random variables implies that the covariance between them is 0. On the other hand, a covariance of 0 between two random variables does not necessarily imply that they are independent. This difference is illustrated in one of the following exercises.

5.6   Exercises

1. Review questions
   a) Name the different moments with which we have become acquainted in this chapter.
   b) How is the expected value of a discrete random variable calculated?
   c) What is the difference between the variance and the standard deviation of a random variable?

d) What is a quantile?

e) What does the covariance between two random variables express? How is it calculated?

f) What is the relationship between the covariance and the correlation coefficient?

g) Which values can the correlation coefficient assume?

h) How is the expectation of a sum of random variables calculated?

i) How is the variance of a sum of random variables calculated?

2. Let X be a discrete random variable with the probability function given in the table below.

a) Determine the expected value of X.

b) Find $E(2 + 5.4 \cdot X)$ and $E(\sqrt{X})$.

c) Calculate $V(X)$.

d) What is the variance of $3 \cdot X$?

x	$f(x) = P(X = x)$
1	0.12
3	0.43
4	0.07
5	0.30
0	0.08

3. Let Y be a continuous random variable with $E(Y) = 3.2$ and $E(Y^2) = 14.1$.

a) Calculate the variance and standard deviation of Y.

b) Also find the variance of $7 \cdot Y + 0.25$.

c) Calculate $E(7 + 2 \cdot Y^2)$.

4. A lottery issues tickets worth DKK 0.00, DKK 100.00 and DKK 100,000.00. There are 90,000 tickets of the first type, 9,999 of the second type and only one of the third type.

a) What is the expected yield on a randomly selected lottery ticket?

b) Assume that all tickets are sold. What would be the minimum cost per ticket to make sure that the organiser breaks even?

c) A ticket costs DKK 25.00. What is the expected profit for the organiser if 9,000 tickets are sold?

5. A random variable, X, has mean value 10 and variance 50.
   a) Calculate the mean value and variance of the random variable,
      $Y = 10 + 5 \cdot X$.
   b) Find the mean value of $Y = (X - 10)^2$ and $Z = X^2$ (exploit the
      fact that $V(X) = E(X^2) - [E(X)]^2$).

6. Let X and Y be two continuous random variables with the following
   distribution functions:

$$F(x) = \begin{cases} 0 & if & x \le 0 \\ \frac{x}{3} & if & 0 < x \le 3 \\ 1 & if & x > 3 \end{cases}$$

$$F(y) = \begin{cases} 0 & if & y \le 4 \\ \left(1 - \frac{y}{4}\right)^2 & if & 4 < y \le 8 \\ 1 & if & y > 8 \end{cases}$$

   a) Find the medians for X and Y.
   b) Find the 0.05-quantiles and the 0.95-quantiles for X and Y.

7. Let Y be a random variable that can assume seven different values.
   The cumulative distribution function for Y is given in the table below.
   a) Determine the median for Y.
   b) Find the 0.1-quantile and the 0.75-quantile.

y	$F(y) = P(Y \le y)$
0	0.0083
1	0.0692
2	0.2553
3	0.5585
4	0.8364
5	0.9723
6	1

8. Consider the experiment from Exercise 4 in Chapter 4, where X and Y were random variables (indicators) for gender and change of job, with joint probabilities as in the table below.
   a) Calculate the covariance between X and Y.
   b) Find the correlation coefficient between X and Y.
   c) What do your results tell you about the relationship between gender and change of job?

	$Y = 1$	$Y = 0$
$X = 1$	0.35	0.23
$X = 0$	0.15	0.27

9. Let X and Y be two random variables with joint probabilities as in the table below.
   a) Calculate the covariance between X and Y.
   b) Are X and Y independent?
   c) Find the marginal probability function for X.
   d) Write up the conditional probability function for X given $Y = 1$.
   e) Interpret your results.
   f) Find the expected values of X and Y.
   g) Find the variances of X and Y.
   h) Let the random variable Z be given by $Z = 2 \cdot X + 3 \cdot Y$. Calculate the expected value and the variance of Z.

	$Y = 0$	$Y = 1$	$Y = 2$
$X = 0$	0.15	0.1	0.15
$X = 1$	0.1	0	0.1
$X = 2$	0.15	0.1	0.15

10. Let X and Y be two random variables with $E(X) = 2.3$ and $E(Y) = 1.4$. Also, let the standard deviations of X and Y be 1.1 and 0.8, respectively, while the covariance is 0.2.
    a) Calculate the expected value of $Z = 2 \cdot X + 3.3 \cdot Y$.
    b) Find the variance of Z.

6 Commonly used distributions

In Chapter 4, we introduced random variables as a method of representing the outcome of an experiment. Random variables are either discrete (e.g. a roll of the dice) or continuous (e.g. amount of a fluid). In this chapter, we will look at some frequently occurring distributions for random variables. Although a random variable may have any distribution, in practice there are certain distributions that we encounter more frequently than others.

Many of the useful distributions are relatively simple to describe. In the previous chapters, we have assigned a probability to every possible value of a random variable. In cases with more than two values, this can be done in the form of a table. However, if a random variable can take on multiple values, then the table used to specify the distribution will become excessively large and unmanageable. In some cases we can, instead, specify the distribution of a random variable with the help of a few parameters. Once these have been described, we can work out the probability for all possible values of the random variable by using a (simple) formula. The distributions we encounter in this chapter can all be specified with the help of a formula and a few parameter values.

In sections 6.1 to 6.4, we will look at four different discrete distributions. In Section 6.5, we will become acquainted with the normal distribution, which is a distribution for a continuous random variable. Finally, in Section 6.6, we will look at a popular joint distribution for several discrete random variables.

6.1   The Bernoulli distribution

A discrete random variable, X, is said to follow a Bernoulli distribution if: i) there are two possible outcomes, i.e. X can assume one of two values (typically 1 and 0); and ii) the probabilities of the two values are p and $1-p$, respectively. In that case, we say that X is Bernoulli-distributed with parameter p. This is written: $X \sim \text{Ber}(p)$, where "$\sim$" is read as "distributed".

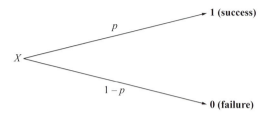

Often, the two possible outcomes for X are denoted as "success" (when $X = 1$) and "failure" (when $X = 0$). These two designations should not be understood as value judgements meaning that one outcome is necessarily better than the other. They are just a way of naming the outcomes. Alternatively, we can say that X "has the property" (when $X = 1$) or "does not have the property" (when $X = 0$). This is just another way of saying essentially the same thing, namely that X can take two, and only two, values.

Perhaps surprisingly, many populations can give rise to Bernoulli-distributed random variables. Here are three examples.

Example 6.1: Heads or tails – part 1

For the "tossing a coin" experiment, the population is "heads" and "tails". We can define a random variable X such that it assumes the value 1 in the case of tails (success) and the value 0 in case of heads (failure). If heads and tails are equally probable, i.e. if it is a "fair" coin, then X is Bernoulli-distributed with the parameter $p = \frac{1}{2}$, i.e. $X \sim \text{Ber}\left(\frac{1}{2}\right)$.

Example 6.2: Yes or no

If we stop a random person in the street and ask whether he or she intends to vote yes or no in an upcoming referendum, and we assume that there are only these two options, then we are dealing with a population consisting of "yes voters" and "no voters". We can therefore define a random variable, X, which takes the value 1 if the person turns out to be a yes voter, and the value 0 if he or she is a no voter. In this case, X is

Bernoulli-distributed with the parameter p, where p is the proportion of the electorate that will vote yes.

Example 6.3: The weather tomorrow

Let Y be a random variable that takes the value 1 if it rains tomorrow, and the value 0 if it does not. The associated population is a super-population with the elements "rain" and "no rain". Thus, Y is Bernoulli-distributed with the parameter p, where p is the probability of rain tomorrow (however this probability is determined).

As the above examples illustrate, the Bernoulli distribution is relevant in situations in which we randomly select an element from a population consisting of only two types of element. This may be from a real population, as in the case of the national electorate in Example 6.2, or from a super-population, as in Example 6.3. Populations with only two types of element are also called Bernoulli populations.

> A **Bernoulli population** is a real population or a super-population that contains only two types of element: successes and failures.

We can also find descriptive measures for a random variable that is Bernoulli-distributed. As there are only two possible values for such a random variable, we can easily calculate the mean value and the variance using the methods presented in Chapter 5:

$$E(X) = 1 \cdot p + 0 \cdot (1 - p) = p$$
$$E(X^2) = 1^2 \cdot p + 0^2 \cdot (1 - p) = p$$
$$V(X) = E(X^2) - E(X)^2 = p - p^2 = p \cdot (1 - p)$$

The properties of a Bernoulli-distributed random variable are summarised in the following box:

> **The Bernoulli distribution**, $X \sim \text{Ber}(p)$
>
> **Probability function**: $f(1) = p$ and $f(0) = 1 - p$
>
> **Mean value and variance**: $E(X) = p$ and $V(X) = p \cdot (1 - p)$
>
> **Interpretation**: X denotes the result of a random draw from a Bernoulli population, where $X = 1$ is success, $X = 0$ is failure, and p is the probability of success.

6.2 The binomial distribution

The binomial distribution arises when you randomly draw n elements independently of each other from a Bernoulli population. In this case, each draw has the probability p of being a success. In other words, if X_1 is the random variable for the outcome of the first draw, so that $X_1 = 1$ indicates a success, then X_1 is Bernoulli-distributed with parameter $p : X_1 \sim \text{Ber}(p)$. Similarly, $X_2 \sim \text{Ber}(p)$, where X_2 indicates the outcome of the second draw, and so on up to X_n. The random variable, Y, indicating the number of successes in the n independent draws, is then said to be binomially distributed with the parameters n and p. We write this as follows: $Y \sim \text{Bin}(n,p)$, where n is the number of draws and p is the probability of success in each draw.

Example 6.4: Heads or tails – part 2

If we toss a coin five times and define the random variable Y as the number of tails in these five attempts, then Y is binomially distributed with $n = 5$ and $p = \frac{1}{2}$: $Y \sim \text{Bin}\left(5, \frac{1}{2}\right)$.

If Y is binomially distributed with the parameters n and p, it means that Y can assume the values $0,1,2,\ldots,n$. More specifically, Y assumes the value 0 if none of the n draws result in a success, i.e. if $X_1 = 0$, $X_2 = 0$, $\ldots$, $X_n = 0$. Similarly, Y assumes the value n if all of the draws result in successes: $X_1 = 1$, $X_2 = 1$, $\ldots$, $X_n = 1$. We can therefore write Y as: $Y = X_1 + X_2 + \ldots + X_n = \sum_{i=1}^{n} X_i$. The value that Y assumes is equal to the number of successes in the n draws, i.e. the sum of the values of the X_is.[7]

Thus, the binomial distribution emerges as the distribution of a sum of independent Bernoulli-distributed random variables. As we will see later, the binomial distribution is extremely useful, for instance, when conducting opinion polls for yes/no votes at a referendum or when analysing the demand for a new product through consumer surveys. In the first case, we draw a sample from a Bernoulli population consisting of yes and no voters. In the second case, the Bernoulli population consists of buyers and non-buyers.

We still need to find a formula for the probability distribution for Y. Example 6.5 shows how we arrive at this formula.

Example 6.5: Heads or tails – part 3

Imagine that we toss a coin twice. Let Y be the number of tails in the two attempts. Y is then binomially distributed with $n = 2$ and $p = \frac{1}{2}$ i.e. $Y \sim \text{Bin}\left(2, \frac{1}{2}\right)$. Let X_i be the outcome of the ith toss, so that $X_1 = 1$ if the first toss is tails, and $X_1 = 0$ if it is heads, and similarly for X_2. Y is then equal to the sum of X_1 and X_2: $Y = X_1 + X_2$. Because the two tosses of the coin are independent, we also know from Chapter 4 that their joint probability, $f(x_1, x_2)$, is given by the product of the marginal probabilities, $f_{X_1}(x_1)$ and $f_{X_2}(x_2)$, i.e.: $f(x_1, x_2) = f_{X_1}(x_1) \cdot f_{X_2}(x_2)$. The probability of getting two tails is equal to the probability of tails in the first toss multiplied by the probability of tails in the second toss, etc. The various possible outcomes of the experiment with associated probabilities and values of Y, can therefore be summarised as in the following table:

Table 6.1:

X_1	X_2	Probability	Y
1	1	$p \cdot p = \frac{1}{2} \cdot \frac{1}{2} = \frac{1}{4}$	2
1	0	$p \cdot (1 - p) = \frac{1}{2} \cdot \frac{1}{2} = \frac{1}{4}$	1
0	1	$(1 - p) \cdot p = \frac{1}{2} \cdot \frac{1}{2} = \frac{1}{4}$	1
0	0	$(1 - p) \cdot (1 - p) = \frac{1}{2} \cdot \frac{1}{2} = \frac{1}{4}$	0

---

7   This also illustrates why it is appropriate to code the two possible outcomes for X_i as 0 and 1 instead of, for example, 13 and 17.

Let the probability function for Y be $f_Y(y)$. From the table above, we know that:

$$f_Y(2) = \frac{1}{4}$$

$$f_Y(1) = \frac{1}{4} + \frac{1}{4} = \frac{1}{2}$$

$$f_Y(0) = \frac{1}{4}$$

The probability of $Y = 1$ is equal to the sum of two probabilities from the table. The reason is that there are two combinations of outcomes of X_1 and X_2, which both result in $Y = 1$, namely heads followed by tails or tails followed by heads.

Example 6.5 illustrates that the probability distribution of Y depends on the number of ways of achieving the same number of successes in n draws. In the world of statistics, this is also called the number of *combinations*. It follows that if $Y \sim \text{Bin}(n,p)$ then $f_Y(y)$, where y is an integer, is given by:

$f_Y(y)$ = "the number of combinations of values of the X_is that result in
$\qquad\qquad Y = y$" · "the probability of such a combination".

In Example 6.5, there are two combinations of values of X_1 and X_2 that result in $Y = 1$. The probability for each of these combinations is $\left(\frac{1}{2}\right)^2$. Therefore, $f_Y(1) = 2 \cdot \left(\frac{1}{2}\right)^2 = \frac{1}{2}$.
   More generally, we can find the number of combinations that result in k successes in n drawings by using the following formula:

The binomial coefficient: $\displaystyle \binom{n}{k} = \frac{n!}{k! \cdot (n - k)!}$

where "$n!$" is the factorial of n and is calculated as:

$$n! = n \cdot (n - 1) \cdot (n - 2) \cdot \ldots \cdot 2 \cdot 1$$

$4! = 4 \cdot 3 \cdot 2 \cdot 1 = 24$ and $2! = 2 \cdot 1 = 2$ and $0!=1$. The latter is by convention.

Example 6.7: Heads or tails – part 4

In Example 6.5, we found that there were two ways in which you could get a single tail ($k = 1$) in two attempts ($n = 2$). Let us check that the binomial coefficient produces the same result:

$$\binom{2}{1} = \frac{2!}{1! \cdot (2-1)!} = \frac{2}{1 \cdot 1} = 2$$

Example 6.8: The binomial coefficient

$$\binom{4}{2} = \frac{4!}{2! \cdot (4-2)!} = \frac{24}{2 \cdot 2} = 6$$

There are six ways of achieving two successes in four selections, for example, two "tails" in four tosses of a coin. One way could be: "head-tail-head-tail". Another could be: "head-head-tail-tail". Try to write up the six different combinations yourself.

The binomial coefficient is our general formula for calculating the number of combinations that give k successes in n selections. Once this is done, we then have to find the probability of each of these combinations. Since the individual elements are selected independently, we know that the probability of a given combination of X_is is equal to the product of their marginal probabilities.

Example 6.9: Heads or tails – part 5

The probability of tossing "head-head-tail-tail" in four (independent) tosses of a coin is:

$$\frac{1}{2} \cdot \frac{1}{2} \cdot \frac{1}{2} \cdot \frac{1}{2} = \left(\frac{1}{2}\right)^4$$

Example 6.10: Probability of a given combination

If we make five independent draws from a Bernoulli population with $p = 0.3$, then the probability of first getting two successes, then two failures and finally one success is given by:
$$0.3 \cdot 0.3 \cdot (1 - 0.3) \cdot (1 - 0.3) \cdot 0.3 = (0.3)^3 \cdot (1 - 0.3)^{5-3}$$

In general, the probability of a given combination of k successes and $n - k$ failures in n independent draws is given by the formula: $p^k \cdot (1 - p)^{n-k}$, where p is the probability of success in each draw. We can therefore write the probability that Y is equal to k as follows:

$$f_Y(k) = \binom{n}{k} \cdot p^k \cdot (1 - p)^{n-k}$$

where $\binom{n}{k}$ is the number of combinations that give k successes, and $p^k \cdot (1 - p)^{n-k}$ is the probability of each of these combinations. $f_Y(k)$ is the probability function for Y, when $\text{Bin}(n, p)$. Note that if n, for example, is equal to 100, then Y can assume 101 different values, which may each have a different probability. But we only need to know n and p in order to use the formula above to calculate all of these 101 probabilities.

We can also calculate descriptive measures for a binomially distributed variable, as in Chapter 5. Here, we use the fact that Y is a sum of independent random variables: $Y = X_1 + \dots + X_n$. Thus, the mean value of Y is given by:

$$E(Y) = E(X_1 + \dots + X_n) = E(X_1) + \dots + E(X_n) = p + \dots + p = n \cdot p$$

while the variance of Y is:

$$V(Y) = V(X_1 + \ldots + X_n) = V(X_1) + \ldots + V(X_n)$$
$$= p \cdot (1 - p) + \ldots + p \cdot (1 - p) = n \cdot p \cdot (1 - p)$$

Here, the variance of $X_1 + \ldots + X_n$ is equal to the sum of the individual variances, because the X_is are independent and the covariances therefore zero, cf. Section 5.5.

The binomial distribution is summarised in the box below:

The binomial distribution, $Y \sim \mathrm{Bin}(n,p)$

Probability function: $f_Y(k) = \binom{n}{k} \cdot p^k \cdot (1 - p)^{n-k}$,

$$k = 0, 1, 2, \ldots, n$$

Mean value and variance: $E(Y) = n \cdot p$ and $V(Y) = n \cdot p \cdot (1 - p)$

Interpretation: Y denotes the number of successes among n independent draws from a Bernoulli population in which there is constant probability, p, for success in each draw.

Example 6.11: Heads or tails – part 6

What is the probability of three heads in Example 6.4, where $Y \sim \mathrm{Bin}\left(5, \frac{1}{2}\right)$?

$$f_Y(3) = \binom{5}{3} \cdot 0.5^3 \cdot (1 - 0.5)^{5-3} = 0.3125$$

In this case, the mean value and variance of Y are:

$$E(Y) = 5 \cdot 0.5 = 2.5 \quad \text{and} \quad V(Y) = 5 \cdot 0.5 \cdot (1 - 0.5) = 1.25$$

Example 6.12: Birthday on a Monday

Imagine we have a group of seven people. What is the probability that two of the seven were born on a Monday? If the seven individuals' birthdays are independent (i.e. there are no twins in the group), then each person can be seen as a draw from a Bernoulli population of "born on a Monday" and "not born on a Monday". The probability of selecting an individual born on Monday (a success) must then be $p = 1/7$. The random variable Y, which indicates the number of children in the group born on a Monday, is therefore binomially distributed with $n = 7$ and $p = 1/7$. Thus, the probability that two people in the group were born on a Monday is given by:

$$P(Y = 2) = \binom{7}{2} \cdot (1/7)^2 \cdot (1 - 1/7)^{7-2} = 0.198$$

What is then the probability that at least two of them were born on a Monday? This probability is equal to 1 minus the probability that at most one of them was born on a Monday. In other words:

$$P(Y \geq 2) = 1 - P(Y \leq 1) = 1 - P(Y = 1) - P(Y = 0)$$

$$= 1 - \binom{7}{1} \cdot (1/7)^1 \cdot (1 - 1/7)^{7-1} - \binom{7}{0} \cdot (1/7)^0 \cdot (1 - 1/7)^7$$

$$= 1 - 0.40 - 0.34 = 0.26$$

Note that if the Bernoulli experiment is conducted by sampling from a finite population, for example selecting students from a class, then the assumption of independence requires "sampling with replacement", otherwise the individual selections will not be independent. In other words, when we have drawn the first student and observed whether it is a girl (success) or a boy (failure), we must "put the person back" into the class (the population) before we draw again. Therefore, in principle, we have the opportunity to draw the same person twice.

What would happen if we did not put the person back? Assume that the first person we sample is a success (a girl). If we do not put her back, it means that the proportion of the remaining girls in the class has become smaller. For example, if at the start there were five girls and five boys, there are now only four girls left. This has reduced the probability of sampling a girl in the second draw – it is now only 4/9, where it was 5/10 in the first draw. Therefore, sampling from a finite population requires replacement of the sampled element after each draw if Y is to be binomially distributed. If we do not sample with replacement, we instead end up with a hypergeometric distribution, which we will look at next.

6.3 The hypergeometric distribution

The hypergeometric distribution is closely related to the binomial distribution. It is obtained when you sample n elements from a real Bernoulli population without replacement. In other words, the same element in the population can only be selected once. The probability of drawing a success (or failure) therefore changes with every draw, because the number of remaining successes (and failures) in the population changes.

Imagine that we draw n times, without replacement, from a population with N elements, of which M are successes and $N - M$ are failures. If we let Y denote the total number of successes in the n draws, then Y is said to be hypergeometrically distributed with parameters n, M and N. We write this as: $Y \sim \text{Hyp}(n, M, N)$. The probability function for Y – i.e. the probability of getting k successes in the n draws – is shown in the following box:

Hypergeometric distribution, $Y \sim \text{Hyp}(n, M, N)$

Probability function: $f_Y(k) = \dfrac{\dbinom{M}{k} \cdot \dbinom{N - M}{n - k}}{\dbinom{N}{n}}$, $k = 0, 1, 2, \ldots, M$

Mean value and variance:

$$E(Y) = n \cdot \frac{M}{N} \quad \text{and} \quad V(Y) = n \cdot \frac{M}{N} \cdot \frac{N - M}{N} \cdot \frac{N - n}{N - 1}$$

Interpretation: Y denotes the number of successes among n draws without replacement from a real Bernoulli population with N elements, of which M have the property "success".

Please note that we can never draw more than M successes (the number of successes in the population). Therefore, the probability of $Y > M$ is equal to zero. Also note that M / N is the proportion of successes in the population to begin with. Therefore, had we drawn with replacement, Y would be binomially distributed with $p = M / N$.

The hypergeometric distribution can be used in connection with, for example, quality control. The following example illustrates this.

Let us assume that a company has produced $N = 10$ machines, of which $M = 3$ are defective. However, the company does not have this information, and since quality control is costly, the company decides to select just three machines at random and test them for defects. Let Y be the number of successes (here, defective machines) among the three machines selected. When the selection is without replacement (there is no point in examining the same machine twice), then Y is hypergeometrically distributed with the parameters $n = 3$, $M = 3$ and $N = 10$. The probability that quality control discovers two defective machines is therefore:

$$f_Y(2) = \frac{\binom{3}{2} \cdot \binom{10-3}{3-2}}{\binom{10}{3}} = \frac{\frac{3!}{2! \cdot 1!} \cdot \frac{7!}{1! \cdot 6!}}{\frac{10!}{3! \cdot 7!}} = 0.175$$

Therefore the probability is $1 - 0.175 = 0.825$ that the company will sell a machine that is defective, namely the machine that was not identified as defective during quality control. The probability of quality control detecting all three defective machines is 0.0083. If the company wants to avoid sending defective machines out onto the market, then the current quality-control process is not good enough, as there is more than a 99% probability that at least one defective machine will slip through undetected.

A company has to select four employees to work the Christmas shift. Management is considering whether to select them at random from among the 19 employees. On the face of it this seems fairest, but management would prefer not to make employees with (small) children work at Christmas. It therefore wishes to calculate the risk (probability) that more than one parent will be working over Christmas if the team is selected randomly among the employees. Seven of the 19 employees have children.

Picking the Christmas shift can be seen as four draws without replacement from a Bernoulli population with seven successes (parents) and twelve failures (non-parents). If we let Y indicate the number of parents among those drawn, we know that $Y \sim \text{Hyp}(4, 7, 19)$. The expected value of Y is therefore $E(Y) = n \cdot M/N = 4 \cdot 7/19 = 1.473$. We have to calculate $P(Y > 1)$. This probability must be equal to:

$$1 - P(Y = 1) - P(Y = 0)$$

$$= 1 - \frac{\binom{7}{1} \cdot \binom{19-7}{4-1}}{\binom{19}{4}} - \frac{\binom{7}{0} \cdot \binom{19-7}{4-0}}{\binom{19}{4}}$$

$$= 1 - \frac{\dfrac{7!}{6! \cdot 1!} \cdot \dfrac{12!}{9! \cdot 3!} - \dfrac{7!}{7! \cdot 0!} \cdot \dfrac{12!}{8! \cdot 4!}}{\dfrac{19!}{15! \cdot 4!}} = 0.475$$

There is therefore a 47.5% chance that more than one parent will be on duty at Christmas.

6.4   The Poisson distribution

The binomial distribution and the hypergeometric distribution emerge when you sample from a Bernoulli population and examine the probability of obtaining a certain number of successes. This could, for example, be a situation where we ask people on the street whether they will vote "yes" ($X_i = 1$) or "no" ($X_i = 0$) in a referendum. Alternative questions might be whether they will "vote" ($X_i = 1$) or "not vote" ($X_i = 0$) at the next election, or whether they are "married" ($X_i = 1$) or "unmarried" ($X_i = 0$). The random variable Y, which indicates the number of yes votes in such an experiment, $Y = X_1 + X_2 + ... + X_n$, is binomially distributed if the n draws are independent, while it is hypergeometrically distributed if the draws are without replacement – and therefore dependent.

Imagine that we are interested in constructing a model of how many customers will come into a shop. We therefore observe the shop for 10 hours, and let the random variable X_1 assume the value 1 if customers enter the shop during the first hour, and the value 0 if no customers enter. Correspondingly, X_2 takes the value 1 if there are customers during the second hour. If we let Y be equal to $X_1 + X_2 +,...,+ X_{10}$, is Y then binomially distributed? Yes, if: i) the "draws" are independent (i.e. if customers entering the shop during a given hour do not affect the probability of customers in the following hours), and ii) the probability of observing customers in each of the 10 hours is the same. In this case, Y is binomially distributed with $n = 10$ and p equal to the probability that customers will enter during a given hour.

However, it might be more interesting to model the total number of customers over the 10 hours. The problem with the binomial model is that X_1 assumes the value 1 regardless of whether there are one or 100 customers in the shop during the first hour. We could address this by shortening the time intervals. Instead of observing whether there are customers over the course of an hour, we could make minute-by-minute observations. If the time interval was one minute and we still observed the shop for 10 hours, we would "draw" 600 ($= 60 \cdot 10$) times instead of 10 times from the Bernoulli population. Even so, we must assume that the selections are independent and that the probability of observing customers is the same in all 600 timeslots. Of course, the probability of observing customers in a given interval of time has now become smaller, and so there is less chance of there being more than one customer per time interval. The value of Y will therefore more closely indicate the actual number of customers entering the shop.

However, there is still a risk that more than one customer will enter the shop during a given time interval. However, if we continue to reduce the time intervals until they become infinitely small, then this risk will eventually disappear. The probability of more than one customer entering the shop in an infinitesimal time interval is zero. In this case, Y will become equal to the actual number of customers over the 10 hours. Because the time intervals have become infinitely small, we must have an infinite number of timeslots in order to cover the 10 hours. It therefore becomes impossible to derive Y's probability function from the binomial distribution. Fortunately, it turns out that the probability function (i.e. the probability of observing k customers during the 10 hours) can now be written as:

$$P(Y = k) = \frac{\lambda^k}{k!} \cdot e^{-\lambda}$$

where λ is the expected number of customers during the 10 hours. In this case, we can say that Y is Poisson-distributed with the parameter λ. A Poisson-distributed variable denotes the number of successes or events (for example, customers) during a time interval (e.g. 10 hours).

We can therefore interpret a Poisson-distributed variable, Y, as the number of successes when we continuously (without interruption) draw from a Bernoulli population throughout a given period of time and then add the number of successes together. This is then the value of Y. Alternatively, we can see it as a situation where we draw once from a super-population of different "numbers of successes". For example, if we draw the element "two customers in 10 hours", Y is then equal to 2.

As is hopefully clear from the above, some underlying assumptions must be met in order for us to model a situation using the Poisson distribution. These are:

i) the number of successes in non-overlapping time intervals must be independent (the number of customers in one hour must be independent of the number of customers in another hour, etc.).

ii) the probabilities in two intervals of equal length must be identical (e.g. there must be the same probability of observing two customers in every hour); and, finally,

iii) the probability of more than one success in a very short time interval must be zero.

Example 6.15: A homepage

An Internet company knows that its website receives, on average, five hits per hour. In connection with the launch of a new product, the company wishes to calculate the probability of at least 10 customers visiting the website in the first hour. Can the Poisson distribution be used for this purpose? To do so requires that the company can reasonably assume: i) that the number of hits in non-overlapping time intervals are independent; ii) that the probabilities for hits in two equally long time intervals are the same; and iii) the probability of more than one hit in a very short time interval is zero.

The company considers these assumptions reasonable, and therefore that the number of hits is Poisson-distributed. Since the expected number of hits per hour is five, this is the value of λ. The probability of exactly 10 hits in the first hour after the launch can then be calculated as:

$$P(Y = 10) = \frac{5^{10}}{10!} \cdot e^{-5} = 0.018$$

To arrive at the probability of a minimum of 10 customers, we must include the probability of 11 customers, the probability of 12 customers, and so on. Alternatively, we may calculate $P(Y \geq 10)$ as $1 - P(Y = 9) - P(Y = 8) - ... - P(Y = 0)$.

The Poisson distribution is summarised in the following box:

The Poisson distribution, $Y \sim \mathrm{Poi}(\lambda)$

Probability function: $f_Y(k) = \dfrac{\lambda^k}{k!} \cdot e^{-\lambda}, \; k = 0, 2, 3, \ldots$

Mean value and variance: $E(Y) = \lambda$ and $V(Y) = \lambda$

Interpretation: Y denotes the number of successes in a given time period where:

- λ is the expected number of successes;
- the number of successes in non-overlapping time intervals are independent;
- the probabilities in two intervals of equal length are identical;
- the probability of more than one success in a very short time interval is zero.

Example 6.16: Ordering pizzas

A pizzeria receives an average of three orders every quarter of an hour. It has promised customers that their pizza will be free if the time between ordering and delivery exceeds 15 minutes. This will happen if it receives more than five orders in any given quarter of an hour. The owner wants to calculate the risk of this. If we assume that Y indicates the number of pizza orders in a quarter of an hour, and that Y follows a Poisson distribution, then $\lambda = 3$. Thus, the probabilities of 0, 1, 2, 3, 4 and 5 orders are, respectively:

$$P(Y = 0) = \frac{3^0}{0!} \cdot e^{-3} = 0.050, \quad P(Y = 1) = \frac{3^1}{1!} \cdot e^{-3} = 0.149,$$

$$P(Y = 2) = \frac{3^2}{2!} \cdot e^{-3} = 0.224, \quad P(Y = 3) = \frac{3^3}{3!} \cdot e^{-3} = 0.224,$$

$$P(Y = 4) = \frac{3^4}{4!} \cdot e^{-3} = 0.168, \quad P(Y = 5) = \frac{3^5}{5!} \cdot e^{-3} = 0.101$$

The probability of more than five orders can then be calculated as:

$$P(Y \geq 6) = 1 - P(Y = 0) - P(Y = 1) - P(Y = 2) - P(Y = 3)$$
$$-P(Y = 4) - P(Y = 5) = 1 - 0.050 - 0.144 - 0.224$$
$$-0.224 - 0.168 - 0.101 = 0.084$$

Therefore, there is an 8.4% probability that, in a given 15-minute period, the owner will have to deliver at least one free pizza.

6.5   The normal distribution

The distributions in Sections 6.1 to 6.4 are all discrete distributions; that is, the random variable can only assume a countable number of values. We will now look at the normal distribution, which is a distribution for a continuous random variable. The normal distribution has gained its popularity for two reasons. Firstly, many real populations have a distribution that resembles the normal distribution. Secondly – as we shall see in subsequent chapters – many estimators and test statistics are normally distributed.

The normal distribution, $Y \sim N(\mu, \sigma^2)$:

A continuous random variable, Y, is normally distributed if it has the probability density function:

$$f(y) = \frac{1}{\sqrt{2\pi\sigma}} e^{-\frac{1}{2}\left(\frac{y-\mu}{\sigma}\right)^2}$$

where $\mu = E(Y)$ is the expected value, and $\sigma^2 = V(Y)$ is the variance.

The probability density function for a normally distributed variable, Y, is illustrated in Figure 6.2 for different values of μ and σ^2. We can see in the figure that the graph for the probability density function depends on both μ and σ^2. The mean value lies in the middle of the graph, where the probability density function "peaks". If the mean value, μ, is high, then the graph is further to the right. There will therefore be a greater probability of higher values of Y. If the variance is high, then the graph has "fatter tails" (i.e. there is a greater probability of getting values of Y that are located far from the mean value).

Figure 6.2:
Probabili-
ty density
function for
normally
distributed
variables

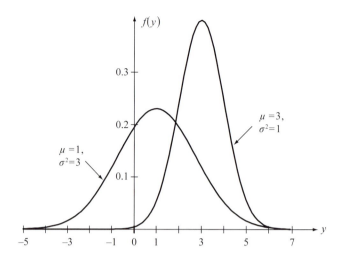

How do we calculate probabilities in the normal distribution? If $Y \sim N(\mu, \sigma^2)$, then the probability of obtaining a value of Y that is less than or equal to y is given by $F(y)$, where F is the cumulative distribution function for Y. Graphically, $F(y)$ is equal to the area under the probability density function to the left of y, as illustrated in Figure 6.3.

Figure 6.3:
Cumulative
probability in
a normal distri-
bution

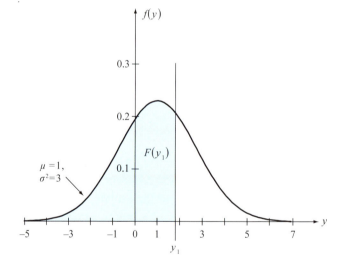

It stands to reason that this area will depend on the sizes of μ and σ^2. If μ is high, the area will be smaller. A higher mean value decreases the probability of observing a low value of Y. The area (i.e. the cumulative distribution function) can be calculated by integrating the density function. Unfortunately, this is impossible – no analytic expression exists for $F(y)$ when Y is normally distributed. This is a bit disappointing if we want to find probabilities for random variables that are normally distributed. Using computer simulations, we can calculate the probability of Y assuming a value less than y for given values of μ and σ^2. However, this is still not a particularly practical solution in many situations.

Fortunately, we can calculate the cumulative probabilities for every normal distribution on the basis of one particular normal distribution, namely the one with mean value $\mu = 0$ and variance $\sigma^2 = 1$. This specific normal distribution, $N(0,1)$, is called the standard normal distribution. It is so important that its cumulative probability function has a special symbol, $\Phi(z)$ and its density function is correspondingly denoted by $\varphi(z)$. The cumulative distribution function, $\Phi(z)$, is tabulated in Table 1 at the back of the book for selected values of z. The next two examples show how to use the table to find probabilities in the standard normal distribution.

Let Z be a standard normal variable, i.e. $Z \sim N(0,1)$. Work out the probability that Z is less than -2.62. We must therefore find $\Phi(z)$, where $z = -2.62$. In Table 1, the first number in each row indicates the value of z up to and including the first decimal place, whereas the first number in each column indicates the second decimal place of z. We must therefore find the value in the table that appears at the intersection of the row with -2.6 and the column with 2. Here we find the value 0.0044. The probability of a value of Z less than -2.62 is therefore 0.0044.

z	0	1	2
-3.0	0.0013	0.0013	0.0013
-2.9	0.0019	0.0018	0.0018
-2.8	0.0026	0.0025	0.0024
-2.7	0.0035	0.0034	0.0033
-2.6	0.0047	0.0045	0.0044
-2.5	0.0062	0.0060	0.0059

Find $P(Z > 1.06)$, where Z is standard normally distributed. From Table 1, we find that $P(Z \leq 1.06) = \Phi(1.06) = 0.8554$. The probability that Z is greater than 1.06 is then:

$$P(Z > 1.06) = 1 - \Phi(1.06) = 1 - 0.8554 = 0.1446 .$$

As we can now find probabilities for the standard normal distribution, we only have to establish the relationship between the standard normal distribution and all the other normal distributions. This is done by *standardisation*. Standardisation changes a random variable with mean value μ and variance σ^2 to a new random variable with mean value 0 and variance 1. If the original random variable is normally distributed, then the new random variable will also be normally distributed, but now with mean value 0 and variance 1:

Standardisation of a random variable:

The random variable Y with mean $E(Y) = \mu$ and variance $V(Y) = \sigma^2$ is standardised by calculating:

$$Z = \frac{Y - \mu}{\sigma} .$$

Z then becomes a random variable with mean value $E(Z) = 0$ and variance $E(Z) = 1$.

Specifically for the normal distribution, if $Y \sim N(\mu, \sigma^2)$, then $Z \sim N(0,1)$.

Example 6.19 shows how to use standardisation to calculate probabilities for a normally distributed variable.

$Y \sim N(10,4)$. We want to calculate the probability $P(Y \leq 8)$. This is done by means of standardisation:

$$P(Y \leq 8) = P(Y - 10 \leq 8 - 10)$$

$$= P\left(\frac{Y - 10}{2} \leq \frac{8 - 10}{2}\right) = P\left(\frac{Y - 10}{2} \leq -1\right) = P(Z \leq -1) = \Phi(-1)$$

where $Z = (Y - 10)/2$. Note that we have used the fact that we can subtract the same number (the mean value 10) and divide by the same positive number (the standard deviation 2) on both sides of an inequality sign. Because Y is normally distributed with mean value 10 and variance 4, the variable $Z = (Y - 10)/2$ must be standard normally distributed. As a result, we can look up the last probability in Table 1. We therefore find that $P(Y \leq 8) = \Phi(-1) = 0.1587$.

The probability that the random variable Y will assume a value less than a is therefore the same as the probability that the standardised variable $Z = (Y - \mu)/\sigma$ assumes a value less than $(a - \mu)/\sigma$, and this probability can be found in Table 1 for the standard normal distribution.

This technique can be summarised as follows:

Probabilities in the normal distribution:

For $Y \sim N(\mu, \sigma^2)$, the following applies:

i) $P(Y \leq a) = \Phi\left(\dfrac{a - \mu}{\sigma}\right)$

ii) $P(Y \geq a) = 1 - \Phi\left(\dfrac{a - \mu}{\sigma}\right)$

iii) $P(b \leq Y \leq a) = \Phi\left(\dfrac{a - \mu}{\sigma}\right) - \Phi\left(\dfrac{b - \mu}{\sigma}\right)$

where a and b are constants, and $\Phi(z)$ is found in Table 1.

Example 6.20: Return on a share

Let the random variable X represent the return on a share (in DKK per year). Suppose also that X is normally distributed with $E(X) = \mu = 20$ and $V(X) = \sigma^2 = 5$. What then is the risk (probability) of a return of less than DKK 15.00 in a given year? We solve this problem in the same manner as in the example above:

$$P(X \leq 15) = P\left(\frac{X - 20}{\sqrt{5}} \leq \frac{15 - 20}{\sqrt{5}}\right) = P\left(\frac{X - 20}{\sqrt{5}} \leq -2.24\right)$$
$$= \Phi(-2.24) = 0.0125$$

The probability of a return of less than DKK 15.00 is therefore 1.25%.

6.6   The multinomial distribution

The multinomial distribution is a generalisation of the binomial distribution. However, instead of sampling from a population with only two different types of elements (a Bernoulli population), we now draw from a population with m different types. An element can therefore assume m different values. As for the binomial distribution, it is assumed that the draws are independent. This means that draws from a real population must be with replacement.

Example 6.21: An EU referendum – part 1

Imagine that we stop five people at random on the street and ask if they will vote yes or no or abstain from voting in a future EU referendum. In this case there are three different types of element in the population (yes, no and abstention). Furthermore, as there is nothing that prevents us from asking the same person twice, we are sampling with replacement from the population.

In the binomial distribution, we let X_i be a random variable, which assumes the value 1 if the ith draw results in a success. The random variable Y (the number of successes in the n draws) was then equal to the sum of the X_is. In Example 6.21, we cannot make do with a single variable. We could let Y indicate the number of yes votes, but this is not sufficient to tell us about the distribution of the no votes and abstentions. The experiment in Example 6.21 requires three random variables.

Example 6.22: An EU referendum – part 2

Let the random variable Y_1 be the number of yes voters in the five draws from Example 6.21, Y_2 the number of no voters and Y_3 the number of abstentions. The distribution of (Y_1, Y_2, Y_3) is then said to be multinomial. Now suppose that the proportion of yes votes in the electorate is 0.4, the proportion who vote no is 0.5 and the proportion who abstain (or spoil their ballot papers) is 0.1. What is the probability that the sample will consist of, say, two yes voters ($Y_1 = 2$), two no voters ($Y_2 = 2$) and one abstention ($Y_3 = 1$)?

When dealing with a multinomial distribution, we must, as illustrated in Example 6.22, calculate the probability of three or more random variables $(Y_1, Y_2, ..., Y_m)$. The multinomial distribution is therefore a joint distribution. In Example 6.22, it is a joint distribution of Y_1, Y_2 and Y_3. The next example shows how the probabilities in the multinomial distribution are worked out.

Based on the population proportions from Example 6.22, we can start to calculate the probability of, first, meeting two yes voters, then two no voters and, finally, one who intends to abstain. This probability is given by: $0.4 \cdot 0.4 \cdot 0.5 \cdot 0.5 \cdot 0.1 = 0.004$. (We sample with replacement, and so the individual draws are independent.) Similarly, there is a probability of 0.004 of meeting the same combination of voters in a different order, for example $0.1 \cdot 0.4 \cdot 0.5 \cdot 0.5 \cdot 0.4 = 0.004$.

To find the total probability, we have to multiply the probability, 0.004, by the number of combinations of outcomes that result in two yes voters, two no voters and one who intends to abstain. This number of combinations can be found using the formula in the box below, called the multinomial coefficient. This is a generalisation of the binomial coefficient from section 6.2. In this case, it gives:

$$\binom{5}{2,2,1} = \frac{5!}{2! \cdot 2! \cdot 1!} = 30$$

In other words, there are 30 different combinations that result in two yes voters, two no voters and one who intends to abstain. The overall probability of selecting two yes voters, two no voters and one who intends to abstain is thus $0.004 \cdot 30 = 0.12$.

Based on the above example, we can write the probability of selecting k_1 elements of type 1, k_2 of the type 2, etc., in n independent draws from a population with m different elements, as follows:

$$P(Y_1 = k_1, Y_2 = k_2, ..., Y_m = k_m) = \binom{n}{k_1, k_2, ..., k_m} \cdot p_1^{k_1} \cdot p_2^{k_2} \cdot ... \cdot p_m^{k_m}$$

where p_1 is the probability of getting an element of type 1 in a given draw, p_2 the probability of getting an element of type 2, etc.

Example 6.24: Rolling a dice

Imagine that we roll a dice 12 times and observe the number of ones, twos, threes, fours, fives and sixes. What is the probability of throwing two of each kind? If we let Y_1 indicate the number of ones, Y_2 the number of twos, etc., then $(Y_1, Y_2, Y_3, Y_4, Y_5, Y_6)$ will be multinomially distributed, with $p_1 = 1/6, p_2 = 1/6, ..., p_6 = 1/6$. We can consider each throw as a draw from the population of the different sides of the dice, where the probability of drawing (throwing) a one is 1/6, and so on. Hence, the probability of getting two ones, two twos, and so on, is:

$$P(Y_1 = 2, Y_2 = 2, ..., Y_6 = 2)$$

$$= \binom{12}{2,2,2,2,2,2} \cdot \left(\frac{1}{6}\right)^2 \cdot \left(\frac{1}{6}\right)^2 \cdot \left(\frac{1}{6}\right)^2 \cdot \left(\frac{1}{6}\right)^2 \cdot \left(\frac{1}{6}\right)^2 \cdot \left(\frac{1}{6}\right)^2$$

$$= \frac{12!}{2! \cdot 2! \cdot 2! \cdot 2! \cdot 2! \cdot 2!} \cdot \left(\frac{1}{6}\right)^{2+2+2+2+2+2}$$

$$= \frac{12!}{2 \cdot 2 \cdot 2 \cdot 2 \cdot 2 \cdot 2} \cdot \left(\frac{1}{6}\right)^{12} = 0.0034$$

Let us conclude by summarising the multinomial distribution as follows:

The multinomial distribution,

$$(Y_1, Y_2, ..., Y_m) \sim M(n, p_1, p_2, ..., p_m)$$

Probability function:

$$P(Y_1 = k_1, Y_2 = k_2, ..., Y_m = k_m) = \binom{n}{k_1, k_2, ..., k_m} \cdot p_1^{k_1} \cdot p_2^{k_2} \cdot ... \cdot p_m^{k_m}$$

Mean value and variance of Y_i: $E(Y_i) = n \cdot p_i$ and $V(Y_i) = n \cdot p_i \cdot (1 - p_i)$

Interpretation:
- n independent draws from a population of m different types of elements.
- Y_1 indicates the number of outcomes of type 1, Y_2 the number of outcomes of type 2, etc., in the n draws.
- There are constant probabilities $p_1, p_2, ..., p_m$ of the m different outcomes in each draw.

6.7   Exercises

1. Review questions:
   a) Provide an example of a Bernoulli-distributed random variable.
   b) What is the relationship between the Bernoulli distribution and the binomial distribution?
   c) Provide an example of a binomially distributed random variable.
   d) What is the difference between the binomial distribution and the hypergeometric distribution?
   e) Illustrate the difference in d) with an example.
   f) Is a Poisson-distributed random variable discrete or continuous?
   g) Think of a phenomenon that might be Poisson-distributed.
   h) Is a normally distributed random variable discrete or continuous?
   i) Give an example of a phenomenon that might be normally distributed.
   j) Explain the difference between a normally distributed and a standard normally distributed random variable.
   k) What is the difference between the multinomial distribution and the binomial distribution?

l) What distinguishes the multinomial distribution from the other distributions in this chapter?

m) Describe a situation in which the multinomial distribution could be relevant.

2. You have a part-time job in a bakery. The master baker says that they plan to introduce 12 new types of cake in the next few years. Experience from previous inventions has shown that 60% of the cakes in the bakery become a success. Let X be the random variable that denotes the number of successful cakes among the 12 new ones.

   a) Focusing on one of the new types of cake, which distribution describes whether that particular type will be a success?

   b) Which distribution does X follow?

   c) The baker wants to retire if none of the 12 cakes becomes a success. What is the probability of this happening?

   d) The baker will give you a pay raise if at least 10 cakes are a success. Find the probability of this.

   e) What is $E(X)$ and $V(X)$?

3. A car factory has a problem: 25% of produced vehicles will not start. A random sample of 10 cars is selected. $X =$ the number of cars in the sample that will not start.

   a) Which distribution does X follow?

   b) What is the probability that more than eight cars in the sample will not start, $P(X > 8)$?

   c) What is the probability that all of the cars will start?

   d) What is the expected number of cars that will not start?

4. You have not done the three assignments set by your statistics teacher in the previous lesson, and you are now considering whether you should turn up for the next class, where students will be called up to the board to solve equations. We assume that the teacher will randomly select one student for each assignment, so that in principle the same student may be asked to answer all three of them. Assume that all 50 students turn up for the class.

   a) What is the probability that you will not be called up to the board?

   b) What is the probability of you being asked to solve all three assignments?

   Now imagine that 20 of the other students have not done the work either, but still show up. If the teacher selects one of these 20 students, she will therefore be obliged to send him or her back to his or her seat and call up a new student. She continues to do this until she finds a student who has done the work.

c) What is the probability that you will not be called up? (Hint: does it make a difference if the 20 students are present or not?)

5. The syllabus for statistics features eight topics. Exam assignments will be set in three of these topics. One of the students has chosen to take a risk, and has only prepared for five topics. Let Y be the random variable that indicates the number of questions the students can answer in the exam if the three subjects for the exam are chosen at random from the eight possibilities.

a) How is Y distributed?
b) Plot the probability function for Y in a table.
c) What is the expected number of questions that the student can answer?

6. You are taken to a casino to play poker. You do not have much money left and choose to gamble everything on the next round. You are therefore calculating the probabilities for your next hand (five cards).

a) If X is the number of aces in your next hand, how is X distributed?
b) What is the probability that you will be dealt four aces? What is the probability of you being dealt three?
c) You dream of a royal straight flush (ace, king, queen, jack and ten, all in hearts). What is the probability of this?

You are dealt three aces and a nine and a five.

d) What is the probability that you get the last ace by swapping the last two cards? (Hint: remember that the parameters in the distribution have now changed.)

7. Alex is on his way home from the city and is waiting for a taxi. He knows that, on average, a taxi comes by every 10 minutes. Let $X =$ number of taxis passing.

a) What distribution can we assume that X follows?
b) Certain properties underlie the probability distribution that X follows. Identify and explain these.

While he is waiting, Alex falls into conversation with a young woman and forgets all about catching a taxi. The conversation lasts one hour.

c) How many taxis would you expect to have passed?
d) What is the probability of seven taxis having passed?
e) What is the probability that at most four taxis have passed?

8. Jack has a summer job working nights at Southampton Oil Mill, where he uses a fishing net to stop jellyfish entering the water inlet. Since there are few people to chat to at night, he starts to use his pocket statistics book to describe his new job. He quickly finds out that the jellyfish are being sucked towards the inlet in a steady stream. From the time he starts work at 11pm until he leaves at 7am, there are on average 90 jellyfish per hour. Let X indicate the random variable that describes the number of jellyfish in a period of one minute.

a) What can we reasonably assume about the way in which X is distributed? In other words, which distribution do you think X follows?

b) What is the probability that two jellyfish will arrive in a period of one minute?

c) How many jellyfish would you expect to arrive in one minute?

Let Y be the random variable describing the number of jellyfish in a period of 15 minutes.

d) How is Y distributed?

e) Jack finds his job quite pleasant when there are only a few jellyfish to be removed, so he wants to find the probability that more than two will arrive in the course of 15 minutes. What is the probability of this?

f) Find $V(Y)$.

9. A normally distributed variable X has the density function:

$$f(x) = \frac{1}{2\sqrt{2 \cdot \pi}} \cdot e^{-\frac{(x-2)^2}{8}}$$

a) What is the mean value of X?

b) What is the variance and the standard deviation of X?

10. Let $X \sim N(3,4)$. Calculate the following probabilities:

a) $P(X \leq 3)$
b) $P(X < 3)$
c) $P(X \leq -1)$
d) $P(X \leq 2)$
e) $P(X \geq 5)$
f) $P(-1 \leq X \leq 5)$
g) Sketch, by means of a probability density function for X, the areas that correspond to the probabilities in questions a) to f).

11. The random variable X is normally distributed with mean value 1 and variance 9.
   a) Standardise X.
   b) What distribution does the standardised variable follow?

12. A consultancy firm is conducting a customer satisfaction survey. It selects 10 former customers at random (and with replacement) and asks whether they were i) very satisfied, ii) satisfied or iii) dissatisfied with the consulting services they received. Let X be the number of very satisfied customers among the 10 surveyed customers, Y the number of satisfied, and Z the number of dissatisfied. Suppose also that 40% of all of the company's customers have been very satisfied, 30% dissatisfied and 30% satisfied.
   a) Which distribution do X, Y and Z follow?
   b) What is the probability that the proportions of respondents are the same as the proportions in the population?
   c) What is the probability that none of the respondents are either satisfied or very satisfied?
   d) What is the probability that half of the respondents are dissatisfied while the other half are very satisfied?

7 Stochastic processes[8]

Situations involving uncertainty often include a time element. One example could be the future development of an exchange rate, another could be the period that will elapse before the next call to the doctor on duty. In this chapter, we will introduce stochastic processes, which are useful tools for dealing with these sorts of situations.

A stochastic process basically consists of a collection of random variables. Hence, even though we define a series of new concepts and introduce new notation in this chapter, we have already covered many of the techniques in earlier chapters.

In Section 7.1, we define a stochastic process, and in Section 7.2 we discuss various transformations of a stochastic process. In Section 7.3, we consider two particularly interesting aspects of stochastic processes: the state of the stochastic process at a given point in time and the waiting time until a specific state in the stochastic process occurs. We explain in Section 7.4 how to divide stochastic processes into four types, and in sections 7.5 to 7.8 we present some widely used examples of each of these. The chapter concludes with a summary of these examples.

7.1   A stochastic process

Imagine a husband and wife who toss a coin each morning to decide which of them will take the car to work and which of them will go by bicycle. If the outcome of the toss of the coin is "heads", he gets the car. If it is "tails", she gets it. Let the random variable Z_t indicate the outcome of the toss of the coin on the tth morning:

$$Z_t = \begin{cases} 0 & \text{if tails (husband gets car) at time } t \\ 1 & \text{if heads (wife gets car) at time } t \end{cases}$$

---

8   You may skip this chapter if you wish, as the rest of the book does not refer back to it.

Several aspects of this situation may be of interest. For example, how many days a year can the wife expect to get the car? What is the probability of the husband getting the car five days in a row? How many days should the husband expect to wait before he gets the car? What is the probability that the wife will have to wait more than three days before she gets the car again? These are the types of question that stochastic processes help us to deal with and eventually answer.

The couple's morning coin tosses can be represented by a collection of random variables: $Z_t, t = 1,2,3,...$ Such a collection, indexed by the subscript t (which represents a point in time), is called a *stochastic process*.

> **A stochastic process,** $\{Z_t, t \in T\}$, is a collection of random variables, Z_t, indexed by time, t, where t belongs to the index set, T. The outcome of a stochastic process, $\{z_t, t \in T\}$, is called a *realisation* or a *sample path*.

In the example above, we had $T = \{1,2,3,...\}$. The index set was thus countable, and we then say that the stochastic process takes place in *discrete time*. Later, we will look at examples of stochastic processes where the index set is uncountable, that is, where there are new realisations of Z_t all the time. These stochastic processes are said to take place in *continuous time*. An example of an uncountable index set is the interval $T = [0,24]$ hours.

In Chapter 4, we learned that a random variable is a function that assumes a numerical value for any outcome of an experiment. The same is also true of stochastic processes. For each outcome of the underlying experiment, there is an associated realisation of the stochastic process.

Example 7.1: Coin toss – part 1

Consider an experiment where you toss a coin three times in succession and look at the upper side of the coin each time. One possible outcome of this experiment is: $\omega =$ (tails, heads, tails). We can also define a stochastic process for this experiment. Let the index set be $T = \{1,2,3\}$. We can then define the random variables in the stochastic process as follows:

$$Z_t = \begin{cases} 0 & \text{if heads in toss } t \\ 1 & \text{if tails in toss } t \end{cases}, \quad t = 1,2,3$$

If the outcome of the experiment is ω = (tails, heads, tails), then the three random variables assume the following values $Z_1(\omega) = 1$, $Z_2(\omega) = 0$ and $Z_3(\omega) = 1$. This is the realisation of the stochastic process for this particular outcome of the experiment. Table 7.1 lists all the possible outcomes of the experiment and the corresponding realisations of the stochastic process. Each row corresponds to a realisation of the process. Note that "T" stands for "tails" and "H" for heads.

Table 7.1: Outcomes of the coin-toss experiment and the associated realisations of the stochastic process

Outcome	Realisation			Probability
ω	$Z_1(\omega)$	$Z_2(\omega)$	$Z_3(\omega)$	$P(\{z_t, t = 1,2,3\})$
(T, T, T)	1	1	1	1/8
(T, T, H)	1	1	0	1/8
(T, H, T)	1	0	1	1/8
(T, H, H)	1	0	0	1/8
(H, T, T)	0	1	1	1/8
(H, T, H)	0	1	0	1/8
(H, H, T)	0	0	1	1/8
(H, H, H)	0	0	0	1/8

In Example 7.1, one possible outcome of the experiment is ω = (tails, heads, tails). Note that all of the elements in ω (in this case: tails, heads and tails) constitute the outcome of the experiment "tossing a coin three times". We refer to each individual element in ω as an *incident*.

Just as we are able to ascribe probabilities to a random variable, it is also possible to ascribe probabilities to a stochastic process. For example, we can calculate the probability of a particular realisation of the stochastic process, as Example 7.2 illustrates.

Example 7.2: Coin toss – part 2

If the coin tosses in Example 7.1 are independent and identically distributed with a probability of 0.5 for both heads and tails, then the probability of a particular realisation is equal to $0.5^3 = 1/8$. These probabilities are listed in the final column of Table 7.1.

7.2 Transformations of a stochastic process

One of the advantages of using stochastic processes is that it makes it easier to model many real-life situations. Once you have characterised a certain aspect of a practical situation by use of a stochastic process, you can transform the original stochastic process to capture another aspect of the situation. In this section, we take a closer look at two such transformations of the original stochastic process.

Consider the stochastic process $\{Z_t, t \in \{1,2,3,...\}\}$. This could, for example, be the stochastic process for the coin toss from Example 7.1. If you are interested in the number of tails that have occurred at a given point in time, you can transform the stochastic process to capture this aspect. The transformation takes the sum of the random variables that comprise the stochastic process up to a certain point in time. Thus $\{X_t, t \in \{1,2,3,...\}\}$ is the transformed stochastic process, which is given by:

$$X_t = Z_1 + Z_2 + ... + Z_t = \sum_{m=1}^{t} Z_m, \quad t = 1,2,3,...$$

We call this a *partial-sum transformation*. As mentioned above, this transformation is a summation of a part of the original process, namely the part up to time t. For example, X_2 is the sum of Z_1 and Z_2. Example 7.3 further clarifies the nature of this relationship.

Example 7.3: Coin toss – part 3

In the coin-toss experiment from Example 7.1, the partial-sum transformation gives a stochastic process, $\{X_t, t \in \{1,2,3\}\}$, where X_t is the number of tails that have occurred up to time t. This transformed stochastic process is formally given by:

$$X_t(\omega) = \sum_{m=1}^{t} Z_m(\omega), \quad t = 1,2,3$$

Here, we have explicitly stated X and Z's dependence on the outcome, ω, of the underlying experiment: "tossing a coin three times". This makes it easier to see the relationship between the two stochastic processes:

$$X_1(\omega) = Z_1(\omega)$$
$$X_2(\omega) = Z_1(\omega) + Z_2(\omega)$$
$$X_3(\omega) = Z_1(\omega) + Z_2(\omega) + Z_3(\omega)$$

This relationship is also illustrated in Table 7.2, which lists the possible realisations of the stochastic process $\{X_t, t \in \{1,2,3\}\}$, along with the associated realisations of the stochastic process $\{Z_t, t \in \{1,2,3\}\}$.

Table 7.2:
Outcome of the coin-toss experiment and associated realisations of the stochastic processes

ω	$Z_1(\omega)$	$Z_2(\omega)$	$Z_3(\omega)$	$X_1(\omega)$	$X_2(\omega)$	$X_3(\omega)$	$P(\omega)$
(T, T, T)	1	1	1	1	2	3	1/8
(T, T, H)	1	1	0	1	2	2	1/8
(T, H, T)	1	0	1	1	1	2	1/8
(T, H, H)	1	0	0	1	1	1	1/8
(H, T, T)	0	1	1	0	1	2	1/8
(H, T, H)	0	1	0	0	1	1	1/8
(H, H, T)	0	0	1	0	0	1	1/8
(H, H, H)	0	0	0	0	0	0	1/8

Other transformations of a stochastic process are also useful in practice. For example, the *first-difference transformation* shows the change of a stochastic process from one point in time until the next. This can be formally written as:[9]

$$X_t = Z_t - Z_{t-1}$$

If Z_t is an individual's income in year t, then X_t is the change in his or her income from year $t-1$ to year t.

Instead of the absolute change from one point in time until the next, we can calculate the relative change. This transformation is given by:

$$X_t = \frac{Z_t - Z_{t-1}}{Z_{t-1}} \cdot 100$$

Note that when the stochastic process $\{Z_t, t = t_{start},...,t_{slut}\}$ is defined for $t = t_{start},...,t_{slut}$, the first-difference transformation (both the absolute and

---

9 Sometimes we use the notation ΔZ_t for $Z_t - Z_{t-1}$, i.e. $\Delta Z_t = Z_t - Z_{t-1}$.

the relative) is only defined for $t = (t_{start} + 1),...,t_{slut}$, as it is impossible to calculate the change for the first period.

7.3   States and waiting times

Two aspects of stochastic processes are particularly interesting: the state of the stochastic process at a certain point in time, and the waiting time until a certain state is achieved for the first time.

The first aspect is interesting if, for example, the stochastic process represents the price of a share or your winnings on a bet. Since the stochastic process consists of elementary outcomes that occur at random, the value at a particular point in time is also random.

More formally: the state at time t_0 of the stochastic process $\{X_t, t \in T\}$ is given by the random variable X_{t_0}. In Example 7.3, for example, X_2 is the number of times that tails has occurred after two tosses of the coin. The distribution of the random variable X_{t_0} is called the *state distribution* of the stochastic process at time t_0.

Figure 7.1 shows a realisation of the stochastic process from Example 7.3. Here, the realised value of X_2 is equal to 1 because the first toss was heads and the second was tails. However, the realised value of X_2 could also have been either 0 or 2, had the outcome been heads twice or tails twice, respectively. Example 7.4 shows how to derive the state distribution.

Figure 7.1:
Realised state
at time $t_0 = 2$

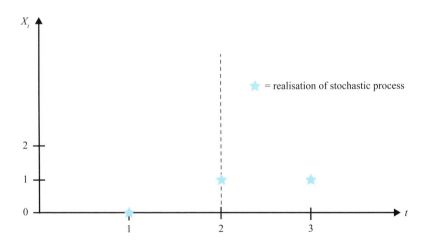

    An insight into statistics for the social sciences

Based on the probabilities in Table 7.2 for the different realisations of $\{Z_t, t = 1,2,3\}$ in the coin-toss experiment, it is relatively easy to calculate the probability that the transformed stochastic process $\{X_t, t \in 1,2,3\}$ will assume a certain value at time t_0. For $t_0 = 3$, the probabilities are given by:

$P(X_3 = 0) = 1/8$ (corresponds to the outcome (H, H, H))

$P(X_3 = 1) = 3/8$ (corresponds to the outcomes (T, H, H) (H, T, H) and (H, H, T))

$P(X_3 = 2) = 3/8$ (corresponds to the outcomes (T, T, H), (H, T, H) and (H, T, T))

$P(X_3 = 3) = 1/8$ (corresponds to the outcome (T, T, T))

This is the state distribution for the stochastic process $\{X_t, t \in 1,2,3\}$ at time $t_0 = 3$. The state distribution for the stochastic process, $\{Z_t, t = 1,2,3\}$ at the same point in time, $t_0 = 3$, is simpler. It is written:

$$P(Z_3 = 0) = 1/2$$
$$P(Z_3 = 1) = 1/2$$

Example 7.4 illustrates the usefulness of stochastic processes. Instead of directly having to specify or calculate the probability distribution for the random variable that indicates the number of tails after n tosses of the coin, it is often easier (or more intuitive) to model the situation "from scratch" using stochastic processes, and thereby arrive at a distribution for the random variable in question.

The second aspect – the waiting time – is about determining how much time will pass before the stochastic process reaches (or passes) a particular state for the first time. Since the stochastic process consists of elementary outcomes that occur at random, the time it takes for the process to reach a certain state will also be random. In the car example from the beginning of the chapter, you might want to know the probability that it takes at least three days before it is the husband's turn to drive to work.

More formally: we want to determine the distribution of a new random variable Y_{x_0}, which we define as the time until the stochastic process $\{X_t, t \in T\}$ reaches a particular state, x_0, i.e. the time until $X_t \geq x_0$ for the first time.[10] This distribution is called a *waiting-time distribution*.

In the coin-toss experiment, we are interested in finding out how long it will be before the outcome is tails for the first time. Thus, let $x_0 = 1$ and let Y_1 be the random variable that indicates how long it takes for the stochastic process $\{X_t, t \in 1, 2, 3\}$ to reach the value 1 for the first time. The probability distribution for this variable can also be calculated from the probabilities listed in Table 7.2:

$P(Y_1 = 1) = 4/8$, because the outcomes (T, T, T), (T, T, P), (T, H, T) and (T, H, H) all have tails as the outcome of the first toss.

$P(Y_1 = 2) = 2/8$, because the outcomes (H, T, T) and (H, T, H) both get tails for the first time in the second toss.

$P(Y_1 = 3) = 1/8$, because the outcome (H, H, T) gets the first tails as the outcome of the third toss.

Note that $P(Y_1 = 1) + P(Y_1 = 2) + P(Y_1 = 3) = 7/8$. In other words, the probabilities do not add up to 1. This is because the outcome (H, H, H) implies that the process $\{X_t, t \in 1, 2, 3\}$ does not reach the value 1 within the three tosses. Hence, $P(Y_1 > 3) = 1 / 8$, even though in principle the experiment ends at $t = 3$. However, all this means is that the stochastic process with probability 1/8 does not reach the value 1 within the first three tosses. We can therefore describe the waiting-time distribution with the four probabilities: $P(Y_1 = 1)$, $P(Y_1 = 2)$, $P(Y_1 = 3)$ and $P(Y_1 > 3)$.

Figure 7.2 shows the realisation of the stochastic process that corresponds to the outcome (H, T, T). This realisation reaches the value $x_0 = 1$ after two periods of time, i.e. $Y_1 = 2$.

---

[10] The formal definition of the random variable, Y_{x_0}, is: $Y_{x_0}(\omega) = \min_t \{t : X_t(\omega) \geq x_0\}$, which is read as: for each outcome, ω, of an experiment you find the shortest time, t, for which $X_t(\omega)$ is at least as large as x_0.

Figure 7.2:
Realised waiting time for $x_0 = 1$

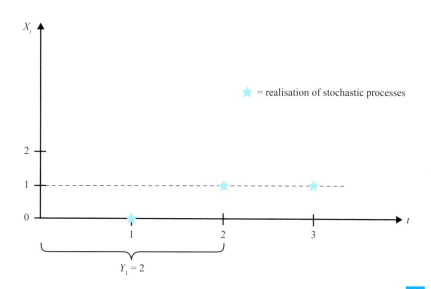

Depending on the application in question, other names are used for the waiting time and its distribution. For example, experiments in which you continue to draw elements from a population until a specific value is reached are referred to as instances of "inverse sampling". Waiting time is also sometimes called "first passage time".

We can calculate descriptive measures for the state distributions and waiting-time distributions of a stochastic process. This is done in the same way as in Chapter 5. For example, we may be interested in knowing the expected waiting time, $E(Y_{x_0})$, or the expected state, $E(X_{t_0})$, of the stochastic process at time t_0. We can also calculate quantiles for these distributions.

7.4 Four types of stochastic processes

In order to be able to use stochastic processes in real-life situations, it is useful to categorise them into four different types. The types depend on: (1) whether the random variable, X_t (or Z_t), i.e. the state of the process, is discrete or continuous; and (2) whether the stochastic process develops in discrete or continuous time. Table 7.3 summarises the resulting four types of process.

As shown in Chapter 4, there are some differences when it comes to making calculations with discrete and continuous random variables, and the same is true of stochastic processes. The categorisation therefore has the added advantage of making it easier to keep track of which tools we need and when.

Table 7.3:
Four types
of stochastic
processes

		State (X_t)	
		Discrete	Continuous
Time (T)	Discrete (countable)	A	C
	Continuous (uncountable)	B	D

The car example from the beginning of the chapter is an example of a stochastic process in discrete time with a discrete state (type A in Table 7.3). As we will see in Section 7.5, the Bernoulli process is an example of a frequently used stochastic process of this type. A Bernoulli process is characterised by the fact that at certain times (e.g. every morning), an incident either occurs or does not occur (e.g. tails as the outcome of a coin toss).

Calls to a doctor constitute an example of a discrete-state, continuous-time stochastic process (type B in Table 7.3). People can call at any time (hence continuous time), but the number of people who do so is always countable, and typically no more than one person calls at a time (therefore discrete state). A frequently used stochastic process of this type is a Poisson process, which we will study in Section 7.6.

An example of a continuous-state, discrete-time stochastic process (type C in Table 7.3) is the calculation of a country's current account. The surplus on the current account can, in principle, be any real number, and therefore the state distribution is continuous. A "Gaussian random walk" is a frequently used stochastic process of this type, as we will see in Section 7.7.

Share prices (while the stock exchange is open) are an example of a continuous-state, continuous-time stochastic process (type D in Table 7.3). Shares can be traded at any point in time, and they can be traded at any non-negative price. A frequently used stochastic process of this type is a Wiener process, as we will see in Section 7.8.

In defining different stochastic processes in the following sections, we are basically specifying four aspects of the processes. As the categorisation of types above indicates, we must specify the time aspect and the possible states. These are the first two items below. In addition, we specify the distribution of outcomes in a time interval and any initial state. Finally, we specify the relationship between outcomes in disjoint (non-overlapping) time intervals:

1. *Time:* the time index set, T
2. *State:* possible states of X_t
3. *Distribution of outcomes* in a time interval
4. *Relationship between outcomes* in disjoint time intervals.

These four fundamental aspects of the specification of a stochastic process provide a useful framework for using stochastic processes to model and interpret many real-life situations.

7.5 The Bernoulli process and the binomial process

In this section, we look at two examples of a discrete-state, discrete-time stochastic process – the Bernoulli process and the binomial process. We have brought them together here because they are transformations of each other (and are both therefore of type A from Table 7.3), as well as being individually interesting in their own right.

7.5.1 Bernoulli process

A *Bernoulli process* is defined by the following four assumptions:

A **Bernoulli process**, $\{Z_t, t \in T\}$, satisfies:

1. *Time*: $T = \{1,2,3,...\}$

2. *State*: $Z_t \in \{0,1\}$

3. *Distribution of outcomes*: $Z_t \sim \text{Ber}(p)$, i.e.:

$$Z_t = \begin{cases} 1 & \textit{with probability} \quad p \\ 0 & \textit{with probability} \ 1-p \end{cases}$$

4. *Relationship between outcomes*: Z_t is statistically independent of Z_s when $t \neq s$

The Bernoulli process is characterised by the fact that at any point in time (1, 2, 3, etc.), an incident either occurs ($Z_t = 1$) or does not occur ($Z_t = 0$). This means that, at each of these points in time, an element is drawn from a Bernoulli population. If it is a "success" ($Z_t = 1$), an incident occurs, and if it is a "failure" ($Z_t = 0$), no incident occurs. Furthermore, the different draws are independent (assumption 4, above).

Figure 7.3 shows a realisation (a sample path), $\{z_t, t \in T\}$, for a Bernoulli process, where $T = \{1,2,...,20\}$.

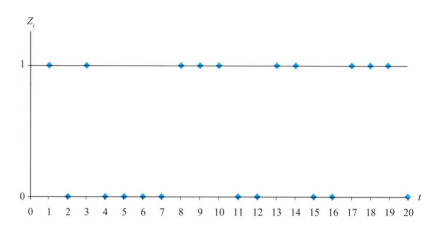

Figure 7.3:
A realisation
of a Bernoulli
process

7.5.2   Binomial process

The number of events (successes) is often of interest when working with a Bernoulli process. This gives rise to a new process called the *binomial process*, which is the partial-sum transformation of the Bernoulli process:

$$X_t = \sum_{m=1}^{t} Z_m$$

where Z_m is the mth element in the Bernoulli process. The binomial process therefore consists of a sum of independent Bernoulli-distributed random variables. We know from Chapter 6 that such a sum is binomially distributed with the parameters n and p, where n is the number of random variables in the sum, and p is the parameter from the Bernoulli distribution. With this result in mind, we are able formally to define a binomial process:

A **binomial process**, $\{X_t, t \in T\}$, satisfies:

1. *Time:* $T = \{1,2,3,...\}$

2. *State:* $X_t \in \{0,1,2,...,t\}$

3. *Distribution of outcomes:* $X_{t+n} - X_t \sim \text{Bin}(n,p)$ and $X_0 = 0$,

   where p is the probability of a success (i.e. an incident occurs) in the underlying Bernoulli distribution

4. *Relationship between outcomes:* $X_{t_1} - X_{t_2}$ is statistically independent of $X_{t_3} - X_{t_4}$ when $t_1 > t_2 > t_3 > t_4$

Assumption 3 says that the number of successes (events) in a time period consisting of n points in time is binomially distributed with the parameters n and p. Note that this assumption implies that the probability of a certain number of outcomes being successes between two points in time depends only on the time difference between these points, and not on when in the process these points occur. Moreover, the number of successes (events) in a given period of time is independent of the number of successes (events) in another, non-overlapping period of time (assumption 4). Both of these assumptions are consequences of the fact that the underlying Bernoulli-distributed variables, Z_t, are independent.

Figure 7.4 shows the realisation, $\{x_t, t \in T\}$, of the binomial process, which corresponds to the realisation $\{z_t, t \in T\}$ of the Bernoulli process in Figure 7.3. In other words, the outcome of the underlying experiment is the same in the two figures. Note, for example, that for $t = 8$, we have $x_8 = 3$ because three events (successes) occurred within the first eight points in time in Figure 7.3.

Figure 7.4:
A realisation
of a binomial
process

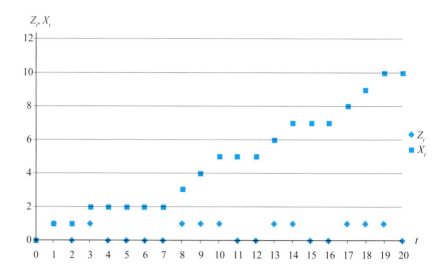

A binomial process is a *counting process*. In other words, it models the number of events that have occurred up to a certain point in time. Counting processes are useful for modelling a wide range of practical problems. In the next subsections, we derive the state distribution and the waiting-time distribution for the binomial process.

7.5.3   The state distribution for a binomial process

The state distribution for X_{t_0} in a binomial process follows directly from assumption 3 above. If we let $t = 0$ and $n = t_0$, then we get $X_{t_0} - X_0 = X_{t_0} \sim \mathrm{Bin}(t_0, p)$, because $X_0 = 0$.

The state distribution for a binomial process:

$$X_{t_0} \sim \mathrm{Bin}(t_0, p)$$

The probability function for X_{t_0} is:

$$f_{X_{t_0}}(x) = \binom{t_0}{x} \cdot p^x \cdot (1 - p)^{t_0 - x}$$

Mean value and variance: $E\left(X_{t_0}\right) = t_0 \cdot p$ and $V\left(X_{t_0}\right) = t_0 \cdot p \cdot (1 - p)$

The different states are countable, and therefore the state distribution is discrete. The probability function, mean value and variance follow directly from inserting into the formulas for the binomial distribution from Chapter 6. We see that the expected state (the mean value) of the binomial process increases with time t_0, and so does the variance.

Example 7.6: Coin toss – part 6

In the coin-toss experiment, the mean value of X_3 according to the above formula is equal to: $t_0 \cdot p = 3 \cdot 0.5 = 1.5$. You can also prove this by calculating the mean value directly from the probability distribution of X_3 in Example 7.4. Correspondingly, the variance is: $t_0 \cdot p \cdot (1 - p) = 3 \cdot 0.5 \cdot (1 - 0.5) = 0.75$.

7.5.4 The waiting-time distribution for a binomial process

Let Y_{x_0} be the time until the binomial process X_t is equal to x_0 for the first time. The distribution of Y_{x_0} is used so often that it has been given its own name: the *negative binomial distribution*. It is summarised in the box below.

The waiting-time distribution for a binomial process (the negative binomial distribution):

$$Y_{x_0} \sim \text{Negbin}(x_0, p)$$

The probability function for Y_{x_0} is:

$$f_{Y_{x_0}}(y) = \binom{y - 1}{x_0 - 1} \cdot p^{x_0} \cdot (1 - p)^{y - x_0}$$

Mean value and variance are: $E\left(Y_{x_0}\right) = x_0 \cdot \dfrac{1}{p}$ and

$$V\left(Y_{x_0}\right) = x_0 \cdot \frac{1 - p}{p^2}$$

Since the set of time indices is countable, the waiting time must be a discrete random variable.

We can use the structure of the stochastic process to derive the negative binomial distribution. First, for the binomial process to reach the state x_0 for the first time at time y, it must be the case that the binomial process is in the state $x_0 - 1$ at time $y - 1$. If not, it cannot possibly be in state x_0 at time y as it can only increase by 1 between two adjacent points in time. Second, it has to increase by 1 at time y, since it will otherwise not reach x_0 at time y. That is, $X_y - X_{y-1} = Z_y = 1$.

Based on this, the probability of reaching state x_0 at time y can be reformulated as the following joint probability:

$$P(Y_{x_0} = y) = P(X_{y-1} = (x_0 - 1), Z_y = 1)$$

Using the rules for conditional probabilities, the right-hand side of the equation above can be rewritten as:

$$P(X_{y-1} = (x_0 - 1), Z_y = 1) = P(X_{y-1} = (x_0 - 1) | Z_y = 1) \cdot P(Z_y = 1)$$

According to assumption 4 of the binomial process, X_{y-1} and Z_y are statistically independent. Thus, we have:

$$P(Y_{x_0} = y) = P(X_{y-1} = x_0 - 1) \cdot P(Z_y = 1)$$

Both probabilities on the right-hand side are known and can be derived from $\text{Bin}(y - 1, p)$ and $\text{Ber}(p)$, respectively. By inserting these probabilities, we arrive at the expression for the probability function for the negative binomial distribution in the box above.

If we want to find the distribution of the waiting time before the first incident occurs, then we just use $x_0 = 1$ and $Y_1 \sim \text{Negbin}(1, p)$. This distribution also has its own name – the *geometric distribution*. It is written $Y_1 \sim \text{Geo}(p)$. The probability function for the geometric distribution is:

$$f_{Y_1}(y) = \binom{y - 1}{1 - 1} \cdot p^1 \cdot (1 - p)^{y-1} = p \cdot (1 - p)^{y-1}$$

which is just the negative binomial distribution with $x_0 = 1$. Since the Bernoulli process is composed of independent Bernoulli-distributed random variables, then it follows that from any point in time in a Bernoulli process, the waiting time to the next incident is geometrically distributed.

Example 7.7: Coin toss – part 7

In the coin-toss example, we can calculate the expected waiting time before the first tails occurs using the formula in the box above:

$$E\left(Y_{x_0}\right) = x_0 \cdot \frac{1}{p} = 1 \cdot \frac{1}{0.5} = 2$$

The expected waiting time is thus two throws.

7.6　Poisson process

A Poisson process is an example of a discrete-state, continuous-time stochastic process. It can be interpreted as a process that, at any point in time, gives you the number of events that have occurred up to that point in time. A Poisson process is, therefore, also a counting process. It is defined on the basis of the following four assumptions:

A **Poisson process**, $\{X_t, t \in T\}$ satisfies:

1. *Time*: $T = (0, \infty)$

2. *State*: $X_t \in \{0,1,2,3,...\}$

3. *Distribution of outcomes*: $X_{t+\tau} - X_t \sim \text{Poi}(\lambda \cdot \tau) \text{ and } X_0 = 0$, where λ is the expected number of events occurring per unit of time

4. *Relationship between outcomes*: $X_{t_1} - X_{t_2}$ is statistically independent of $X_{t_3} - X_{t_4}$ when $t_1 > t_2 > t_3 > t_4$

According to assumption 3, the number of events in a time interval of length τ is Poisson-distributed with the parameter $\lambda \cdot \tau$, where λ is the expected number of events per unit of time. Assumption 3 means that only the length, τ, of the time interval matters for the distribution of the number of events, whereas the point in time at which the interval starts is not important.

7.6.1　The state distribution for a Poisson process

The state distribution for X_{t_0} can be taken directly from assumption 3 above. If we set $t = 0$ and $\tau = t_0$, we arrive at: $X_{t_0} \sim \text{Poi}(\lambda \cdot t_0)$.

The state distribution for a Poisson process:

$$X_{t_0} \sim \text{Poi}(\lambda \cdot t_0)$$

The probability function for X_{t_0} is:

$$f_{x_{t_0}}(x) = \frac{(\lambda \cdot t_0)^x}{x!} \cdot e^{-(\lambda \cdot t_0)}$$

Mean value and variance are: $E(X_{t_0}) = \lambda \cdot t_0$ and $V(X_{t_0}) = \lambda \cdot t_0$

Since the number of states is countable, the state distribution is discrete. The probability function, mean value and variance follow directly from inserting into the formulas for the Poisson distribution from Chapter 6. As with the binomial process, we see that the mean value increases with time t_0. The same applies to the variance.

Information about the state of a Poisson process at a given point in time, s, can be used to revise the probabilities for the state of the process at a later point in time, t. This is done using conditional probabilities. If b events have occurred at time s, then the probability that, at time t, x_t events will have occurred is equal to the probability of the occurrence of $x_t - b$ events between time s and time t:

$$P(X_t = x_t \mid X_s = b) = P(X_t - X_s = x_t - b)$$

This follows from assumption 4 in the box above and, thus, it holds independently of the distribution of X_t and X_s. Furthermore, from assumption 3, we know the distribution of $X_t - X_s$. This means that we are able to compute the conditional probability using the Poisson distribution with the parameter $\lambda \cdot (t - s)$.

Example 7.8: Calls to the doctor – part 1

In a small district, the doctor's surgery receives an average of 10 calls per hour. We assume that the number of calls follows a Poisson process with $\lambda = 10$. After 15 minutes, the probability that three people will have called is as follows:

$$P(X_{0.25} = 3) = \frac{(10 \cdot 0.25)^3}{3!} \cdot e^{-(10 \cdot 0.25)} = 0.214$$

as $X_{0.25} \sim \text{Poi}(10 \cdot 0.25)$.

The probability that 12 people will have called after one hour is:

$$P(X_1 = 12) = \frac{(10 \cdot 1)^{12}}{12!} \cdot e^{-(10 \cdot 1)} = 0.095$$

as $X_1 \sim \text{Poi}(10 \cdot 1)$.

If we know that three people have called after 15 minutes, the probability that 12 will have called after an hour is given by:

$$P(X_1 = 12 \mid X_{0.25} = 3) = P(X_1 - X_{0.25} = 12 - 3)$$

$$= P(X_1 - X_{0.25} = 9) = \frac{(10 \cdot 0.75)^9}{9!} \cdot e^{-(10 \cdot 0.75)} = 0.114$$

as $(X_1 - X_{0.25}) \sim \text{Poi}(10 \cdot (1 - 0.25))$.

Note that the probability of 12 people calling within an hour is higher if we know that three called within the first 15 minutes. If, conversely, we knew that nobody called during the first 15 minutes, then the probability of 12 calling within an hour would be less than if we did not know how many people had called during the first 15 minutes.

7.6.2   The waiting-time distribution for a Poisson process

Let Y_{x_0} be the time until the Poisson process reaches the value x_0. The distribution of Y_{x_0} also has its own name, the *Erlang distribution*. It is described in the following box:

> **The waiting-time distribution for a Poisson process (the Erlang distribution):**
>
> $$Y_{x_0} \sim \text{Erlang}(\lambda, x_0)$$
>
> The probability density function for Y_{x_0} is:
>
> $$f_{Y_{x_0}}(y) = \frac{\lambda^{x_0} \cdot y^{x_0-1}}{(x_0 - 1)!} \cdot e^{-\lambda \cdot y}$$
>
> And the cumulative distribution function is:
>
> $$F_{Y_{x_0}}(y) = 1 - \sum_{k=0}^{x_0-1} \frac{(\lambda \cdot y)^k}{k!} \cdot e^{-\lambda \cdot y}$$
>
> Mean value and variance are: $E\left(Y_{x_0}\right) = \dfrac{x_0}{\lambda}$ and $V\left(Y_{x_0}\right) = \dfrac{x_0}{\lambda^2}$

Because in this case the set of time indices is uncountable (it is an interval), the waiting time is a continuous random variable.

We can derive the Erlang distribution as follows: if you have to wait longer than time y until the number of events is x_0, then it must imply that there were fewer than x_0 events at time y. In terms of probabilities, it is therefore the case that:

$$P(Y_{x_0} > y) = P(X_y < x_0)$$

where X_y is the state at time y, and $X_y \sim \text{Poi}(\lambda \cdot y)$ according to the state distribution for the Poisson process from the section above. Since $P(X_y < x_0) = P(X_y \le x_0 - 1)$, we get $P(Y_{x_0} > y) = P(X_y \le x_0 - 1)$. Finally, we can use that $P(Y_{x_0} \le y) = 1 - P(Y_{x_0} > y)$ to arrive at the Erlang distribution:

$$P(Y_{x_0} \le y) = 1 - P(Y_{x_0} > y) = 1 - P(X_y < x_0) = 1 - P(X_y \le x_0 - 1)$$

If you are interested in when the next incident will occur in a Poisson process, you insert $x_0 = 1$ into the Erlang distribution. This gives the following probability density function and cumulative distribution function for Y_1 (the time until the next incident):

$$f_{Y_1}(y) = \lambda \cdot e^{-\lambda \cdot y} \text{ and } F_{Y_1}(y) = 1 - e^{-\lambda \cdot y}$$

This distribution – which is a special case of the Erlang distribution – is also called the *exponential distribution* and is written: $Y_1 \sim \text{EXP}(\lambda)$

Example 7.9: Calls to the doctor – part 2

In Example 7.8, we assumed that the calls to the doctor followed a Poisson process with $\lambda = 10$. The probability of having to wait 15 minutes before two people call is given by:

$$P(Y_2 \le 0.25) = F_{Y_2}(0.25)$$
$$= 1 - \frac{(10 \cdot 0.25)^0}{0!} \cdot e^{-10 \cdot 0.25} - \frac{(10 \cdot 0.25)^1}{1!} \cdot e^{-10 \cdot 0.25}$$
$$= 1 - 0.082 - 0.205 = 0.713$$

since $Y_2 \sim \text{Erlang}(10,2)$. Correspondingly, the probability of waiting more than an hour for 12 people to call is: $P(Y_{12} > 1) = 1 - P(Y_{12} \le 1)$, where $Y_{12} \sim \text{Erlang}(10,12)$. Try to work this probability out yourself!

The probability of waiting a maximum of two minutes for a call is $P(Y_1 \le 2/60)$, where $Y_1 \sim \text{Erlang}(10,1) = \text{EXP}(10)$. This probability is:

$$P\left(Y_1 \le \frac{1}{30}\right) = F_{Y_1}\left(\frac{1}{30}\right) = 1 - e^{-10 \cdot \left(\frac{1}{30}\right)} = 0.283$$

7.7   Gaussian random walk

A Gaussian random walk is an example of a continuous-state, discrete-time stochastic process, and is one of many specifications of a random walk. In general, a random walk is a stochastic process in which each random variable X_t can be written as a partial sum of independent and identically distributed random variables.[11] The binomial process is therefore also an example of a random walk. As the name suggests, random walk processes are used to illustrate, for example, the kind of motion observed after drunken parties – where each step could be either forwards or backwards.

In a Gaussian random walk, the outcome at a given point in time is normally distributed (also referred to as Gaussian). The Gaussian random walk is defined by the following four assumptions:

A **Gaussian random walk**, $\{X_t, t \in T\}$, satisfies:

1. *Time: $T = \{0,1,2,3,...\}$*

2. *State: $X_t \in (-\infty, \infty)$*

3. *Distribution of outcomes: $(X_{t+n} - X_t) \sim N(n \cdot \mu, n \cdot \sigma^2)$ and $X_0 = 0$,*

    where μ is called the drift parameter and σ^2 is called the diffusion parameter

4. *Relationship between outcomes: $X_{t_1} - X_{t_2}$ is statistically independent of $X_{t_3} - X_{t_4}$ when $t_1 > t_2 > t_3 > t_4$*

A Gaussian random walk is a stochastic process with a continuous state. This means that X_t may assume any value. Assumption 3 tells us that the change in the process within a given period of time is normally distributed where the mean value and the variance depend on the length, n, of the time period: $N(n \cdot \mu, n \cdot \sigma^2)$. Furthermore, assumption 4 says that this change in the process is independent of the previous evolution of the process.

---

11   A random walk $\{X_t, t = 1,2,3,...\}$ satisfies that: (i) $X_t = Z_1 + Z_2 + ... + Z_t = \sum_{m=1}^{t} Z_m$; (ii) Z_t is statistically independent of Z_s when $t \neq s$; and (iii) the distribution of Z_t is the same irrespective of t.

7.7.1   The state distribution for a Gaussian random walk

We can derive the state distribution directly from assumption 3 above. If we set $t = 0$ and $n = t_0$, we get: $X_{t_0} \sim N(t_0 \cdot \mu, \, t_0 \cdot \sigma^2)$.

> **The state distribution for a Gaussian random walk:**
>
> $$X_{t_0} \sim N(t_0 \cdot \mu, \, t_0 \cdot \sigma^2)$$
>
> The probability density function for X_{t_0} is:
>
> $$f_{X_{t_0}}(x) = \frac{1}{\sqrt{2 \cdot \pi \cdot t_0 \cdot \sigma^2}} \cdot e^{-\frac{1}{2} \frac{(x - t_0 \cdot \mu)^2}{t_0 \cdot \sigma^2}}$$
>
> Mean value and variance are: $E(X_{t_0}) = t_0 \cdot \mu$ and $V(X_{t_0}) = t_0 \cdot \sigma^2$

The condition that the Gaussian random walk $\{X_t, t \in T\}$ starts in $X_0 = 0$ is not restrictive. If you want a stochastic process $\{\tilde{X}_t, t \in T\}$ that starts at a different value than zero, for example, $\tilde{X}_0 = a$, but otherwise has the same properties as a Gaussian random walk, then its distribution can be derived from the Gaussian random walk in the following way:

$$P(\tilde{X}_t < \tilde{x}) = P(\tilde{X}_t - a < \tilde{x} - a) = P(X_t < \tilde{x} - a)$$

The stochastic process $\{\tilde{X}_t, t \in T\}$ is also called a Gaussian random walk with starting point at a.

It is also possible to compute the conditional probability of the state of the process being, for example, less than a particular value at a given point in time, t, given that we know where it was at an earlier point in time, s. As with the Poisson process, we can use that:

$$P(X_t \leq x_t \mid X_s = b) = P(X_t - X_s \leq x_t - b)$$

due to assumption 4.

Then we can calculate the conditional probability by using the normal distribution with mean, $(t - s) \cdot \mu$, and variance, $(t - s) \cdot \sigma^2$.

Imagine a country that has an average foreign exchange deficit of DKK 20 billion p.a. Let us therefore assume that, on an annual basis, the content of the currency reserve follows a Gaussian random walk, with $\mu = -20$ (DKK billion) and $\sigma^2 = 625$. The currency reserve contains DKK 60 billion at the starting point (year 0). The probability of the currency reserve being depleted after two years is given by:

$$P(\tilde{X}_2 < 0) = P(X_2 < 0 - 60)$$

where $\tilde{X}_t$ is a Gaussian random walk with initial value 60. According to the above, X_2 is normally distributed with mean value $2 \cdot (-20) = -40$ and variance $2 \cdot 625 = 1250$. We can therefore calculate the above probability as:

$$P(X_2 < -60) = \Phi\left(\frac{-60 - (-40)}{\sqrt{1250}}\right) = \Phi(-0.567) = 0.29$$

Note that even though the reserve is not empty after the first two years, it may well have been empty at some point along the way. To calculate the probability of this, we must look at the waiting-time distribution.

7.7.2   The waiting-time distribution for a Gaussian random walk

The waiting-time distribution for a Gaussian random walk is complicated and cannot be stated in a simple formula. We have therefore chosen not to discuss it further here. However, you can use the waiting-time distribution of a Wiener process, as discussed in the next section, as an approximation.

7.8   Wiener process

A Wiener process is an example of a continuous-state, continuous-time stochastic process, defined on the basis of the following four assumptions:

A **Wiener process**, $\{X_t, t \in T\}$ satisfies:

1. *Time:* $T = (0,\infty)$

2. *State:* $X_t \in (-\infty,\infty)$

3. *Distribution of outcomes:* $(X_{t+\tau} - X_t) \sim N(\mu \cdot \tau, \sigma^2 \tau)$ *and* $X_0 = 0$, where μ *is called the drift parameter and* σ^2 *is called the diffusion parameter*

4. *Relationship between outcomes:* $X_{t_1} - X_{t_2}$ *is statistically independent of* $X_{t_3} - X_{t_4}$ *when* $t_1 > t_2 > t_3 > t_4$

The Wiener process is also called a *Brownian motion*. The Wiener process is very similar to the Gaussian random walk, the difference being that the former takes place in continuous time, while the Gaussian random walk is a discrete-time process. In other words, the Wiener process is constantly changing, while the Gaussian random walk only changes at specified points in time (1, 2, 3, etc.). Figure 7.5 shows examples of realisations of a Gaussian random walk and a Wiener process, respectively.

Figure 7.5:
Realisations
of a Gaussian
random walk
and a Wiener
process

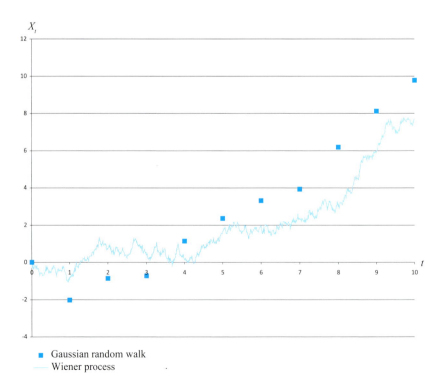

Gaussian random walk
Wiener process

An insight into statistics for the social sciences

7.8.1 The state distribution for a Wiener process

The state distribution follows directly from assumption 3 and is completely identical to the state distribution for a Gaussian random walk:

> **The state distribution for a Wiener process:**
>
> $$X_{t_0} \sim N(t_0 \cdot \mu, \, t_0 \cdot \sigma^2)$$
>
> The probability density function for X_{t_0} is:
>
> $$f_{X_{t_0}}(x) = \frac{1}{\sqrt{2 \cdot \pi \cdot t_0 \cdot \sigma^2}} \cdot e^{-\frac{1}{2} \cdot \frac{(x - t_0 \cdot \mu)^2}{t_0 \cdot \sigma^2}}$$
>
> Mean value and variance are: $E(X_{t_0}) = t_0 \cdot \mu$ and $V(X_{t_0}) = t_0 \cdot \sigma^2$

As with the Gaussian random walk, the condition that the process starts at $X_0 = 0$ is not restrictive. If you want a Wiener process $\{\tilde{X}_t, t \in T\}$ to start at the value a, then you can simply use that $P(\tilde{X}_t \leq \tilde{x}) = P(X_t \leq \tilde{x} - a)$, where $\{X_t, t \in T\}$ is a standard Wiener process, as defined in the box above.

7.8.2 The waiting-time distribution for a Wiener process

Let Y_{x_0} be the time until the Wiener process X_t reaches x_0 for the first time. The distribution of Y_{x_0} is called the *inverse Gaussian distribution*, or the *Wald distribution*. It is described in the next box:

The waiting-time distribution for a Wiener process (the inverse Gaussian distribution):

For $x_0 > 0$ and $\mu > 0$:

$$Y_{x_0} \sim IG\left(\frac{x_0}{\mu}, \frac{x_0^2}{\sigma^2}\right)$$

The probability density function for Y_{x_0} is:

$$f_{Y_{x_0}}(y) = \left[\frac{\frac{x_0^2}{\sigma^2}}{2 \cdot \pi \cdot y^3}\right]^{1/2} \cdot \exp\left(\frac{-\frac{x_0^2}{\sigma^2} \cdot \left(y - \frac{x_0}{\mu}\right)^2}{2 \cdot \left(\frac{x_0}{\mu}\right)^2 \cdot y}\right)$$

And the cumulative distribution function is:

$$F_{Y_{x_0}}(y) = \Phi\left(\sqrt{\frac{x_0^2}{y \cdot \sigma^2}} \cdot \frac{\mu}{x_0} \cdot \left[y - \frac{x_0}{\mu}\right]\right)$$

$$+ \exp\left(2 \cdot x_0 \cdot \frac{\mu}{\sigma^2}\right) \cdot \Phi\left(-\sqrt{\frac{x_0^2}{\sigma^2 \cdot y}} \cdot \frac{\mu}{x_0} \left[y + \frac{x_0}{\mu}\right]\right)$$

Mean value and variance are: $E\left(Y_{x_0}\right) = \frac{x_0}{\mu}$ and $V\left(Y_{x_0}\right) = \frac{x_0}{\mu} \cdot \frac{\sigma^2}{\mu^2}$

The waiting time is defined as the time it takes the process to reach or pass the value x_0. We can also analyse how long it takes before the process becomes less than or equal to a certain value. For a Wiener process, we can use the above formulas directly, based on the following consideration: let W_t be a Wiener process with negative drift parameter, $\mu_W < 0$. The time that it takes W_t to reach the value $w_0 < 0$ corresponds to the time it takes for the "inverted" process X_t (where X_t is similar to W_t, only with positive drift parameter $\mu_X = -\mu_W$) to reach the value $-w_0 > 0$. Example 7.11 illustrates this.

In Example 7.10, we assumed that the content of the currency reserve follows a Gaussian random walk with $\mu = -20$ and $\sigma^2 = 625$. If the currency reserve is calculated continuously, then a Wiener process with the same parameters will better describe its contents.

Let Y_{-60} be the waiting time until the Wiener process with a starting value of 0 passes minus 60 for the first time. As the currency reserve will start off at DKK 60 billion, this corresponds to finding the waiting time until the reserve is depleted for the first time. This also equals the waiting time for the inverted process with a starting value of 0 to reach 60, and Y_{-60} therefore follows the following inverse Gaussian distribution:

$$Y_{-60} \sim IG\left(\frac{60}{20}, \frac{(60)^2}{625}\right)$$

The probability of the currency reserve being emptied within the next two years is $P(Y_{-60} < 2)$. This probability can be calculated by inserting into the expression for the cumulative distribution function in the box above:

$$P\left(Y_{-60} < 2\right) = F_{Y_{-60}}(2) = \Phi\left(\sqrt{\frac{5.76}{2}} \cdot \left[\frac{2}{3} - 1\right]\right)$$
$$+ \exp\left(2 \cdot \frac{5.76}{3}\right) \cdot \Phi\left(-\sqrt{\frac{5.76}{2}} \cdot \left[\frac{2}{3} + 1\right]\right) = 0.39$$

In Example 7.10, we calculated the probability that the currency reserve would be empty after two years. This probability – which is the same for the Gaussian random walk and the Wiener process – was lower than the probability of it being emptied for the first time within two years. This is because the currency reserve may be temporarily emptied before the two years are up, without being empty at the two-year point.

7.9 Summary of selected stochastic processes

In this chapter, we have examined the idea of a stochastic process and shown various examples of stochastic processes. The most common ones are summarised in Table 7.4.

Table 7.4:
Selected
stochastic
processes

Stochastic process	Time index	State	State distribution	Waiting-time distribution
Binomial process	Disc.	Disc.	$\text{Bin}(t_0, p)$	$\text{Negbin}(x_0, p)$
Poisson process	Cont.	Disc.	$\text{Poi}(t_0 \cdot \lambda)$	$\text{Erlang}(\lambda, x_0)$
Gaussian random walk	Disc.	Cont.	$N(\mu \cdot t_0, \sigma^2 \cdot t_0)$	Omitted
Wiener process	Cont.	Cont.	$N(\mu \cdot t_0, \sigma^2 \cdot t_0)$	$IG\left(\dfrac{x_0}{\mu}, \dfrac{x_0^2}{\sigma^2}\right)$

7.10 Exercises

1. Review questions:
   a) What is a stochastic process? How is it defined?
   b) What do we mean by a realisation or a sample path?
   c) Explain what we mean when we say that a stochastic process takes place in discrete time and continuous time, respectively.
   d) Explain what you understand by a partial-sum transformation.
   e) Explain what you understand by a first-difference transformation.
   f) Explain how the state distribution and waiting-time distribution, respectively, of a stochastic process are defined and what they can be used for.
   g) Explain the difference between the four types of stochastic process in Section 7.4.

2. Consider a binomial process, $\{X_t, t = 1,...,3\}$ with $p = 0.5$. Let $W_t = 2 \cdot X_t - t$. The process $\{W_t, t = 1,...,3\}$ is called a simple random walk because each step is either +1 or –1.
   a) Write down all sample paths for $\{W_t, t = 1,...,3\}$ and the probability of each of them.
   b) Find the state distribution for W_t at time $t = 3$.

c) Find the probability that W_t is greater than or equal to 2 at time $t = 3$.

d) Find the probability that W_t is less than 1 at time $t = 3$.

e) Find the waiting-time distribution for Y_{w_0} when $w_0 = 1$.

f) Find the probability that the waiting time is longer than 2 when $w_0 = 1$.

3. Changes in house prices in a particularly attractive residential area can be described by a Gaussian random walk, $\{X_t, t = 1,...\}$, with a drift parameter equal to 2 and a diffusion parameter equal to 1. The process starts at $X_0 = 0$, but this does not mean that the starting price for houses is zero. Rather, the starting point is normalised to 0 because what is of interest is the development in the price level, not the price level in absolute terms.

a) Find the state distribution for the following transformation of the Gaussian random walk: $W_t = a + b \cdot X_t$, where a and b are constants. This transformation is assumed to be capable of describing the evolution of house prices in the same area when $a = -1$ and $b = 1.2$.

b) Work out the probability that X_t is less than 4 for $t = 2$.

c) Work out the probability that W_t is less than 4 for $t = 2$.

d) Work out the probability that X_t is larger than 2 for $t = 3$.

e) Work out the probability that W_t is larger than 2 for $t = 3$.

f) Find the state distribution for the following transformation of the Gaussian random walk: $W_t = X_t - X_{t-1}$.

g) Work out the probability that W_t is less than 4 for $t = 2$.

h) Work out the probability that W_t is larger than 2 for $t = 3$.

4. The price of a financial asset follows a Wiener process with drift parameter $\mu = 0.1$ and diffusion parameter $\sigma^2 = 0.2$. The time is measured in days. At the turn of the year, the asset price is DKK 274.

a) What is the probability that the asset will have a lower price at the end of January than at the start of the month (i.e. after 31 days)?

b) What is the probability of you having to wait more than 31 days before the asset price is higher than DKK 280?

c) What is the expected price of the asset after one year (365 days)?

8 From deductive reasoning to inductive reasoning

The previous chapters described situations in which the distribution of the random variable was known. This distribution was then used to calculate the probabilities of realising certain values. We also interpreted the random variable as the result of selecting from a population – either a real population or a super-population – where the probability distribution of the random variable was determined by the distribution (composition) of the population and by the selection mechanism. We assumed that the population and the selection mechanism were known. This type of analysis is called *deductive reasoning*, because it involves analysing from the more general (the population and the selection mechanism) to learn about the more specific (the sample).

In the remaining chapters, we will reverse this procedure. Often, the purpose of statistical methods is to help us learn about the population or the selection mechanism. This information is obtained by selecting a sample. This type of analysis is called *inductive reasoning* because it involves analysing from the more specific outcome (the sample) to learn about the more general (the population and the selection mechanism).

The knowledge we acquire about the population and the selection mechanism using this type of inductive reasoning can in turn be used to make predictions. A prediction is a statement about what you think a future sample will look like. In other words, first we use an (existing) sample to learn about the population and the selection mechanism. This is inductive reasoning. We then use what we have learned about the population and the selection mechanism to predict a future sample. This is deductive reasoning.

Section 8.1 looks at inductive reasoning. Section 8.2 provides an overview of the different types of analyses that social scientists may encounter. This also provides an explanation of the book's structure. Section 8.3 gives a brief overview of the remaining chapters.

8.1   Inductive reasoning

In advance of an EU referendum, an opinion poll is conducted in order to find out the proportion of yes and no voters in the electorate (the population). Similarly, a company conducts market research to quantify consumer (population) demand for a new product. The information obtained is then used to predict the proportion of the electorate that will vote yes, or how many consumers will want the product. In other words, we observe a few elements (the sample) from a real population and use these to comment on the whole population.

In the case of a super-population, it is often the selection mechanism itself that is of interest. For example, a company that produces screws might be interested to know the range of lengths of the screws that emerge from its production process. It may know that the screws always measure between 12 mm and 17 mm but would like to know the mean length. The screws are not a sample from a real population. Rather, they are a sample from a super-population of possible screw lengths, which belong to the interval between 12 mm and 17 mm. This super-population is fully described; what is unknown is how the selection mechanism works. It is the selection mechanism that determines the distribution of the screw lengths. Here, the company uses the sample of screws to learn about the probability distribution of a random variable, namely the random variable that gives the length of a randomly selected screw.

Samples can therefore be used to learn about both real populations and probability distributions of random variables. Remember, however, that a real population can also be represented by the distribution of a random variable. If the value of the random variable is given by the value of the selected element, and all elements have the same chance of selection, then the distribution of the random variable is given by the relative frequency function of the real population (as discussed in Chapter 4).

We can therefore think of all situations in which samples are used in an inductive analysis as being situations where we want to learn something about the distribution of a random variable. This abstraction is particularly useful.

8.2   Types of analyses

In this section, we provide a brief overview of when, and for what purpose, deductive and inductive reasoning are used in statistics. Table 8.1

shows the possible situations in which we may find ourselves when we conduct an analysis. The population and selection mechanism may either be known or unknown.

Table 8.1:
Types of analyses

Selection mechanism \ Population	Known	Unknown
Known	(1)	(2)
Unknown	(3)	(4)

In situation (1) in Table 8.1, both the population and the selection mechanism are known. Here, the purpose of the analyses is to predict a future sample. The task is purely deductive, so we need only apply probability theory, not statistics. If, for example, we roll a dice, then both the population (one, two, ... six) and the selection mechanism (all outcomes have the same chance of being selected) are known. The job is to calculate the probability of rolling, say, a six. Even if we had a sample at our disposal, we would have no use for it in this situation. It is the outcome of a future sample that we are trying to predict. This is the type of analysis we have conducted so far in the book.

Situation (2), with an unknown population and a known selection mechanism, occurs when we want to learn something about a real population – for example, opinions regarding a television programme, how people will vote in an election, and so on. If we have a sample where we know that everybody in the population has the same probability of being selected, then the task is purely inductive – in other words, we must use the sample to predict the properties of the population.

Situation (3), with a known population but an unknown selection mechanism, was illustrated by the example of the screws above. This situation typically occurs when we have to make a prediction. This re-quires that we possess knowledge of both the population and the selection mechanism. Since the selection mechanism is unknown, the first task is to form an estimate of this mechanism based on the sample. This task is inductive. We can then use our knowledge of the population and the estimated selection mechanism to make a prediction of a future sample (e.g. the length of future screws). This task is deductive.

Another example of this is when we want to predict the future price of a bond. Here, we have at our disposal the previous prices of the same bond. This sample is selected from a super-population of all possible prices (ranging from 0 to infinity). However, we do not know how the selection mechanism works on this super-population. It is possible to use the sample to form estimates of the probabilities of the various prices in the super-population. We are then able to use these probabilities to predict, for example, the price of the bond in two weeks' time, as this constitutes a new (future) sample. Here, the inductive analysis is again followed by a deductive analysis.

Situation (4), where both the population and the selection mechanism are unknown, happens in cases involving real populations where we are interested in learning about the population or making a prediction. For example, we might want to know the local population's opinion of the quality of a restaurant. If our sample consists of all those persons who visit the restaurant, then the selection mechanism in relation to the whole population is also unknown, since we do not know the probability of a given person eating at this specific restaurant. This probability typically depends on the person's opinion of the restaurant's quality, which is unknown.

8.3   Estimators and tests

In Chapter 9, we will look at how to obtain a representative sample from a population, and at the problems that often arise in connection with this. As mentioned above, the sample is used in an inductive analysis to form an estimate of the distribution (of a random variable) or an aspect of a distribution (e.g. the mean value). An *estimator* is a function that, based on the sample, helps us create an estimate of the aspect that we are interested in. Chapter 10 illustrates this by focusing on an estimator for the mean value of a distribution, when we have at our disposal a simple random sample. In Chapter 11, we look at other estimators for the mean value under alternative sampling mechanisms. Chapter 12 provides an overview of various estimators, including estimators for the other parameters in the distribution (e.g. the variance).

Since an estimator is based on a sample, the estimator is also random. Therefore, the estimator does not allow us to conclude anything with certainty about the underlying parameter. However, we can say something about its probable size. We do this by constructing confidence intervals or by testing hypotheses about the parameter.

In the construction of confidence intervals, we use the sample to compute an interval of values (instead of just a single estimate) within which the "true" parameter value is likely to be found. We will look at confidence intervals in Chapter 13.

If, for example, we have a hypothesis that a distribution's mean value is 5, then we can use the sample to form an estimate of the mean value and compare this with the hypothetical value. If the two values are far apart, then it is unlikely that the mean value of the distribution is 5, and we therefore reject the hypothesis. This is the underlying concept of hypothesis testing, which we will look at in Chapter 14.

Chapters 15 and 16 look at methods of testing hypotheses regarding relationships between random variables. A typical example is when we want to investigate whether two groups in a population (e.g. men and women) are identical. Chapter 15 focuses on situations in which we have quantitative data, and shows, for example, how to test whether two mean values are different when corrected for the uncertainty caused by the samples. In Chapter 16, we present corresponding tests for qualitative data.

Finally, Chapters 17 and 18 introduce regression analysis, which is used to form estimates of specific relationships between random variables. In connection with this, we will also see how to test hypotheses about relationships of this type.

9 The sampling process

The main purpose of statistical inference is to obtain knowledge about an unknown distribution. This could be the distribution of a particular characteristic, such as income or attitudes, in a real population. It is usually not feasible to obtain complete knowledge about a whole population. Instead, we have to rely on a sample. In this chapter, we discuss how to extract a sample from a real population, as well as common sources of errors in sampling.

The quality of the sample is essential to the subsequent analysis. Without a proper sample, we have a "rubbish in, rubbish out" situation. Even the most advanced of statistical methods is of little use if the underlying data is not of sufficient quality. In practice, the process of data acquisition (the sampling) – which some people take too lightly in their haste to get to the analysis stage – is vital to whether the results are useful or just "rubbish out" at the other end.

In Chapter 3, we introduced the concepts of the "statistical experiment" and the "probability model". Sampling is an important aspect of both concepts. Until now, we have ignored this aspect, apart from noting that some random sampling takes place. The sampling implies that we can define random variables and their distribution in the probability model. In practice, selecting a sample from a real population is a complicated matter and there are many potential sources of error, which can lead to samples being uninformative or even entirely misleading. In this chapter, we will therefore look in detail at sample selection and analyse various sources of error.

In Section 9.1, we present the four key points in the design of the sampling process: Choice of population and characteristics of interest; specification of sampling units and sampling frame; specification of sampling method; and measurement of the characteristics of interest. These are discussed in sections 9.2 to 9.5. Sections 9.6 and 9.7 are a bit more technical and establish a model for the sample. This model allows us to define a representative sample in Section 9.8 and to discuss the consequences of non-representative samples in Section 9.9. Finally, in sections 9.10 and 9.11, we discuss sources of error in the sampling process and observation errors, respectively.

9.1   Designing the sampling process

In Chapter 3, we defined a statistical experiment as the selection of a sample from a population. In this chapter, we focus on how to design a sampling process from a real population. The concepts we employ are also useful for super-populations, but focusing exclusively on real populations means that the elements and their associated characteristics have a physical interpretation.

The four main points that need careful consideration when designing a sampling process are:

1. Choice of population and characteristics of interest
2. Specification of sampling units and sampling frame
3. Specification of sampling method
4. Measurement of the characteristics of interest.

The choice of the population and the characteristics of the elements in which we are interested follow from the purpose of the study. However, determining the actual purpose of a study is not always as simple as you might think. It is important, therefore, that this is clarified and specified. We cannot ignore the fact that a study may involve many actors with conflicting interests. They will usually want to help shape the design of the study, because this can have a major influence on the results. We will look at this in Section 9.2.

While the purpose of the study forms the basis for the choice of population and the characteristics of interest, the specification of sampling units and the sampling frame is a more technical issue. The *sampling units* are the subsets of elements from the population that we extract. In many cases the sampling units are just the elements of the population but it could be the case that, for example, married couples constitute the sampling units, although we are interested in each of the two individuals separately. The *sampling frame* is a way of writing up all of the possible sampling units and describing how each of them can be reached. This may take the form, for example, of a postal address for each of the sampling units. We look more closely at sampling units and frames in Section 9.3.

The selection from the sampling frame gives us our sample. The main difference between different sampling methods is whether or not they are described by a known probability distribution. For example, do all of the sampling units have the same probability of selection? We will look at this in Section 9.4.

Once we have extracted a sampling unit, we have to measure the characteristics of interest of the elements in that unit. In cases where the samples are human beings, this may take the form of asking questions in order to measure the values of different characteristics. We will look at this in more depth in Section 9.5.

Example 9.1 illustrates the different elements in the design of a sampling process.

Example 9.1: Attitudes towards the EU

Let us look at a study of Danish voters' attitudes towards EU membership. The purpose is therefore to study attitudes towards the EU (the relevant characteristic) among Danes aged 18 and over (the population). We can identify the population elements on the basis of their main residence (the sampling unit). A complete list of addresses (the sampling frame) can be used to contact all of the people who live at a particular place of residence. We can select sampling units by numbering the residences in the sampling frame consecutively, and letting a computer randomly select from these numbers (the sampling method). Finally, we can send an interviewer to the residence and ask the people who live there about their attitudes towards the EU (the measurement of characteristics).

Although Example 9.1 suggests a particular order of the stages in the sampling process, in practice we will often jump back and forth between the different stages. Often, you test the design of a sampling process by running a *pilot study* – a mini version of the actual sample survey. The following sections consider in detail each of the steps in the design of a sample process.

9.2   Population and characteristics of interest

The first task in the design of a sample process is the choice of population and the characteristics of the elements that we are interested in. The population and characteristics of interest are not necessarily the same as those that we are actually studying. They are specified as a result of the purpose of the study. For example, it may be that you want to study the impact of a hazardous substance on human health. However, for ethical reasons, we do not wish to give a person a big dose of the substance to observe the effect. Instead, we can investigate the effect on synthetic cells in a laboratory. Thus, the population to be studied comprises the collection of synthetic cells, and the relevant characteristic is their reproductive capability. The aim is to use this population as a substitute for the population of interest, which is the human population.

The population of interest is called the *target population*. As we have seen above, this is not necessarily the population used in the statistical experiment. For practical reasons, we may sometimes have to study a different population. We use the concept of population as the designation for the collection of elements from which the sample is taken. Used on its own, "population" therefore refers to the population involved in the statistical experiment, which may differ from the target population.

As we have seen, one reason the population in a statistical experiment sometimes differs from the target population may be that it is impossible in practice to select a sample from the target population. In this case, there is no overlap between the population from which the sample is taken and the target population. Another reason may be that it can be prohibitively expensive to select a sample from the whole of the target population. It may be cheaper to conduct a study within a limited area (e.g. in one city) and then extrapolate the results to the whole country. In this case, the population from which the sample is taken is a subset of the target population.

When the target population is not the same as the population being studied, it raises the question of how well the population being studied mimics the target population. Statistical theory cannot help us answer this question. It is therefore up to the researcher to argue (using his or her knowledge of the problem) that the results obtained can be transferred to the target population. If, for example, we want to transfer results from a sample survey conducted in one city to the whole country, then we must be able to argue that this city is "similar" in some sense to the whole country.

The specification of the elements' characteristics of interest can be difficult. For example, if we want to study the quality of various secondary schools by measuring pupils' grades in written exams, then it would be useful to know the skills of the pupils before they enrolled at the schools. This would ensure that we do not mistakenly come to the conclusion that one school is better than another if the reality is that the difference is due to the innate abilities of the pupils. However, abilities are anything but well defined, let alone quantifiable. One solution could be to use the values from an IQ test taken by the pupils prior to enrolment in the schools.

The problem is therefore that it can be difficult to define relevant characteristics. Statistical theory cannot help us with this problem either. The people conducting the study must, on the basis of their knowledge of the problem, justify the choice of characteristics to be measured.

Example 9.2: Youth crime

The Ministry of Education wants to shed light on youth crime and hires a consultancy company to conduct a study. This raises a number of questions: Who are the youngsters? What kind of crime are we talking about? Should the study be based on offenders, on crimes reported or on crimes committed? The consultancy company decides to define the target population as all individuals aged 15–18. The population from which the sample is selected, on the other hand, consists of all those aged 15–18 who have been charged with crimes. Finally, as the characteristic of interest, the consultancy company chooses the number of break-ins by each person. Discuss these choices.

9.3   Sampling units and the sampling frame

The units to be selected are called *sampling units*, each of which may consist of more than one element. Often, it is cheaper to select many elements together, for example, an entire school class, rather than selecting the elements individually. The collection of all sampling units is called the *sampling frame*.

In practice, the sampling frame must contain information about how to make contact with the different sampling units. Typically, this involves making a list, for example, of company registration numbers and addresses. The list enables us to reach the sampling units and hence the elements in the population.

Sometimes, the description of how to reach all the sampling units in the sampling frame can be less specific. For instance, if we select our sample by interviewing people who are at a certain place at a certain time – say at a particular airport on a Thursday afternoon – the sampling frame is precise in terms of the sampling units (in this case, people) but not in terms of how to get in touch with all of them. Only those who happen to be in the airport on that Thursday can be selected for the sample.

The information about how to get in contact with an element is often a characteristic of that particular element. For example, a social security number or an address is a characteristic of a person. We call such a characteristic a *selection characteristic.* It may also be useful to think of other, less precise information as selection characteristics of the elements. For example, "to be at a particular airport on a given Thursday afternoon" can be seen as selection characteristic of a person in this context.

Establishing a precise sampling frame is important because we do not usually work alone when conducting a study. To be able to evaluate the quality of the study in retrospect, you must have an accurate idea of how it was conducted. Again, this depends on how the researchers' tasks have been delineated. Part of this delineation lies in the specification of the sampling frame.

9.4   Sampling method

The methods used to select the sampling units from the sampling frame have important implications for the quality of the sample, and, in particular, for the possibility of evaluating its quality. In the next subsections, we divide the different sampling methods into *probability sampling* and *non-probability sampling.*

9.4.1   Probability sampling

How to select the sampling units from the sampling frame is an important strategic consideration in the design of the sampling process. Probability sampling means that the probability of selecting a particular sampling unit is known. One example could be that all sampling units have the same probability of being selected. In this book, we look at three types of probability sampling: simple random sampling, stratified sampling and cluster sampling. In the following chapters, we will consider these three sampling methods in detail. In particular, we will focus on simple random sampling, not only because it makes the calculations relatively simple but also because the more complicated methods of selection involve an element of simple random sampling.

One advantage of probability sampling is that it makes it possible to quantify the quality of the study. Another advantage of probability sampling is that it is easier to obtain a sample that provides a "true" picture of the population.

9.4.2   Non-probability sampling

Non-probability sampling means that the probability of selecting a given sampling unit is unknown, which effectively makes it impossible to assess the quality of a study. However, non-probability sampling is widely used in practice because it is relatively inexpensive. In addition, in some cases it may be difficult to perform probability sampling. Some of the sources of error discussed later in this chapter stem from treating a sample as if it were a result of probability sampling, when it is actually (at least partially) a result of non-probability sampling. Below are four examples of non-probability sampling: convenience sampling, purposive sampling, quota sampling and snowball sampling.

Convenience sampling is where the researcher allows convenience to determine the selection of the sampling units – for example, conducting interviews with shoppers in a shopping centre. The advantage of this method is that it is inexpensive, as there is no need to identify specific individuals. However, this is also the method's main disadvantage, because the researcher does not know the probability of a particular person being included in the sample. The main problem is that the probabilities of the different values of the characteristic you are investigating can be dependent on the probability of being included in the sample. If, for example, we are interviewing people about their attitudes towards shopping in big shopping centres by interviewing people in those very centres, then there is a fair chance that those people will be more positive than the population as a whole, otherwise they would probably not be in the centre in the first place. In this case, the sample does not provide a true picture of the population. We will look at this in greater detail in Section 9.10.

Purposive sampling, also called judgment sampling, is where the researcher identifies who is to be studied. This method is sometimes used when we want to interview people who are assumed to have a particularly good knowledge of the survey topic. This allows us to interview fewer people and conduct a less expensive study. The main problem with purposive sampling is that the people selected often do not give a true picture of the whole population.

Quota sampling is where we decide in advance that the sample must contain a certain quota, or proportion, of people with certain characteristics that are not the direct focus of the study. These are also called *background characteristics*. For example, in a study of young people's Internet usage, we might require that half of the individuals selected should be from rural areas and the other half from urban conurbations. A good thing about quota sampling is that it ensures that people with different background characteristics are represented in the sample.

Problems can occur, however, if these background characteristics influence the characteristic we are studying. Here too, we run the risk of the sample not giving a true picture of the population. However, if we know the distribution of the background characteristics used (e.g. the shares living in urban and rural areas, respectively), then we can use this information to correct the sample's results and hence improve the quality of the study. The idea behind *stratification*, which we will look at in Chapter 11, is that knowledge of the distribution of a background characteristic can be used to improve the sampling method.

Snowball sampling is where the selected sampling unit identifies the next sampling unit to be examined. This method can be used in cases where it is difficult to find people with certain characteristics. For instance, if we wanted to study the amount of illegal gambling among poker players, we could let the first poker player studied identify the next element in the sample, because these players typically know each other from the "community".

9.5   Measurement of characteristics

Once we have selected an element, we have to measure its characteristics. Depending on the problem being studied, there are various methods of doing this. We will consider methods of measurement based on both observation and self-reporting.

Measurement by observation is when the researcher observes the relevant characteristics. This is often the case both in anthropological studies and in clinical studies.

When we observe a person's behaviour, it is important not to influence it – for example, a school class may behave better (or worse) if there is a researcher sitting at the back of the classroom. If we use instruments to take measurements, there is also a risk, of course, that the instruments are insufficiently precise.

A physical examination of an element's characteristics may also sometimes imply that the element examined is destroyed – for example, a study that involves lighting a firework to evaluate whether it works.

In *self-reporting*, the element itself measures its own characteristics. It is therefore important to consider whether the element is willing and able to provide a correct measurement. One advantage of self-reporting is that it enables us also to study characteristics not present at the time of the examination. For example, in addition to finding out about how much of a product a person has consumed, we can also ask how much of it they intend to consume in the future. The first measurement reveals what has been done, and is called a *revealed preference*. The second reveals what someone wants to do, and is called a *stated preference*.

A widely used method of self-reporting is answering questions, be it orally or in writing. In this context, we have to consider how we will present the questions. For example, we can ask questions during a personal interview, send a questionnaire by mail or e-mail, make a phone call, set up an online questionnaire or ask the person to keep a diary. Each of these different methods has advantages and disadvantages that affect the probability of getting answers, the probability of getting correct answers and the costs of the study.

The question formulation also has a major influence on the probability that a person will answer and that the answer will be correct. Among other things, we need to consider whether the questions are understandable, value-laden, easy to answer, sensitive or misleading. The number and order of the questions, as well as the response options, can also be important in obtaining precise measurements. Finally, it is often a good idea to formulate some open questions that the subject is able to expand upon. This can be particularly useful in a pilot study.

In order to have confidence in the answers, we should ideally be able to repeat the sample selection and measurement and get similar answers. This is called the *reliability* of the study. In other words, other people should be able to repeat the experiment and get more or less the same result. We must also make sure that what we are measuring is what we set out to measure. This is called the *validity* of the study.

We will look at the consequences of measurement errors in greater depth in Section 9.11.

9.6   Random sampling

When probability sampling is used to select a sample, we can model the uncertainty associated with the sample by representing it with random variables. Unless otherwise mentioned, we assume in the rest of this book that probability sampling has been used. In this section we will formalise the representation of a sample and its distribution.

The statistical representation of a sample utilises random variables. We can write the value of element i (or to be precise: the value of the studied characteristic of element i) as a random variable with subscript i, e.g. X_i. A sample consisting of n elements can therefore be represented by n random variables, $X_1,...,X_n$.

> **A sample** with n elements is represented by n random variables, $X_1,...,X_n$. It is written as $(X_1,...,X_n)$.

Before the sample is selected, we do not know what values the random variables in the sample will assume. Once it has been selected, we have n tangible values. This is called the *realised sample:*

> **A realised sample** with n elements is n values, $x_1,...,x_n$, of the random variables, $X_1,...,X_n$. This is written as $(X_1,...,X_n) = (x_1,...,x_n)$, or simply $(x_1,...,x_n)$.

Each random variable, X_i, has a distribution given by $f_{X_i}(x_i)$. The sample also has an overall distribution, which is the joint distribution of $X_1,...,X_n$. For example, if the sample size n is equal to 2, then X_1 has the distribution $f_{X_1}(x_1)$, X_2 has the distribution $f_{X_2}(x_2)$, and the sample (X_1,X_2) has the distribution $f(x_1,x_2)$.

> The **sample distribution** is the joint distribution of the n random variables, $(X_1,...,X_n)$, given by $f(x_1,...,x_n)$, which is a probability function if the random variables are discrete, and a probability density function if (at least one of) the random variables is continuous.

Example 9.3: A Bernoulli population – part 1

Consider a population in which all of the elements have a characteristic that has either the value 0 or the value 1. For example, this could be the coding for the intention to vote "no" ($= 0$) or "yes" ($= 1$) in a referendum on a new constitution. Let the proportion of 1s in the population be p. Suppose you select $n = 2$ elements independently of each other (i.e. with replacement). This leads to $X_1 \sim \text{Ber}(p)$ and $X_2 \sim \text{Ber}(p)$ and therefore:

$$f_{X_1}(x_1) = \begin{cases} p & \text{if } x_1 = 1 \\ 1-p & \text{if } x_1 = 0 \end{cases} \quad \text{and} \quad f_{X_2}(x_2) = \begin{cases} p & \text{if } x_2 = 1 \\ 1-p & \text{if } x_2 = 0 \end{cases}$$

These are the marginal distributions for the two random variables, X_1 and X_2. The sample's overall distribution can be worked out on the basis of the two marginal distributions, as it is assumed that X_1 and X_2 are independent:

$$f(x_1, x_2) = f_{X_1}(x_1) \cdot f_{X_2}(x_2) = \begin{cases} p \cdot p & \text{if } x_1 = 1 \text{ and } x_2 = 1 \\ p \cdot (1-p) & \text{if } x_1 = 1 \text{ and } x_2 = 0 \\ (1-p) \cdot p & \text{if } x_1 = 0 \text{ and } x_2 = 1 \\ (1-p) \cdot (1-p) & \text{if } x_1 = 0 \text{ and } x_2 = 0 \end{cases}$$

The first equal sign follows from the assumption of independence. The probability that the first selected element will answer no, and the second yes, is equal to $(1-p) \cdot p$, because this is the probability of the realised sample $(x_1, x_2) = (0, 1)$.

9.7   A model for the sample

In practice, a sample is selected from a real population on the basis of a characteristic for each element other than the one in which we are actually interested. This characteristic is specified in the sampling frame. We denote it with z and refer to it as the *selection characteristic*. It could, for example, be a civil registration number. In this section, we present a model for the relationship between the selection mechanism (determined by the sampling method), the distribution of the chosen selection characteristic in the sample and the distribution of the characteristic that we are interested in studying. This model can subsequently be used to define a representative sample and to illustrate the consequences of different sources of errors in the sampling process.

Let Z_i be a random variable that indicates the value of the selection characteristic for the ith element in the sample. $f_{Z_i}(z)$ then expresses the selection mechanism. For example, if the sampling method selects a person on the basis of their civil registration number, and each number has an equal chance of selection, then $f_{Z_i}(z) = 1/N$, in which N is the number of people in the population and z is a civil registration number in the population. If instead we select only women for the sample, then $f_{Z_i}(z) = 0$ for all male civil registration numbers and $f_{Z_i}(z) = 1/N_{women}$ for all female civil registration numbers in the population, where N_{women} is the number of women in the population.

Different elements of the population can sometimes have the same value of a selection characteristic. This depends on how precisely the sampling frame is specified. Later in the chapter, we illustrate the type of problems this may give rise to. It is therefore important to know whether an element has a unique value of the selection characteristic. If this is the case, we say that the element is *identified*:

An element in a real population is **identified** if no other elements in the population have the same value of the selection characteristic. If this is not the case, the element is said to be non-identified.

If we use the individuals' civil registration numbers as the selection characteristic, then all elements are identified, as everybody has a unique number. However, this is not the case if we use phone numbers, because multiple people can share the same phone number and some people do not have a phone.

The relationship between the selection characteristic used and the characteristic in which we are interested can be expressed by the conditional distribution, $f_{X_i|Z_i}(x|z)$. The conditional distribution gives us the probability of selecting a specific value, x, of our characteristic of interest, given a certain value, z, of the selection characteristic.

If an element in a real population is identified with the value $z^{\#}$ of the selection characteristic, then $f_{X_i|Z_i}(x^{\#}|z^{\#}) = 1$, where $x^{\#}$ is the same element's value of the characteristic of interest. If the element is non-identified, then $f_{X_i|Z_i}(x^{\#}|z^{\#}) \leq 1$, where the equality sign only applies if all elements with the value $z^{\#}$ of the selection characteristic have the same value, $x^{\#}$, of the characteristic of interest.

We are now ready to express the distribution of the ith element in the sample, $f_{X_i}(x)$, as a function of $f_{X_i|Z_i}(x|z)$ and $f_{Z_i}(z)$. As in Chapter 4, we can find a marginal probability by summing over the joint probabilities:

$$f_{X_i}(x) = \sum_z f_{X_i,Z_i}(x,z)$$

From the definition of a conditional probability, we can also express the joint probability as:

$$f_{X_i,Z_i}(x,z) = f_{X_i|Z_i}(x|z) \cdot f_{Z_i}(z)$$

By inserting this formula into the first formula, we get an expression for the distribution of the ith element in the sample, which depends on the selection mechanism, $f_{Z_i}(z)$, and the conditional distribution of X_i given the value of the selection characteristic:

$$f_{X_i}(x) = \sum_z f_{X_i|Z_i}(x|z) \cdot f_{Z_i}(z)$$

Example 9.4 illustrates this relationship.

Example 9.4: Sampling from a small population

Imagine that we draw (with replacement) from a population of only four elements, in which each element is identified by the values 1, 2, 3 and 4 of the selection characteristic, z. These values are listed in Table 9.1, along with the values of the characteristic in which we are interested, x.

Table 9.1:
Selection characteristic and characteristic of interest

Selection characteristic, z	Characteristic of interest, x
1	5
2	7
3	7
4	8

All of the elements are identified via the selection characteristic used, which means, for example, that $f_{X_i|Z_i}(7|2) = 1$, as only one element has the value $z = 2$, and for this element $x = 7$. The element with $z = 3$ also has the value $x = 7$, but this is irrelevant when the conditional probability requires that $z = 2$.

Assume that the sampling method assigns all four elements an equal chance of selection. As a consequence:

$$f_{X_i}(x) = \begin{cases} \frac{1}{4} & \text{if} \quad x = 5 \\ \frac{2}{4} & \text{if} \quad x = 7 \\ \frac{1}{4} & \text{if} \quad x = 8 \end{cases}$$

where, for example, the second probability is calculated using the formula above in the following manner:

$$f_{X_i}(7) = f_{X_i|Z_i}(7|1) \cdot f_{Z_i}(1) + f_{X_i|Z_i}(7|2) \cdot f_{Z_i}(2) + f_{X_i|Z_i}(7|3) \cdot f_{Z_i}(3)$$
$$+ f_{X_i|Z_i}(7|4) \cdot f_{Z_i}(4) = 0 \cdot \frac{1}{4} + 1 \cdot \frac{1}{4} + 1 \cdot \frac{1}{4} + 0 \cdot \frac{1}{4} = \frac{2}{4}$$

Another sampling method can result in a different distribution of X_i. Assume that the element with $z = 1$ has no chance of selection, while the other elements all have the same chance ($= 1/3$) of selection. In this case, we get:

$$f_{X_i}(x) = \begin{cases} 0 & if \quad x = 5 \\ \frac{2}{3} & if \quad x = 7 \\ \frac{1}{3} & if \quad x = 8 \end{cases}.$$

9.8   Representative sample

In most cases, the purpose of sampling is to obtain a "true picture" of the population without having to study the whole population. This section specifies what we mean by a true picture.

In a real population, the relative frequency function tells us how often a characteristic, x, occurs among the elements. A true picture of a real population should therefore reflect the relative frequency function. As discussed in Chapter 4, we can let the relative frequency function be represented by a random variable, X, with the probability function, $f_X(x)$. Similarly, we can let the relative frequency function for our selection characteristic be represented by a random variable, Z, with the probability function, $f_Z(z)$.

We will now define what we mean by a representative sample.[12] The sample is *representative* for X if the probability (density) function, $f_{X_i}(x)$, for each element in the sample is the same as the probability (density) function, $f_X(x)$, for X:

> **A sample is representative** for X, if $f_{X_i}(x) = f_X(x)$ for $i = 1,...,n$, where $f_X(x)$ is equal to the relative frequency function, if the sample is selected from a real population. If $f_{X_i}(x) \neq f_X(x)$ for at least one i, the sample is non-representative.

In the case of selection from a super-population, we can interpret f_X as representing the existing (or actual) selection mechanism about which we want to learn.

---

12   Note that there is no consensus in the literature on a precise definition of a representative sample, and the concept is often used without a precise definition. The definition below is our attempt to flesh out the meaning of the concept.

The sample from the Bernoulli population in Example 9.3 was drawn with replacement and is therefore representative, as the proportion of 1s in the population is p and the proportion of 0s is $(1-p)$, which correspond to the probabilities in both $f_{X_1}(x_1)$ and $f_{X_2}(x_2)$.

We can get a better understanding of what constitutes a representative sample by considering the model for the sample from Section 9.7:

$$f_{X_i}(x) = \sum_z f_{X_i|Z_i}(x|z) \cdot f_{Z_i}(z)$$

The sample is automatically representative, i.e $f_{X_i}(x) = f_X(x)$ if:

(i) $f_{Z_i}(z)$ is equal to $f_Z(z)$, i.e. the selection probabilities of the different values of the applied selection characteristic are equal to these values' proportions in the population; and

(ii) $f_{X_i|Z_i}(x|z)$ is equal to $f_{X|Z}(x|z)$ for all values of x and z, i.e. for a given value of the selection characteristic, the probability of selecting a given value of X_i is equal to the proportion of this value among the elements in the population that have the given value of the selection characteristic.

In the following, we will focus on how the selection mechanism, $f_{Z_i}(z)$, can result in non-representative samples. We therefore assume throughout that point (ii) above is satisfied. The distribution of X_i is therefore given by:

$$f_{X_i}(x) = \sum_z f_{X|Z}(x|z) \cdot f_{Z_i}(z)$$

Consider a population in which the persons (the elements) have two characteristics: x, which is the number of shopping trips made per week, and z, which is equal to 1 if the person is shopping on a Saturday and 0 otherwise. Assume that the following ten elements (x, z), are included in the population: (8,1), (3,1), (4,0), (8,1), (4,1), (5,0), (8,0), (3, 1), (8,1), (5,0).

The population shares are represented by the joint and marginal probabilities for the corresponding stochastic variables, X and Z, in Table 9.2.

Table 9.2:

Joint and marginal probabilities

	$Z = 0$	$Z = 1$	$f_X(x)$
$X = 3$	0.0	0.2	0.2
$X = 4$	0.1	0.1	0.2
$X = 5$	0.2	0.0	0.2
$X = 8$	0.1	0.3	0.4
$f_Z(z)$	0.4	0.6	1.0

In Table 9.3, we have listed the probabilities for X given Z:

Table 9.3:

Conditional probabilities for X

X	$f_{X|Z}(x|0)$	$f_{X|Z}(x|1)$
3	0.00	0.33
4	0.25	0.17
5	0.50	0.00
8	0.25	0.50
	1.00	1.00

Now, suppose that we select the element i for the sample via a selection mechanism represented by the following probability distribution for Z_i:

$$f_{Z_i}(z) = \begin{cases} 0.1 & \text{if } z = 0 \\ 0.9 & \text{if } z = 1 \end{cases}$$

In other words, there is a 90% probability that the person selected will be one of those who shops on a Saturday. This distribution is different from the distribution of our selection characteristic in the population, which (based on Table 9.2) is given by:

$$f_Z(z) = \begin{cases} 0.4 & \text{if } z = 0 \\ 0.6 & \text{if } z = 1 \end{cases}$$

The selection mechanism therefore ascribes a higher probability of selection to people who shop on Saturday ($z = 1$) than their proportion of the population. The consequence of this for the distribution of X_i in the sample is:

$$f_{X_i}(x) = f_{X_i|Z_i}(x \mid 0) \cdot f_{Z_i}(0) + f_{X_i|Z_i}(x \mid 1) \cdot f_{Z_i}(1) = \begin{cases} 0.300 & \text{if } x = 3 \\ 0.175 & \text{if } x = 4 \\ 0.050 & \text{if } x = 5 \\ 0.475 & \text{if } x = 8 \end{cases}$$

Note that $f_{X_i}(x) \neq f_X(x)$. For example, the probability of $x = 8$ is higher in this non-representative sample than the proportion of people in the population with the characteristic $x = 8$.

It is possible to obtain a representative sample even if the sampling probabilities of the different values of the selection characteristic, $f_{Z_i}(z)$, are different from the distribution of the selection characteristic in the population, $f_Z(z)$. The most important example is a situation where X and Z are independent. This implies that $f_{X|Z}(x|z) = f_X(x)$ for all values of z. Insertion into the above formula gives us:

$$f_{X_i}(x) = \sum_z f_X(x) \cdot f_{Z_i}(z) = f_X(x) \sum_z f_{Z_i}(z) = f_X(x)$$

It can be seen that $f_{X_i}(x) = f_X(x)$, regardless of which selection mechanism, $f_{Z_i}(z)$, we use. In other words, when the selection characteristic is independent of the characteristic of interest, it does not matter that we use selection probabilities that are different from the population shares.

For example, if the shopping pattern is the same for people from two different parts of the country, and hence is statistically independent of where they live, then we can select the sample from either of the two regions.

9.9   Consequences of a non-representative sample

The consequences of a non-representative sample depend on what we are studying. Generally speaking, non-representative samples provide misleading results, for example in calculations of descriptive measures.

To illustrate this, we can consider the mean value of a characteristic in a real population. This population's mean value is the same as the mean value of the random variable, X, i.e. $E_X(X)$:

$$E_X(X) = \sum_x x \cdot f_X(x)$$

whereas the mean value of the ith selected element in the sample is given by:

$$E_{X_i}(X_i) = \sum_x x \cdot f_{X_i}(x)$$

Whether $E_{X_i}(X_i)$ differs from $E_X(X)$ depends on the selection mechanism. In general, they will be different if the sample is non-representative. Example 9.7 illustrates this.

Example 9.7: Shopping trips – part 2

In the shopping trips example, we calculated both $f_{X_i}(x)$ and $f_X(x)$. This results in the following mean values:

$$E_X(X) = 5.60$$

$$E_{X_i}(X_i) = 5.65$$

If we know the distribution of the selection characteristic in the population, then it is possible to correct a non-representative sample in order to provide accurate results. When this option is available, it can actually be advantageous to select a non-representative sample. A prominent example of this is stratified sample selection, which we will look at in Chapter 11. However, this requires that we are able to model the way in which the sample is non-representative.

9.10 Sources of error in the sampling process

In practice, we obtain a representative sample if we select the elements according to the distribution of the selection characteristic, z, in the population. However, it is often not easy to select according to this distribution.

Moreover, it is often mistakenly believed that the selection is done according to the distribution of z in the population, even though this is not the case. This section looks at various reasons why the selection mechanism represented by the probability function, $f_{Z_i}(z)$, may differ from the probability function, $f_Z(z)$, and illustrates the importance of the sample's representativeness with the help of the model from Section 9.7.

9.10.1 Errors in the sampling frame

The sampling frame specifies the sampling units that can be selected, where the sampling units can each consist of multiple elements from the population. However, sometimes the sampling frame is not very precise. A possible error can be that parts of the population are omitted. Example 9.8 shows how this can lead to a non-representative sample.

Example 9.8: Hybrid cars

Consider an online survey of people's attitudes to hybrid cars. Let $z = 1$ for a person who has access to (and can use) a computer and let $z = 0$ for a person who does not have access to (or cannot use) a computer. This sampling method implies that:

$$f_{Z_i}(z) = \begin{cases} 0 & if\ z = 0 \\ 1 & if\ z = 1 \end{cases}$$

(i.e. only those with a computer will have a chance of being selected for the sample). Let X be a binary random variable that is equal to 1 if the person selected is positive about hybrid cars and 0 if he or she is neutral or negative. Assume that the population is such that $f_{X|Z}(1 \mid 1) = 0.6$. and $f_{X|Z}(1 \mid 0) = 0.3$. The distribution of X_i using an online survey can then be calculated using the formula from section 9.7:

$$f_{X_i}(x) = f_{X|Z}(x \mid 0) \cdot 0 + f_{X|Z}(x \mid 1) \cdot 1 = f_{X|Z}(x \mid 1) = \begin{cases} 0.6 & if\ x = 1 \\ 0.4 & if\ x = 0 \end{cases}$$

If $f_Z(1) = 0.8$,(i.e. 80% of the population has access to a computer), then the distribution of X (i.e. the shares of the population) is:

$$f_X(x) = f_{X|Z}(x \mid 0) \cdot f_Z(0) + f_{X|Z}(x \mid 1) \cdot f_Z(1) = \begin{cases} 0.54 & if\ x = 1 \\ 0.46 & if\ x = 0 \end{cases}$$

The sample is therefore non-representative, as it will tend to overvalue the proportion of the population that is positive.

In general, errors in the sampling frame lead to $f_{Z_i}(z) = 0$ for elements in the population with certain values, z, of the selection characteristic. In Example 9.8, the sample is therefore only representative if $f_X(x) = f_{X|Z}(x|1)$. Since Z is a binary variable, this implies that X and Z must be statistically independent.

9.10.2 Non-respondents

Not everybody can, or wants to, take part in a study, and some people will not want to answer certain questions. These people are called *non-respondents*. If there is a relationship between the answer to a question and whether the interviewee is a non-respondent, this will generally lead to a non-representative sample.

There are several reasons for the existence of non-respondents. One may be that we have asked a sensitive question. For example, in a study of tax avoidance, there could be a relationship between willingness to respond and avoiding tax. Another reason may be that a person does not want to (or cannot) devote time to answering questions.

The consequences of non-respondents can be examined in the same manner as errors in the sampling frame. Let Z be a binary variable equal to 1 if the person will answer and 0 if the person is a non-respondent. The selection mechanism can then be represented by:

$$f_{Z_i}(z) = \begin{cases} 0 & \text{if } z = 0 \\ 1 & \text{if } z = 1 \end{cases}$$

As in Example 9.8, this gives us:

$$f_{X_i}(x) = f_{X|Z}(x \mid 1)$$

The distribution of X_i is therefore equal to the distribution of X for those who are willing to answer. The distribution function, $f_{X_i}(x)$, is therefore only equal to the distribution function, $f_X(x)$, if there is no relationship between X and whether or not the person concerned will answer, i.e. Z.

The elements in the population above (and in Example 9.8) are not identified, as Z only assumes two values. We have opted to use this formulation because it makes it easier to see the effect of non-respondents. If the elements are identified via, for example, their civil registration number, then we reach the same conclusion by identifying the elements that are non-respondents and ascribing them the probability 0 in the selection mechanism.

Both non-respondents and errors in the sampling frame mean that some elements have zero probability of selection. Such errors are called *errors of non-observation*.

9.10.3　Self-selection in the sample

Self-selection occurs if someone's behaviour affects the probability that the person will be selected for the sample. For example, if we study attitudes to green issues by interviewing customers at an organic green-grocer, then it is highly likely that we will obtain a sample that reflects a more positive attitude to ecology than that of the population as a whole. This is because there is likely to be a connection between the customers of an organic greengrocer and their attitudes towards ecology.

Non-respondents are an example of extreme self-selection, as the probability of selection for non-respondents is zero. In a milder form of self-selection, the selection probabilities differ from the distribution of the selection characteristic in the population. In other words, the selection mechanism leads to $f_{Z_i}(z) > f_Z(z)$ for elements whose behaviour leads to a higher probability of inclusion in the sample than is justified by their proportion of the population – they "self-select" for the sample.

Example 9.6 contained an example of self-selection. Here is another.

Example 9.9: Evaluation of teachers

Students of two different subjects are to evaluate two teachers, Professor Smith and Associate Professor Jones. They can grade them good (= 1), medium (= 2) or poor (= 3). The evaluations are conducted in connection with the lectures. As a result, only students who attend the lectures are involved in the evaluations. Let X represent a student's mark for Professor Smith and Y for Associate Professor Jones. A student's decision to come to a lecture is represented by Z, which is equal to 0 if absent and equal to 1 for present. The distribution of marks to Professor Smith in the whole population of students (both those attending and those not attending the lectures) is given in Table 9.4, while the corresponding distribution for Associate Professor Jones is found in Table 9.5.

Table 9.4: Distribution of marks to Professor Smith

$f(x,z)$	$Z = 0$	$Z = 1$	$f_X(x)$
$X = 1$	0.35	0.25	0.60
$X = 2$	0.07	0.30	0.37
$X = 3$	0.03	0.00	0.03
$f_Z(z)$	0.45	0.55	

Table 9.5:
Distribution of marks to Associate Professor Jones

$f(y,z)$	$Z=0$	$Z=1$	$f_Y(y)$
$Y=1$	0.01	0.08	0.09
$Y=2$	0.03	0.02	0.05
$Y=3$	0.86	0.00	0.86
$f_Z(z)$	0.90	0.10	

The evaluation results for Professor Smith and Associate Professor Jones are selected from the distribution of attendees, i.e.:

$$f_{X|Z}(x \mid 1) = \frac{f(x,1)}{f_Z(1)} = \begin{cases} 0.45 & \text{if } x = 1 \\ 0.55 & \text{if } x = 2 \\ 0 & \text{if } x = 3 \end{cases}$$

$$f_{Y|Z}(y \mid 1) = \frac{f(y,1)}{f_Y(1)} = \begin{cases} 0.80 & \text{if } y = 1 \\ 0.20 & \text{if } y = 2 \\ 0 & \text{if } y = 3 \end{cases}$$

Associate Professor Jones gets a significantly better evaluation than Professor Smith, with 80% of the students saying Jones is good, whereas this figure would drop to 9% if the entire population were involved in the evaluation of him. Associate Professor Jones is therefore more highly rated in the evaluations than Professor Smith, although Smith's score would significantly improve if all of the students were forced to participate in the evaluation. Students who think Jones is poor have a tendency to select themselves out of the sample – perhaps precisely because Jones' lectures are dreary!

9.11   Observation errors

In this section, we consider the problems that arise if the observed value of a characteristic is not the same as the actual value, for example, if we are using scales that do not measure weights accurately. We divide such *observation errors* into *response errors* and *measurement errors*. Then we show how to develop a model that can be used to assess the consequences of errors of observation.

9.11.1 Types of observation error

Response errors arise if a respondent misunderstands a question or if the answer is reported incorrectly in the data. This could be a question that the respondent misunderstands and therefore answers in a way that is incompatible with what we are trying to measure. This type of response error is known as a *question error*. The interviewer can also influence the respondent to answer incorrectly, which is called an *interview error*. Finally, an answer can be recorded or coded incorrectly. These errors are called *recording- and coding errors*.

Measurement errors are usually attributed to errors that occur when it is physically difficult to obtain an accurate measurement of a characteristic. Most, if not all, measuring instruments are imprecise. Some even indicate the degree of uncertainty involved. Alternatively, we can use repeated measurements with different instruments to work out the extent of the uncertainty ourselves.

Overall, we model the consequences of observation errors by assuming that the observed value of a characteristic is a function of the correct value and an observation error. In this context, we call the correct value the *latent value* and denote it with the superscript *. For example, we may have selected a person who smokes six cigarettes a day, $(x^* = 6)$, but by mistake we write on the form that the number is 16 $(x = 16)$. In this example, there is an observation error of 10 $(= x - x^*)$. Generally, the observation error, ε, is given by:

$$observation\ error = \varepsilon = X - X^*$$

where X^* is the latent variable and X is the observable variable. Below, we will consider the consequences of observation errors.

9.11.2 Consequences of observation errors

Suppose we want to measure the random variable X^*, which is the latent variable. Unfortunately, observation errors occur. Let the random variable, ε, be the observation error. The observable random variable, X, can then be written as:

$$X = X^* + \varepsilon$$

In other words, we would like to observe X^*, but due to the observation error we instead observe X.

The consequences of observation error depend on what it is we want to study and the type of observation error. We assume first that the observation error has the mean value zero, $E(\varepsilon) = 0$. If we are interested in the mean value of X^* in the population, then the observation error does not prevent us from doing this. The reason for this is that:

$$E(X) = E(X^*) + E(\varepsilon) = E(X^*)$$

If the observation error systematically pulls in a certain direction, however, as in the case of an improperly calibrated scale, so that $E(\varepsilon) = \mu_\varepsilon \neq 0$, then $E(X) \neq E(X^*)$.

The variance of the observable variable is affected differently by the observation error. If the error is statistically independent of the latent variable, X^*, which we are interested in measuring, we get:

$$V(X) = V(X^*) + V(\varepsilon)$$

The result is that we overestimate the variance of X^* when using the variance of X, even when the observation error is independent of X^*.

The correlation coefficient is a useful summary measure to describe the relationship between two random variables. If we are to find the correlation between X^* and a random variable Y (without observation errors), then it is given by:

$$\rho(X^*, Y) = \frac{Cov(X^*, Y)}{\sqrt{V(X^*) \cdot V(Y)}}$$

This is the correlation of interest. The observable correlation is instead given by:

$$\rho(X, Y) = \frac{Cov(X, Y)}{\sqrt{V(X) \cdot V(Y)}}$$

Above, we found an expression for $V(X)$ when the observation error was independent of X^*. If we further assume that the observation error is also independent of Y, then the covariance between X and Y is given by:

$$Cov(X, Y) = Cov(X^* + \varepsilon, Y) = Cov(X^*, Y) + Cov(\varepsilon, Y) = Cov(X^*, Y)$$

In this case, the covariance is unaffected by the observation error. If we insert this into the expression for the correlation coefficient, we get:

$$\rho(X,Y) = \frac{Cov(X^*,Y)}{\sqrt{(V(X^*) + V(\varepsilon)) \cdot V(Y)}}$$

In other words, the correlation is affected by the observation error. The observable correlation, $\rho(X,Y)$, is only equal to the correlation of interest, $\rho(X^*,Y)$, if there are no observation errors, i.e. if $V(\varepsilon) = 0$.

If we assume that the variance of the observation error is a proportion, s, of the variance of X^*:

$$V(\varepsilon) = s \cdot V(X^*)$$

Then it applies that:

$$\rho(X,Y) = \frac{Cov(X^*,Y)}{\sqrt{(1+s) \cdot V(X^*) \cdot V(Y)}} = \rho(X^*,Y) \cdot \frac{1}{\sqrt{(1+s)}}$$

Note that the observable correlation, $\rho(X,Y)$, is less than the correlation of interest, $\rho(X^*,Y)$. In other words, the observation error introduces some "noise" and this makes the relationship between X^* and Y seem weaker. For example, if the observation error constitutes 20% of the variation in X^* (which is not unrealistic in many contexts), then the observable correlation is around 8% lower than the correlation of interest.

We can set up a variety of models for observation errors. Above, we assumed that the expected value of the observation error was zero, and that it was independent of the latent variable. In each case, we must determine which assumptions best describe the type of measurement error that we suspect may be present. For example, we can change the model above by assuming that the observation error is correlated with the latent variable, such that a high value of the latent variable will typically result in a high value of the observation error. If we use such a model, the covariance will also be affected by the observation error.

Observable quantiles can also be affected by observation errors. However, the median is not affected if we assume that the median is zero in the distribution of the observation error.

The consequences of errors of observation underline the importance of precise measurement. This can be achieved by being very careful in the formulation of questions. For example, there are typically far fewer observation errors when people are asked about their annual income rather than their hourly wage and hours worked.

9.12 Exercises

1. Review questions
   a) Outline, briefly, the four main points in a sampling process.
   b) What is a pilot study?
   c) Explain what we mean by the target population, and why it may differ from the population being studied.
   d) Explain what we understand by sampling units and sampling frames.
   e) Explain the difference between probability and non-probability sampling, and what is meant by convenience sampling, purposive sampling, quota sampling and snowball sampling.
   f) Explain, briefly, the different methods of measuring characteristics, and what is meant by the terms "reliability" and "validity".
   g) Explain what makes a sample random, and what we mean by the sample distribution.
   h) Define a selection characteristic, and explain what it means when an element in a real population is identified.
   i) What is a representative sample?
   j) Explain how a non-representative sample can be caused by errors in the sampling frame, by non-respondents and by self-selection.
   k) Briefly explain the different types of observation error and their consequences.

2. You are about to conduct a study of young students' working habits, i.e. how many hours a week they spend on lectures and preparation.
   a) Explain how you will select your population and the characteristics on which you wish to focus.
   b) Explain how you will select your sampling units, and outline how a sampling frame can be set up.
   c) Discuss the advantages and disadvantages of different ways of selecting the sample from the sampling frame.
   d) Discuss how the characteristics you selected in a) can best and most easily be measured.
   e) Discuss the factors that can give rise to a non-representative sample, and how to avoid this.

3. The Association of Ambitious Medical Students is conducting a study of young people's drinking habits. With a little help, they have established their sampling frame, and they have actually obtained a representative sample – or so they think. However, they run into a problem in that not all of the selected elements want to answer

the question posed. In such cases, they select a new person until they find one who will answer. They think this is problem-free, but would like you to check it for them. Let X specify the consumption of alcohol and let Z be the willingness of a randomly selected individual from the population to respond. The table below summarises the joint probabilities of X and Z, which are given by the population shares. $X = 1$ when consumption is moderate (fewer than 6 units per day) and $X = 2$ when consumption is high (6 or more units per day).

$f_{X,Z}(x,z)$	$Z = 0$ (unwilling to answer)	$Z = 1$ (willing to answer)
$X = 1$ (moderate consumption)	0.1	0.6
$X = 2$ (high consumption)	0.2	0.1

a) Calculate the marginal distribution of X (in the population).
b) Calculate the distribution of X_i for the ith element of the sample.
c) Is the sample representative?

10 Estimating the mean value using a simple random sample

Information derived from a sample can be used to construct estimates of the unknown distribution. It is therefore important to have efficient methods for extracting the relevant information from the sample. There are many different aspects of the unknown distribution in which we can be interested. Often it is a descriptive measure, such as the mean consumption level of a product, that we wish to know. The purpose of this chapter is to show how to use the sample to construct an estimate of the mean value of a distribution, and how to evaluate the quality of this estimate.

As an example, our screw manufacturer from Chapter 8 would like to know the mean length of the screws produced. The length of a screw can be represented by a random variable, X. However, the probability distribution of this, $f(x)$, is unknown. By taking a sample of screws already produced, the company hopes to obtain an estimate of the mean value of the distribution, μ.

In this chapter, we look at estimates of the mean value in the case where we have a so-called *simple random sample*. In this case, the calculations involved are relatively simple, but is it also a relevant case to study because other forms of sampling often partially build on simple random sampling. In Section 10.1, we look at the properties of a simple random sample. In Section 10.2, we show how a simple random sample can be used to construct an estimate of the mean value in a distribution. We evaluate the quality of how the estimate is constructed in sections 10.3 and 10.4.

10.1   Simple random sampling

A sample is a simple random sample if all of the observations in the sample are statistically independent and if they all follow the distribution, that we are interested in, $f_X(x)$. This is summarised in the box below.

> The sample $(X_1,...,X_n)$ is a **simple random sample** if:
>
> 1. $X_1,...,X_n$ are statistically independent
>
> 2. $X_1,...,X_n$ have the same (marginal) distribution $f_X(x)$ (the distribution of interest).

Condition 2) above implies that a simple random sample is representative for X (see the definition of a representative sample in Chapter 9).

The distribution of a simple random sample, $f(x_1,...,x_n)$, can be easily derived. Since $X_1,...,X_n$ are independent according to 1), the joint distribution is equal to the product of all of the marginal distributions:

$$f(x_1,...,x_n) = f_{X_1}(x_1) \cdot f_{X_2}(x_2) \cdot ... \cdot f_{X_n}(x_n)$$

In addition, 2) means that all of the marginal distributions are identical:

$$f_{X_i}(x_i) = f_X(x_i), \quad i = 1,...,n$$

The result is summarised in the box below.

> A simple random sample has the distribution:
>
> $$f(x_1,...,x_n) = f_X(x_1) \cdot f_X(x_2) \cdot ... \cdot f_X(x_n)$$

Example 10.1: A TV programme – part 1

Suppose that we want to study attitudes to a particular television programme. We conduct a market survey in which we ask a number of people whether they think that the programme is "good" or "bad". In statistical language, we are dealing with a real population of "good" and "bad" elements, comprising all those who saw the programme. A population like this, with two possible values, is a Bernoulli population (see Chapter 6). The purpose of the market survey is to estimate the proportion, p, who think it is a good programme.

In Chapter 4, we showed how a real population can be represented by a random variable with a probability function that is equal to the relative frequency function for the population. If we select an element at random in the population, and let X be a random variable that indicates the individual's opinion of the programme:

$$X = \begin{cases} 1 & \text{if good} \\ 0 & \text{if bad} \end{cases}$$

then X is Bernoulli-distributed with parameter p: $X \sim \text{Ber}(p)$. The mean value of X is then $E(X) = \mu = p$. The purpose of the market survey – to estimate p – is therefore the same as working out an estimate of the mean value of X.

To keep the calculations manageable, let us assume that we only interview three people about their opinion of the programme. The sample is then three random variables, (X_1, X_2, X_3). The first random variable, X_1, is the answer from the first respondent, and can be either 1 (= good) or 0 (= bad). The same options are available to X_2 and X_3. The realised sample will therefore be given by one of the following eight possibilities: (0,0,0), (0,0,1), (0,1,0), (0,1,1), (1,0,0), (1,0,1), (1,1,0), (1,1,1).

Suppose that the sample is a simple random sample. Using the formula in the box above, we can now calculate the probabilities for the various realised samples. The probability that the first observation will be "good" ($X_1 = 1$) is p. The same applies to the second and third observations. The probabilities for the various samples can therefore be summarised as in Table 10.1.

Table 10.1:
Possible samples and their probabilities

Possible samples	Probability	Probability if: $p = 0.7$
(1,1,1)	$p \cdot p \cdot p$	0.343
(1,1,0)	$p \cdot p \cdot (1 - p)$	0.147
(1,0,1)	$p \cdot (1 - p) \cdot p$	0.147
(1,0,0)	$p \cdot (1 - p) \cdot (1 - p)$	0.063
(0,1,1)	$(1 - p) \cdot p \cdot p$	0.147
(0,1,0)	$(1 - p) \cdot p \cdot (1 - p)$	0.063
(0,0,1)	$(1 - p) \cdot (1 - p) \cdot p$	0.063
(0,0,0)	$(1 - p) \cdot (1 - p) \cdot (1 - p)$	0.027

The various possible samples have different probabilities of becoming the realised sample. The probability for each sample is calculated in the third column of Table 10.1 – here, we imagine that $p = 0.7$ (i.e. 70% of the population thought the programme was good). Note that the sample (1,1,1), where all three respondents say the programme was good, is the most probable. It is significantly less probable that we will obtain a sample in which all three respond that the programme was bad, (0,0,0). In practice, however, we cannot calculate the probabilities in column three, as the proportion p is unknown.

10.2   Constructing an estimator of the mean value

The purpose of this chapter is to construct an estimate of the mean value μ for the distribution $f_X(x)$ in a simple random sample. In a simple random sample, the n observations $X_1,...,X_n$ all have the distribution $f_X(x)$, and therefore they also all have the mean value μ. This suggests that there is information in each observation to estimate μ. In this section, we look at how to combine the observations to get a better estimate of the mean value.

First, let us consider each of the observations separately. Since X_1 has the mean value μ, we can use the realised value of X_1 as an estimate of the mean value μ. However, we can also use the realised value of X_2 as an estimate of μ, as X_2 has the same distribution as X_1. We can therefore use each of the n realised values of $X_1,...,X_n$ as an estimate of μ. Thus, we have n (different) estimates of the mean value. This suggests that we do not use the information particularly well when we use only one of the realized values since they are all estimates of the mean value.

The inspiration to construct an estimate that includes all of the observations can be derived using the *analogy principle of estimation.* This principle says that we should use the formulas that we would use if we knew the unknown distribution, $f_X(x)$, but then replace all the unknown quantities with their corresponding sample quantities. Thus, if we knew $f_X(x)$, we would (for a discrete random variable) calculate the mean as:

$$\mu = E(X) = \sum_{i=1}^{N} x \cdot f_X(x) = x_1 \cdot f_X(x_1) + x_2 \cdot f_X(x_2) + ... + x_N \cdot f_X(x_N)$$

In this formula, $x_1,...,x_N$ are the N possible values that the random variable X can assume, and $f_X(x)$ gives us the probability of each of these values. With a real population, $f_X(x_1)$ is the percentage of the population that has a value equal to x_1. In practice, we do not know $f_X(x)$ and perhaps we do not even know the possible values of X. Instead, the sample gives us n values, $x_1,...,x_n$, of X, each of which represents the proportion $1/n$ of the sample. We will therefore use these n values $x_1,...,x_n$ instead of the N possible values for the random variable X, and use their weight, $1/n$, in the sample instead of the N probabilities,

$f_X(X_1),\ldots,f_X(X_N)$. When the estimator is constructed in this way it is called the *sample average*, $\overline{X}$:

> **The sample average, $\overline{X}$ is defined as:**
> $$\overline{X} = X_1 \cdot \frac{1}{n} + X_2 \cdot \frac{1}{n} + \ldots + X_n \cdot \frac{1}{n}$$
> $$= \frac{1}{n} \cdot (X_1 + X_2 + \ldots + X_n) = \frac{1}{n} \sum_{i=1}^{n} X_i$$

Since the sample consists of n random variables $X_1,\ldots,X_n$, their average, $\overline{X}$, is also a random variable. We call $\overline{X}$ an *estimator* of μ. It is important to stress that $\overline{X}$ is a random variable, whereas μ is a constant. This difference between the estimator, $\overline{X}$, and that for which it is an estimator (i.e. the mean value) is important if we are to understand statistical methods.

When we insert the realised sample in the expression in the box above, we get the realised sample average, $\overline{x}$. We call $\overline{x}$ an *estimate* of μ. In the next section, we will show that the sample average is a good estimate of the mean value, and is preferable to using only one of the observations from the sample as an estimate.

<h3>Example 10.2: A TV programme – part 2</h3>

The estimate of the mean value (the proportion p) from Example 10.1 is shown in Table 10.2 for each of the possible realised samples. Thus, if the realised sample is (1,0,1), our estimate of the mean value is $(1 + 0 + 1) / 3 = 0.67$.

Table 10.2:
Samples and sample averages

Possible samples	Sample average, $\overline{X}$
(1,1,1)	1.00
(1,1,0)	0.67
(1,0,1)	0.67
(1,0,0)	0.33
(0,1,1)	0.67
(0,1,0)	0.33
(0,0,1)	0.33
(0,0,0)	0.00

Table 10.2 shows that three of the possible samples will result in an estimate of 0.67. If the true value of p is 0.7, then none of the possible samples will result in an estimate that is exactly equal to the true value.

We conclude this section with a formal definition of an estimator. An estimator is a function of the sample, i.e. a function of $X_1,...,X_n$. Generally, we define an estimator as follows:

> An **estimator**, Y, for a parameter, θ, is a random variable that is a function, $h(\ )$, of the sample:
>
> $$Y = h(X_1,...,X_n)$$
>
> A realised value of the estimator is called an **estimate** of θ.

When we have a realised sample, we also have a realised value of the estimator. The realised value of the estimator is called an *estimate*. The estimate is our guess of the unknown parameter, which in this chapter is the mean value of the distribution $f_X(x)$.

10.3   Properties of estimators

What makes a good estimator? Since the estimator is a random variable, we know that sometimes it will result in a good estimate and sometimes it will result in a bad (or at least worse) estimate. This depends on the realised sample, as illustrated in Example 10.2. In order to be able to say anything more specific about the estimator's accuracy, we need to examine its properties.

10.3.1   Unbiased estimator

If we were able to repeat an experiment by selecting a sample and calculating an estimate many times, it would be desirable for our estimator to be accurate "on average". In order to investigate whether this is the case, we need to find the estimator's expected value (i.e. its mean value). If its mean value is equal to the parameter we are trying to estimate, the estimator is said to be *unbiased*.

The mean value of the estimator $\bar{X}$ in a simple random sample can be calculated as follows:

$$E(\overline{X}) = E\left(\frac{1}{n} \cdot (X_1 + X_2 + \dots + X_n)\right)$$

$$= \frac{1}{n} \cdot (E(X_1) + E(X_2) + \dots + E(X_n))$$

$$= \frac{1}{n} \cdot (\mu + \mu + \dots + \mu) = \frac{1}{n} \cdot n \cdot \mu = \mu$$

where we exploit the fact that the mean value of a sum is equal to the sum of the mean values, which in this case are all μ. The estimator's mean value therefore corresponds to the value it is supposed to estimate.

> **The sample average**, $\overline{X}$, in a simple random sample is an **unbiased estimator** for the mean value, μ, in the distribution of interest:
>
> $$E\left(\overline{X}\right) = \mu$$

Since the estimator is a random variable, it has a distribution around the mean value. Here, it is important to keep in mind that, although the estimator's mean value is μ, the estimate in a given situation will be based on a realised sample, and may thus be miles away from μ. This is not a failure of methodology, but a natural consequence of the fact that the sample only shows us part of the population.

10.3.2   Efficiency and consistency

If the estimator's distribution is dispersed widely around its mean value, then the estimator is not as precise as if the distribution was concentrated around the mean value. The variance of the estimator $\overline{X}$ in a simple random sample can be calculated as follows:

$$V(\overline{X}) = V\left(\frac{1}{n} \cdot (X_1 + \dots + X_n)\right) = \frac{1}{n^2} \cdot V(X_1 + \dots + X_n)$$

$$= \frac{1}{n^2} \cdot [V(X_1) + \dots + V(X_n)] = \frac{1}{n^2} \cdot (\sigma^2 + \dots + \sigma^2)$$

$$= \frac{1}{n^2} \cdot n \cdot \sigma^2 = \frac{\sigma^2}{n}$$

where $V(X_1) = \ldots = V(X_n) = \sigma^2$. Here, we have exploited the fact that the sample's observations are independent, such that the variance of their sum is equal to the sum of their variances.

> **The variance of the sample average**, $\overline{X}$, in a simple random sample is:
>
> $$V(\overline{X}) = \frac{\sigma^2}{n}$$
>
> where σ^2 is the variance in the distribution of interest.

The variance of an estimator can help us to choose between several estimators of the same parameter. In section 10.1, we pointed out that we could use the first observation, X_1, as an estimate of the mean value. In this case, we would ignore the other observations, $X_2, \ldots, X_n$. But why is this worse than using the average $\overline{X}$? We have already shown that $E(X_1) = \mu$ and $E(\overline{X}) = \mu$, so both estimators are unbiased. But they do not have the same variance! Above, we showed that $V(\overline{X}) = \sigma^2/n$, whereas $V(X_1) = \sigma^2$. If the sample consists of 100 observations, then the variance is 100 times smaller when the average, rather than a single observation, is used as the estimator. In general, we say that one estimator is more *efficient* than another, if it has a smaller variance.

The estimator $\overline{X}$ has the property that it becomes more accurate when sample size is increased. We can see this from the formula for the variance, where we have to divide by the sample size n. If we had a very large sample size, the variance would tend to 0. In this case, the distribution of $\overline{X}$ becomes concentrated around the mean value, μ. This means that, in all likelihood, the estimate would be close to the mean value. In general, we say that an estimator is *consistent* if its distribution becomes concentrated around its mean value when the sample size becomes sufficiently large.

We conclude this section by summarising the properties of an estimator, Y:

Properties of estimators

An estimator Y of a parameter θ is:

1. unbiased if $E(Y) = \theta$

2. consistent if $E(Y) \rightarrow \theta$ and $\text{Var}(Y) \rightarrow 0$ when $n \rightarrow \infty$ [13]

3. more efficient than the estimator Z, if $\text{Var}(Y) < \text{Var}(Z)$, and Y and Z are both unbiased.

10.4   The distribution of the estimator $\overline{X}$

The sample average in a simple random sample is a central and consistent estimator for the distribution's mean value. Above, we calculated the estimator's mean value, μ, and its variance, σ^2/n, but in a more general analysis we may be interested in knowing the entire distribution of the sample average.

Using the joint probability function, $f(x_1,...,x_n)$, for the n random variables in the sample, we can in principle calculate the probabilities for all of the possible realised samples. For a simple random sample, we can use the formula in Section 10.1 to calculate the distribution of the estimator, as the following example illustrates.

Example 10.3: A TV programme – part 3

We can calculate the probabilities for the different realised sample averages in Example 10.2 by using the probabilities for obtaining a particular sample from Example 10.1. For this reason, Tables 10.1 and 10.2 are combined in Table 10.3:

---

13   The symbol "$\rightarrow$" is read "converges to". In this case it thus means that $E(Y)$ converges to θ, when n converges to infinity.

Table 10.3:
Realised
sample
averages
and their
probabilities

Possible samples	Average, $\overline{X}$	Probability	Probability when $p = 0{,}7$
(1,1,1)	1.00	$p \cdot p \cdot p$	0.343
(1,1,0)	0.67	$p \cdot p \cdot (1 - p)$	0.147
(1,0,1)	0.67	$p \cdot (1 - p) \cdot p$	0.147
(1,0,0)	0.33	$p \cdot (1 - p) \cdot (1 - p)$	0.063
(0,1,1)	0.67	$(1 - p) \cdot p \cdot p$	0.147
(0,1,0)	0.33	$(1 - p) \cdot p \cdot (1 - p)$	0.063
(0,0,1)	0.33	$(1 - p) \cdot (1 - p) \cdot p$	0.063
(0,0,0)	0.00	$(1 - p) \cdot (1 - p) \cdot (1 - p)$	0.027

Table 10.3 shows that 0.67 is the estimate for three different realised samples. The overall probability of an estimate of 0.67 (when we select a simple random sample) is therefore the sum of the probabilities for each of these realised samples:

$$P(\overline{X} = 0.67) = p \cdot (1 - p) \cdot p + p \cdot p \cdot (1 - p) + (1 - p) \cdot p \cdot p = 3 \cdot p \cdot p \cdot (1 - p)$$

In the case where $p = 0.7$, this probability is equal to: $3 \cdot 0.147 = 0.441$. Similarly, we can find the probability of all the other possible values of the sample average $\overline{X}$:

$$f_{\overline{X}}(x) = P(\overline{X} = x) = \begin{cases} (1 - p)^3 & \text{for } x = 0.00 \\ 3 \cdot (1 - p)^2 \cdot p & \text{for } x = 0.33 \\ 3 \cdot p^2 \cdot (1 - p) & \text{for } x = 0.67 \\ p^3 & \text{for } x = 1.00 \end{cases}$$

This is the estimator's probability function (its distribution), which depends on the unknown parameter p – the value that we are trying to estimate.

Working out the distribution of an estimator is not always quite so straightforward. Simple random samples in which the observations are normally distributed are an important special case, as discussed in Example 10.4.

Example 10.4: A normally distributed sample

Let us assume that the length of a manufactured screw is normally distributed with mean value μ and variance σ^2. We now select a simple random sample with n screws: $X_1, X_2,...,X_n$. The individual random variables in the sample are then independent, normally distributed variables with mean value μ and variance σ^2: $X_i \sim N(\mu,\sigma^2)$, $i = 1,....,n$. The estimator of the mean value μ is the sample average:

$$\overline{X} = \frac{1}{n} \cdot (X_1 + X_2 + ... + X_n) = \frac{1}{n} \cdot X_1 + \frac{1}{n} \cdot X_2 + ... + \frac{1}{n} \cdot X_n$$

When a random variable X is normally distributed, $X \sim N(\mu,\sigma^2)$, the random variable $Y = k \cdot X$, where k is a constant, will also normally be distributed with mean value $k \cdot \mu$ and variance $k^2 \cdot \sigma^2$. Hence it follows that:

$$\frac{X_i}{n} \sim N\left(\frac{\mu}{n}, \frac{\sigma^2}{n^2}\right), \quad i = 1,...,n$$

because $X_i \sim N(\mu,\sigma^2)$. The average $\overline{X}$ is a sum of such independent normally distributed variables, X_i / n. Such a sum will also be normally distributed with a mean value that is equal to the sum of the mean values of the individual parts and a variance equal to the sum of the variances:

$$\overline{X} \sim N(\mu, \sigma^2/n)$$

because the sum of the mean values is μ, and the sum of the variances is σ^2/n. We note that the mean value and variance of $\overline{X}$ are, of course, the same as in the general case from Section 10.3. What we have shown here is that $\overline{X}$ is normally distributed when the underlying distribution is normally distributed.

The above example is a special case in which the observations in the sample are normally distributed. In this case, it turns out that the sample average, $\overline{X}$, is also normally distributed. Often, we do not know which distribution the sample observations follow. However, even when the distribution of the observations is unknown, it is still possible to find an approximation to the distribution of the sample average that is close to its correct distribution when the sample size, n, is large. Here we can use the following result:[14]

The central limit theorem

Suppose we have a simple random sample of n elements, $X_1, X_2, ..., X_n$, where $E(X_i) = \mu$ and $V(X_i) = \sigma^2$, $i = 1, ..., n$. When n is large, the sample average, $\overline{X}$, will then be approximately normally distributed with mean value μ and variance σ^2/n:

$$\overline{X} \sim^A N(\mu, \sigma^2/n)$$

where $\sim^A$ means approximately distributed.

The central limit theorem decrees that, regardless of the distribution of the observation in a simple random sample, the sample average is approximately normally distributed as long as the sample is sufficiently large. This is a very useful result, which we will often use in later chapters. It is also illustrates why the normal distribution is so important.

10.5   Exercises

1. Review questions
   a) What do we use samples for and why is this relevant?
   b) Explain the difference between a sample and a realised sample.
   c) What do we understand by a simple random sample?
   d) Explain in your own words what a simple random sample is when we are dealing with a real population. What is the relationship between the population's distribution and the distribution of the sample's observations?
   e) What is an estimator? And what is an estimate?
   f) What is meant by an unbiased estimator?
   g) What does it mean when an estimator is said to be efficient? And consistent?
   h) Explain briefly the central limit theorem.

---

14   Formally, the central limit theorem says that the standardised sample average asymptotically following a standard normal distribution: $(\overline{X} - \mu)/\sqrt{\sigma^2/n} \to N(0, 1)$ when $n \to \infty$.

An insight into statistics for the social sciences

2. The police want to determine the proportion of guests at a club, p, who are aged under 18. To this end, they decide to select a simple random sample of five people from the 235 guests in the club.

   a) What is the probability that everybody in the sample is aged 18 years or older?

   Let X_i assume the value 1 if the ith person in the sample is under 18, and the value 0 if he/she is not.

   b) Find the expected value of the sample average, $\overline{X}$. Also, find the variance of $\overline{X}$. (Hint: what is the variance of a Bernoulli-distributed variable?)

   c) Calculate the expected value and the variance from question b) in the case where $p = 0.3$.

   d) Discuss any problems that may be associated with ensuring that the sample is a simple random one.

3. A school nurse selects a simple random sample of 200 children's heights from a school with a population of 2,000 pupils. Assume that the (unknown) population's mean value is $\mu = 140$ cm, and that its variance is $\sigma^2 = 64$.

   a) Explain how the sample should be selected so that it becomes a simple random sample.

   b) What is the expected value of the sample average, $\overline{X}$?

   c) What is the variance of $\overline{X}$?

   d) Determine the approximate distribution of the sample average.

   e) Using the distribution in d), compute the probability of obtaining a sample with an average of less than 136 cm.

   f) Find the probability that the sample average will be within 2 cm of the population's mean value.

   g) If the nurse wants a sample with 90% probability of the average being within 1 cm of the population's mean value, how large a sample must she then use?

11 Estimating the mean value using stratified sampling and cluster sampling

Often, we have knowledge about characteristics of a real population other than the particular characteristic we want to study. If this is the case, then it may be possible to use this knowledge to select a sample in a way that gives us more information about the unknown characteristic of interest than by merely selecting a simple random sample. In this chapter, we will show how such knowledge of other characteristics can be used to improve the estimate of the mean value in a real population, compared to the estimate from Chapter 10.

In Section 11.1, we define the stratified sample average, which is an estimator of the population's mean value when we have a stratified sample. In Section 11.2, we then look at the properties of the stratified sample average. There are many ways to stratify, and Section 11.3 discusses some of them. We end the chapter by discussing cluster sampling, which is an alternative way of selecting a sample that is often used in practice.

11.1 Stratification

Stratification is a method of achieving greater precision in an estimate of, for example, the mean value, than if we select a simple random sample. We can use stratification if we have prior knowledge of the distribution of some characteristic in the population. To illustrate, assume that each element in the population has at least two characteristics. We would like to know the distribution of the first of these characteristics, but we already know the distribution of the second characteristic, for example, the age or the gender of the individuals in the population. Stratification divides the population into groups – also called *strata* – based on the known characteristic. These could be "men" and "women" or "children" and "adults". We then select a simple random sample from each stratum. We therefore need a model that can bring the information in the samples from the various strata together to obtain information about the total population.

As in Chapter 10, we will let the random variable X represent the characteristic we are interested in studying. In addition, we will let the known characteristic be represented by the variable Y.

Stratification:

Stratification is possible if the elements of the real population have at least one known characteristic, Y.

A stratum consists of all of the elements in the population with the same value of Y: $Y = y_j$.

From the box above, it follows that all elements of the population that have the same value of Y are grouped in the same stratum. If Y assumes m different values in the population, there will be m different strata.

Example 11.1: Advertising in stores – part 1

A major Danish manufacturer markets its products through 400 small stores. The manufacturer wants to conduct a study into how many square metres each shop devotes to these products. This is the unknown characteristic of interest, which we will represent by the random variable X. Since it is too expensive for the manufacturer to survey the whole population of 400 stores, it will try to estimate the mean value of X with the help of a sample. The manufacturer knows the location of each store, which we will represent with the variable Y. For example $Y = 0$ means that the shop is located in Jutland. The manufacturer hopes to work out a better estimate of floor space devoted to its products by taking advantage of this geographical information during the sample selection process.

11.1.1 Stratified sample average

When we use stratification, we should be able to find the mean value of X in the population based on the mean values of X in the various strata. This is done by using the following formula, which is also called the law of iterated expectations:[15]

$$\mu = E_X(X) = E_{X|Y}(X|Y = y_1) \cdot f_Y(y_1) + \ldots + E(X|Y = y_m) \cdot f_Y(y_m)$$

$$= \sum_{j=1}^{m} E_{X|Y}(X|Y = y_j) \cdot f_Y(y_j) = E_Y\left(E_{X|Y}(X|Y)\right)$$

where μ is the mean value of X in the population, m is the number of different outcomes for Y (here, the number of strata), $f_Y(y_j)$ is the probability function for Y, and $E_{X|Y}(X|Y = y_j)$ is the mean value of X in stratum j, which is the same as the conditional mean value of X given $Y=y_j$. The mean value of X is thus a weighted average of the means in the strata. As weights, we use the shares of the different strata in the population, which are also given by the probability function for Y, $f_Y(y_j)$, in the case where all elements have the same chance of selection:

$$f_Y(y_j) = N_j/N_{pop} = w_j$$

where N_j is the number of elements in stratum j, (i.e. the number of elements with $Y = y_j$) and N_{pop} is the total number of elements in the population. Therefore, w_j is the proportion of elements in stratum j in relation to the whole population. This is summarised in the box below:

---

15   For discrete random variables, X and Y, we can verify the formula by use of the rules for joint and conditional probabilities as follows:

$$\mu = E_X(X) = \sum_x x \cdot f_X(x) = \sum_x x \cdot \sum_y f(x,y) = \sum_x x \cdot \sum_y f_{X|Y}(x|y) \cdot f_Y(y)$$

$$= \sum_x \sum_y x \cdot f_{X|Y}(x|y) \cdot f_Y(y) = \sum_y \sum_x x \cdot f_{X|Y}(x|y) \cdot f_Y(y) = \sum_y \left(\sum_x x \cdot f_{X|Y}(x|y)\right) \cdot f_Y(y)$$

$$= \sum_y E_{X|Y}(X|Y = y) \cdot f_Y(y)$$

The latter can also be written as:

$$\sum_y E_{X|Y}(X|Y = y) \cdot f_Y(y) = E_Y\left(E_{X|Y}(X|Y)\right).$$

It thus follows that $E_X(X) = E_Y\left(E_{X|Y}(X|Y)\right)$. This result is called the law of iterated expectations.

> **The population's mean value,** $E(X) = \mu$, can be calculated as
> a weighted sum of the m stratum mean values:
>
> $$\mu = E(X) = \sum_{j=1}^{m} \mu_j \cdot w_j$$
>
> where $\mu_j = E(X|Y = y_j)$ is the mean value of X in stratum j (el-
> ements with $Y = y_j$), and $w_j = N_j / N_{pop}$ is stratum j's proportion
> of the total population.

Example 11.2: Advertising in stores – part 2

The manufacturer in Example 11.1 expects all the stores in Jutland to
be comparable to each other and those on the Danish islands to be relatively similar to each other. However, he thinks that there is a general
difference between stores in Jutland and elsewhere. The manufacturer therefore defines a "Jutland" stratum, which includes all stores in
Jutland, and an "islands" stratum, comprising all stores on the Danish
islands. Let the variable Y indicate whether a store is located in Jutland
or on the islands:

$$Y = \begin{cases} 0 & \textit{if Jutland} \\ 1 & \textit{if islands} \end{cases}$$

There are a total of $N_{pop} = 400$ stores: $N_{jut} = 160$ in Jutland and $N_{isl} = 240$
on the islands. It follows from this that:

$$w_{jut} = N_{jut}/N_{pop} = 160/400 = 0.4$$

$$w_{isl} = N_{isl}/N_{pop} = 240/400 = 0.6$$

where w_{jut} and w_{isl} are the proportions of the population belonging to
the stratum "Jutland" and the stratum "islands", respectively. Thus, the
mean value of X in the total population can be written as:

$$\mu = \mu_{jut} \cdot w_{jut} + \mu_{isl} \cdot w_{isl} = \mu_{jut} \cdot 0.4 + \mu_{isl} \cdot 0.6$$

where $\mu_{jut} = E_{X|Y}(X|Y = 0)$ is the mean value of X in Jutland, and
$\mu_{isl} = E_{X|Y}(X|Y = 1)$ is the mean value of X on the islands.

In practice, we find an estimate of the mean value, μ, by replacing all unknown quantities in the formula above with estimates based on the samples from each stratum. In Chapter 10, we called this approach to estimation the *analogy principle of estimation*. We assume that the population shares, w_j, are known, and therefore all we lack are estimates of the mean values of X in the various strata.

We select a simple random sample from each stratum. We can therefore use the techniques from Chapter 10 to obtain estimates of the mean values in each of these samples. Thus, if we select a simple random sample $(X_{1,j}, X_{2,j}, \ldots, X_{nj,j})$ of size n_j from the stratum j, then the estimate of the mean value in this stratum, $\mu_j = E_{X|Y}(X \mid Y = y_j)$, is given by the sample average:

$$\overline{X}_j = \frac{1}{n_j} \cdot \sum_{i=1}^{n_j} X_{i,j}$$

To find the estimate of the mean value μ in the total population, we replace μ_j with $\overline{X}_j$ in the above formula for the population's mean value.

The stratified sample average

$$\overline{X}_{st} = \sum_{j=1}^{m} \overline{X}_j \cdot w_j$$

is used as an estimator of the population's mean value, μ, in which $\overline{X}_j$ is the sample average from stratum j, m is the number of strata, and w_j is stratum j's proportion of the total population.

$\overline{X}_{st}$ is thus a weighted sum of the m strata's sample averages.

Example 11.3: Advertising in stores – part 3

The manufacturer from Examples 11.1 and 11.2 selects a sample from each of the two strata, the sizes of which are n_{jut} and n_{isl}. Based on these, the manufacturer can construct the following two estimators of the mean value in Jutland, μ_{jut}, and the mean value on the islands, μ_{isl}, respectively:

$$\overline{X}_{jut} = \frac{1}{n_{jut}} \cdot \sum_{i=1}^{n_{jut}} X_{i,jut} \quad \text{og} \quad \overline{X}_{isl} = \frac{1}{n_{isl}} \cdot \sum_{i=1}^{n_{isl}} X_{i,isl}$$

The estimators $\overline{X}_{jut}$ and $\overline{X}_{isl}$ can then be weighted together to form an estimator for the population's overall average, μ:

$$\overline{X}_{st} = \overline{X}_{jut} \cdot w_{jut} + \overline{X}_{isl} \cdot w_{isl} = \overline{X}_{jut} \cdot 0.4 + \overline{X}_{isl} \cdot 0.6$$

If the realised samples resulted in $\overline{X}_{jut} = 1.5$ and $\overline{X}_{isl} = 1.1$, then $\overline{X}_{st} = 1.26$.

11.2   Properties of the stratified sample average

In this section, we study the properties of the stratified sample average, and we also make a comparison with the sample average from a simple random sample.

In general, stratified samples are non-representative. Specifically, this is the case if $n_j/n \neq N_j/N_{pop}$, and if there is dependence between the characteristic Y, which is used to define strata, and the characteristic X, which we are interested in.

One consequence of a non-representative sample is that the simple sample average is not an unbiased estimator of the population's mean value. This is most easily illustrated by an example.

Example 11.4: A biased estimator

Consider two strata, with an equal number of elements: $N_1/N_{pop} = N_2/N_{pop} = 1/2$. Assume that the mean values are $\mu_1 = 10$ and $\mu_2 = 20$. The population's mean value is therefore $\mu = 15$. If we choose the sample sizes so that $n_1/n = 3/4$ and $n_2/n = 1/4$, then the expected value of the sample average is:

$$E(\overline{X}) = 10 \cdot 3/4 + 20 \cdot 1/4 = 12.5$$

Since $E(\overline{X}) = 12.5 \neq 15 = E(X)$, the sample average is a biased estimator. The problem is that the sample average does not correct for the fact that the sample is not representative, since the elements in stratum one have three times the probability of selection as those in stratum two.

Thus, in the case of a stratified sample, we should not use the simple sample average as an estimator of the population's mean value.

The stratified sample average, $\overline{X}_{st}$, is designed to correct the unrepresentative sample so that we can obtain an unbiased estimate of the population's mean value. To see this, note that:

$$E(\overline{X}_{st}) = E(\sum_{j=1}^{m} \overline{X}_j \cdot w_j) = \sum_{j=1}^{m} E(\overline{X}_j) \cdot w_j = \sum_{j=1}^{m} \mu_j \cdot w_j = \mu$$

where the last equality sign follows from the first box in Section 11.1.1. The stratified sample average is therefore an unbiased estimator.

An important purpose of stratification is that, with a given sample size, we are able to achieve greater precision than with a simple random sample. The effect of stratification can be seen on the variance of the stratified sample average, $\overline{X}_{st}$, which is a function of the variances of the sample averages, $\overline{X}_j$, from the various strata:

$$V(\overline{X}_{st}) = V(\sum_{j=1}^{m} \overline{X}_j \cdot w_j) = \sum_{j=1}^{m} V(\overline{X}_j \cdot w_j) = \sum_{j=1}^{m} w_j^2 \cdot V(\overline{X}_j)$$

Above, we have exploited the fact that the sample averages from the different strata are independent, and therefore the variance of their (weighted) sum is equal to the (weighted) sum of their variances. However, we still lack an expression for $V(\overline{X}_j)$.

As an estimator of μ_j, $\overline{X}_j$ has the same properties as the sample average, $\overline{X}$, had as an estimator of μ. This is not surprising if we think of a stratum as a subpopulation from which we select a simple random sample of size n_j. We then know from Chapter 10 that the variance of $\overline{X}_j$ must be:

$$V(\overline{X}_j) = V(\overline{X}|Y = y_j) = \frac{V(X|Y = y_j)}{n_j} = \frac{\sigma_j^2}{n_j}$$

where $V(X|Y = y_j)$ is the variance of X, given that Y assumes the value y_j (called the conditional variance of X given Y). This conditional variance is equal to σ_j^2, which is the variance of X in stratum j.

The total variance of the stratified sample average, $\overline{X}_{st}$, is therefore:

$$V(\overline{X}_{st}) = \sum_{j=1}^{m} w_j^2 \cdot V(\overline{X}_j) = \sum_{j=1}^{m} w_j^2 \cdot \frac{\sigma_j^2}{n_j}$$

Note that the variance of $\overline{X}_{st}$ depends on the sample size in each stratum, n_j, the proportion of elements in each stratum relative to the whole population, w_j, as well as the variance of X in each stratum, σ_j^2. The total sample size is: $n_1 + n_2 + \ldots + n_m = n$.

As an alternative to the stratified sample average's estimate of μ, we could have selected a simple random sample with n observations from the whole population, and then used the sample average, $\overline{X}$, from Chapter 10 as an estimator of μ. This estimator is also unbiased, but it often has a different variance than $\overline{X}_{st}$. In Chapter 10, we found the variance of $\overline{X}$ to be: $V(\overline{X}) = \sigma^2/n$. This should be compared with the expression for $V(\overline{X}_{st})$ above. The best estimator will be the one with least variance. This depends on the sizes of σ_j^2 and n_j, and therefore on how the strata are defined. If the stratum variances, σ_j^2, are small compared to the population's variance, σ^2, then the stratified sample average will be a better (more precise) estimator. We can also say that the stratified sample average is more efficient than the simple sample average.

Example 11.5: Advertising in stores – part 4

In the study of the stores, the variances of $\overline{X}_{st}$ and $\overline{X}$, (i.e. the stratified sample average and the simple sample average) are given by:

$$V\left(\overline{X}_{st}\right) = w_{jut}^2 \cdot V\left(\overline{X}_{jut}\right) + w_{isl}^2 \cdot V\left(\overline{X}_{isl}\right) = w_{jut}^2 \cdot \frac{\sigma_{jut}^2}{n_{jut}} + w_{isl}^2 \cdot \frac{\sigma_{isl}^2}{n_{isl}}$$

$$V\left(\overline{X}\right) = \frac{\sigma^2}{n} = \frac{\sigma^2}{n_{jut} + n_{isl}}$$

where $n = n_{jut} + n_{isl}$, since we assume that both approaches use the same total sample size. This means that $\overline{X}_{st}$ is a more "precise" estimator than $\overline{X}$ if σ_{jut}^2 and σ_{isl}^2 are small compared to σ^2. This could be the case if there were a large difference between stores in Jutland and those on the islands, for example if Jutland stores generally use more space for products, and as such are clustered around a mean value, μ_{jut}, that is somewhat larger than that of the shops on the islands, μ_{isl}. This possibility is illustrated in Figure 11.1.

Figure 11.1:
Population and strata

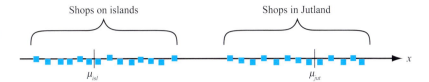

Shops on islands   Shops in Jutland

μ_{isl} μ_{jut} x

In Figure 11.1, there will be a large variance for the population as a whole, whereas there is a small variance in each of the two strata. The two estimators of the strata's mean values are therefore relatively precise. This also gives a more precise estimate of the total mean value of the population, when the correct weights are used: $w_{jut} = N_{jut}/N_{pop}$ and $w_{isl} = N_{isl}/N_{pop}$. If instead we select randomly from the whole population, there is a high probability of getting "too many" observations from one of the two strata. Consequently, the estimate will be pulled toward that stratum's mean value. However, this is a natural consequence of simple random samples, because a randomly selected sample from the whole population will rarely be fully representative in the sense that it contains elements from the two strata in exactly the same proportions that the two strata are represented in the population.

As the example illustrates, the characteristic we know, Y, must be correlated with the characteristic that we want to study, X, if stratification is to make the estimate of the mean value more precise. Technically, we can see this in the formula for $V(\bar{X}_{st})$, which depends on $V(X|Y = y_j)$. If there is no relationship between X and Y (i.e. X and Y are independent), then the variance of X is independent of whichever stratum we are looking at. This implies that $V(X|Y = y_j) = \sigma^2$ for all $j = 1,...,m$. If we insert this into the formula for $V(\bar{X}_{st})$, then $V(\bar{X}_{st}) = \sigma^2/n$, which is just the variance of the sample average with simple random selection. The examples also illustrate that stratification is closely linked to the concept of conditional expectation. The reason for stratifying is precisely that we expect that the conditional means (the means in the strata) will be different from the unconditional mean (the mean in the whole population).

> **Properties of the stratified sample average**
>
> The estimator $\bar{X}_{st}$ has the following properties:
>
> $$E\left(\bar{X}_{st}\right) = \mu$$
>
> $$V\left(\bar{X}_{st}\right) = \sum_{j=1}^{m} w_j^2 \cdot \frac{\sigma_j^2}{n_j}$$
>
> where σ_j^2 is the variance of X in stratum j, w_j is stratum j's proportion of the total population, and n_j is the size of the sample from stratum j.

Having defined the different strata, we have to determine how large a sample we want to select from each of these. In the examples above, we simply assumed that there were given sizes of the samples $n_1, n_2, ..., n_m$. In the following section, we will look at various methods of determining these sample sizes.

11.3   Choice of stratum sample size

There are many ways to determine the sample size from each stratum. One is called *optimal allocation*, which is optimal with regard to the stratified sample average having the least possible variance. Another way, which is easier to implement in practice, is *proportional allocation*.

11.3.1   Optimal allocation

The box above shows that the variance of the stratified sample average, $\bar{X}_{st}$, depends on both σ_j^2 and n_j. If we know the variances in the different strata, $(\sigma_1^2, \sigma_2^2, ..., \sigma_m^2)$, we can deduce the sample sizes, $(n_1, n_2, ..., n_m)$, which for a given total sample size, n, ensures that the variance of $\bar{X}_{st}$ is minimised. These optimal sample sizes are given by:

$$n_j^* = n \cdot \frac{\sigma_j \cdot w_j}{\sum_{j=1}^{m} \sigma_j \cdot w_j} \quad , \quad j = 1, 2, ..., m$$

where the denominator is a weighted sum of the standard deviations in the different strata. This formula reveals that if the variance, σ_j^2, in a stratum j is large, we should select a relatively large sample, n_j^*, from this stratum. Similarly, we should take a large sample from the stratum j, if the proportion, w_j, of this stratum in the whole population is large.

When using the optimal sample size n_j^* for each stratum, the variance of the stratified sample average, $\overline{X}_{st,opt}$, is given by:

$$V^*(\overline{X}_{st,opt}) = \frac{\left(\sum_{j=1}^{m} \sigma_j \cdot w_j\right)^2}{n}$$

If we compare this with the variance of the simple sample average, $\overline{X}$, it follows that the stratified sample average with optimal allocation, $\overline{X}_{st,opt}$, has less variance than $\overline{X}$ if $\sum_{j=1}^{m} \sigma_j \cdot w_j < \sigma$. This will always be the case if the variances in the individual strata are less than in the population as a whole.

Example 11.6: Red wine and income strata

A wine importer wants to study the mean consumption of red wine from the Haut-Medoc district. The importer commissions a market-research company to conduct interviews in private homes. The company charges DKK 500.00 per interview. The importer expects that a simple random sample will be selected, and that achieving a satisfactory level of precision will require 1,000 interviews. The total cost of this study will therefore be DKK 500,000.

However, the research company thinks that consumption of Haut-Medoc red wine depends heavily on household income. The higher the income, the higher the consumption. It suggests, therefore, that the population be divided into two strata – one for households with an income over DKK 400,000 and one for those with an income below DKK 400,000. It also expects that the standard deviation in each stratum will be half as big as the standard deviation for the whole population: $\sigma_{low\ income} = \sigma_{high\ income} = \frac{1}{2} \cdot \sigma$. If households with an income below DKK 400,000 represent 40% of the population, then the variance of the stratified sample average with optimal allocation of the sample sizes in strata is given by:

$$V(\overline{X}_{st,opt}) = \frac{(\sigma_{low} \cdot 0.4 + \sigma_{high} \cdot 0.6)^2}{n}$$

$$= \frac{\left(\frac{1}{2} \cdot \sigma \cdot 0.4 + \frac{1}{2} \cdot \sigma \cdot 0.6\right)^2}{n} = \frac{1}{4} \cdot \frac{\sigma^2}{n}$$

This shows that $V(\overline{X}) = \sigma^2/n$ is four times lower than the variance of the sample average, $V(\overline{X}_{st,opt})$. To achieve the same precision when using the stratified estimator, it is therefore only necessary to interview $1,000/4 = 250$ people, which will "only" cost DKK 125,000. Stratification can therefore save the importer DKK 375,000.

In order to be able to use optimal allocation, we have to know the variance of X in each stratum, which will not normally be the case. Instead, we can try to estimate the variance in each stratum (as we will see in the next chapter) by conducting a pilot study. Then we can use the formula for n_j^*, where σ_j is replaced with the estimate of σ_j. This approach is also called optimal allocation.

The optimal sample size from stratum j is:

$$n_j^* = n \cdot \frac{\sigma_j \cdot w_j}{\sum_{j=1}^{m} \sigma_j \cdot w_j}, \quad j = 1,2,...,m$$

where n is the total sample size, σ_j is the standard deviation of X in stratum j, and w_j is the proportion of stratum j in the population. The variance of the stratified sample average with optimal allocation is:

$$V(\overline{X}_{st,opt}) = \frac{(\sum_{j=1}^{m} \sigma_j \cdot w_j)^2}{n}$$

11.3.2 Proportional allocation

Even if we are not using the optimal stratum sample sizes, stratifying is often still worthwhile. One possible allocation is to choose the sample sizes for the various strata in such a way that they are proportional to the sizes of the strata, i.e. $n_j/n = N_j/N_{pop} = w_j$. In this case, the stratified sample average becomes equal to the average of all of the observations selected from the m strata. The reason for this is that the stratum sample sizes have been chosen to reflect the size of the individual strata. There is therefore no need for a further weighting of the observations. Formally, this can be shown in the following way:

$$\bar{X}_{st,prop} = \sum_{j=1}^{m} w_j \cdot \bar{X}_j = \sum_{j=1}^{m} \frac{N_j}{N_{pop}} \cdot \bar{X}_j = \sum_{j=1}^{m} \left(\frac{N_j}{N_{pop}} \cdot \frac{1}{n_j} \sum_{i=1}^{n_j} X_{i,j} \right)$$

$$= \sum_{j=1}^{m} \left(\frac{N_j}{n_j} \cdot \frac{1}{N_{pop}} \sum_{i=1}^{n_j} X_{i,j} \right) = \sum_{j=1}^{m} \left(\frac{N_{pop}}{n} \cdot \frac{1}{N_{pop}} \sum_{i=1}^{n_j} X_{i,j} \right)$$

$$= \frac{1}{n} \sum_{j=1}^{m} \sum_{i=1}^{n_j} X_{i,j}$$

Although the stratified sample average in this case is an average of all of the observations, it is not the same as the simple sample average calculated without stratification. The reason for this is that the number of elements selected from each stratum is determined before the sampling takes place and is given by the proportion of the whole population that the stratum represents. In a simple random sample, we can, in principle, end up with elements from only one stratum.

> With **proportional allocation**, the sample size from stratum j is:
>
> $$n_j^* = n \cdot \frac{N_j}{N_{pop}} = n \cdot w_j, \quad j = 1, 2, ..., m$$
>
> where n is the total sample size and w_j is the proportion of stratum j in the population. The variance of the stratified estimator with proportional allocation is:
>
> $$V\left(\bar{X}_{st,prop} \right) = \frac{1}{n} \sum_{j=1}^{m} w_j \cdot \sigma_j^2$$

11.3.3   Predetermined stratification

Until now, we have discussed stratification in a context where we can control the sample size in each stratum. However, if we buy a pre-selected stratified sample from Statistics Denmark, for example, then the sample sizes for each stratum are already given. In order to be able to use such a sample, it is imperative that, for each stratum, we know both the sample size, n_j, and the proportion, w_j, of the stratum in the population. We can then use the formula from Section 11.1.1 to construct a stratified estimate of the mean value of the population.

11.3.4   Stratification without replacement

So far, we have assumed that we are selecting a simple random sample from each stratum. Since we are dealing with real populations, this means that we must be sampling with replacement. However, in most real situations, we would sample without replacement. This means that the individual observations in a sample from a stratum will not be independent.

However, the estimators for the mean values are calculated in the same manner as before, but their variances and distributions are different. If we select a simple random sample from the whole population *without replacement*, then the sample average, $\bar{X}_{without}$, will have the following variance:

$$V\left(\bar{X}_{without}\right) = \frac{\sigma^2}{n} \cdot \frac{N_{pop}}{N_{pop} - 1} \cdot \left(1 - \frac{n}{N_{pop}}\right)$$

The variance of the stratified sample average, $\bar{X}_{st,without}$, changes accordingly, as does the expression for the optimal sample sizes, since these have to minimise the estimator's variance. The following box provides the necessary formulas:

With **stratified sampling without replacement,** the variance of the stratified estimator is given by:

$$V\left(\bar{X}_{st,without}\right) = \sum_{j=1}^{m} w_j^2 \cdot \frac{\sigma_j^2}{n_j} \cdot \frac{N_j}{\left(N_j - 1\right)} \cdot \left(1 - \frac{n_j}{N_j}\right)$$

and the **optimal sample size** from stratum *j* is:

$$n_j^* = n \cdot \frac{w_j \cdot \sigma_j \cdot \sqrt{\dfrac{N_j}{N_j - 1}}}{\displaystyle\sum_{j=1}^{m} \left(w_j \cdot \sigma_j \cdot \sqrt{\dfrac{N_j}{N_j - 1}}\right)}$$

If the sample size, n_j, is small compared to the size of the stratum, N_j, then these corrections will have little practical importance.

11.4   Cluster sampling

Often, a large part of the cost of conducting a study is determined by how difficult it is to obtain information about the selected elements. If information is obtained by interviews with selected elements that are geographically widely dispersed, then transport costs can quickly escalate. It may also be that we want to study a product by means of a laboratory experiment. In this case, it is typically less expensive to explore many elements at the same time, instead of performing the same test many times. It can therefore sometimes be practical (cheaper) to divide elements into groups – called *clusters* in statistical language – and then select one or more clusters instead of selecting individual elements.

After a real population has been divided into clusters, we use simple random sampling to select some of the clusters. Within the selected clusters, we can use all of the elements (the one-step method) or select some of the elements by simple random sampling (the two-step method). In any case, we call this *cluster sampling*.

Note that with cluster sampling we only select some clusters, whereas in stratification we select elements from all strata. Because of this, the division of elements into clusters should also be done differently from the division of elements into strata. With stratification, we seek to divide the elements into *homogeneous* groups (strata). With cluster sampling, we aim to divide the elements into *heterogeneous* groups (clusters) so that each individual cluster's composition is representative of the population's composition.

Figure 11.2:
Heterogeneous strata vs. heterogeneous clusters

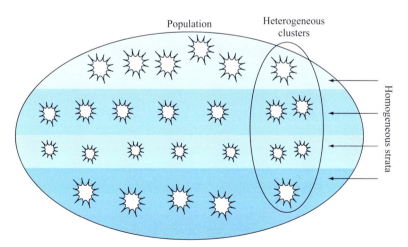

If the manufacturer from Example 11.5 considers Jutland and the is-lands as two clusters rather than two strata, and selects some elements from one cluster (e.g. Jutland) to constitute the sample (the two-step method), this will give a biased estimator of the mean value of the pop-ulation (see Figure 11.1). This is because none of the clusters by them-selves provide a representative picture of the population. To use cluster sampling successfully, the manufacturer must divide up the population differently.

> **Cluster sampling** is useful when it is expensive to sample or study elements individually, and when the individual clusters are heterogeneous.

With stratification, we strive to make each stratum as homogeneous as possible, so that the variance of X in each stratum is small. This reduc-es the variance of the stratified estimator of the mean value. The main motivation for cluster sampling is that it is cheaper. In other words, it is motivated more by costs than by statistical considerations. However, a cheaper study, of course, means that we can study more elements for the same money.

If the population is divided into K clusters of the same size, $\bar{N} = N_{pop}/K$, and the number of the selected clusters is k, then the clus-ter estimator for the mean value of the population, μ, is given by:

$$\bar{X}_{cluster} = \frac{1}{k}\sum_{j=1}^{k}\bar{X}_j = \frac{1}{k \cdot \bar{N}}\sum_{j=1}^{k}\sum_{i=1}^{\bar{N}}X_{i,j}$$

where $\bar{X}_j$ is the sample average in cluster j. This cluster estimator is thus calculated as a simple average of all of the selected elements.

11.5   Exercises

1. Review questions
   a) What is the basic idea behind stratifying a population?
   b) What do you have to know about the population to conduct a stratification, and how is a stratum defined?
   c) What is the relationship between the mean value of the popula-tion and the strata's mean values?
   d) Explain how the stratified sample average is calculated.

e) What is the stratified sample average an estimator for? And what properties does it have as an estimator?

f) What determines whether the stratified sample average, $\overline{X}_{st}$, is a better estimator than the simple sample average, $\overline{X}$?

g) Explain what is meant by *optimal allocation* of the sample sizes.

h) Explain what is meant by *proportional allocation*, and how the stratified sample average, $\overline{X}_{st,prop}$, can be calculated in this case.

i) Why does the optimal allocation of the sample sizes change when sampling is *without replacement?*

j) How is cluster sampling conducted?

k) When is cluster sampling advantageous (compared with stratified sampling)?

2. A stratified population consists of four strata. The sizes of these strata, and the mean values and variances of X in each stratum are as follows:

Stratum	N_j	μ_j	σ_j^2
1	105	6.5	4.34
2	76	8.4	2.33
3	57	12.4	3.52
4	89	3.6	2.12

a) Determine the mean value of X in the whole population. The variance of X in the whole population is equal to 11.86 (can you verify this?). Assume that the total sample size is $n = 40$.

b) Find the variance of the sample average if you use simple random sampling from the whole population.

c) Determine the sample sizes to be used from each stratum if you use proportional allocation and simple random sampling from the individual strata. Determine also the variance of the stratified sample average in this case.

d) Determine the sample sizes if you use optimal allocation. Determine also the variance of the stratified sample average in this case.

e) Compare the variances from questions b)–d).

f) Calculate the optimal sample sizes from the various strata if you select without replacement instead. Determine also the variance of the stratified sample average in this case.

3. A Danish company would like to study how many of its products are bought in 347 shops around the country. The shops can be classified as small (238), medium (90) and large (19).

    As the company expects that sales of its products will be positively correlated with the size of the shops, it decides to use a stratified sampling procedure with replacement.

    a) Find the sample sizes for the different strata with proportional allocation of a total sample size of $n = 30$.

    b) Find the optimal sample sizes if the variance among the large shops is assumed to be four times as great as among the small shops and twice as great as among the medium shops:

    $$\sigma^2_{big} = 2 \cdot \sigma^2_{medium} = 4 \cdot \sigma^2_{small}$$

    c) Explain the difference between the results in a) and b).

12 Estimators of other descriptive measures

In Chapter 10, we looked at the sample average as an estimator of the mean value of a distribution when we have a simple random sample at our disposal. In Chapter 11, we extended this to other types of sampling that are often used when sampling from real populations. In this chapter, we return to the assumption of a simple random sample in order to study estimators of other descriptive measures of a distribution.

In Chapter 5, we divided descriptive measures up into moments, for example the mean value, and into quantiles, such as the median. In this chapter, we will look at estimators of these different descriptive measures, all of which are based on the analogy principle of estimation. This principle, which we discussed in Chapters 10 and 11, says that we should take the definition of a descriptive measure and replace all the unknown quantities with their corresponding sample quantities.

In Section 12.1, we introduce an estimator of the variance, and we look at estimators of moments more generally in Section 12.2. The estimation of descriptive measures of relationships between two random variables is the subject of Section 12.3. In Section 12.4, we show how to estimate the entire distribution of a characteristic. This forms the basis for discussing estimators of quantiles in Section 12.5.

12.1   An estimator of the variance

In this section, we present an estimator for the variance of a distribution. Since the estimator is derived in the same way as the sample average, we start by summarising the idea behind the sample average as an estimator of the mean value.

In Chapter 10, we showed that we can use the *sample average*, $\overline{X}$, as an estimator for the mean value, μ. The motivation for this estimator is found in the *analogy principle of estimation:* we take the expression for the mean value of a discrete random variable and replace all the unknown quantities in this expression with their corresponding sample quantities. The mean value of a discrete random variable, X, is given by:

$$\mu = E(X) = \sum_{i=1}^{N} x_i \cdot f_X(x_i)$$

where you sum over all the possible values, x_i, which X can assume, weighted by their probabilities, $f_X(x_i)$. When we use the sample, we sum over all the elements in the sample and replace the probabilities with the weight of each observation in the sample, namely $1/n$. Thus, the sample average is:

$$\bar{X} = \frac{1}{n} \cdot (X_1 + X_2 + \dots + X_n) = \frac{1}{n} \sum_{i=1}^{n} X_i$$

We do the same when we want to calculate an estimator for the variance, σ^2. The variance for a discrete random variable, X, is given by:

$$V(X) = \sum_{i=1}^{N} (x_i - \mu)^2 \cdot f_X(x_i)$$

When we calculate an estimator for this, we again replace $f_X(x_i)$ by the weight, $1/n$, and sum up all of the elements in the sample. In addition, we replace the unknown mean value, μ, with the sample average, $\bar{X}$:

$$b^2 = \frac{1}{n} \sum_{i=1}^{n} (X_i - \bar{X})^2$$

$$= \frac{1}{n} \cdot (X_1 - \bar{X})^2 + \frac{1}{n} \cdot (X_2 - \bar{X})^2 + \dots + \frac{1}{n} \cdot (X_n - \bar{X})^2$$

It can be shown that $E(b^2) = \sigma^2 \cdot (n-1)/n$. Since $E(b^2) \neq \sigma^2$, b^2 is not an unbiased estimator of the variance. However, since n is a known constant value, we can correct b^2 in order to obtain a new, unbiased estimator. This estimator is called the *sample variance*, S^2, and it is given by:

$$S^2 = \frac{n}{n-1} \cdot b_2 = \frac{1}{n-1} \sum_{i=1}^{n} (X_i - \bar{X})^2$$

S^2 is an unbiased estimator of σ^2 since $E(S^2) = \sigma^2$. In practice, there is not a big difference between b^2 and S^2 when the sample size, n, is large.

We can use the sample standard deviation, $S = \sqrt{S^2}$, as an estimator of the standard deviation, σ. Note that although S is a consistent estimator of σ, it is not an unbiased estimator.

In a study of young people's consumption of cola, a simple random sample of 10th grade pupils in a local authority area has been selected and asked about their weekly consumption of half-litre bottles of cola. The result of the study was the following realised sample:

$$2, 3, 1, 1, 4, 1, 4, 6, 2$$

The sample average and the sample variance are:

$$\overline{X} = \frac{1}{9} \cdot (2 + 3 + 1 + 1 + 4 + 1 + 4 + 6 + 2) = 2.67$$

$$S^2 = \frac{1}{9-1} \cdot (2 - 2.67)^2 + \frac{1}{9-1} \cdot (3 - 2.67)^2 + \frac{1}{9-1} \cdot (1 - 2.67)^2 +$$

$$\frac{1}{9-1} \cdot (1 - 2.67)^2 + \frac{1}{9-1} \cdot (4 - 2.67)^2 + \frac{1}{9-1} \cdot (1 - 2.67)^2 +$$

$$\frac{1}{9-1} \cdot (4 - 2.67)^2 + \frac{1}{9-1} \cdot (6 - 2.67)^2 + \frac{1}{9-1} \cdot (2 - 2.67)^2 = 3$$

As a result, the sample standard deviation is: $S = \sqrt{3}$.

The sample variance is an estimator. As such, it has a distribution, because different samples result in different estimates. It turns out that it is easier to find an approximate distribution for the random variable, Y, defined by :

$$Y = S^2 \cdot \frac{(n-1)}{\sigma^2}$$

than for S^2 itself. Once we know the distribution for Y we can use it in the following way to calculate the relevant probabilities for S^2:

$$P(S^2 \le a) = P\left(S^2 \cdot \frac{n-1}{\sigma^2} \le a \cdot \frac{n-1}{\sigma^2}\right) = P\left(Y \le a \cdot \frac{n-1}{\sigma^2}\right)$$

It can be shown that Y is approximately χ^2-distributed (chi-square distributed) with $n - 1$ degrees of freedom. The χ^2-distribution with $n - 1$ degrees of freedom is one of a whole family of distributions: the χ^2 distribution with one degree of freedom, the χ^2-distribution with two degrees of freedom, and so on. In Table 4 at the back of the book, we have tabulated the most commonly used quantiles for different χ^2-distributions. To illustrate the χ^2-distribution, the probability density functions for the χ^2-distribution with 3 and 10 degrees of freedom, respectively, are depicted in Figure 12.1. We can see that, in contrast to the standard normal distribution and the t-distribution, the χ^2-distribution is not symmetric. The next example shows how to use the above formula.

Figure 12.1:
χ^2-distributions with 3 and 10 degrees of freedom

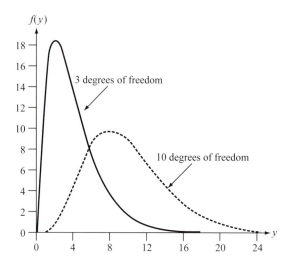

Example 12.2: Precision of sample variance

We wish to assess the precision of an estimator of the variance of a population. To do so, we assume that the true value of the variance in the population is $\sigma^2 = 5$.

Suppose we have a simple random sample of $n = 30$ observations from this population. The probability that we will estimate a value of σ^2 that is, say, less than 6, can be calculated as:

$$P(S^2 < 6) = P\left(Y < 6 \cdot \frac{n-1}{\sigma^2}\right) = P\left(Y < 6 \cdot \frac{30-1}{5}\right)$$
$$= P(Y < 34.8) \approx 0.80$$

We arrive at the final number as follows. The random variable Y is approximately χ^2-distributed with $(n-1) = 29$ degrees of freedom. Table 4 at the back of the book contains percentiles for the χ^2-distribution. Under 29 degrees of freedom, you will find the values 32.5 and 35.1, as the 0.7- and 0.8-quantiles, respectively. Since 35.1 is closer to the value 34.8 that we found above, we use the probability in this column, which is 0.8.

We have compiled the above results in the box below:

The sample variance:

$$S^2 = \frac{n}{n-1} \cdot b_2 = \frac{1}{n-1}\sum_{i=1}^{n}\left(X_i - \overline{X}\right)^2$$

The sample standard deviation: $S = \sqrt{S^2}$

Properties of the sample variance in a simple random sample:

$$E\left(S^2\right) = \sigma^2$$

$$V\left(S^2\right) = \frac{1}{n} \cdot \left(E\left(X^4\right) - \frac{n-3}{n-1}\left(E\left(X^2\right)\right)^2 \right)$$

$$S^2 \cdot \frac{(n-1)}{\sigma^2} \sim^A \chi^2(n-1)$$

12.2   Estimators for higher-order moments

In addition to the mean value and the variance, we sometimes study other central moments. The third central moment provides a measure of the skewness of the distribution while the fourth gives a characterisation of the tails of the distribution (see Section 5.2.5 in Chapter 5).

We can find estimators for higher-order moments in the same way as we found estimators of the mean value and the variance. In Section 5.2.5, we defined the $k$te central element as:

$$m_k^* = E\left([X - E(X)]^k\right)$$

If X is a discrete random variable, we can calculate the kth central moment as:

$$m_k^* = \sum_{i=1}^{N}\left(x_i - \mu\right)^k f_X(x_i)$$

We can then use the analogy principle of estimation to arrive at the following estimator of the kth central moment:

$$\hat{m}_k^* = \sum_{i=1}^{n} (X_i - \bar{X})^k \cdot \frac{1}{n} = \frac{1}{n} \sum_{i=1}^{n} (X_i - \bar{X})^k$$

Similarly, we can estimate the kth moment, $m_k = E(X^k)$, with the following estimator:

$$\hat{m}_k = \frac{1}{n} \sum_{i=1}^{n} X_i^k$$

The moments depend on the scaling of the variable. For example, if we go from measuring in DKK to measuring in thousands of DKK, the value of the moments changes. For example, the mean value would decrease by a factor of 1,000. To avoid this, we sometimes report standardised coefficients, which are not affected by scaling of the variables. As a scale-independent measure of the skewness of a distribution, we thus often use the third standardised central moment:

$$\gamma_3 = \frac{m_3^*}{\sigma^3}$$

As before, the estimator of the skewness can be derived from the analogy principle of estimation:

$$\hat{\gamma}_3 = \frac{\hat{m}_3^*}{S^3}$$

The standardised fourth central moment is:

$$\gamma_4 = \frac{m_4^*}{\sigma^4}$$

This moment is also called the *kurtosis* of a distribution. Again, the estimator is found using the analogy principle:

$$\hat{\gamma}_4 = \frac{\hat{m}_4^*}{S^4}$$

We can use the skewness and kurtosis measures to assess whether a distribution resembles a normal distribution. For a normal distribution, the skewness is equal to 0 and the kurtosis is equal to 3. We can therefore calculate the estimates of the skewness and the kurtosis for a given sample, and compare how close they are to 0 and 3, respectively.

Example 12.3. Share yields

When studying, for example, the monthly yields on shares, we often find that the kurtosis is significantly higher than 3, which would have been the value if the yields were normally distributed. A kurtosis in excess of 3 means that there is a higher probability of extreme outcomes than if the yields were normally distributed. In theoretical models of yields and optimal portfolio choices, we often use the normal distribution to model the yield. As a result, such models typically underestimate the probability of extreme outcomes, such as those observed during periods of financial turmoil.

12.3   Estimators of the covariance and the correlation coefficient

In Chapter 5, we presented the covariance and correlation coefficient as descriptive measures for the relationship between two random variables. In this section, we use the analogy principle of estimation to derive estimators of these.

The covariance between two random variables, X and Y, is:

$$Cov(X,Y) = E\big((X - \mu_X) \cdot (Y - \mu_Y)\big)$$

For two discrete random variables, X and Y, we calculate the covariance as (see Section 5.5.2):

$$Cov(X,Y) = \sum_{x_i}\sum_{y_j}(x_i - \mu_X) \cdot (y_j - \mu_Y) \cdot f(x_i, y_j)$$

According to the analogy principle of estimation, we can replace x_i and y_j with the observations X_i and Y_j, the probability $f(x_i, y_j)$ with $1/n$, and the mean values with the sample averages. This gives us the following estimator of the covariance:

$$\widehat{Cov}(X,Y) = \frac{1}{n}\sum_{i=1}^{n}(X_i - \bar{X}) \cdot (Y_i - \bar{Y})$$

This estimator is also called the sample covariance.

We often use the correlation coefficient $\rho(X,Y)$ to assess the strength of the relationship between X and Y. As shown in Section 5.5.3, the correlation coefficient is given by:

$$\rho = \rho(X,Y) = \frac{Cov(X,Y)}{\sqrt{V(X) \cdot V(Y)}}$$

We have already found estimators for each of the quantities that appear in the formula for the correlation coefficient. Hence, we simply substitute these estimators into the formula above in order to arrive at an estimator for the correlation coefficient:

$$\hat{\rho} = \frac{\widehat{Cov}(X,Y)}{\sqrt{S_X^2 \cdot S_Y^2}}$$

This estimator is also called the sample correlation coefficient.

In order to assess the quality of the estimator of the correlation coefficient, it is necessary to find its distribution. As above, we can only find an approximate distribution, which is useful when the sample size is large. An approximate distribution is:

$$\hat{\rho} \sim^A N\left(\rho, \frac{\left(1 - \rho^2\right)^2}{n - 2}\right)$$

The approximate variance of $\hat{\rho}$ is thus $V(\hat{\rho}) \approx (1 - \rho^2)^2/(n - 2)$. Note that if the true value of ρ is close to 1, then the variance of the estimator $\hat{\rho}$ is less than if the true value of ρ is close to 0.

12.4   Estimating a distribution

Sometimes an estimate of the entire distribution of a characteristic is required, instead of just an estimate of one or more descriptive measures of the distribution. The distribution of a characteristic is described by the probability (density) function $f_X(x)$ or by the cumulative distribution function $F_X(x)$. We focus on the latter in the following, as it always exists, regardless of whether X is discrete or continuous.

Based on the sample, we can derive an estimate of the cumulative distribution function $F_X(x)$. Suppose we have a simple random sample $(X_1,...,X_n)$ of the characteristic that we want to study. The cumulative distribution function is defined as $F_X(x) = P(X \leq x)$ (see Section 4.2.2 in Chapter 4). We will now use the analogy principle of estimation once more: the probability of getting an outcome of X that is less than or equal to x corresponds in the sample to the proportion of observations that are less than or equal to x. Thus, we get the following estimator,

$\hat{F}_X(x)$, of the cumulative distribution function $F_X(x)$, which is called the *empirical distribution function.*

Empirical distribution function:

$$\hat{F}_X(x) = \frac{number\ of\ X_i\text{'s with value} \le x}{n}$$

Example 12.4: Cola consumption – part 2

In Example 12.1, the realised sample was given by:

$$2, 3, 1, 1, 4, 1, 4, 6, 2$$

The estimate of the empirical distribution function is then:

$$\hat{F}(x) = \begin{cases} 0 & if\ x < 1 \\ \frac{3}{9} & if\ 1 \le x < 2 \\ \frac{5}{9} & if\ 2 \le x < 3 \\ \frac{6}{9} & if\ 3 \le x < 4 \\ \frac{8}{9} & if\ 4 \le x < 6 \\ 1 & if\ x \ge 6 \end{cases}$$

The empirical distribution function is illustrated in Figure 12.2

Figure 12.2:
Empirical
distribution
function and
sample median

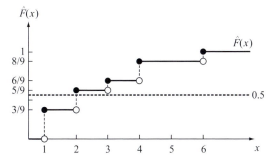

We can find the properties of the empirical distribution function in the same way that we found properties for the sample average. This is important for assessing the quality of the estimate. The empirical distribution function is an unbiased and consistent estimator of the cumulative distribution function. Using the central limit theorem, we can also show that the empirical distribution function for a given value of x is approximately normally distributed. The next box summarises these properties.

Properties of the empirical distribution function. Assuming we have a simple random sample, then:

1. $E\left(\hat{F}_X(x)\right) = F_X(x)$

2. $V\left(\hat{F}_X(x)\right) = \dfrac{F_X(x) \cdot (1 - F_X(x))}{n}$

3. $\hat{F}_X(x) \sim^A N\left(F_X(x), \dfrac{F_X(x) \cdot (1 - F_X(x))}{n}\right)$

Note that the larger the sample (larger n), the smaller the variance, and therefore we get a higher precision.

Example 12.5. Taxes

A regional tax office is interested in how much time people spend completing standard income tax returns. Let X denote the time (measured in hours) needed to fill in the forms. The cumulative distribution function, $F_X(x)$, is therefore the proportion of the population that spends at most x hours on the forms.

In order to assess the quality of the planned study, the tax office considers a number of scenarios. One scenario is to select a simple random sample with $n = 100$ observations. If the reality is that 60% of people spend a maximum of one hour filling out their returns, then the tax office wants to know the probability of the study arriving at an estimate that is within five percentage points of this number.

We can calculate this probability by using the approximate distribution. We want to find $P(0.55 \leq \hat{F}_X(1) \leq 0.65)$. This can be rewritten as:

$$P(0.55 \leq \hat{F}_X(1) \leq 0.65) = P(\hat{F}_X(1) \leq 0.65) - P(\hat{F}_X(1) < 0.55)$$

As we have assumed that $F_X(1) = 0.6$, we can use standardisation to find that:

$$P(\hat{F}_X(1) \le 0.65) = P\left(\frac{\hat{F}_X(1) - F_X(1)}{\sqrt{\dfrac{F_X(1) \cdot (1 - F_X(1))}{n}}} \le \frac{0.65 - F_X(1)}{\sqrt{\dfrac{F_X(1) \cdot (1 - F_X(1))}{n}}}\right)$$

$$= P\left(Z \le \frac{0.65 - 0.6}{\sqrt{\dfrac{0.6 \cdot (1 - 0.6)}{100}}}\right) = P(Z \le 1.02) \approx 0.8461$$

where $Z \sim^A N(0,1)$ according to the box above. Similarly, we can find that:

$$P(\hat{F}_X(1) < 0.55) = P(\hat{F}_X(1) \le 0.55) = P(Z \le -1.02) \approx 0.1539$$

We therefore arrive at:

$$P(0.55 \le \hat{F}_X(1) \le 0.65) \approx 0.8461 - 0.1539 = 0.6922$$

The conclusion is that if indeed 60% of citizens spend a maximum of one hour on their tax returns, then with a probability slightly above 0.69, the study will result in an estimate that lies between 55% and 65%.

12.5 Estimators for quantiles

Quantiles constitute our second group of descriptive measures for a distribution. A p-quantile is a value such that the probability of obtaining an outcome less than the p-quantile is at most p, while the probability of an outcome greater than the p-quantile is at most $(1 - p)$. The formal definition of a p-quantile for a distribution was provided in Section 5.3. In order to use the definition of a p-quantile, we need to know the cumulative distribution function, $F_X(x)$. Since the cumulative distribution function is unknown, we can instead use the empirical distribution function, $\hat{F}_X(x)$, to construct an estimate of a p-quantile.

Let us start by illustrating the idea behind this by considering the most commonly used quantile: the median. The analogy principle of estimation dictates that we must do the same with the sample as we would do with a discrete random variable. Here we would find the median as the value $q_{0.5}$, where the graph for the cumulative distribution function, $F_X(x)$, crosses (or jumps above) the 0.5-line. Since the graph of $F_X(x)$

is a step function (as illustrated in Figure 5.4 in Chapter 5), it can either jump above the 0.5-line at one point or be equal to 0.5 across a whole step. In the latter case, the median is often chosen as the value of x in the middle of the step, although all values within the step are, in principle, median values.

To find the sample median, we replace the unknown cumulative distribution function, $F_X(x)$, with the empirical distribution function, $\hat{F}(x)$, which we introduced in Section 12.4. We can then find the sample median and other sample quantiles using $\hat{F}(x)$, in exactly the same way as we find the median and other quantiles using $F_X(x)$.

If the sample consists of an odd number of elements, the graph for $\hat{F}(x)$ jumps above the 0.5-line exactly at the middle observation in the sample. The middle observation is therefore the sample median. However, if there is an even number of observations, $\hat{F}(x)$ will be equal to 0.5 for all values between the two middle values in the sample. We therefore use the average of these as our sample median. Example 12.6 illustrates this.

For the sample in Example 12.1, the empirical distribution function is:

$$\hat{F}(x) = \begin{cases} 0 & \text{if } x < 1 \\ \frac{3}{9} & \text{if } 1 \leq x < 2 \\ \frac{5}{9} & \text{if } 2 \leq x < 3 \\ \frac{6}{9} & \text{if } 3 \leq x < 4 \\ \frac{8}{9} & \text{if } 4 \leq x < 6 \\ 1 & \text{if } x \geq 6 \end{cases}$$

This was illustrated in Figure 12.1. In this case, the sample median is seen to be equal to 2.

If there were an extra observation in the sample with, for example, the value 6, the empirical distribution function would instead look like this:

$$\hat{F}(x) = \begin{cases} 0 & \text{if } x < 1 \\ \frac{3}{10} & \text{if } 1 \leq x < 2 \\ \frac{5}{10} & \text{if } 2 \leq x < 3 \\ \frac{6}{10} & \text{if } 3 \leq x < 4 \\ \frac{8}{10} & \text{if } 4 \leq x < 6 \\ 1 & \text{if } x \geq 6 \end{cases}$$

Figure 12.3:
Empirical distribution function and sample median

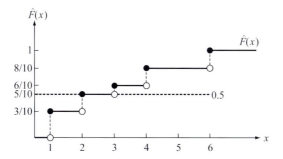

This is illustrated in Figure 12.3. Now the sample median is equal to 2.5.

There is another method of estimating a p-percentile, which gives the same result. In Chapter 2 (Section 2.3.2), we defined a p-quantile for a real population. Using that definition, we sorted the values of a characteristic in size order. The value that separates the largest and smallest values into two equal groups is the median. We can do something similar using the sample, but first we have to define an *order statistic*.

> The **kth-order statistic** is the kth smallest observation in the sample, and is written as $X_{(k)}$.

The first-order statistic is the smallest observation in the sample, and the nth-order statistic is the largest.

Example 12.7: Order statistics

Assume the realised sample is (3,8,5,9,5,1). The realised order statistics are therefore: $x_{(1)} = 1$, $x_{(2)} = 3$, $x_{(3)} = 5$, $x_{(4)} = 5$, $x_{(5)} = 8$, $x_{(6)} = 9$. Note that several order statistics can assume the same value.

We can determine sample quantiles with the help of order statistics. The box below shows the formulas, and the subsequent example illustrates the calculations.

Estimators for quantiles using order statistics. In a simple random sample, the estimator, $\hat{q}_p$, for a p-quantile is:

$$\hat{q}_p = \begin{cases} X_{([n \cdot p+1])} & \text{if } [n \cdot p] \neq n \cdot p \\ \dfrac{1}{2} \cdot \left(X_{(n \cdot p)} + X_{(n \cdot p+1)} \right) & \text{if } [n \cdot p] = n \cdot p \end{cases}$$

where $[n \cdot p + 1]$ is the integer value of $n \cdot p + 1$.

Specifically, the estimator, $\hat{q}_{0.5}$, for the median is:

$$\hat{q}_{0.5} = \begin{cases} X_{\left(\frac{n+1}{2}\right)} & \text{if } n \text{ is odd} \\ \dfrac{1}{2}\left(X_{\left(\frac{n}{2}\right)} + X_{\left(\frac{n}{2}+1\right)} \right) & \text{if } n \text{ is even} \end{cases}$$

Using the formulas in the box above, we can find estimates of p-quantiles without first having to find the empirical distribution function, $\hat{F}(x)$.

Example 12.8: Cola consumption – part 4

Using the sample of nine observations from the previous examples, the sorted sample becomes:

$$1, 1, 1, 2, 2, 3, 4, 4, 6$$

Let us find the estimator for the 0.25-quantile. Since $n \cdot p = 9 \cdot 0.25 = 2.25$, the integer value of $n \cdot p$ is equal to 2. Since $[n \cdot p + 1] = [3.25] = 3$, we have to use observation number 3 in the sorted sample as the estimator for the 0.25-quantile, i.e. the value 1. Similarly, $n \cdot p = 9 \cdot 0.5 = 4.5$, whereby the estimator of the median becomes the fifth (the middle) observation in the sorted sample.

We can work out an approximate distribution for the estimator of a p-quantile. The result applies only for $0 < p < 1$ and when X is continuous. If $f_X(x)$ is the probability density function for X, then:

$$\hat{q}_p \sim^A N\left(q_p, \frac{p \cdot (1-p)}{\left(f_X(q_p) \right)^2} \cdot \frac{1}{n} \right)$$

We can see that the variance is generally highest when we want to estimate the median, where $p = 0.5$.

12.6   Exercises

1. Review questions
   a) Explain the analogy principle of estimation.
   b) What is the sample variance and for what is it an estimator?
   c) What are the properties of the sample variance?
   d) How do we estimate higher order moments?
   e) How do we estimate the covariance and the correlation coeffi-
      cient?
   f) Explain how we derive the empirical distribution function.
   g) How can we use the empirical distribution function to estimate
      p-quantiles?

2. The quality-control team in a soft drinks factory selects a simple
   random sample of 18 bottles and measures their content in centilitres. They get the following results:

24.82	25.12	25.15	25.09	24.98	25.03
25.23	25.11	25.38	25.19	24.87	25.04
24.89	24.96	25.03	25.10	25.03	24.94

   a) Depict the sample in a histogram with width 0,1 centilitres.
   b) Calculate the sample average.
   c) Determine the sample variance.
   d) Calculate the sample median and compare with the sample aver-
      age. Is there a difference?
   e) Calculate the sample quartiles.

3. A newspaper held a vote about attitudes to smoking bans in Danish
   educational institutions. The survey was conducted via the Internet,
   and 634 people participated in it. A total of 429 replied that they
   were in favour, while the rest were against.
   a) What is the relevant population in this example?
   b) What type of population is it? (Hint: see Section 6.1)
   c) Discuss under which circumstances we can reasonably consider
      the participants as a simple random sample from this population.
   d) What is the sample estimate of the proportion of opponents of
      smoking in the population?

4. A study wants to examine the correlation between two random variables, X and Y. Assume that you have a simple random sample with $n = 20$ observations, and you want to find the probability of getting a sample correlation coefficient of between -0.10 and 0.10 if the true value of the correlation coefficient is 0.

a) Calculate the above probability with the help of approximate distribution of the sample correlation coefficient given in Section 12.3.

b) An alternative approximate distribution of the sample correlation coefficient is based on the following result:

$$\sqrt{n-3} \cdot \frac{1}{2} \cdot \left(\log\left[\frac{1+\hat{\rho}}{1-\hat{\rho}}\right] - \log\left[\frac{1+\rho}{1-\rho}\right] \right) \sim^{A} N(0,1)$$

This should provide a better approximation than the one given in Section 12.3 when the sample size is small. Calculate the above probability using this approximation instead and compare it with the result from a).

13 Confidence intervals

In chapters 10 to 12, we considered how to construct estimators of unknown descriptive measures of a distribution – or the distribution itself – by means of a sample. The typical example is to use the sample average, $\overline{X}$ as an estimate of the mean value, μ. As the estimates are constructed from a sample, different samples can result in different estimates. There is thus a natural element of uncertainty involved in constructing an estimate, and $\overline{X}$ will only rarely be equal to μ. The hope is that $\overline{X}$ is close to μ, and we can also use the distribution for $\overline{X}$ to work out the probability of $\overline{X}$ being close to μ. The idea behind *confidence intervals* is to include aspects of the distribution of $\overline{X}$, in order to say something about the uncertainty of the estimate in a simple manner.

While $\overline{X}$ is an estimate in the form of a single number, a confidence interval is an estimate in the form of a range of numbers. Confidence intervals are used as estimates because it is possible to construct them in such a way that they also say something about the uncertainty of the estimators, and thereby become more informative than a single number. In principle, we could report the whole distribution of $\overline{X}$, because it contains all of the relevant information about the uncertainty of $\overline{X}$. However, we might easily lose sight of the important features when looking at the entire distribution. This was the reason that we defined various descriptive measures in Chapter 5 that try to extract the most relevant aspects of a distribution.

In order to construct a confidence interval for an unknown mean value, for example, we find the lower and upper limits of the interval, such that the unknown value lies within these limits with a certain probability.

The confidence intervals in this chapter are constructed from the results about the different estimators and their distributions from chapters 10 to 12. In Section 13.1, we look at the confidence interval for a mean value when we have a simple random sample. We also use this section to illustrate the general idea behind confidence intervals. Stratified random samples are covered in Section 13.2. In Section 13.3, we look at confidence intervals for the variance, while sections 13.4 and 13.5 deal with confidence intervals for differences between two mean values, and two variances, respectively. Finally, in Section 13.6, we look at how to determine the sample size in order to achieve a certain degree of precision in an estimate, as measured by the width of the confidence interval.

13.1 Confidence interval for the mean value with a simple random sample

In this section we will show how to construct a confidence interval for the mean value, μ, with a simple random sample. The section also serves to illustrate the general principle in the construction of a confidence interval. A confidence interval consists of a lower limit, W_{lower} and an upper limit, W_{upper}, within which lies – with a certain probability – the unknown value that we are studying. The question is how to choose the limits W_{lower} and W_{upper}, so that the interval $\hat{I} = [W_{lower}, W_{upper}]$ contains the unknown value with this prespecified probability. In this section, we address that question in the case of a confidence interval for the mean value.

We know that the sample average, $\overline{X}$, is an unbiased estimate of the mean value μ. The obvious choice is therefore to build on $\overline{X}$ when constructing the interval. Since the approximate distribution of $\overline{X}$ is a normal distribution, which is symmetrical, we will also make the confidence interval symmetrical around $\overline{X}$. Formally, this can be written as:

$$\hat{I} = [W_{lower}, W_{upper}] = [\overline{X} - k; \overline{X} + k]$$

where k is a positive number. Because $\overline{X}$ is random (the estimate is uncertain), the confidence interval will not always contain the true mean value, μ. This depends on the concrete value of $\overline{X}$. Sometimes it may miss μ by a wide margin, but with the help of the distribution for $\overline{X}$, we can calculate the probability that the interval will contain μ, as the following example shows.

Suppose we have selected a simple random sample of 10 normally distributed observations with an unknown mean value, μ, and a known variance, $\sigma^2 = 16$. In this particular case, we know from Chapter 10 that the sample average, $\overline{X}$, is also normally distributed: $\overline{X} \sim N(\mu, \sigma^2/n) = N(\mu, 16/10)$. We now construct the following confidence interval for the mean value, μ, by setting $k = 1$:

$$\hat{I} = [W_{lower}, W_{upper}] = [\bar{X} - 1, \bar{X} + 1].$$

We can work out the probability of obtaining a value of $\bar{X}$ so that the interval $[\bar{X} - 1, \bar{X} + 1]$ contains μ:

$$P(\mu \in \hat{I}) = P(\mu \in [\bar{X} - 1, \bar{X} + 1]) = P(\bar{X} - 1 \leq \mu \leq \bar{X} + 1)$$

where "$\in$" means "belongs to". This probability can be rewritten as:

$$
\begin{aligned}
P(\bar{X} - 1 \leq \mu \leq \bar{X} + 1) &= P(-1 \leq \mu - \bar{X} \leq 1) \\
&= P(-1 - \mu \leq -\bar{X} \leq 1 - \mu) \\
&= P(1 + \mu \geq \bar{X} \geq -1 + \mu) \\
&= P(\mu - 1 \leq \bar{X} \leq \mu + 1)
\end{aligned}
$$

We can now use the fact that $\bar{X}$ is normally distributed, $\bar{X} \sim N(\mu, 16/10)$, to determine this probability with the help of the rules outlined in Section 6.5:

$$
\begin{aligned}
P(\mu - 1 \leq \bar{X} \leq \mu + 1) &= \Phi\left(\frac{\mu + 1 - \mu}{\sigma}\right) - \Phi\left(\frac{\mu + 1 - \mu}{\sigma}\right) \\
&= \Phi\left(\frac{1}{\sqrt{16/10}}\right) - \Phi\left(\frac{1}{\sqrt{16/10}}\right) \\
&= 0.79 - 0.21 = 0.58
\end{aligned}
$$

As can be seen, the probability that the confidence interval will contain the unknown mean value, μ, is 58%. The range is therefore called a 0.58-confidence interval.

In Example 13.1, we started by defining the confidence interval as the sample average plus and minus one: $\hat{I} = [W_{lower}, W_{upper}] = [\bar{X} - 1, \bar{X} + 1]$. We then calculated the probability of obtaining a value of the sample average $\bar{X}$, so that the interval, $[\bar{X} - 1, \bar{X} + 1]$, would contain the mean value, μ. In this context, it is important to remember that it is the interval that is stochastic, whereas the mean value, μ, is fixed – it is just unknown.

Typically, however, and unlike Example 13.1, we do it the other way around. We set the probability for the confidence interval in advance, and instead calculate the lower and upper limits necessary to achieve this probability. Therefore, if we want the confidence interval to contain the true mean value, μ, with the probability $1 - \alpha$, then we must find the constant, k, that satisfies the following:

$$
\begin{aligned}
1 - \alpha &= P\left(\mu \in \hat{I}\right) \\
&= P\left(\mu \in [\bar{X} - k; \bar{X} + k]\right) \\
&= P\left(\bar{X} - k \leq \mu \leq \bar{X} + k\right) \\
&= P\left(\mu - k \leq \bar{X} \leq \mu + k\right)
\end{aligned}
$$

In other words, we must determine k so the probability that the stochastic variable $\bar{X}$ will assume a value between $\mu - k$ and $\mu + k$, is $1 - \alpha$. We call $1 - \alpha$ the confidence level.

13.1.1   The general case with a simple random sample

In order to calculate k, we must know the distribution of $\bar{X}$. We only have this information in special cases, as in Example 13.1, where the observations in the sample are normally distributed. However, from the central limit theorem we know that $\bar{X}$ is approximately normally distributed when the sample size, n, is sufficiently large: $\bar{X} \sim^A N\left(\mu, \sigma^2/n\right)$. The standardised sample average therefore approximately follows a standard normal distribution:

$$
Z = \frac{\bar{X} - \mu}{\sqrt{\sigma^2/n}} \sim^A N(0, 1)
$$

We can exploit this in the pursuit of k by rewriting the above probability as an expression for Z:

$$
\begin{aligned}
1 - \alpha &= P\left(\mu - k \leq \bar{X} \leq \mu + k\right) = P\left(-k \leq \bar{X} - \mu \leq k\right) \\
&= P\left(\frac{-k}{\sqrt{\sigma^2/n}} \leq \frac{\bar{X} - \mu}{\sqrt{\sigma^2/n}} \leq \frac{k}{\sqrt{\sigma^2/n}}\right) \\
&= P\left(-\frac{k}{\sqrt{\sigma^2/n}} \leq Z \leq \frac{k}{\sqrt{\sigma^2/n}}\right)
\end{aligned}
$$

We have now rewritten our confidence interval as a probability for the random variable Z. We can now use the fact that the approximate distribution for Z is known.

Let $a = k/\sqrt{\sigma^2/n}$. We must then find the value of a where:

$$1 - \alpha = P\big(-a \le Z \le a\big)$$

Since $Z \sim^A N(0,1)$, the solution is to set a equal to the $(1-\alpha/2)$-quantile of the standard normal distribution, and $-a$ equal to the $(\alpha/2)$-quantile: $a = Z_{1-\alpha/2}$ and $-a = Z_{\alpha/2} = -Z_{1-\alpha/2}$. We can see that this is the solution by inserting in the expression above:

$$P\big(-a \le Z \le a\big) =^A \Phi\big(a\big) - \Phi\big(-a\big) = \Phi\big(Z_{1-\alpha/2}\big) - \Phi\big(Z_{\alpha/2}\big)$$
$$= 1 - \alpha/2 - \alpha/2 = 1 - \alpha$$

where $=^A$ indicates that the result is only approximately true because Z is approximately normally distributed.

Figure 13.1:
$Z_{\alpha/2}$ and $Z_{1-\alpha/2}$

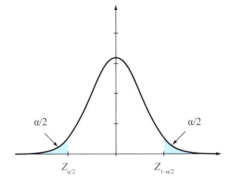

$\alpha/2$ $\alpha/2$

$Z_{\alpha/2}$ $Z_{1-\alpha/2}$

After determining that $a = Z_{1-\alpha/2}$, we can solve for k:

$$k = Z_{1-\alpha/2} \cdot \sqrt{\sigma^2/n}$$

By inserting this expression in $\hat{I} = [\bar{X} - k, \bar{X} + k]$, we obtain the $(1-\alpha)$-confidence interval as:

$$\left[\bar{X} - Z_{1-\alpha/2} \cdot \sqrt{\sigma^2/n} \ , \ \bar{X} + Z_{1-\alpha/2} \cdot \sqrt{\sigma^2/n} \right]$$

However, we can only use this confidence interval if we know the variance, σ^2. In practice, the variance is typically unknown, but we can estimate it with the sampling variance, S^2. In general, therefore, it is possible to approximate the $(1-\alpha)$-confidence interval for the mean value with the following interval:

Confidence interval for the mean value – the general case

With a simple random sample, $(X_1,...,X_n)$, where $E(X_i) = \mu$ and $V(X_i) = \sigma^2$, the approximate $(1 - \alpha)$-confidence interval for the mean value, μ, is:

$$\left[\overline{X} - Z_{1-\alpha/2} \cdot \sqrt{S^2/n} \;,\; \overline{X} + Z_{1-\alpha/2} \cdot \sqrt{S^2/n} \right]$$

where $Z_{1-\alpha/2}$ is the $(1 - \alpha/2)$-quantile from the standard normal distribution, and S^2 (the sampling variance) is the estimator for σ^2. If σ^2 is known, S^2 is just replaced by σ^2.

The difference between a confidence interval for the mean value and the sample average is that the confidence interval provides information about the uncertainty of the sample average, rather than just a single number. An estimator that results in a single estimate is known as a *point estimator*, while the confidence interval is known as an *interval estimator*.

The confidence interval above is approximate because we have not assumed anything about the distribution of the observations in the sample. However, there are a number of special cases, where we can use information about the distribution of the observations to derive exact confidence intervals. Some of these special cases are the subject of the following subsections.

13.1.2 Simple random sample of normally distributed observations with known variance

If the sample observations are normally distributed with known variance, σ^2, then we know that the exact distribution of the standardised sample average, Z, is standard normal, and this is also the case when the sample size is small. Therefore, the confidence interval above is also exact, since it is derived from the distribution of Z:

13.1.3 Simple random sample of normally distributed observations with unknown variance

If the sample observations are normally distributed with unknown variance, it can be shown that $\left(\overline{X} - \mu \right) / \sqrt{S^2/n}$ follows a so-called t-distribution with $n - 1$ degrees of freedom. This is written in the following way:

$$\frac{\overline{X} - \mu}{\sqrt{S^2/n}} \sim t(n - 1)$$

The t-distribution with $n - 1$ degrees of freedom is very similar to the normal distribution. The graph of the density function has "fatter tails", indicating a slightly higher probability of extreme values. In fact, the t-distribution is a whole family of distributions: the t-distribution with one degree of freedom, the t-distribution with two degrees of freedom, and so on. The more degrees of freedom, the closer the t-distribution gets to the standard normal distribution, as shown in Figure 13.2.

Figure 13.2:
The standard normal distribution and two t-distributions

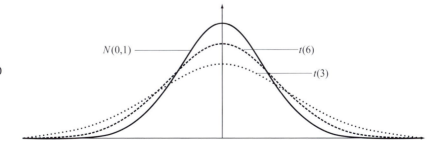

Since the probabilities depend on the degrees of freedom, tabulating all of the cumulative probabilities would be beyond the scope of this book. Instead, Table 3 contains the most important quantiles for a range of different degrees of freedom. For example, the 0.975-quantile of a t-distribution with 15 degrees of freedom is 2.13. Therefore, the 0.025-quantile in a t-distribution with 15 degrees of freedom is equal to -2.13 because all t-distributions are symmetric around 0. If the degrees of freedom exceed 50, the quantiles from the standard normal distribution are used, since the t-distribution with 50 (or more) degrees of freedom is almost identical to the normal distribution.

We can now write up the exact confidence interval in this case. It is very similar to the confidence interval from the previous subsection, only with $Z_{1-\alpha/2}$ replaced by the $(1 - \alpha/2)$-quantile from the t-distribution with $n - 1$ degrees of freedom: $t_{1-\alpha/2}(n - 1)$.

Confidence interval for mean value – normally distributed observations and unknown variance

With a simple random sample, $(X_1,...,X_n)$, where $X_i \sim N(\mu,\sigma^2)$ and σ^2 is unknown, the exact $(1 - \alpha)$-confidence interval for the mean value, μ, is:

$$\left[\overline{X} - t_{1-\alpha/2}(n - 1) \cdot \sqrt{S^2/n} \ , \ \overline{X} + t_{1-\alpha/2}(n - 1) \cdot \sqrt{S^2/n} \right]$$

where $t_{1-\alpha/2}(n - 1)$ is the $(1 - \alpha/2)$-quantile from the t-distribution with $n - 1$ degrees of freedom, and S^2 (the sampling variance) is the estimator for σ^2.

Although this result differs from the general case in Section 13.1.1, it does not mean that the latter is wrong. The reason for the difference is that the result in 13.1.1 is only approximate, while the result above is exact. When n is large, the t-distribution looks like the standard normal distribution, and the difference between the two confidence intervals disappears.

Example 13.2: Milk in daycare institutions – part 1

In order to determine the expected weekly demand for milk at a children's daycare institution, 31 kindergartens are asked about their consumption of milk in the previous week. The sample average is found to be $\overline{X} = 117.43$ litres and the sample variance is $S^2 = 125.21$. It is assumed that the 31 kindergartens constitute a simple random sample of normally distributed observations. Therefore, the exact 0.95-confidence interval ($\alpha = 0.05$) for the expected demand (the mean value) is given by:

$$\hat{I} = \left[117.43 - 2.02 \cdot \sqrt{125.21/31} \; , \; 117.43 + 2.02 \cdot \sqrt{125.21/31}\right]$$

$$= \left[117.43 - 4.06 \; , \; 117.43 + 4.06\right]$$

$$= \left[113.37 \; , \; 121.49\right]$$

since we are using the 97.5%-percentile from the t-distribution with $31-1 = 30$ degrees of freedom, which is 2.02. If, on the other hand, we have doubts about whether the observations are normally distributed, then we can use the approximate formula from Section 13.1.1. In that case, we must use the standard normal distribution instead of the t-distribution. In the standard normal distribution, the 97.5%-percentile is equal to 1.96:

$$\hat{I} = \left[117.43 - 1.96 \cdot \sqrt{125.21/31} \; , \; 117.43 + 1.96 \cdot \sqrt{125.21/31}\right]$$

$$= \left[117.43 - 3.94 \; , \; 117.43 + 3.94\right]$$

$$= \left[113.49 \; , \; 121.37\right]$$

This result is only approximate but, on the other hand, we are not relying on the observations being normally distributed. Note, however, that the difference between the two intervals above is relatively small.

13.1.4 Simple random sample of Bernoulli-distributed observations

For some distributions, the variance can be written as a function of the mean value. This is the case for a Bernoulli-distributed random variable, $X \sim \text{Ber}(p)$, where p is the probability that $X = 1$. As we showed in Chapter 6.1, $E(X) = \mu = p$ and $V(X) = p \cdot (1 - p)$. This means that we can use the estimator of the mean value to estimate the variance, instead of relying on the sample variance. The result is usually a more precise estimator of the variance because this method uses more information about the distribution than the sample variance does.

When the observations are Bernoulli-distributed, we therefore use $\bar{p} \cdot (1 - \bar{p})$ as the estimator of the variance instead af S^2, where $\bar{p}$ is the sample average, i.e. the estimate of the unknown probability or proportion, p. The confidence interval for the mean value, which in this case is also the proportion, p, is therefore calculated as follows:

Confidence interval for a proportion – Bernoulli-distributed observations

With a simple random sample, $(X_1,...,X_n)$, where $X_i \sim \text{Ber}(p)$, the approximate $(1 - \alpha)$-confidence interval for the mean value (the proportion), p, is:

$$\left[\overline{p} - Z_{1-\alpha/2} \cdot \sqrt{\frac{\overline{p} \cdot (1 - \overline{p})}{n}} \ , \ \overline{p} + Z_{1-\alpha/2} \cdot \sqrt{\frac{\overline{p} \cdot (1 - \overline{p})}{n}} \right]$$

where $Z_{1-\alpha/2}$ is the $(1 - \alpha/2)$-quantile from the standard normal distribution, and $\overline{p}$ is the sample average.

Example 13.3: A supermarket chain – part 1

A supermarket chain wants to set up a 0.95-confidence interval for the unknown proportion of a region's population who shop with it. Out of a simple random sample of 400 individuals, 116 shopped with the chain, i.e. $\overline{p} = 116/400 = 0.29$. The approximate confidence interval is therefore:

$$\hat{I} = \left[0.29 - 1.96 \cdot \sqrt{\frac{0.29 \cdot (1 - 0.29)}{400}} \ , \ 0.29 + 1.96 \cdot \sqrt{\frac{0.29 \cdot (1 - 0.29)}{400}} \right]$$

$$= \left[0.29 - 0.044 \ , \ 0.29 + 0.044 \right]$$

$$= \left[0.246 \ , \ 0.334 \right]$$

because $Z_{1-\alpha/2} = Z_{1-0,05/2} = Z_{0,975} = 1.96$.

13.1.5 Confidence intervals for the mean value with a simple random sample – an overview

Table 13.1 summarises the general cases from Section 13.1.1 and the special cases in sections 13.1.2 to 13.1.4.

Table 13.1: Confidence intervals for mean value with simple random sample

The general case: Large sample size (section 13.1.1)	
σ^2 known:	$\left[\bar{X} - Z_{1-\alpha/2} \cdot \sigma/\sqrt{n} \ , \ \bar{X} + Z_{1-\alpha/2} \cdot \sigma/\sqrt{n} \right]$
σ^2 unknown:	$\left[\bar{X} - Z_{1-\alpha/2} \cdot S/\sqrt{n} \ , \ \bar{X} + Z_{1-\alpha/2} \cdot S/\sqrt{n} \right]$
Normally distribution observations (sections 13.1.2 and 13.1.3)	
σ^2 known:	$\left[\bar{X} - Z_{1-\alpha/2} \cdot \sigma/\sqrt{n} \ , \ \bar{X} + Z_{1-\alpha/2} \cdot \sigma/\sqrt{n} \right]$
σ^2 unknown:	$\left[\bar{X} - t_{1-\alpha/2}(n-1) \cdot S/\sqrt{n} \ , \ \bar{X} + t_{1-\alpha/2}(n-1) \cdot S/\sqrt{n} \right]$
Confidence interval for a proportion: $X_i \sim \text{Ber}(p)$ **and large sample size (section 13.1.4)**	
σ^2 unknown:*	$\left[\bar{p} - Z_{1-\alpha/2} \cdot \sqrt{\bar{p} \cdot (1 - \bar{p})/n} \ , \ \bar{p} + Z_{1-\alpha/2} \cdot \sqrt{\bar{p} \cdot (1 - \bar{p})/n} \right]$

Notes:
1. $Z_{1-\alpha/2}$ is the $(1 - \alpha/2)$-quantile from the standard normal distribution.
2. $t_{1-\alpha/2}(n-1)$ is the $(1 - \alpha/2)$-quantile from the t-distribution with $n - 1$ degree of freedom.
3. $1 - \alpha$ is the confidence interval.
* If σ^2 is known in this case, p will also be known.

13.2 Confidence interval for the mean value with stratified sampling

In Chapter 11, we looked at stratified sampling. The idea is that, by dividing the population into m homogeneous strata and then selecting simple random samples from each of those strata, we can obtain a more precise estimate of the unknown population's mean value, μ, than with a simple random sample of the same size. In this case, to calculate the confidence interval for μ we have to use the stratified sample average and its variance, which we derived in Chapter 11.

The stratified sample average is:

$$\bar{X}_{st} = \sum_{j=1}^{m} w_j \cdot \bar{X}_j = \sum_{j=1}^{m} \frac{N_j}{N_{pop}} \cdot \bar{X}_j$$

where w_j is stratum j's proportion of the in the total population, and $\bar{X}_j$ is the sample average from stratum j:

$$\overline{X}_j = \frac{1}{n_j}\sum_{i=1}^{n_j} X_{i,j}$$

and n_j is the size of the sample from stratum j. The variance of the stratified sample average $\overline{X}_{st}$ is:

$$V\left(\overline{X}_{st}\right) = \sum_{j=1}^{m} w_j^2 \cdot \frac{\sigma_j^2}{n_j}$$

where σ_j^2 is the variance in stratum j. Since σ_j^2 is typically unknown, we can estimate the variance of $\overline{X}_{st}$ by replacing σ_j^2 with the sample variance, S_j^2:

$$\hat{V}\left(\overline{X}_{st}\right) = \sum_{j=1}^{m} w_j^2 \cdot \frac{\sigma_j^2}{n_j} = \sum_{j=1}^{m} w_j^2 \cdot \frac{S_j^2}{n_j}$$

where the sample variance from stratum j is given by:

$$S_j^{2} = \frac{1}{n_j - 1}\sum_{i=1}^{n_j}\left(X_{i,j} - \overline{X}_j\right)^2$$

To construct a confidence interval for the unknown mean, μ, we exploit the fact that the estimator, $\overline{X}_{st}$, is approximately normally distributed with mean value μ and variance $V(\overline{X}_{st})$ when the sample size is large. The confidence interval therefore looks exactly the same as before:

Confidence interval for mean value – stratified sample

With stratified random sampling from a population divided into m strata, the approximate $(1 - \alpha)$-confidence interval for the mean value, μ, is:

$$\left[\bar{X}_{st} - Z_{1-\alpha/2} \cdot \sqrt{\hat{V}\left(\bar{X}_{st}\right)} \; , \; \bar{X}_{st} + Z_{1-\alpha/2} \cdot \sqrt{\hat{V}\left(\bar{X}_{st}\right)} \right]$$

where $Z_{1-\alpha/2}$ is the $(1 - \alpha/2)$-quantile from the standard normal distribution and $\bar{X}_{st}$ is the stratified sample average with estimated variance:

$$\hat{V}\left(\bar{X}_{st}\right) = \sum_{j=1}^{m} w_j^2 \cdot \frac{S_j^2}{n_j} \; , \text{ where: } S_j^2 = \frac{1}{n_j - 1} \sum_{i=1}^{n_j} \left(X_{i,j} - \bar{X}_j\right)^2$$

Where $\bar{X}_j$ is the sample average from stratum j with sample size n_j, and $w_j = N_j / N_{pop}$ is stratum j's proportion of the total population. If the stratum variances are known, then σ_j^2 replaces S_j^2.

Example 13.4: Advertising in stores

The manufacturer in Examples 11.1 to 11.3 divided the population into two strata (stores in Jutland and stores on the islands) containing 160 and 240 elements, respectively. He has now selected a sample of eight observations from Jutland and 12 observations from the islands. The results are as follows:

$$\bar{X}_{jut} = 1.5 \qquad S_{jut}^2 = 1.73$$
$$\bar{X}_{isl} = 1.1 \qquad S_{isl}^2 = 1.32$$

The stratified sample average is:

$$\bar{X}_{st} = \sum_{j=1}^{2} w_j \cdot \bar{X}_j = 0.4 \cdot 1.5 + 0.6 \cdot 1.1 = 1.26$$

If the selection from the individual strata is a simple random sample, then the estimated variance is:

$$\hat{V}\left(\bar{X}_{st}\right) = \sum_{j=1}^{2} w_j^2 \cdot \frac{S_j^2}{n_j} = 0.4^2 \cdot \frac{1.73}{8} + 0.6^2 \cdot \frac{1.32}{12} = 0.0742$$

and the 0.95 confidence interval is therefore given by:

$$\hat{I} = \left[1.26 - 1.96 \cdot \sqrt{0.0742} \ , \ 1.26 + 1.96 \cdot \sqrt{0.0742} \right] = [0.73 \ , \ 1.79]$$

As we saw in Chapter 11, the variance for $\bar{X}_{st}$ changes slightly if the selection from each stratum is *without* replacement. In such cases, in the box above we would have to use the following expression for the estimated variance of $\bar{X}_{st}$:

$$\hat{V}\left(\bar{X}_{st} \right) = \sum_{j=1}^{m} w_j^2 \cdot \frac{S_j^2}{n_j} \cdot \frac{N_j}{N_{j-1}} \cdot \left(1 - \frac{n_j}{N_j} \right)$$

13.3   Confidence interval for the variance

We can also construct a confidence interval for an unknown variance, σ^2. The derivation of the confidence interval follows the same recipe as for the mean value above. We must find an interval:

$$\hat{I} = \left[W_{lower}, W_{upper} \right]$$

where W_{lower} is the lower limit, and W_{upper} is the upper limit.

As with the mean value, the construction of the confidence interval is based on the estimator of the unknown value (here, the variance) and the distribution of this estimator. The estimator is the sample variance S^2. One important difference between a mean value and a variance, however, is that a variance can never be negative. Therefore, we will not – as with the mean value – construct a symmetrical confidence interval around the estimate, S^2. The reason is that this would run the risk of the confidence interval including negative values, which we know with certainty the variance, σ^2, cannot assume.

To find the lower and upper limit of the interval, we can use the result from Chapter 12 about the approximate distribution of the sample variance, S^2. There, the result was that:

$$\frac{\left(n - 1 \right) \cdot S^2}{\sigma^2}$$

is approximately χ^2-distributed with $n - 1$ degrees of freedom. The χ^2-distribution was also described in Chapter 12. We use the above expression to construct a confidence interval for the unknown variance, σ^2. If $\chi^2_{\alpha/2}(n-1)$ and $\chi^2_{1-\alpha/2}(n-1)$ are the $\alpha/2$- and $1 - \alpha/2$-quantiles, respectively, from the χ^2-distribution with $n - 1$ degrees of freedom, then we know that there must (approximately) be the probability $1 - \alpha$ of obtaining a value of $(n-1) \cdot S^2/\sigma^2$ that lies between $\chi^2_{\alpha/2}(n-1)$ and $\chi^2_{1-\alpha/2}(n-1)$:

$$P\left(\chi^2_{\alpha/2}(n-1) \leq \frac{(n-1) \cdot S^2}{\sigma^2} \leq \chi^2_{1-\alpha/2}(n-1) \right) =^A 1 - \alpha$$

Note how this corresponds precisely to the procedure in Section 13.1.1, where we also started out by expressing the confidence interval as an interval for the stochastic variable Z, whose approximate distribution we knew. Now, correspondingly, we have an interval for the random variable $(n-1) \cdot S^2/\sigma^2$, which we know the approximate distribution of. We then rewrite this as an interval for the unknown variance, σ^2, as follows:

$$1 - \alpha =^A P\left(\chi^2_{\alpha/2}(n-1) \leq \frac{(n-1) \cdot S^2}{\sigma^2} \leq \chi^2_{1-\alpha/2}(n-1) \right)$$

$$= P\left(\frac{\chi^2_{\alpha/2} \cdot (n-1)}{(n-1) \cdot S^2} \leq \frac{1}{\sigma^2} \leq \frac{\chi^2_{1-\alpha/2} \cdot (n-1)}{(n-1) \cdot S^2} \right)$$

$$= P\left(\frac{(n-1) \cdot S^2}{\chi^2_{1-\alpha/2}(n-1)} \leq \sigma^2 \leq \frac{(n-1) \cdot S^2}{\chi^2_{\alpha/2}(n-1)} \right)$$

This formula gives both lower and upper limits for an approximate $(1 - \alpha)$-confidence interval for the variance. Note that in the case where the observations in the sample are normally distributed, the expression for the confidence interval is exact. The results are summarised in the following box:

Confidence interval for variance

With a simple random sample, $(X_1,...,X_n)$, where $E(X_i) = \mu$ and $V(X_i) = \sigma^2$, the approximate $(1 - \alpha)$-confidence interval for the variance, σ^2 is:

$$\left[\frac{(n-1) \cdot S^2}{\chi^2_{1-\alpha/2}(n-1)} , \frac{(n-1) \cdot S^2}{\chi^2_{\alpha/2}(n-1)} \right]$$

where S^2 (the sample variance) is the estimator for σ^2 and $\chi^2_{\alpha/2}(n-1)$ and $\chi^2_{1-\alpha/2}(n-1)$ are, respectively, the $\alpha/2$- and $(1 - \alpha/2)$-quantiles from the χ^2-distribution with $n-1$ degrees of freedom.

If the observations are normally distributed, $X_i \sim N(\mu,\sigma^2)$, then the confidence interval is exact.

The confidence interval is not symmetrical around S^2 because the χ^2-distribution is not symmetrical. This is in line with our desire not to include negative values in the confidence interval, because we know in advance that variances cannot be negative.

Example 13.5: A stock-market analyst

A stock-market analyst wants to set up a confidence interval for the variance of share dividends from companies in the service industry, and has therefore selected a simple random sample of 51 dividends. The value of the variance estimator is calculated as $S^2 = 59.6$. An approximate 0.95-confidence interval for the unknown variance is therefore:

$$\left[\frac{(51-1) \cdot 59.6}{71.4} , \frac{(51-1) \cdot 59.6}{32.4} \right] = [41.74 , 92.98]$$

because the 0.025-quantile and the 0.975-quantile from the χ^2-distribution with 50 degrees of freedom are, respectively, 32.4 and 71.4.

13.4   Confidence interval for the difference between two mean values

Sometimes, we are interested in examining the difference between two different groups in a population. For example, we might want to study the difference in the average level of education attained by women and men. In this section, we consider confidence intervals for the difference between two mean values, μ_1 and μ_2, for two groups in a population.

13.4.1   The general case

As in the other cases in this chapter, the construction of the confidence interval is based on an estimate of the unknown quantity. The unknown quantity is here $\mu_1 - \mu_2$, where μ_1 is the mean value of a distribution (the first group in the population) and μ_2 is the mean value of another distribution (the second group in the population). We assume that we have a simple random sample from group and that the two samples are independent of each other: $\left(X_{1,1}, \ldots, X_{1,n_1} \right)$ and $\left(X_{2,1}, \ldots, X_{2,n_2} \right)$ where $E\left(X_{1,i} \right) = \mu_1$, $V\left(X_{1,i} \right) = \sigma_1^2$, $E\left(X_{2,i} \right) = \mu_2$ and $V\left(X_{2,i} \right) = \sigma_2^2$. The estimate of $\mu_1 - \mu_2$ is $\overline{X}_1 - \overline{X}_2$, (i.e. the difference between the sample averages from the two samples).

When constructing a confidence interval, the trick, as before, is to find a value whose approximate distribution is known. We know from the central limit theorem that both $\overline{X}_1$ and $\overline{X}_2$ are approximately normally distributed and, because the samples are independent, their difference, $\overline{X}_1 - \overline{X}_2$, is also approximately normally distributed with mean value:

$$E\left(\overline{X}_1 - \overline{X}_2 \right) = E\left(\overline{X}_1 \right) - E\left(\overline{X}_2 \right) = \mu_1 - \mu_2$$

and variance:

$$V\left(\overline{X}_1 - \overline{X}_2 \right) = V\left(\overline{X}_1 \right) + V\left(\overline{X}_2 \right) = \frac{\sigma_1^2}{n_1} + \frac{\sigma_2^2}{n_2}$$

Therefore, the standardised difference:

$$\frac{\left(\overline{X}_1 - \overline{X}_2 \right) - \left(\mu_1 - \mu_2 \right)}{\sqrt{\left(\dfrac{\sigma_1^2}{n_1} + \dfrac{\sigma_2^2}{n_2} \right)}}$$

is approximately standard normal. The probability of obtaining a value of the standardised difference, which is between $Z_{\alpha/2}$ and $Z_{1-\alpha/2}$, i.e. between the $\alpha/2$- and the $(1 - \alpha/2)$-quantiles of the standard normal distribution, is $1 - \alpha$.

Figure 13.3:
$Z_{\alpha/2}$ and $Z_{1-\alpha/2}$

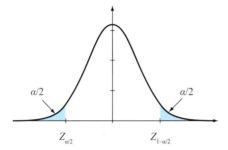

Because of the symmetry of the standard normal distribution, $Z_{\alpha/2} = -Z_{1-\alpha/2}$, and we can therefore write this probability as:

$$P\left(-Z_{1-\alpha/2} \leq \frac{\left(\bar{X}_1 - \bar{X}_2\right) - \left(\mu_1 - \mu_2\right)}{\sqrt{\dfrac{\sigma_1^2}{n_1} + \dfrac{\sigma_2^2}{n_2}}} \leq Z_{1-\alpha/2}\right) =^A 1 - \alpha$$

This can be rewritten as a confidence interval for the unknown difference, $\mu_1 - \mu_2$. Since the variances, σ_1^2 and σ_2^2 are, typically, unknown, then we can replace them with the sample variances, S_1^2 and S_2^2. The result is summarised in the box below.

Confidence interval for difference between two mean values – the general case

With two independent simple random samples, $\left(X_{1,1},\ldots,X_{1,n_1}\right)$ and $\left(X_{2,1},\ldots,X_{2,n_2}\right)$, where $E\left(X_{1,i}\right) = \mu_1, V\left(X_{1,i}\right) = \sigma_1^2, E\left(X_{2,i}\right) = \mu_2$ and $V\left(X_{2,i}\right) = \sigma_2^2$, the approximate $(1 - \alpha)$-confidence interval for the difference between the mean values, $\mu_1 - \mu_2$, is given by:

$$\left[(\bar{X}_1 - \bar{X}_2) - Z_{1-\alpha/2} \cdot \sqrt{\frac{S_1^2}{n_1} + \frac{S_2^2}{n_2}}, \; (\bar{X}_1 - \bar{X}_2) + Z_{1-\alpha/2} \cdot \sqrt{\frac{S_1^2}{n_1} + \frac{S_2^2}{n_2}}\right],$$

where $Z_{1-\alpha/2}$ is the $(1 - \alpha/2)$-quantile from the standard normal distribution, $\bar{X}_1$ and $\bar{X}_2$ are the sample averages, and S_1^2 and S_2^2 are the sample variances. If σ_1^2 and σ_2^2 are known, they replace S_1^2 and S_2^2.

A company has two types of employee in its production department: employees who have undergone a particular training module, and those who have not. When recruiting new employees, the company is in a quandary about whether to hire people with or without previous training. It commissions a consultancy company to study whether there is any difference in average productivity between the two types of worker. The consultant has selected two simple random samples of 30 and 50 observations among individuals with and without training, respectively. The consultancy company finds that two sample averages are $\bar{X} = 22.54$ and $\bar{X} = 19.34$ and that the sample variances are $S_1^2 = 19.13$ and $S_2^2 = 22.25$. A 0.95-confidence interval for the difference between the two mean values can then be constructed as:

$$\left[(22.54 - 19.34) - 1.96 \cdot \sqrt{\frac{19.13}{30} + \frac{22.25}{50}} \right.,$$

$$\left. (22.54 - 19.34) + 1.96 \cdot \sqrt{\frac{19.13}{30} + \frac{22.25}{50}} \right] = \left[1.16 \; , \; 5.24\right]$$

because $Z_{1-0.05/2} = Z_{0.975} = 1.96$. It can be seen that the 0.95-confidence interval does not include 0, which indicates that there is indeed a difference between the two types of worker.

If we know (or believe) that the two variances, σ_1^2 and σ_2^2 are the same, a more accurate estimate of the variance of $\bar{X}_1 - \bar{X}_2$ is obtained by using what is known as the pooled variance estimator. This is given by:

$$S_p^2 = \frac{(n_1 - 1) \cdot S_1^2 + (n_2 - 1) \cdot S_2^2}{n_1 + n_2 - 2}$$

We can then write the confidence interval as:

$$\left[(\bar{X}_1 - \bar{X}_2) - Z_{1-\alpha/2} \cdot \sqrt{S_p^2 \cdot \left(\frac{1}{n_1} + \frac{1}{n_2} \right)} \right.,$$

$$\left. (\bar{X}_1 - \bar{X}_2) + Z_{1-\alpha/2} \cdot \sqrt{S_p^2 \cdot \left(\frac{1}{n_1} + \frac{1}{n_2} \right)} \right]$$

In Example 13.6, the pooled variance estimator is:

$$S_p^{\,2} = \frac{(30-1)\cdot 19.13 + (50-1)\cdot 22.25}{30 + 50 - 2} = 21.09$$

which gives the following confidence interval:

$$\left[(22.54 - 19.34) - 1.96 \cdot \sqrt{21.09 \cdot \left(\frac{1}{30} + \frac{1}{50} \right)} \, , \right.$$

$$\left. (22.54 - 19.34) + 1.96 \cdot \sqrt{21.09 \cdot \left(\frac{1}{30} + \frac{1}{50} \right)} \right] = [1.12 \, , \, 5.28]$$

13.4.2 Confidence interval for the difference between two mean values – an overview

As with confidence intervals for a simple mean value, there are a number of special cases where we can calculate more precise confidence intervals than the approximate interval from Section 13.4.1.

The first case is where the two samples consist of normally distributed observations with known variance. Here, we can show that the confidence interval from Section 13.4.1 is exact, and not just approximate.

Another special case occurs when the observations are normally distributed with unknown variance. Here, we can achieve an exact confidence interval by replacing the quantile from the standard normal distribution, $Z_{1-\alpha/2}$, with the corresponding quantile from the t-distribution with $n_1 + n_2 - 2$ degrees of freedom, $t_{1-\alpha/2}(n_1 + n_2 - 2)$.

The last special case we will mention is when the observations in the samples are Bernoulli-distributed. Here, we calculate $S_1^{\,2}$ and $S_2^{\,2}$ as $\bar{p}_1 \cdot (1 - \bar{p}_1)$ and $\bar{p}_2 \cdot (1 - \bar{p}_2)$, respectively, where $\bar{p}_1$ and $\bar{p}_2$ are the two sample averages (or sample proportions). The results for these special cases are summarised in the box below, along with the general case from Section 13.4.1.

A business school wants to study whether the probability of passing an exam depends upon the teacher who has taught the subject. Let $\bar{p}_1$ be the probability of passing with teacher 1, and $\bar{p}_2$ the probability of passing with teacher 2. The school now selects two simple random samples independently of each other, comprising 25 and 36 students, respectively, from the two teachers' exams. It finds that the proportion of those selected who passed with teacher 1 was $7/25 = 0.28$, while the proportion for teacher 2 was $14/36 = 0.389$. Using the formula from the box above, we can now establish a 0.95-confidence interval for the difference between the true but unknown probabilities, $\bar{p}_1 - \bar{p}_2$:

$$\left[\left(0.28 - 0.389\right) - 1.96 \cdot \sqrt{\frac{0.28 \cdot \left(1 - 0.28\right)}{25} + \frac{0.389 \cdot \left(1 - 0.389\right)}{36}} \right. ,$$

$$\left. \left(0.28 - 0.389\right) + 1.96 \cdot \sqrt{\frac{0.28 \cdot \left(1 - 0.28\right)}{25} + \frac{0.389 \cdot \left(1 - 0.389\right)}{36}} \right]$$

$$= [-0.346 , 0.128]$$

Note that the interval includes the value 0 and therefore, with a confidence level of 0.95, we cannot rule out that the risk of failing the exam is the same with both teachers.

Table 13.2: Confidence interval for the difference between two mean values, $\mu_1 - \mu_2$, using two independent random samples.

The general case: Large sample sizes (section 13.4.1)

σ_1^2 and σ_2^2 known:

$$\left[\left(\bar{X}_1 - \bar{X}_2\right) - Z_{1-\alpha/2} \cdot \sqrt{\frac{\sigma_1^2}{n_1} + \frac{\sigma_2^2}{n_2}}, \ \left(\bar{X}_1 - \bar{X}_2\right) + Z_{1-\alpha/2} \cdot \sqrt{\frac{\sigma_1^2}{n_1} + \frac{\sigma_2^2}{n_2}}\right]$$

σ_1^2 and σ_2^2 unknown:

$$\left[\left(\bar{X}_1 - \bar{X}_2\right) - Z_{1-\alpha/2} \cdot \sqrt{\frac{S_1^2}{n_1} + \frac{S_2^2}{n_2}}, \ \left(\bar{X}_1 - \bar{X}_2\right) + Z_{1-\alpha/2} \cdot \sqrt{\frac{S_1^2}{n_1} + \frac{S_2^2}{n_2}}\right]$$

σ_1^2 and σ_2^2 unknown, but identical:

$$\left[\left(\bar{X}_1 - \bar{X}_2\right) - Z_{1-\alpha/2} \cdot \sqrt{S_p^2 \cdot \left(\frac{1}{n_1} + \frac{1}{n_2}\right)}, \ \left(\bar{X}_1 - \bar{X}_2\right) + Z_{1-\alpha/2} \cdot \sqrt{S_p^2 \cdot \left(\frac{1}{n_1} + \frac{1}{n_2}\right)}\right]$$

hvor: $S_p^2 = \dfrac{(n_1 - 1) \cdot S_1^2 + (n_2 - 1) \cdot S_2^2}{n_1 + n_2 - 2}$

Normally distributed elements:

σ_1^2 and σ_2^2 known:

$$\left[\left(\bar{X}_1 - \bar{X}_2\right) - Z_{1-\alpha/2} \cdot \sqrt{\frac{\sigma_1^2}{n_1} + \frac{\sigma_2^2}{n_2}}, \ \left(\bar{X}_1 - \bar{X}_2\right) + Z_{1-\alpha/2} \cdot \sqrt{\frac{\sigma_1^2}{n_1} + \frac{\sigma_2^2}{n_2}}\right]$$

σ_1^2 and σ_2^2 unknown:

$$\left[\left(\bar{X}_1 - \bar{X}_2\right) - t_{1-\alpha/2}\left(n_1 + n_2 - 2\right) \cdot \sqrt{\frac{S_1^2}{n_1} + \frac{S_2^2}{n_2}}, \ \left(\bar{X}_1 - \bar{X}_2\right) + t_{1-\alpha/2}\left(n_1 + n_2 - 2\right) \cdot \sqrt{\frac{S_1^2}{n_1} + \frac{S_2^2}{n_2}}\right]$$

σ_1^2 and σ_2^2 unknown, but identical:

$$\left[\left(\bar{X}_1 - \bar{X}_2\right) - t_{1-\alpha/2}\left(n_1 + n_2 - 2\right) \cdot \sqrt{S_p^2 \cdot \left(\frac{1}{n_1} + \frac{1}{n_2}\right)}, \ \left(\bar{X}_1 - \bar{X}_2\right) + t_{1-\alpha/2}\left(n_1 + n_2 - 2\right) \cdot \sqrt{S_p^2 \cdot \left(\frac{1}{n_1} + \frac{1}{n_2}\right)}\right]$$

hvor: $S_p^2 = \dfrac{(n_1 - 1) \cdot S_1^2 + (n_2 - 1) \cdot S_2^2}{n_1 + n_2 - 2}$

Confidens interval for difference between two proportions: $X_i \sim \text{Ber}(p)$ and large sample sizes:

σ_1^2 and σ_2^2 unknown:

$$\left[\left(\bar{p}_1 - \bar{p}_2\right) - Z_{1-\alpha/2} \cdot \sqrt{\frac{\bar{p}_1 \cdot \left(1 - \bar{p}_1\right)}{n_1} + \frac{\bar{p}_2 \cdot \left(1 - \bar{p}_2\right)}{n_2}}, \ \left(\bar{p}_1 - \bar{p}_2\right) + Z_{1-\alpha/2} \cdot \sqrt{\frac{\bar{p}_1 \cdot \left(1 - \bar{p}_1\right)}{n_1} + \frac{\bar{p}_2 \cdot \left(1 - \bar{p}_2\right)}{n_2}}\right]$$

Notes:
1. $Z_{1-\alpha/2}$ is the $(1 - \alpha/2)$-quantile from the standard normal distribution.
2. $t_{1-\alpha/2}(n_1 + n_2 - 2)$ is the $(1 - \alpha/2)$-quantile from the t-distribution with $n_1 + n_2 - 2$ degrees of freedom.
3. $1 - \alpha$ is the confidence level.

13.5 Confidence interval for the ratio of two variances

The last type of confidence interval we will look at is for the ratio of two variances. As in Section 13.4, we assume that we are dealing with two independent simple random samples, $\left(X_{1,1}, \ldots, X_{1,n_1}\right)$ and $\left(X_{2,1}, \ldots, X_{2,n_2}\right)$. We will also assume that the observations in the two samples are normally distributed, i.e. $X_{1,i} \sim N\left(\mu_1, \sigma_1^2\right)$ and $X_{2,i} \sim N\left(\mu_2, \sigma_2^2\right)$. We can then construct a confidence interval for the ratio between the two unknown variances, σ_2^2 / σ_1^2, with the help of the estimators of the variances, S_1^2 and S_2^2.

The basis for this confidence interval is that we can show that the value:

$$\frac{S_1^2 / \sigma_1^2}{S_2^2 / \sigma_2^2} = \frac{S_1^2 \cdot \sigma_2^2}{S_2^2 \cdot \sigma_1^2}$$

is F-distributed with $\left(n_1 - 1, n_2 - 1\right)$ degrees of freedom, where n_1 and n_2 are the sizes of the two samples from the two groups in the population. As with the t-distribution and the χ^2-distribution, the F-distribution is a family of distributions. However, unlike the other two, the F-distribution is characterised by two parameters, or two sets of degrees of freedom. We have illustrated one of the distributions in Figure 13.4. Selected quantiles for the F-distribution are listed in Tables 5 and 6 at the back of the book.

Figure 13.4: F-distribution with (5, 9) degrees of freedom

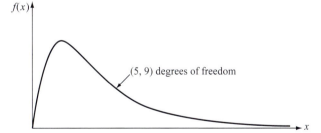

$(5, 9)$ degrees of freedom

If $F_{\alpha/2}\left(n_1 - 1, n_2 - 1\right)$ and $F_{1-\alpha/2}\left(n_1 - 1, n_2 - 1\right)$ are, respectively, the $\alpha/2$- and the $1 - \alpha/2$-quantile from the F-distribution with $\left(n_1 - 1, n_2 - 1\right)$ degrees of freedom, then the probability of observing a value of the above quantity between these two values is equal to $1 - \alpha$:

$$P\left(F_{\alpha/2}(n_1 - 1, n_2 - 1) \leq \frac{S_1^2 \cdot \sigma_2^2}{S_2^2 \cdot \sigma_1^2} \leq F_{1-\alpha/2}(n_1 - 1, n_2 - 1) \right) = 1 - \alpha$$

Figure 13.5:
$F_{\alpha/2}(n_1 - 1, n_2 - 1)$
and
$F_{1-\alpha/2}(n_1 - 1, n_2 - 1)$

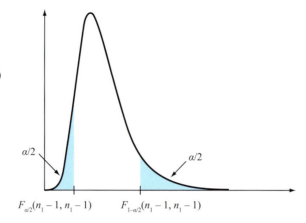

$\alpha/2$ $\alpha/2$

$F_{\alpha/2}(n_1 - 1, n_1 - 1)$ $F_{1-\alpha/2}(n_1 - 1, n_1 - 1)$

This can be rewritten as a confidence interval by isolating σ_2^2/σ_1^2. The result is summarised in the box below.

Confidence interval for the ratio of two variances

With two independent simple random samples, $(X_{1,1},...,X_{1,n_1})$ and $(X_{2,1},...,X_{2,n_2})$, where $X_{1,i} \sim N(\mu_1,\sigma_1^2)$ and $X_{2,i} \sim N(\mu_2,\sigma_2^2)$, the exact $(1 - \alpha)$-confidence interval for the ratio of the two variances σ_2^2/σ_1^2 is:

$$\left[\frac{S_2^{\,2}}{S_1^{\,2}} \cdot F_{\alpha/2}(n_1 - 1, n_2 - 1) \,,\, \frac{S_2^{\,2}}{S_1^{\,2}} \cdot F_{1-\alpha/2}(n_1 - 1, n_2 - 1) \right]$$

where $F_{\alpha/2}(n_1 - 1, n_2 - 1)$ and $F_{1-\alpha/2}(n_1 - 1, n_2 - 1)$ are, respectively, the $\alpha/2$- and $1 - \alpha/2$-quantile from the F-distribution with $(n_1 - 1, n_2 - 1)$ degrees of freedom, and $S_1^{\,2}$ and $S_2^{\,2}$ are the sample variances.

Example 13.9: Training – part 3

Let us try to construct a confidence interval for the ratio of the two sample variances from Example 13.7. The sample variances were $S_1^{\,2} = 19.13$ and $S_2^{\,2} = 22.25$. A 0.95-confidence interval will then look like this:

$$\left[\frac{22.25}{19.13} \cdot 0.50 \,,\, \frac{22.25}{19.13} \cdot 1.88 \right] = [0.582 \,,\, 2.187]$$

since the 0.025-quantile and the 0.975-quantile of the F-distribution with (29,49) degrees of freedom are 0.50 and 1.88, respectively. Since 1 is in the confidence interval, we cannot rule out that the variances are the same with a confidence level of 0.95.

13.6 Determining the sample size based on a confidence interval

The sample size has a direct impact on the estimators' precision and hence the width of a confidence interval. If we want a certain precision, and are also able to decide the sample size, then we can use the confidence interval to determine how large the sample must be in order to achieve the desired precision. For example, we can calculate how large a sample is necessary for the 0.95-confidence interval (and therefore the uncertainty of the estimate) to be no more than two units wide. In this section, we will illustrate this technique in the case where we estimate a mean value.

The confidence interval for a mean value with known variance from Section 13.1.1 is:

$$\left[\bar{X} - Z_{1-\alpha/2} \cdot \sqrt{\sigma^2/n} \; , \; \bar{X} + Z_{1-\alpha/2} \cdot \sqrt{\sigma^2/n} \right]$$

The width of the confidence interval is $2 \cdot Z_{1-\alpha/2} \cdot \sqrt{\sigma^2/n}$. If we want the maximum interval width to be $2 \cdot K$, then we have to choose the sample size n, such that:

$$Z_{1-\alpha/2} \cdot \sqrt{\sigma^2/n} \le K$$

which is the same as:

$$\sigma^2/n \le \frac{K^2}{Z^2_{1-\alpha/2}} \quad \Leftrightarrow \quad \frac{\sigma^2 \cdot Z^2_{1-\alpha/2}}{K^2} \le n$$

The required sample size, n^*, which ensures that we can achieve the desired width $2 \cdot K$ of the confidence interval, is repeated in the box below:

Confidence interval-based sample size for estimating a mean value

In order to obtain a $(1 - \alpha)$-confidence interval for the mean value with a width of (at most) $2 \cdot K$, we need a sample size of (at least):

$$n^* = \frac{\sigma^2}{K^2} \cdot Z^2_{1-\alpha/2}.$$

Note that a narrow confidence interval (a small value of K), requires a large sample size, n^*. Similarly, a large variance, σ^2, of the observations in the sample, or a high level of confidence, $1 - \alpha$, requires a larger sample.

However, in order to calculate n^*, it is necessary to know the variance, σ^2, or an estimate thereof from another study. This is why we sometimes run a pilot study, in which we select a small sample in order to estimate the variance, σ^2.

Example 13.10: Milk in daycare institutions – part 2

In Example 13.2, a sample of 31 kindergartens was selected and the sample variance was calculated as $S^2 = 125.21$. The study is repeated the following year, using the existing estimate of the variance to determine the sample size, which ensures that the 0.95-confidence interval will have a width of (at most) 5 (litres), i.e. $2 \cdot K = 5$. If we use the 0.975-quantile of the standard normal distribution, which is 1.96, then n^* can be calculated as:[16]

$$n^* = \frac{S^2}{K^2} \cdot Z^2_{1-\alpha/2} = \frac{125.21}{(5/2)^2} \cdot 1.96^2 = 76.96$$

A sample of 77 kindergartens is therefore needed in order to achieve the desired precision.

---

16   If, as in Example 13.2, we assume that the elements in the sample are normally distributed, then we should actually use the 0.975-quantile from the relevant t-distribution. However, as this distribution depends on the unknown n, it is somewhat difficult – therefore, we just use the standard normal distribution.

If the sample elements are Bernoulli-distributed, then we know that the variance is $\sigma^2 = p \cdot (1 - p)$, where p is the probability (or proportion) we want to study. Here, the required sample size is given by:

$$n^* = \frac{p \cdot (1 - p)}{K^2} \cdot Z^2_{1-\alpha/2}$$

where p, of course, is unknown. However, we can show that n^* is greatest when $p = 0.5$. We are therefore on the safe side, if we choose:

$$n^* = \frac{0.5 \cdot (1 - 0.5)}{K^2} \cdot Z^2_{1-\alpha/2} = \frac{0.25}{K^2} \cdot Z^2_{1-\alpha/2}$$

Example 13.11: A supermarket chain – part 2

The supermarket chain from Example 13.3 wants a 0.95-confidence interval with a maximum width of 0.1. In that case, it has to select a sample of size:

$$n^* = \frac{0.25}{(0.1/2)^2} \cdot 1.96^2 = 384.16$$

It can therefore conduct 15 fewer interviews compared to the sample from Example 13.3.

13.7 Exercises

1. Review questions
   a) What do you understand by a confidence interval?
   b) Explain in brief how a confidence interval is constructed for a mean value.
   c) Which different types of confidence intervals do we use in connection with a mean value? Explain when the different confidence intervals should be used.
   d) What does the confidence interval look like when we have a stratified sample?
   e) How do you construct the confidence interval for a variance? What assumptions underlie this?

f) Explain the different confidence intervals used for the difference between two mean values.

g) What does a confidence interval for the ratio of two variances look like?

h) Explain how to find the sample size required to achieve a given width of a confidence interval.

2. The soft drinks factory from Exercise 2 in Chapter 12 would like to establish a confidence interval for the mean volume of a drink, based on the selected sample.

a) Write up the 0.95-confidence interval, assuming that the content of a randomly selected drink is normally distributed with a variance of 0.02.

b) Construct a 0.95-confidence interval when the variance is unknown, and compare with the result from question a).

3. In the study in Exercise 3 in Chapter 12, 429 people out of a total of 634 responded that they were against smoking in Danish educational institutions.

a) Construct a 0.95-confidence interval for the proportion of opponents of smoking in the population.

b) Also set up a 0.90- and a 0.99-confidence interval.

4. In a local authority area with 3,431 children, a health visitor selects a simple random sample of 100 children's heights. The sample average is $\overline{X} = 138.4$ cm and the sample variance is $S^2 = 62.32$.

a) Construct a 0.95-confidence interval for the mean height in the population.

b) Does the height 140 cm lie within this interval?

c) If the health visitor instead uses a 0.90- or a 0.99-confidence interval, does that change your conclusion from question b)?

5. A stock-market analyst has two simple random samples with 50 and 43 observations. In the first sample, the sample average is calculated as $\overline{X}_1 = 11.43$ and the sample variance as $S_1^2 = 86.8$. In the second, they are $\overline{X}_2 = 14.47$ and $S_2^2 = 142.7$, respectively.

a) Construct a 0.95-confidence interval for each of the two unknown variances. What assumptions underlie these intervals?

b) Do the two intervals overlap? How would you interpret this?

c) Construct two 0.95-confidence intervals for the mean values. What are the assumptions in this case?

d) Do the intervals from question c) overlap?

e) Construct a 0.95-confidence interval for the difference between the two mean values.

f) Finally, construct a 0.95-confidence interval for the ratio of the two variances.

6. A polling company found that in 1997 and 2002, 74% and 72%, respectively, were against alcohol advertising on TV. The sample size was 957 in 1997 and 1,012 in 2002.

   a) Construct 0.90-, 0.95- and 0.99-confidence intervals for the difference in the two unknown proportions in 1997 and 2002.

   b) Is the value 0 included in these intervals?

   c) What level of significance should we use for the value 0 to be just outside the confidence interval?

7. A bank wants to compare the mean turnover among corporate customers in two of its branches. It selects two samples, one from each branch's clientèle. The results of the two samples are:

	n	$\bar{X}$ (DKK 1,000)	S
Branch 1:	25	1,267.7	210.8
Branch 2:	30	1,443.4	278.0

   a) Construct a 0.95-confidence interval without the use of the pooled variance estimator.

   b) Perform the same procedure using the pooled estimator.

8. In a study of consumption of Spanish red wine in Denmark, the adult population is divided into four income strata. The results of the study are summarised in the table below.

Stratum	N_j	n_j	$\bar{X}_j$	S_j^2
1	1,105	67	6.5	3.34
2	676	61	8.4	6.33
3	957	73	12.4	4.52
4	389	22	3.6	2.12

   a) Construct 0.95-confidence intervals for each of the four unknown stratum mean values, assuming that we have simple random samples from each of the four strata.

b) Construct a 0.95-confidence interval for the mean value of the
   total population.

Now, consider the four samples as a single simple random sample
from the whole population.

c) Calculate the sample average.
d) Construct a 0.95-confidence interval for mean value of the population in this case.
e) Compare your results in questions b) and d).

14 Testing hypotheses

In chapters 10 to 13, we used our sample to construct estimates of various descriptive measures. In this chapter, we will use these estimates to test the theories that might initially have led us to draw a sample. For example, we might have a theory that says that, on average, adult Danes spend more than two hours a week exercising. If our sample results in an estimate of 2.1 hours per week, is this enough to conclude that our theory is correct?

Since we only have a sample from the population at our disposal, it is not immediately possible to either accept or reject the theory. Therefore, in order to answer the above question, we need to assess the inherent uncertainty in the sample, and decide how big a risk we are willing to take in terms of drawing the wrong conclusions. All this leads to the procedure known as *hypothesis testing*.

Hypothesis testing involves formulating a theory as two hypotheses, one of which confirms the theory while the other rejects it. In order to implement the test, we select what is known as a *test statistic*, which summarises, in a single numerical value, the information in the sample that is relevant for the assessment of the hypotheses. Finally, we choose a *decision rule,* which enables a final decision to be made about which hypothesis we will accept.

This chapter will focus primarily on testing hypotheses about a mean value, partly because this is useful in practice and partly because these tests help illustrate how to construct a hypothesis test in general. In Section 14.1, we show how to develop hypotheses, and discuss the possible conclusions that can be drawn on the basis of hypothesis testing. In Section 14.2, we review the main elements in the construction of a hypothesis test based on a simple example. In sections 14.3 to 14.5, we look at different situations in which hypothesis testing is used. In Section 14.6, we introduce an alternative formulation of a decision rule. In Section 14.7, we provide an overview of hypothesis testing of a mean value, while the choice of sample size is discussed in Section 14.8. In Section 14.9, we test hypotheses about the variance, while sections

14.10 and 14.11 explain the difference between statistical significance and practical significance, as well as the relationship between hypothesis tests and confidence intervals.

14.1 Hypotheses and types of error

The motivation for conducting a study usually comes from some underlying theory, which may be more or less precisely formulated. We then end up selecting a sample in order to test whether the theory is correct. As we only have a sample at our disposal, we do not have a sufficient basis on which to reliably accept or reject the theory. In other words, it is possible that we may reach the wrong conclusion. In this section, we will look at the concepts used to deal with this situation.

14.1.1 Constructing hypotheses

First, we formulate our theory as two hypotheses – one that supports the theory and one that does not. We call them the *null hypothesis*, written H_0, and the *alternative hypothesis*, H_1. Which of the hypotheses we choose as the null hypothesis and which as the alternative depends on the given situation and on the risks and costs associated with drawing a wrong conclusion.

Example 14.1: Accused – part 1

A man is accused of theft and summoned to appear in court. The null hypothesis is that the man is innocent, while the alternative hypothesis is that he is guilty:

$$H_0 : \text{innocent}$$

$$H_1 : \text{guilty}$$

The judge must either *accept* the null hypothesis (i.e. acquit the accused) or *reject* it (i.e. accept the alternative hypothesis), in which case the man will be punished. The judge must make this decision without knowing for certain whether the null hypothesis is true. Rather, he or she must act only on the basis of circumstantial evidence.

Like Example 14.1, a statistical study uses circumstantial evidence as a basis on which to make a decision about whether a hypothesis can be accepted or has to be rejected. In our case, the circumstantial evidence consists of a sample. Both for the judge and for us, the problem is that decisions have to be based on incomplete knowledge.

In statistics, hypotheses are usually about values in a population or distribution. For example, we might be interested in testing whether the mean value, μ, in a population is equal to μ_0 or equal to μ_1 (assuming that these are the only two possibilities). This leads to the two hypotheses $H_0: \mu = \mu_0$ and $H_1: \mu = \mu_1$. In another case, we might be interested in testing whether the mean value μ is equal to μ_0 or whether μ is not equal to μ_0. In this situation, the two hypotheses are: $H_0: \mu = \mu_0$ and $H_1: \mu \neq \mu_0$. We might also be interested in comparing two different groups in the population. For example, we can test whether the average male income, μ_{men}, is equal to the average female income, μ_{women}. This leads to the two hypotheses $H_0: \mu_{women} = \mu_{men}$ and $H_1: \mu_{women} \neq \mu_{men}$.

We have to decide which of the two hypotheses will be the null hypothesis. Traditionally, the one that supports the theory we are testing is made the alternative hypothesis, which we will only accept if there is overwhelming evidence against the null hypothesis. In Example 14.1, the null hypothesis is "innocent". Under the rule of law, a person is innocent until proven guilty – or deemed so with a very high degree of probability. In other words, only when there is overwhelming evidence of lack of innocence do we reject the null hypothesis in favour of the alternative hypothesis and conclude that the person is guilty. In a statistical test, e.g. of unequal pay between men and women, we typically let the null hypothesis be that there *is* equal pay ($H_0: \mu_{women} = \mu_{men}$). Only in the face of overwhelming evidence of unequal pay do we reject the null hypothesis and accept that pay is not equal. As such, if we end up accepting the alternative hypothesis, then we have a compelling case, because we only reject the null hypothesis in the face of massive evidence that it is wrong. We will return to this in sections 14.2.4 and 14.2.5.

14.1.2 Conclusions and types of error

Since we do not know the truth, we risk making mistakes. The example of the accused can be used to illustrate this.

For the judge, it is important to sentence the accused if he is guilty and acquit him if he is innocent. Because the evidence is uncertain, the judge runs the risk of committing two types of error. Firstly, the judge may impose a sentence on the accused (reject the null hypothesis) even though he is innocent. Errors of this type are called type I errors. The judge may also acquit the person (accepting the null hypothesis) even though he is in fact guilty. This is called a type II error.

A *type I error* occurs if we reject a null hypothesis that is true. A *type II error* occurs if we accept a null hypothesis that is false. As long as the evidence or basis for making the decision is not complete, there is always a risk of making such an error. Table 14.1 summarises the possible conclusions and errors when testing hypotheses.

Table 14.1: Conclusions and types of error in hypothesis testing

	Null hypothesis true	Null hypothesis false
Null hypothesis accepted	Correct conclusion	Type II error
Null hypothesis rejected	Type I error	Correct conclusion

In statistical studies, we can assess the likelihood of an error because the decision is based on a sample. To do so, we first write up a decision rule, which for every conceivable outcome of the sample tells us whether we must accept or reject the null hypothesis. We can therefore perceive a decision rule as a random variable, which for every outcome of the statistical experiment (the sample) furnishes us with a conclusion about the null hypothesis. In the following section, we will see how to establish such a decision rule in different situations.

Assume that we have already established such a decision rule. We can then write up the probabilities of type I and type II errors. These probabilities characterise the properties of the test. The probability of committing a type I error is labelled α, and defined by the following conditional probability:

$$P(\text{Type I error}) = P(\text{reject H}_0 | \text{H}_0 \text{ true}) = \alpha$$

This is read as: "The probability of rejecting H$_0$, given that H$_0$ is true, is equal to α". The probability of committing a type II error is labelled β, and is also defined as a conditional probability:

$$P(\text{Type II error}) = P(\text{accept } H_0 | H_0 \text{ false}) = \beta$$

The *power* of a test is equal to $1 - \beta$. A high power of a test (i.e. a power close to 1 and therefore a probability of a type II error close to 0) means that the test is very likely to reject a false null hypothesis.

It is worth re-emphasising that the decision we make has an element of randomness, since it depends on the sample available. However, whether the hypothesis is true or false is by no means random.[17]

The probabilities of type I and type II errors are expressions of the test's properties: low probabilities indicate a good test. In the following sections, we will use the probabilities of type I and type II errors as a basis for constructing decision rules.

14.2   Construction of a hypothesis test

We approach the construction of a hypothesis test as follows: first, we define a measure that, with a single number, indicates whether the null hypothesis is true or false. We use this measure to define a test statistic that has the same interpretation as the measure, but with more appropriate statistical properties. The decision to accept or reject the null hypothesis is based on the value of the test statistic. The test statistic follows a given distribution, which means that we can calculate the relationship between the decision rule and the probabilities of type I and type II errors. This relationship, and our desire to control the size of the probabilities of the two types of error, determines the final form of the decision rule.

In this section, we illustrate the construction of a hypothesis test with a simple example. The hypotheses are:

$$H_0: \mu = \mu_0$$

$$H_1: \mu = \mu_1$$

where μ is the mean value, and μ_0 and μ_1 are known values (and the only possible values of μ in this case). Assume also that $\mu_0 < \mu_1$ and that we have a simple random sample with n observations at our disposal,

---

17   The expressions for type I and type II errors above are conditional on whether the hypothesis is true or false. Strictly speaking, this is not consistent with the definition of a conditional probability, in which conditions are based on stochastic variable. However, it rarely gives rise to misunderstandings, and it helps illustrate the conditions under which the probabilities are calculated.

$(X_1, \ldots, X_n)$, where each observation, X_i, is normally distributed with mean value μ and variance σ^2:

$$X_i \sim N(\mu, \sigma^2), \quad i = 1, \ldots, n$$

To keep the example as simple as possible, we shall in this section assume that the variance, σ^2, is known.

14.2.1 Hypothesis measure

The first tool we use in constructing a hypothesis test is a measure that, with a single number, indicates whether the null hypothesis is true or false. We will call this measure a *hypothesis measure*.[18] If we could use the true mean value in calculating the hypothesis measure, then it should, of course, unambiguously identify the correct hypothesis. In practice, however, we do not know the true mean value, but we can use the sample to work out an estimate of the hypothesis measure.

A hypothesis measure could be $h(\mu) = \mu - \mu_0$, where $h(\mu)$ is the hypothesis measure, which is a function of the unknown value, μ. If the null hypothesis is true, then $\mu = \mu_0$ and the hypothesis measure is therefore $h(\mu_0) = 0$. If instead the null hypothesis is false, then $\mu = \mu_1$ and the hypothesis measure is therefore $h(\mu_1) = \mu_1 - \mu_0$. Since we assumed that $\mu_0 < \mu_1$, then $h(\mu_1) > 0$ in this case. When we insert the true mean value, the hypothesis measure leaves us in no doubt about whether the null hypothesis is true or false.

In practice, we replace the true (but unknown) value with an estimate. We know from Chapter 10 that the sample average:

$$\bar{X} = \frac{1}{n} \sum_{i=1}^{n} X_i$$

is an estimator for μ. When this is inserted into the hypothesis measure, we arrive at the estimated hypothesis measure:

$$h(\bar{X}) = \bar{X} - \mu_0$$

We can interpret the estimated hypothesis measure as an estimate of whether the null hypothesis is true or false. Since $\bar{X}$ is an estimate of μ, the value of $\bar{X}$ is typically different from μ. From this, it follows that

---

18   Traditionally, this measure does not have a specific name in the academic literature. We have chosen to highlight (and name) it to draw attention to this particular step in the construction of a hypothesis test.

the estimated hypothesis measure, $h(\bar{X})$, typically also deviates from the true hypothesis measure, $h(\mu)$, calculated with the help of the true mean value. In our example, the estimated hypothesis measure is thus typically different from 0 even if $\mu = \mu_0$, and it will typically also be different from $\mu_1 - \mu_0$, even when $\mu = \mu_1$. In practice, there is a risk of obtaining the same realised sample and therefore the same value of the estimated hypothesis measure, when $\mu = \mu_0$ and when $\mu = \mu_1$. The difference between the two situations lies in the probability of obtaining certain values of the estimated hypothesis measure. For example, it is more probable that we will obtain values of the estimated hypothesis measure that are close to 0, when $\mu = \mu_0$, rather than when $\mu = \mu_1$. We will make use of this fact in the next stages of constructing the hypothesis test.

14.2.2   Test statistic

Some values of the estimated hypothesis measure are more probable or likely if the null hypothesis is true than if it is false. This leads us towards a decision rule that accepts the null hypothesis for certain values of the estimated hypothesis measure and rejects it for others. However, instead of using the estimated hypothesis measure and its distribution to construct the decision rule, we rewrite the estimated hypothesis measure as what is known as a *test statistic*. The advantage of using a test statistic rather than a hypothesis measure is partly that it is easier to derive the distribution of the test statistic, and partly that the test statistic has better statistical properties.[19]

We can rewrite the estimated hypothesis measure for our test of a mean value as a test statistic, Z, as follows:

$$Z = \frac{h(\bar{X})}{\sqrt{\sigma^2/n}} = \frac{\bar{X} - \mu_0}{\sqrt{\sigma^2/n}}$$

As we shall see, Z has a distribution that is easier to work with than the distribution of $h(\bar{X})$, but this does not mean that Z contains less information than $h(\bar{X})$. When the sample average is close to μ_0, which indicates that μ_0 is the true value, then Z, like $h(\bar{X})$, is close to 0. And when the sample average is close to μ_1, then Z, like $h(\bar{X})$, is greater than 0.

We can find the distribution of Z because we assumed that $X_i \sim N(\mu,\sigma^2)$. In Chapter 10, we argued that in this case $\bar{X}$ is also normally distributed with mean μ and variance σ^2/n: $\bar{X} \sim N(\mu,\sigma^2/n)$. Fur-

---

19   It is, however, beyond the scope of this book to explain why the statistical properties are better.

thermore, from Chapter 10, we know that if we scale a normally distributed variable by a constant, then the resulting variable is still normally distributed. Dividing $\overline{X}$ by the constant $\sqrt{\sigma^2/n}$ therefore results in another normally distributed variable, this time with mean $\mu/\sqrt{\sigma^2/n}$ and variance 1 according to the rules for calculating mean values and variances:

$$\frac{\overline{X}}{\sqrt{\sigma^2/n}} \sim N\left(\frac{\mu}{\sqrt{\sigma^2/n}}, 1\right)$$

Finally, the value $\dfrac{\mu_0}{\sqrt{\sigma^2/n}}$ is constant. If we deduct a constant from a normally distributed random variable, the resulting variable will still be normally distributed; only its mean value changes. We therefore arrive at:

$$Z = \frac{\overline{X} - \mu_0}{\sqrt{\sigma^2/n}} = \frac{\overline{X}}{\sqrt{\sigma^2/n}} - \frac{\mu_0}{\sqrt{\sigma^2/n}} \sim N\left(\frac{\mu - \mu_0}{\sqrt{\sigma^2/n}}, 1\right)$$

The test statistic, Z, is thus normally distributed with a mean value, which depends on the true mean value, μ, and a variance that is equal to 1. This turns out to be useful!

We are particularly interested in knowing the distribution of Z when the null hypothesis is true. A true null hypothesis is the same as $\mu = \mu_0$ and therefore $Z \sim N(0, 1)$. This means that Z follows the standard normal distribution under H_0. A false null hypothesis (i.e., a true alternative hypothesis) is the same as $\mu = \mu_1$, and therefore $Z \sim N\left(\dfrac{\mu_1 - \mu_0}{\sqrt{\sigma^2/n}}, 1\right)$ under H_1.

Example 14.3: A sample from a normal distribution – part 1

Assume we have a simple random sample with 12 observations, which are normally distributed with the mean value μ and variance $\sigma^2 = 16$. The hypotheses are H_0: $\mu = 1$ and H_1: $\mu = 3$. We apply the hypothesis measure $h(\mu) = \mu - 1$, and we use the sample average $\overline{X}$ as an estimator of μ.

We can then find the probability that the test statistic, Z, is less than or equal to 1.5. Under the null hypothesis, the probability is:

$$P(Z \leq 1.5 \mid H_0 \text{ true}) = \Phi(1.5) = 0.9332$$

Under the alternative hypothesis, $Z \sim N\left(\dfrac{3-1}{\sqrt{16/12}}, 1\right)$. The probability is therefore:

$$P(Z \leq 1.5 \mid \mathrm{H_1\ true}) = \Phi\left(\dfrac{1.5 - \dfrac{(3-1)}{\sqrt{16/12}}}{\sqrt{1}}\right) = \Phi(-0.23) = 0.4090$$

14.2.3 Decision rule

We can now establish a decision rule and calculate its consequences for the probabilities of type I and type II errors. Since $\mu_0 < \mu_1$, large values of $\bar{X}$ and hence Z are an indication that the null hypothesis is false and the alternative hypotheses is true. Small values of $\bar{X}$ and hence Z, on the other hand, are an indication that the null hypothesis is true. We therefore define a decision rule as follows:

$$\text{accept } \mathrm{H_0} \quad \textit{if} \quad Z \leq cv$$
$$\text{reject } \mathrm{H_0} \quad \textit{if} \quad Z > cv$$

where cv is a numerical value that separates the values of Z, for which we accept the null hypothesis from the values where we reject the null hypothesis. For this reason, cv is called a *critical value*. It is worth stressing (again) that accepting/rejecting a hypothesis does not make it true or false. There is always a risk of committing a type I error or a type II error.

But given the decision rule, we can work out the probability of committing type I and type II errors. The probability of committing a type I error is the probability of rejecting the null hypothesis when it is actually true. That is:

$$P(\text{type I error}) = P(Z > cv \mid \mathrm{H_0\ true})$$

The probability of committing a type II error is the probability of accepting the null hypothesis when it is false (i.e. rejecting the alternative hypothesis when it is true). That is:

$$P(\text{type II error}) = P(Z \leq cv \mid H_1 \text{ true})$$

In Example 14.3, we calculated the probability of Z being less than 1.5. If the critical value in the decision rule is set to 1.5, then the decision rule is given by:

$$\text{accept } H_0 \quad \text{if} \quad Z \leq 1.5$$
$$\text{reject } H_0 \quad \text{if} \quad Z > 1.5$$

In Example 14.3, we found that $P(Z \leq 1.5 \mid H_0 \text{ true}) = P(Z \leq 1.5 \mid \mu = 1)$ = 0.9332. This leads to:

$$P(\text{type I error}) = P(Z > 1.5 \mid \mu = 1) = 1 - P(Z \leq 1.5 \mid \mu = 1)$$
$$= 0.0668$$

We also found that $P(Z \leq 1.5 \mid H_0 \text{ false}) = P(Z \leq 1.5 \mid \mu = 3) = 0.4090$. This leads to:

$$P(\text{type II error}) = P(Z \leq 1.5 \mid \mu = 3) = 0.4090$$

14.2.4 Choice of critical value based on the type I error

When choosing the critical value, there is a tradition in statistics of focusing on the risk of type I errors. Typically, it is decided to fix the probability of a type I error at some low level, say, 0.05, and then pick a critical value that achieves this. One reason for this focus on type I errors is that we usually formulate the theory that we want to test as the alternative hypothesis, and we only want to conclude that this theory is correct if there is solid evidence in favour of it, which corresponds to a low probability of committing a type I error.

To illustrate this approach, assume that we want a test that commits a type I error with a probability not higher than α. We call α the *significance level*. We can now work backwards to find the required critical value, *cv*. This critical value must satisfy the following condition:

$$\text{accept } H_0 \quad \text{if} \quad Z \leq cv$$
$$\text{reject } H_0 \quad \text{if} \quad Z > cv$$

such that:

$$P(\text{type I error}) = P(Z > cv \mid H_0 \text{ true}) = \alpha$$

Since Z follows a standard normal distribution under H_0, *cv* must be equal to the $(1 - \alpha)$-quantile of the standard normal distribution, $Z_{1-\alpha}$. The decision rule therefore becomes:

$$\text{accept } H_0 \quad \text{if} \quad Z \leq Z_{1-\alpha}$$
$$\text{reject } H_0 \quad \text{if} \quad Z > Z_{1-\alpha}$$

Note that it is only the probability of committing a type I error (the significance level, α), that is needed to determine the critical value. This is one of the advantages of using a test statistic rather than the hypothesis measure itself.

Example 14.5: A sample from a normal distribution – part 3

Suppose that, in Example 14.3, a sample is selected that results in a realised sample average of $\bar{x} = 2.85$. The realised test statistic then becomes:

$$z = \frac{2.85 - 1}{\sqrt{16/12}} = 1.60$$

If we choose a significance level of $\alpha = 0.05$, then the critical value is $cv = Z_{0.95} = 1.6449$. Since $z \leq cv$, we accept the null hypothesis. Note that the choice of $\alpha = 0.05$ means that the probability of a type II error is:

$$P(\text{type II error}) = P(Z < 1.6449 \mid \mu = 3) = \Phi\left(1.6449 - \frac{3 - 1}{\sqrt{16/12}}\right)$$
$$= \Phi(-0.0872) = 0.4641$$

14.2.5　The trade-off between type I and type II errors

If we were able to choose the probabilities of committing type I and type II errors independently of each other, we should, of course, set both of them equal to 0. Unfortunately, this is not possible. In practice, we have to trade off the risks of committing a type I and a type II error, respectively, when choosing the critical value in our decision rule. A lower risk of committing a type I error means a higher risk of committing a type II error, and vice versa. If we want to make sure not to convict a man who is innocent, the evidence has to be so strong before we find him guilty that in many cases we will have to let a guilty man walk free (a type II error).

Example 14.6: A sample from a normal distribution – part 4

We can see the trade-off between type I and type II errors in Examples 14.4 and 14.5. In Example 14.4, we assumed that the critical value was 1.5. This led to P(type I error) = 0.0668 and P(type II error) = 0.4090. In Example 14.5, we chose P(type I error) = 0.05, which led to a critical value of 1.6449 and P(type II error) = 0.4641. The lower probability of a type I error in Example 14.5 thus resulted in a higher probability of a type II error.

The choice of α and β should in principle be based on an assessment of the consequences of drawing erroneous conclusions, which must depend on the question we are studying. However, as explained above, there is a tradition of focusing exclusively on the probability of type I errors. Typically, people set α equal to 0.10, 0.05 or 0.01, and find the corresponding critical value – just as we did in Example 14.5 above. The flip side of this is that we will in many cases fail to reject a false null. Thus, in Example 14.5, there is almost a 50% chance of a type II error. In other words, if the null hypothesis is false, we will only "discover" that half of the time.

The decision rule above suggests that one can phrase the decision as "we accept the null hypothesis" or "we reject the null hypothesis", and we will also use these phrases here. But when following the traditional approach of picking a low value of α, many people prefer to say "we cannot reject the null hypothesis" rather than "we accept the null hypothesis", because this wording emphasises the (sometimes high) risk of committing a type II error.

Focusing exclusively on the risk of committing a type I error and completely ignoring the risk of a type II error typically does not provide a good balance between the two types of error and thus between the null hypothesis and the alternative hypothesis. A more sensible approach is explicitly to choose a combination of α and β that is both feasible and that best supports the purpose of our study. Since there is a relationship between α and β, it is actually possible to calculate the consequences for β of choosing different values of α.

In the case of $H_0: \mu = \mu_0$ against $H_1: \mu = \mu_1$, the relationship between α and β can be written as follows: since $cv = Z_{1-\alpha}$, the probability of a type II error is given by:

$$\beta = P(\text{type II error}) = P(Z \leq cv \mid H_0 \text{ false}) = P(Z \leq Z_{1-\alpha} \mid H_0 \text{ false})$$

$$= \Phi\left(\frac{Z_{1-\alpha} - \dfrac{\mu_1 - \mu_0}{\sqrt{\sigma^2/n}}}{\sqrt{1}}\right)$$

Here, we can see that the smaller the value of α, the greater is $Z_{1-\alpha}$, and the greater β becomes. Example 14.7 illustrates this more clearly.

Example 14.7: A sample from a normal distribution – part 5

In the example of the sample with 12 normally distributed observations with variance $\sigma^2 = 16$, the probability of a type II error β, as a function of α is given by:

$$\beta = \Phi\left(\frac{Z_{1-\alpha} - \dfrac{\mu_1 - \mu_0}{\sqrt{\sigma^2/n}}}{\sqrt{1}}\right) = \Phi\left(\frac{Z_{1-\alpha} - \dfrac{3-1}{\sqrt{16/12}}}{\sqrt{1}}\right) = \Phi\left(Z_{1-\alpha} - 1.73\right)$$

In Figure 14.1, we illustrate this relationship between α and β.

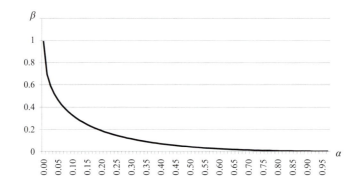

Here, we can clearly see the negative trade-off between α and β: if we require a lower probability of a type I error, then we have to accept a higher probability of a type II error. If, for example, we want the probability of a type I error to be no greater than 0.10, then we have to accept a probability of a type II error of about 0.3.

14.2.6 The case of $\mu_0 > \mu_1$

Until now, we have assumed that $\mu_0 < \mu_1$ in connection with the hypotheses $H_0: \mu = \mu_0$ and $H_1: \mu = \mu_1$. In this subsection, we will show how the decision rule changes when we instead assume that $\mu_0 > \mu_1$. As above, we use the hypothesis measure, $h(\mu) = \mu - \mu_0$, and the test statistic:

$$Z = \frac{h(\bar{X})}{\sqrt{\sigma^2/n}} = \frac{\bar{X} - \mu_0}{\sqrt{\sigma^2/n}}$$

The distribution of the test statistic is also the same as before:

$$Z \sim N\left(\frac{\mu - \mu_0}{\sqrt{\sigma^2/n}}, 1\right)$$

The difference arises when it comes to the decision rule. If H_0 is true, then $h(\mu) = 0$, and if H_1 is true, then $h(\mu) = \mu_1 - \mu_0 < 0$. Hence, the inequality sign under H_1 has changed. This means that negative values of the estimated hypothesis measure, $h(\bar{X})$, now indicate that the alternative hypothesis is true and the null hypothesis false. The same reasoning can be applied to the sign of the test statistic. We therefore now choose a decision rule that looks like this:

$$accept\ H_0 \quad if \quad Z \geq cv$$

$$reject\ H_0 \quad if \quad Z < cv$$

If the significance level is α, the probability of a type I error can now be written as:

$$P(\text{type I error}) = P(Z < cv \mid H_0\ \text{true}) = \alpha$$

Hence, the critical value must be $cv = Z_\alpha$, where Z_α is the α-quantile from the standard normal distribution. This results in the following decision rule:

$$accept\ H_0 \quad if \quad Z \geq Z_\alpha$$

$$reject\ H_0 \quad if \quad Z < Z_\alpha$$

The probability of a type II error is therefore:

$$\beta = P(\text{type II error}) = P(Z \geq cv \mid H_0\ \text{false}) = P(Z \geq Z_\alpha \mid H_0\ \text{false})$$

$$= 1 - \Phi\left(Z_\alpha - \frac{\mu_1 - \mu_0}{\sigma/\sqrt{n}}\right)$$

14.2.7 Summary

We conclude with a summary of the steps in the construction of a hypothesis test.

Construction of a hypothesis test

1. Define the null hypothesis, H_0, and the alternative hypothesis, H_1.

2. Choose the hypothesis measure and the test statistic.

3. Select the significance level, α, taking into account the effect on the power, $1 - \beta$, of the test.

4. Define the decision rule and find the critical value.

5. Calculate the realised test statistic with the help of the sample.

6. Reject or accept H_0.

Note that the trade-off between type I and type II errors means that it may be necessary to solve points 3 and 4 at the same time, since we need the decision rule in order to be able to calculate the power of the test. In practice, however, we often just use $\alpha = 0.05$ or 0.10 without considering the consequences for the power of the test. The box below sums up the first four steps in the construction of the hypothesis test for the recurring example used in this section.

Example of construction of a hypothesis test

Assume that we have a simple random sample with n normally distributed observations with known variance, σ^2.

1. Hypotheses: $H_0: \mu = \mu_0$ versus $H_1: \mu = \mu_1$

2. Test statistic: $Z = \dfrac{\bar{X} - \mu_0}{\sqrt{\sigma^2/n}} \sim N\left(\dfrac{\mu - \mu_0}{\sqrt{\sigma^2/n}}, 1\right)$

3. Significance level: α

4. Decision rule:

a) If $\mu_1 > \mu_0$, then the decision rule is:

$$\begin{aligned} accept\ H_0 \quad & if \quad Z \leq Z_{1-\alpha} \\ reject\ H_0 \quad & if \quad Z > Z_{1-\alpha} \end{aligned}$$

where $Z_{1-\alpha}$ is the $(1-\alpha)$-quantile from the standard normal distribution. The probability of a type II error is then:

$$\beta = \Phi\left(Z_{1-\alpha} - \dfrac{\mu_1 - \mu_0}{\sigma/\sqrt{n}}\right)$$

b) If $\mu_1 < \mu_0$, the decision rule is:

$$\begin{aligned} accept\ H_0 \quad & if \quad Z \geq Z_{\alpha} \\ reject\ H_0 \quad & if \quad Z < Z_{\alpha} \end{aligned}$$

where Z_{α} is the α-quantile from the standard normal distribution. The probability of a type II error is then:

$$\beta = 1 - \Phi\left(Z_{\alpha} - \dfrac{\mu_1 - \mu_0}{\sigma/\sqrt{n}}\right)$$

Note that a test statistic is a random variable, which implies that we accept the null hypothesis if the test statistic's values fall within a certain interval, while we reject the null hypothesis if its values fall in a different, non-overlapping interval. The formal and more general definition of a test statistic, T, and a decision rule are given in the following box:

Test statistic and decision rule

Let T be a stochastic variable and R a set of numbers. T is a test statistic when it is part of the decision rule:

$$accept\, H_0 \quad if \quad T \notin R$$
$$reject\, H_0 \quad if \quad T \in R$$

R is called the *rejection region*, and the end points in R are called the *critical values*.

In the recurring example in this section, Z has the role of the test statistic, T. The rejection region is $R = (cv\,,\,\infty)$ in the case where $\mu_0 < \mu_1$, and cv is a critical value. In the case where $\mu_0 > \mu_1$, the rejection region is $R = (-\infty\,,\,cv)$.

14.3 Test of mean value under different distributional assumptions

In the previous section, we examined the construction of a hypothesis test in the case of a specific hypothesis about the mean value and an assumption that the observations in the sample were normally distributed with a known variance. In this section we will consider the same hypothesis as above, but with different assumptions about the distribution of the observations in the sample. In sections 14.3.1 and 14.3.2, we will look at the general case, where the distribution of the observations in the sample is unknown but we assume that the variance can be either known or unknown. In sections 14.3.3 and 14.3.4, we will look at the two special cases in which the observations in the sample are normally distributed with known and unknown variance, respectively. The different cases are summarised in a table in Section 14.7.

Throughout this section, the hypotheses are as in Section 14.2, i.e.:

$$H_0 : \mu = \mu_0$$

$$H_1 : \mu = \mu_1$$

where μ_0 and μ_1 are known values (and the only possible values of μ), and it is assumed that $\mu_0 < \mu_1$. Since the hypotheses are the same as in the previous section, we also use the same hypothesis measure and the same test statistic:

$$Z = \frac{\overline{X} - \mu_0}{\sqrt{\sigma^2/n}}$$

14.3.1   Unknown distribution, known variance

When we do not know the distribution of the observations in the sample, we cannot find the exact distribution of the sample average, $\overline{X}$, and therefore we cannot find the exact distribution of the test statistic, Z. Instead, we can use the central limit theorem from Chapter 10, which tells us that the sample average is approximately normally distributed, with mean value μ, and variance σ^2/n, when the sample size is large. Hence it follows that:

$$\frac{\overline{X}}{\sqrt{\sigma^2/n}} \overset{A}{\sim} N\left(\frac{\mu}{\sqrt{\sigma^2/n}}, 1\right)$$

The precision of this approximation depends on the sample size, n – the larger the sample, the better the approximation. As in Section 14.2, we can use this result to find the distribution of the test statistic:

$$Z = \frac{\overline{X}}{\sqrt{\sigma^2/n}} - \frac{\mu_0}{\sqrt{\sigma^2/n}} \overset{A}{\sim} N\left(\frac{\mu - \mu_0}{\sqrt{\sigma^2/n}}, 1\right)$$

Since the second term, $\mu_0 / \sqrt{\sigma^2/n}$, is just a constant, it only affects the mean value of Z. This result can be used to find the approximate distributions of the test statistic, Z, under H_0 and under H_1:

$$Z = \frac{\overline{X} - \mu_0}{\sqrt{\sigma^2/n}} \overset{A}{\sim} N(0, 1) \text{ under } H_0$$

and

$$Z = \frac{\overline{X} - \mu_0}{\sqrt{\sigma^2/n}} \overset{A}{\sim} N\left(\frac{\mu_1 - \mu_0}{\sqrt{\sigma^2/n}}, 1\right) \text{ under } H_1$$

The only difference compared to Section 14.2, where we assumed that the observations in the sample were normally distributed, is that Z is now only approximately normally distributed under the null and the alternative hypotheses.

Based on the approximate distributions for Z, we can write up the decision rule in exactly the same manner as before:

$$accept\ H_0 \quad if \quad Z \le cv$$

$$reject\ H_0 \quad if \quad Z > cv$$

where $cv = Z_{1-\alpha}$ is the $(1 - \alpha)$-quantile of the standard normal distribution.

14.3.2 Unknown distribution, unknown variance

When the variance is unknown, as is often the case in practice, we can replace it with an estimator. An estimator for the variance σ^2 is the sample variance:

$$S^2 = \frac{1}{n-1}\sum_{i=1}^{n}(X_i - \bar{X})^2$$

The test statistic is therefore now given by:

$$Z = \frac{\bar{X} - \mu_0}{\sqrt{S^2/n}}$$

which is still approximately normally distributed, even though we have replaced σ^2 with S^2. The decision rule is therefore the same as in the case with a known variance. In most cases, the same approximate distribution of the test statistics can be used when we replace an unknown variance with an estimator of the unknown variance.

14.3.3 Normally distributed observations, known variance

When the observations in the sample are normally distributed, we can, of course, still use the general results from the previous two sections. However, in these cases, we can typically use more precise and therefore better results.

We found in Section 14.2 that when σ^2 is known, Z is exactly normally distributed. The decision rule is therefore exactly the same as in the previous two subsections, the only difference being that the distribution of the test statistic is now exact. Therefore, the test statistic is useful even in relation to small samples.

14.3.4   Normally distributed observations, unknown variance

When the observations in the sample are normally distributed, but σ^2 is unknown and replaced by S^2, the test statistic becomes t-distributed with $n-1$ degrees of freedom under the null hypothesis.[20] This test can therefore also be used with small samples. The t-distribution, which was described in Chapter 13, is very similar to the standard normal distribution. Table 3 at the back of this book presents selected quantiles of the t-distribution. Furthermore, the test statistic is often denoted T, in this case to indicate that, with unknown variance and normally distributed observations, the test statistic is t-distributed.

Example 14.8: A sample from a normal distribution – part 6

In Example 14.5, the realised sample average was $\bar{x} = 2.85$. Now, suppose that the variance is unknown and that the realised sample variance is $s^2 = 13.6$. As a consequence, the realised test statistic becomes:

$$z = \frac{2.85 - 1}{\sqrt{13.6/12}} = 1.74$$

The test statistic is t-distributed with $(12-1)$ degrees of freedom under the null hypothesis. With a significance level of $\alpha = 0.05$ the critical value becomes: $cv = t_{0.95}(11) = 1.80$. Since $z < cv$, we accept the null hypothesis in this case.

Example 14.5 shows that when the variance is unknown, the critical value becomes greater. This is because we use the t-distribution instead of the standard normal distribution. The underlying intuition is that the unknown variance reduces the information in the test statistic, and therefore we need stronger evidence to reject the null hypothesis with a given significance level.

---

20   The distribution of the test statistic under the alternative hypothesis is given by what is known as a non-central t-distribution.

14.4   Simple and composite hypotheses about a mean value

In this section, we treat hypotheses about the mean value other than those we considered in sections 14.2 and 14.3. Throughout this section, we focus on the case in which we have a simple random sample with normally distributed observations, $X_i \sim N(\mu, \sigma^2)$, where the variance is known. When the variance is unknown, we just replace it with the sample variance in the calculation of the test statistic and use the t-distribution instead of the standard normal distribution. When the observations are not normally distributed, the distribution of the test statistic is only approximate, and therefore it cannot be used in small samples.

We distinguish between two types of hypothesis. A hypothesis is *simple* if it is satisfied for only one value. For example, the hypothesis $\mu = \mu_0$ is a simple hypothesis because only one value of the mean satisfies this hypothesis. Often we do not have a theory that leads to such precise hypotheses. The hypothesis $\mu \neq \mu_0$, for example, only says that the mean is not equal to μ_0, and the hypothesis is therefore satisfied for all other values of the mean. A hypothesis that is satisfied for more than one value is called a *composite hypothesis*. In the previous section, both the null and alternative hypotheses were simple hypotheses.

14.4.1   Simple null hypothesis and composite two-sided alternative hypothesis

In the social sciences, a frequently occurring hypothesis is that a particular policy intervention will have an effect. Without the intervention, we know that the mean value is μ_0. If the intervention has an effect, then the mean value will differ from μ_0. When we want to study whether there is an effect, we usually establish this as the alternative hypothesis. Therefore, the hypotheses become:

$$H_0 : \mu = \mu_0$$

$$H_1 : \mu \neq \mu_0$$

The alternative hypothesis is composite because multiple values of the mean value satisfy the hypothesis. It is also called *two-sided*, because the values on both sides of the null hypothesis satisfy the alternative hypothesis.

We use the same hypothesis measure and test statistic as before. The hypothesis measure is $h(\mu) = \mu - \mu_0$. It is only equal to 0 when the null hypothesis is true, while it is always different from 0 when the null hypothesis is false. The hypothesis measure can, therefore, be used to discriminate between the null hypothesis and the alternative hypothesis. The estimated hypothesis measures enter the test statistic in the same way as before:

$$Z = \frac{\bar{X} - \mu_0}{\sqrt{\sigma^2/n}}$$

The test statistic also follows the same distribution as previously:

$$Z \sim N\left(\frac{\mu - \mu_0}{\sqrt{\sigma^2/n}}, 1\right)$$

The decision rule must reflect the fact that both values greater than μ_0 and values less than μ_0 satisfy the alternative hypothesis. This reasoning implies that we reject the null hypothesis when the value of the test statistic is sufficiently far from 0, either in a positive or negative direction. We therefore get two critical values, cv_1 and cv_2, in this case. The decision rule thus reads:

$$\begin{aligned} accept\ H_0 \quad & if \quad cv_1 \leq Z \leq cv_2 \\ reject\ H_0 \quad & if \quad Z < cv_1\ or\ Z > cv_2 \end{aligned}$$

Since Z follows a standard normal distribution under the null hypothesis, and this distribution is symmetric around 0, we choose the two critical values such that $cv_1 = -cv_2$. As above, we use the significance level α to find the values of cv_1 and cv_2. To do this, we must solve the following equation:

$$P(\text{type I error}) = P(Z < cv_1 \mid \mu = \mu_0) + P(Z > cv_2 \mid \mu = \mu_0) = \alpha$$

The solution is to let $cv_1 = z_{\alpha/2}$ and $cv_2 = z_{1-\alpha/2}$, where $Z_{\alpha/2}$ and $Z_{1-\alpha/2}$ are, respectively, the $\alpha/2$- and the $(1 - \alpha/2)$-quantile of the standard normal distribution. Figure 14.2 illustrates the case with a significance level of 0.05.

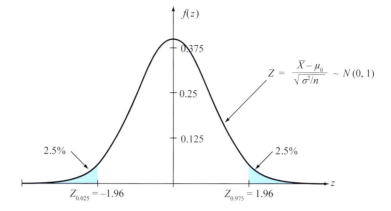

Since the alternative hypothesis is a composite hypothesis, there are multiple values of μ that will satisfy it. For any of these values, we can calculate the probability of a type II error. We could thus think of the probability of a type II error, β, as a function of the true mean value, μ, and write it as $\beta(\mu)$. Since $1 - \beta$ is the power of the test, we call $1 - \beta(\mu)$ the *power function* of the test.

Example 14.9: A sample from a normal distribution – part 7

Suppose that in Example 14.5 we want to test the null hypothesis against $H_1 : \mu \neq 1$. With a chosen significance level of 0.05, the critical values become: $Z_{0.05/2} = -1.96$ and $Z_{1 - 0.05/2} = 1.96$. The decision rule is therefore:

$$accept\ H_0 \quad if \quad -1.96 \leq Z \leq 1.96$$

$$reject\ H_0 \quad if \quad Z < -1.96\ \ or\ \ Z > 1.96$$

The realised test statistic was $z = 1.60$. We therefore accept the null hypothesis.

The probability of committing a type II error depends on the true value of the mean under the alternative hypothesis. If the true value is $\mu = 4$, then we can work out the probability of committing a type II error by using our knowledge about Z's distribution:

$$P(\text{type II error} \mid \mu = 4) = P(-1.96 \le Z \le 1.96 \mid \mu = 4)$$

$$= \Phi\left(\frac{1.96 - \dfrac{4-1}{\sqrt{16/12}}}{\sqrt{1}}\right) - \Phi\left(\frac{-1.96 - \dfrac{4-1}{\sqrt{16/12}}}{\sqrt{1}}\right)$$

$$= \Phi(-0.6381) - \Phi(-4.5581) = 0.2611 - 0 = 0.2611$$

14.4.2 Simple null hypothesis and composite one-sided alternative hypothesis

Above, we had an alternative hypothesis that did not distinguish between whether the mean value was greater or less than the hypothetical value under the null hypothesis. When we have a theory that says, for example, that an intervention should have a positive effect, then the focus is only on whether the mean value is greater than the mean value under the null hypothesis. This leads to the following hypotheses:[21]

$$H_0 : \mu = \mu_0$$
$$H_1 : \mu > \mu_0$$

Here, the alternative hypothesis is satisfied by all values of the mean value that are greater than μ_0. The alternative hypothesis is still composite, as several values of μ satisfy H_1, but now it is one-sided, as only values in one direction from the null hypothesis satisfy H_1. The decision rule is therefore similar to the decision rule from Section 14.2, where we tested $H_0 : \mu = \mu_0$ against $H_1 : \mu = \mu_1$ in the case where $\mu_0 < \mu_1$. The decision rule thus reads:

$$accept\ H_0 \quad if \quad Z \le Z_{1-\alpha}$$
$$reject\ H_0 \quad if \quad Z > Z_{1-\alpha}$$

---

21   Note that there are values of μ that are not included in either the null hypothesis or the alternative hypothesis, namely, all negative values. Implicitly it is assumed that those values are not of practical relevance.

Had the hypotheses instead been:

$$H_0 : \mu = \mu_0$$
$$H_1 : \mu < \mu_0$$

then the decision rule would have been:

$$\textit{accept } H_0 \quad \textit{if} \quad Z \geq Z_\alpha$$
$$\textit{reject } H_0 \quad \textit{if} \quad Z < Z_\alpha$$

The only difference between the situation above and the situation in Section 14.2 is that there are multiple values of the mean value that satisfy the alternative hypothesis. We can therefore calculate the probability of a type II error for each of them.

Figure 14.3 summarises the three situations with composite alternative hypotheses, and shows how to find the critical value in each individual case.

Figure 14.3:
Critical values
with two-sided
and one-sided
H_1

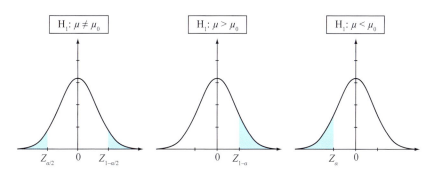

14.4.3 Composite null hypothesis

Sometimes, a null hypothesis of the type $H_0 : \mu \leq \mu_0$ is posited against an alternative hypothesis of the type $H_1 : \mu > \mu_0$. The null hypothesis is now also composite, as several values of the mean value satisfy the null hypothesis. The procedure for testing this null hypothesis is the same as in the test of $H_0 : \mu = \mu_0$ versus $H_1 : \mu > \mu_0$ in Section 14.4.2 above. Actually, unless we can a priori rule out that the mean value can be less than μ_0, a composite null hypothesis of the form $H_0 : \mu \leq \mu_0$ is a more appropriate specification of the null hypothesis than $H_0 : \mu = \mu_0$ when the alternative hypothesis is $H_1 : \mu > \mu_0$.

With a composite null hypothesis, we wish to control the probability of committing a type I error, regardless of which value of μ under the null hypothesis is the true one. However, the probability of committing a type I error for a value of $\mu < \mu_0$ is less than the probability of committing a type I error when $\mu = \mu_0$, because the distance to the critical value is greater in the former case. We therefore find the critical value for the case where $\mu = \mu_0$, which is the same as in a test of $H_0 : \mu = \mu_0$ versus $H_1 : \mu > \mu_0$.

Similarly, a test of the null hypothesis, $H_0 : \mu \geq \mu_0$, versus the alternative hypothesis, $H_1 : \mu < \mu_0$, is carried out in the same way as a test of the null hypothesis, $H_0 : \mu = \mu_0$, versus the alternative hypothesis, $H_1 : \mu < \mu_0$.

14.5 Testing the mean value with Bernoulli-distributed observations

We have already looked at the special case in which we assume that the observations in the sample are normally distributed. In this section, we look at another practically relevant situation, in which the sample is drawn from a Bernoulli population. A test of the mean value of a Bernoulli population is the same as a test of the proportion of successes in the population.

Assume that the observations in the sample are Bernoulli-distributed with the parameter p. The hypotheses are:

$$H_0 : \mu = p = p_0$$

$$H_1 : \mu = p > p_0$$

Because the observations are Bernoulli-distributed, we know that the variance of the individual observations in the sample is: $V(X_i) = p \cdot (1 - p)$. Under H_0, the variance is therefore: $\sigma^2 = p_0 \cdot (1 - p_0)$. We can use this instead of σ^2 in the test statistic:

$$Z = \frac{\overline{X} - p_0}{\sqrt{p_0 \cdot (1 - p_0)/n}}$$

When n is large ($n > 20$), we again use the general result, based on the central limit theorem, that Z is approximately standard normally distributed under the null hypothesis.

Example 14.10: Supermarket customers

A supermarket chain has made a study of the proportion of the population who shop with them. Out of 400 respondents, 116 said they shopped at the chain. The owners of the supermarket want to clarify whether they can deduce from this that more than a quarter of the general population shops with them. They therefore want to test: $H_0 : p \leq \frac{1}{4}$ versus $H_1 : p > \frac{1}{4}$, where p is the proportion of those who shop at the chain. For this purpose, we use the test statistic above. The critical value of this at a 5% significance level is $Z_{0.95} = 1.64$, because the alternative hypothesis is one-sided. The value of the test statistic is calculated as:

$$Z = \frac{\frac{116}{400} - 0.25}{\sqrt{(0.25 \cdot (1 - 0.25)/400)}} = 1.85$$

The supermarket can therefore reject H_0, and the owners can therefore conclude that more than a quarter of the general population shops with them.

Note that it is possible to calculate the exact distribution for Z with the help of the binomial distribution. This is because the sample average is a sum of Bernoulli-distributed variables (divided by n). If you want to compute the exact probabilities for Z, this can be done as follows:

$$P(Z < cv) = P\left(\frac{\overline{X} - p_0}{\sqrt{p_0 \cdot (1 - p_0) / n}} < cv \right)$$

$$= P\left(\overline{X} < p_0 + cv \cdot \sqrt{p_0 \cdot (1 - p_0) / n} \right)$$

$$= P\left(\frac{1}{n} \sum_{i=1}^{n} X_i < p_0 + cv \cdot \sqrt{p_0 \cdot (1 - p_0) / n} \right)$$

$$= P\left(\sum_{i=1}^{n} X_i < n \cdot \left[p_0 + cv \cdot \sqrt{p_0 \cdot (1 - p_0) / n} \right] \right)$$

Since $\sum_{i=1}^{n} X_i$ is a sum of independent Bernoulli-distributed stochastic variables, then

$$\sum_{i=1}^{n} X_i \sim \text{Bin}(n, p_0) \text{ under } H_0$$

However, unless the sample size is very small, we usually rely on the result above based on the central limit theorem.

In this section, we will look at an alternative way of expressing the decision rule. Instead of using a critical value, we can use a so-called *p-value*. As we will see, a p-value is a bit more informative than a critical value.

First, consider the general example from Section 14.2. The hypotheses about the mean value are: $H_0 : \mu = \mu_0$ versus $H_1 : \mu = \mu_1$, where $\mu_0 < \mu_1$. The sample contains normally distributed observations with known variance, σ^2. The test statistic is therefore:

$$Z = \frac{\overline{X} - \mu_0}{\sqrt{\sigma^2/n}}$$

which follows the distribution:

$$Z \sim N\left(\frac{\mu - \mu_0}{\sqrt{\sigma^2/n}}, 1\right)$$

As before, we reject the null hypothesis if the values of the test statistic are high, and accept it if the values are low. Previously, the decision rule was written as:

$$accept\ H_0 \quad if \quad Z \leq cv$$
$$reject\ H_0 \quad if \quad Z > cv$$

Instead of determining the critical value, cv, we can start by calculating the realised value of the test statistic, z. We can then find the probability, under the null hypothesis, of observing a value of the test statistic that is at least as extreme in the direction of the alternative hypothesis as the realised value, z. This probability is called the p-value and is given by:

$$\text{p-value} = P(Z > z | H_0\ true).$$

The p-value expresses the probability of committing a type I error if we use the realised value of the test statistic, z, as the critical value (i.e., if we reject the null hypothesis when the value of Z is greater than or equal to z).

Since Z follows a standard normal distribution, the p-value in the above case is calculated as:

$$\text{p-value} = 1 - \Phi(z)$$

If the null hypothesis is a composite hypothesis, then the p-value is calculated using the value of μ under H_0, which gives the greatest probability of a type I error. This is exactly the same approach as in Section 14.4.3.

The decision can now be made using the significance level, α, which is the probability of committing a type I error that we are willing to accept:

$$accept\ H_0 \quad if \quad \text{p-value} \geq \alpha$$

$$reject\ H_0 \quad if \quad \text{p-value} < \alpha$$

Example 14.11. A sample from a normal distribution – part 8

In Example 14.5, the realised test statistic was $z = 1.60$. Thus, the p-value becomes:

$$\text{p-value} = 1 - \Phi(1.60) = 1 - 0.9452 = 0.0548$$

If the significance level is $\alpha = 0.05$, then we accept (or do not reject) the null hypothesis in this case. This was also the conclusion in Example 14.5.

In the situation where $\mu_0 > \mu_1$, the p-value is given by:

$$\text{p-value} = \Phi(z)$$

when Z follows a standard normal distribution. The decision rule is the same as above.

In the case of the alternative hypothesis being two-sided, $H_1 : \mu \neq \mu_0$, the p-value is given by:

$$\text{p-value} = P(Z < -|z|\ \text{or}\ Z > |z| \,|\, H_0\ \text{true})$$

When Z follows a standard normal distribution, this probability can be calculated as:

$$\text{p-value} = \Phi(-|z|) + 1 - \Phi(|z|) = 2 \cdot \Phi(-|z|)$$

Example 14.12. A sample from a normal distribution – part 9

In Example 14.5, the realised test statistic was $z = 1.60$. Thus, the p-value for $H_1 : \mu \neq \mu_0$ is given by:

$$\text{p-value} = \Phi(-1.60) + 1 - \Phi(1.60) = 0.0548 + 1 - 0.9452 = 0.1096$$

If the significance level is $\alpha = 0.05$, then we accept the null hypothesis.

In the general case, where we do not know the distribution of the population, we replace the variance, σ^2, with the sample variance, S^2, in the calculation of the test statistic. Since in this case the test statistic is only approximately normally distributed, then the p-values, calculated as above, are also only approximate.

14.7   Summary of hypothesis tests of mean value

The results from this chapter so far are summarised in the box below:

Table 14.2: Test of mean value with a simple random sample $H_0 : \mu = \mu_0$

	Alternative hypotheses		
	$H_1 : \mu \neq \mu_0$	$H_1 : \mu > \mu_0$	$H_1 : \mu < \mu_0$
Test statistic and distribution under H_0			
The general case: Large sample size (Sections 14.3.1 and 14.3.2)			
σ^2 known: $Z = \dfrac{\overline{X} - \mu_0}{\sqrt{\sigma^2/n}} \sim^A N(0,1)$	p-value: $2 \cdot \Phi(-|z|)$	p-value: $1 - \Phi(z)$	p-value: $\Phi(z)$
σ^2 unknown: $Z = \dfrac{\overline{X} - \mu_0}{\sqrt{S^2/n}} \sim^A N(0,1)$	Critical values: $Z_{\alpha/2}$ and $Z_{1-\alpha/2}$	Critical value: $Z_{1-\alpha}$	Critical value: Z_α
Normally distributed observations (Sections 14.3.3 and 14.3.4)			
σ^2 known: $Z = \dfrac{\overline{X} - \mu_0}{\sqrt{\sigma^2/n}} \sim N(0,1)$	p-value: $2 \cdot \Phi(-|z|)$ Critical values: $Z_{\alpha/2}$ and $Z_{1-\alpha/2}$	p-value: $1 - \Phi(z)$ Critical value: $Z_{1-\alpha}$	p-value: $\Phi(z)$ Critical value: Z_α

$\rightarrow$

	p-value: $2 \cdot P(T < -|t|)$	p-value: $P(T > t)$	p-value: $P(T < t)$
σ^2 unknown: $T = \dfrac{\overline{X} - \mu_0}{\sqrt{S^2/n}} \sim t(n-1)$	Critical values: $t_{\alpha/2}(n-1)$ and $t_{1-\alpha/2}(n-1)$	Critical values: $t_{1-\alpha}(n-1)$	Critical values: $t_{\alpha}(n-1)$ and $t_{1-\alpha/2}(n-1)$

Test of a proportion: $X_i \sim$ Ber (p) and large sample size (Section 14.5)

	p-value: $2 \cdot \Phi(-|z|)$	p-value: $1 - \Phi(z)$	p-value: $\Phi(z)$
$Z = \dfrac{\hat{p} - p_0}{\sqrt{p_0 \cdot (1 - p_0)/n}} \sim^A N(0,1)$	Critical values: $Z_{\alpha/2}$ and $Z_{1-\alpha/2}$	Critical value: $Z_{1-\alpha}$	Critical value: Z_{α}

Notes:
1. z and t are the observed values of the test statistic.
2. α is the significance level.
3. Z_{α} is the α-quantile from the standard normal distribution.
4. $t_{\alpha}(n-1)$ is the α-quantile of the t-distribution with $n-1$ degrees of freedom.
5. Column $H_1 : \mu > \mu_0$ also covers the case where $H_1 : \mu = \mu_1$ when $\mu_0 < \mu_1$.
6. Column $H_1 : \mu < \mu_0$ also covers the case where $H_1 : \mu = \mu_1$ when $\mu_0 > \mu_1$.

Table 14.3: The power of the test of the mean value $H_0 : \mu = \mu_0$

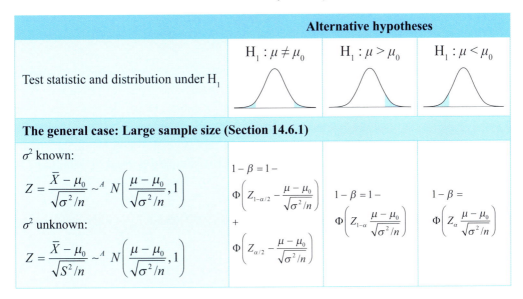

	Alternative hypotheses		
	$H_1 : \mu \neq \mu_0$	$H_1 : \mu > \mu_0$	$H_1 : \mu < \mu_0$
Test statistic and distribution under H_1			

The general case: Large sample size (Section 14.6.1)

σ^2 known:
$$Z = \dfrac{\overline{X} - \mu_0}{\sqrt{\sigma^2/n}} \sim^A N\left(\dfrac{\mu - \mu_0}{\sqrt{\sigma^2/n}}, 1\right)$$

σ^2 unknown:
$$Z = \dfrac{\overline{X} - \mu_0}{\sqrt{S^2/n}} \sim^A N\left(\dfrac{\mu - \mu_0}{\sqrt{\sigma^2/n}}, 1\right)$$

$$1 - \beta = 1 - \Phi\left(Z_{1-\alpha/2} - \dfrac{\mu - \mu_0}{\sqrt{\sigma^2/n}}\right) + \Phi\left(Z_{\alpha/2} - \dfrac{\mu - \mu_0}{\sqrt{\sigma^2/n}}\right)$$

$$1 - \beta = 1 - \Phi\left(Z_{1-\alpha} - \dfrac{\mu - \mu_0}{\sqrt{\sigma^2/n}}\right)$$

$$1 - \beta = \Phi\left(Z_{\alpha} - \dfrac{\mu - \mu_0}{\sqrt{\sigma^2/n}}\right)$$

Note that some people prefer to use the T-test instead of the Z-test when σ^2 is unknown – even though the observations in the sample are not normally distributed. However, when the sample size, n, is large – as is required when the observations are not normally distributed – the difference between the t-distribution and the standard normal distribution is not very big.

14.8 Choice of sample size based on type I and type II errors

In a situation where we can determine the sample size, we do so based on the purpose of the study. We showed in Section 13.6 how to determine the sample size, n, in cases where the primary objective is to estimate the mean value with a particular degree of precision. In this section, we show how to choose the sample size if the primary purpose of the study is to test a hypothesis with a certain degree of control against the probabilities of type I and type II errors.

As in Section 14.2, we look at a test of the two hypotheses:

$$H_0 : \mu = \mu_0$$
$$H_1 : \mu = \mu_1$$

where $\mu_0 < \mu_1$. In Section 14.2.5, we found the relationship between α and β to be:

$$\beta = \Phi\left(Z_{1-\alpha} - \frac{\mu_1 - \mu_0}{\sigma / \sqrt{n}} \right)$$

For a given choice of α and therefore $Z_{1-\alpha}$, we can use the above equation to find out how large a sample size, n, is required to obtain a given level of β. Note that since $\mu_0 < \mu_1$, β must always be less than $1 - \alpha$ because the second term in the parenthesis above is positive. From the definition of a quantile, we can see that the expression inside the brackets must equal the β-quantile from the standard normal distribution:

$$Z_\beta = Z_{1-\alpha} - \frac{\mu_1 - \mu_0}{\sigma / \sqrt{n}}$$

If we isolate the sample size, n, in the above expression, we get:

$$n = \left(\frac{Z_{1-\alpha} - Z_\beta}{\mu_1 - \mu_0} \cdot \sigma \right)^2$$

This gives us the sample size required to obtain a given level of α and β, when $\beta < 1 - \alpha$.

If we are to decide the size of the sample in Example 14.3 so that the probability of a type I error is no more than 0.05 and the probability of a type II error is no more than 0.10, then we would need a sample of at least the following size:

$$n = \left(\frac{Z_{1-0.05} - Z_{0.10}}{\mu_1 - \mu_0} \cdot \sigma \right)^2 = \left(\frac{1.6449 - (-1.2816)}{3-1} \cdot 4 \right)^2 = 34.26$$

We would therefore select a sample with at least 35 observations in order to keep the probabilities of type I and type II errors to the desired levels.

The formula shows that we can make do with a smaller sample size if there is a greater distance between μ_1 and μ_0. It is also the case that a lower variance, σ^2, allows for a smaller sample size. Finally, the formula also shows that the higher α and β we tolerate, the smaller the sample size required.

> **Calculation of sample size based on desired type I and type II errors:**
> 1. Decide the values of α and β.
> 2. Find the distribution of the test statistic under H_0 and H_1.
> 3. Calculate the relationship between α and β.
> 4. Based on the relationship between α and β, find the sample size.

14.9 Test of variance

In this section, we consider testing a hypothesis about the variance, σ^2. In some financial theories, the variance, σ^2, measures the risk inherent in an investment. In a situation like this, we are often interested in finding out whether the variance assumes a certain value or is higher or lower than this value. If we are studying income inequality, it might be interesting to test whether the variance in income in the Danish population exceeds a certain threshold. A test of the variance can also be part of a test of a more wide-ranging theory. In all of these situations, we need to be able to test a hypothesis about the variance, σ^2, in a distribution.

Let us look at the following null hypothesis and alternative hypothesis:

$$H_0 : \sigma^2 = \sigma_0^{\,2}$$
$$H_1 : \sigma^2 \neq \sigma_0^{\,2}$$

where $\sigma_0^{\,2}$ is the value of the variance under our null hypothesis. First, we must find a hypothesis measure that is able to distinguish between the null hypothesis and the alternative hypothesis. It turns out that $\sigma^2 / \sigma_0^{\,2}$ is a suitable measure. It is equal to 1 if the null hypothesis is true ($\sigma^2 = \sigma_0^{\,2}$), whereas it is different from 1 if the alternative hypothesis is true ($\sigma^2 \neq \sigma_0^{\,2}$). Since the alternative hypothesis is two-sided, $H_1 : \sigma^2 \neq \sigma_0^{\,2}$, both values of the hypothesis measure that are greater than 1 and those that are less than 1 can be considered as evidence against the null hypothesis. If, however, the alternative hypothesis is one-sided, $H_1 : \sigma^2 > \sigma_0^{\,2}$ (or $H_1 : \sigma^2 < \sigma_0^{\,2}$), only large (or small) values compared to 1 will serve as evidence against the null hypothesis.

To run the test, we first replace the unknown variance, σ^2, in the hypothesis measure with the sample variance, S^2. Then, all we have to do is write up a test statistic and find its distribution under H_0. The test statistic is in this case given by:

$$Y = (n-1) \cdot \frac{S^2}{\sigma_0^{\,2}}$$

Part of the reason for choosing this test statistic is that it can be shown that Y is approximately χ^2-distributed with $n - 1$ degrees of freedom under H_0 for large sample sizes. We described the χ^2-distribution in Chapter 12.1. Because we have not predicated anything about the distribution of the observations in the sample, the χ^2-distribution is only an approximation of the exact – but unknown – distribution of the test statistic, Y, under the null hypothesis. This means that the exact distribution of Y only resembles the χ^2-distribution when the sample size, n, is large.

As in the case where we test a hypothesis about the mean value, there are special cases where we can work out the exact distribution of the test statistic, Y, under H_0. One such case is when the observations in the sample are normally distributed. In this case, the distribution of Y under H_0 is exactly equal to a χ^2-distribution with $n - 1$ degrees of freedom, regardless of the sample size.

Table 14.4: Test of variance with simple random test $H_0 : \sigma^2 = \sigma_0^2$

	Alternative hypotheses		
	$H_1 : \sigma^2 \neq \sigma_0^2$	$H_1 : \sigma^2 > \sigma_0^2$	$H_1 : \sigma^2 < \sigma_0^2$
Test statistic and distribution under H_0			
Large sample size			
$Y = (n-1) \cdot \dfrac{S^2}{\sigma_0^2} \sim^A \chi^2(n-1)$ where $S^2 = \dfrac{1}{n-1} \sum_{i=1}^{n} (X_i - \overline{X})^2$	Critical values: $\chi^2_{1-\alpha/2}(n-1)$ and $\chi^2_{\alpha/2}(n-1)$	Critical values: $\chi^2_{1-\alpha}(n-1)$	Critical values: $\chi^2_{\alpha}(n-1)$
Normally distributed observations			
$Y = (n-1) \cdot \dfrac{S^2}{\sigma_0^2} \sim \chi^2(n-1)$ where $S^2 = \dfrac{1}{n-1} \sum_{i=1}^{n} (X_i - \overline{X})^2$	Critical values: $\chi^2_{\alpha/2}(n-1)$ and $\chi^2_{\alpha/2}(n-1)$	Critical values: $\chi^2_{1-\alpha}(n-1)$	Critical values: $\chi^2_{\alpha}(n-1)$

Notes:
1. α is the significance level.
2. $\chi^2_\alpha(n-1)$ is the α-quantile from the χ^2-distribution with $n-1$ degrees of freedom.

Example 14.14: Share dividends

A portfolio manager wants to test the variance of dividends from companies in the service sector and has selected a sample of 51 observed dividends. Based on the 51 observations, she has calculated the sample variance as $S^2 = 11.59$. She now wants to test the following hypothesis about the variance, σ^2:

$$H_0 : \sigma^2 = 10$$

$$H_1 : \sigma^2 > 10$$

In this case, the value of the test statistic is:

$$Y = (51-1) \cdot \frac{11.92}{10} = 59.6$$

If she insists on a significance level of 5%, she must use the 0.95-quantile from the χ^2-distribution with 50 degrees of freedom, because the alternative hypothesis is one-sided. From Table 4 at the back of the book, we find this to be 67.5. Therefore, she cannot reject the null hypothesis that the variance is 10 in favour of an alternative hypothesis, which says that the variance is greater than 10.

14.10 Statistical significance versus practical significance

Until now, we have focused on whether to accept the null or the alternative hypothesis. As previously mentioned, we usually phrase the theory we want to test as the alternative hypothesis. We then say that a result is significant if we reject the null hypothesis and accept the alternative hypothesis. This type of significance is called *statistical significance*.

We might be tempted to think that a statistically significant result is necessarily also of practical importance. However, we must bear in mind what hypothesis testing is all about. A hypothesis test is based on a sample, and the realised test statistic is affected by sample uncertainty. This means, among other things, that it is possible for a result to be statistically significant when the sample is large, while the same result might not be statistically significant with a smaller sample. But whether the result is also important in practice, also called *practical significance,* is a quite different matter that may not have anything to do with the statistical significance of the result.

Example 14.15: Monthly income

Assume that our null hypothesis is that the average income in a certain area of Denmark is DKK 50,000 per month, while the true (but unknown) average income is in fact DKK 50,070 per month. Furthermore, assume that we select a sample and find that the sample average is equal to DKK 50,060 per month. If the sample size is sufficiently large and the variance of our estimator is therefore small, this will probably cause us to reject the null hypothesis. As such, the result is statistically significant. However, is it also a significant finding – from a practical or economic point of view – that the average income is DKK 60 more per month than we thought? In another area of the country, the true average income might be DKK 30,000 per month. If we only have a small sample from this area and find a sample average of DKK 35,000 per month, this may not be enough to reject the null hypothesis of an average income of DKK 50,000 per month. But is this difference still more important from a practical point of view?

With Example 14.15, we want to point out two things: firstly, that statistical significance is a concept that relates to the sample uncertainty. Practical significance is an assessment of the social (or other) consequences of the problem being studied. Secondly, the choice of significance level should depend on the size of the sample, as well as the power of the test.

14.11 Relationship between confidence intervals and hypothesis testing

We conclude this chapter by discussing the close relationship between a $(1 - \alpha)$ confidence interval, which was the subject of Chapter 13, and a hypothesis test with a significance level of α.

Let us imagine that we want to test a null hypothesis about a mean value, $H_0 : \mu = \mu_0$, against the alternative hypothesis, $H_1 : \mu \neq \mu_0$. A $(1 - \alpha)$ confidence interval for μ will contain the true μ with the probability $1 - \alpha$. If the null hypothesis is true, the confidence interval will thus contain μ_0 with the probability $1 - \alpha$. In other words, the probability that the confidence interval does not include μ_0 when the null hypothesis is true, is α. However, this is also the probability of rejecting the null hypothesis in our test, given that the null hypothesis is actually true. In other words, this is the probability of committing a type I error.

As a consequence, we could just as well test our null hypothesis by constructing a $(1 - \alpha)$-confidence interval for μ and examining whether μ_0 lies within the interval. If not, then we can reject H_0. This corresponds exactly to what the hypothesis test does. This is not so surprising if we consider that the confidence interval was constructed from the distribution of the standardised sample average, Z – exactly as the hypothesis test in this chapter was based on the distribution of the standardised sample average under H_0.

The intuitive difference between the two approaches is as follows: in the hypothesis test, the test statistic directly measures the distance between the sample average, $\bar{X}$, and the value under the null hypothesis, μ_0. If this distance is too large (i.e. the test statistic is large), then the null hypothesis must be rejected. This conclusion is based on the distribution of the test statistic, which comes from the distribution of $\bar{X}$. When constructing a confidence interval, we set an interval around $\bar{X}$ based on the distribution of $\bar{X}$, and look at whether μ_0 lies within this interval. In other words, we indirectly study the distance between $\bar{X}$ and μ_0.

14.12   Exercises

1. Review questions
   a) Explain briefly what is meant by a null hypothesis and an alternative hypothesis.
   b) What does it mean to commit, respectively, a type I and a type II error? Give an example of each.
   c) What do you understand by the significance level?
   d) Account in brief for the different steps in the construction of a hypothesis test.
   e) What is your interpretation of the p-value and the critical values?
   f) Explain the difference between a one-sided and a two-sided alternative hypothesis. What implications does this have for the calculation of p-values and critical values?
   g) What do you understand by a test's power?
   h) Briefly explain the conditions under which the various test statistics can be used when you want to test a hypothesis about a mean value. Also specify their distributions under H_0.
   i) Explain briefly how you choose your sample size so as to obtain certain probabilities of committing type I and type II errors.
   j) Explain which test statistic you use to test a hypothesis about a variance
   k) What is the difference between statistical and practical significance?
   l) Explain the relationship between hypothesis testing and confidence intervals.

2. Assume you have a simple random sample of 100 normally distributed observations, $(X_1,...,X_{100})$, where $X_i \sim N(\mu, \sigma^2 = 24)$. The sample average is calculated as $\bar{X} = 20.9$. You now want to test the following null hypothesis: $H_0 : \mu = 20$ against the alternative hypothesis: $H_1 : \mu \neq 20$.
   a) Find the relevant test statistic.
   b) State the test statistic's distribution under H_0.
   c) Calculate the value of the test statistic as well as the p-value.
   d) Can you reject H_0 at a 5% level of significance? At a 10% significance level?
   e) Find the p-value if the alternative hypothesis is instead $H_1 : \mu > 20$.
   f) Can you now reject H_0 at a 5% significance level?

3. The soft drinks factory from Exercise 2 in Chapter 12, with the help of its simple random sample of 18 drinks, wants to test the null hypothesis that the average content of a drink is 25 cl. It is assumed in this context that the content of a randomly selected drink is normally distributed with a variance of 0.02.

a) Set up the test statistic.

b) What is the distribution of the test statistic under H_0?

c) Calculate the value of the test statistic, as well as the p-value with a two-sided alternative hypothesis.

d) What are the critical values of the test statistic with a two-sided alternative hypothesis and a 5% significance level? Can you reject H_0 at a 5% significance level?

e) Suppose instead that you use a one-sided alternative hypothesis, $H_1 : \mu > \mu_0$. Find the critical values in tests with a significance level of 5% and 10%, respectively.

f) Can you reject H_0 in these cases?

Now suppose that the variance of the content of a randomly selected drink is unknown.

g) Set up the test statistic for this case.

h) What is the distribution of the test statistic under H_0?

i) Calculate the value of the test statistic, as well as the p-value with a two-sided alternative hypothesis.

j) Find the critical values with a two-sided alternative hypothesis and a 5% significance level. Can you reject H_0?

k) Can you reject H_0 if you instead use a one-sided alternative hypothesis $H_1 : \mu > 25$ and a 5% significance level?

4. The school nurse from Exercise 3 in Chapter 10 selects a simple random sample of 100 children's heights in a local authority area with 3,431 children. She finds that the sample average is $\bar{X} = 138.4$ cm, and that the sample variance is $S^2 = 62.32$. She now wants to test whether the mean value of the population is equal to 140 cm.

a) Write up the null hypothesis and the alternative hypothesis for this test, assuming that the nurse wants to conduct a two-sided alternative hypothesis.

b) What is the relevant test statistic for this example?

c) What is the distribution of the test statistic under H_0, and under what assumptions?

d) What are the critical values at, respectively, 5% and 10% significance levels?

e) Calculate the value of the test statistic as well as the p-value.

f) Can H_0 be rejected at a 5% significance level? At a 10% level?

g) Assume, instead, that the alternative hypothesis is that the average height is under 140 cm.

h) At what significance levels can we now reject H_0?

5. In Example 1.3 from Chapter 1, the car manufacturer wanted to study whether there was a similar risk of faults on the factory's new production line as there was with the original system. From experience, the company knew that the error rate was 0.8% with the original system. The factory collates information about 800 of the cars produced on the new line and finds that 11 of them have faults. The factory now wants to test whether this error rate is significantly different from 0.8%.

a) Discuss whether you can reasonably consider the 800 cars as a simple random sample.

b) Assume that it is indeed a simple random sample and let X_i indicate whether the ith car in the sample is defective or not.

c) What distribution does X_i follow?

d) Set up the null hypothesis for the test that the factory wants to perform.

e) Set up the alternative hypothesis for a two-sided alternative.

f) What does the test statistic look like, and what is its distribution under the null hypothesis?

g) What are the critical values at a significance level of 5%?

h) Calculate the value of the test statistic as well as the p-value. Can you reject H_0?

i) What are the critical values at a significance level of 10%? Can you reject H_0?

j) Assume, instead, that the relevant alternative hypothesis is that the error rate is higher on the new production line.

k) Find the critical values of the test statistic at 5% and 1% significance levels, respectively.

l) Can you reject H_0 in these cases?

15 Testing relationships using quantitative data

In Chapter 14, we introduced the idea behind hypothesis testing by testing hypotheses about descriptive measures (the mean value and the variance) for a distribution. We may also be interested in testing hypotheses about whether two or more distributions have the same mean or variance. If there is a difference in, for example, the mean value between two distributions, then this suggests a possible relationship between the characteristic that distinguishes the two distributions (e.g. men and women) and the characteristic being measured (e.g. height).

An important example of a test of a difference between two distributions is when we examine whether a treatment has an effect. Note that in this context, the word "treatment" has a much broader meaning than the narrow medical interpretation of it. For example, a treatment could consist of people taking part in a job-training programme, while the effect could be their income a year later. We can then test whether people who have received the treatment (the training) earn more than they did before, or we can compare them with people who have not received the treatment. If there are differences in the mean values between these two groups, it suggests that the treatment has had an effect.

The tests in this chapter are introduced in the same way as in Chapter 14. First, we define the null-and alternative hypotheses, then we construct a hypothesis measure to distinguish between them. Finally, we run the test by constructing a test statistic and using its distribution under the null hypothesis to calculate critical values or p-values. Based on these, we determine whether the null hypothesis should be rejected or accepted.

In Section 15.1, we will show how to test whether the mean values in two distributions are the same. We then generalise this in Section 15.2 to cases in which there are more than two distributions. In Section 15.3, we consider three ways to test the effect of a treatment. We can also test for differences in variances between distributions, as we will see in Section 15.4.

We can study whether there is a difference between two groups in a population by testing whether they have different mean values. For example, we can test whether there is a difference between the amount of housework done by men and women when both partners have full-time jobs. We might also want to test whether a person's life expectancy depends on his or her upbringing.

Example 15.1: Educational background – part 1

A company has two types of employee in its production department: those who have completed an apprenticeship, and those with formal vocational training from a technical college. When hiring new employees, the company is unsure as to whether apprenticeships are better than technical college, so it hires a consultancy company to study whether there is an average productivity difference between the two types of employees.

Let Y specify the group to which the element belongs in the population, for example, whether an individual did an apprenticeship ($Y = 1$) or went to technical college ($Y = 2$). Let X be the characteristic we want to compare for the two types. We are then interested in comparing the mean values in the following two conditional distributions for X: $f(x|y = 1)$ and $f(x|y = 2)$, i.e. the distribution of X for group 1 and the distribution of X for group 2.

Other examples could be the expected yield on two shares or the expected grade in two different exams. These examples can also be formulated in exactly the same way: namely that we want to compare $f(x|y = 1)$ with $f(x|y = 2)$, where X is the yield (or grade), and Y indicates the share (or exam) concerned.

The mean values in the two conditional distributions, $f(x|y = 1)$ and $f(x|y = 2)$, are unknown. It is assumed that we have a simple random sample of n_1 observations from the first conditional distribution and n_2 observations from the second conditional distribution.[22] We also assume that the number of observations from each distribution is predetermined. As such, the number of observations we select from each of the two conditional distributions is not random.

---

22   It is often said that there are two samples, one from each conditional distribution.

15.1.1 The general case

As described in Chapter 14, the first task in the construction of a test is to define the hypotheses. In the following, we focus on a two-sided alternative hypothesis:

$$H_0 : \mu_1 = \mu_2$$

$$H_1 : \mu_1 \neq \mu_2$$

where μ_1 is the mean value of X in the distribution $f(x|y = 1)$, and μ_2 is the mean value of X in the distribution $f(x|y = 2)$. The null hypothesis is that there is no difference between the mean values of the two distributions, while the alternative hypothesis states that there is a difference. The sizes of the mean values are unimportant. We only care about whether they are identical or not. We could also choose a one-sided alternative hypothesis, as will be shown in Example 15.2.

The next step is to find a hypothesis measure capable of distinguishing between the null hypothesis and the alternative hypothesis when we insert the true values. An appropriate hypothesis measure in the present case is: $h(\mu_1, \mu_2) = \mu_1 - \mu_2$. If this hypothesis measure is 0 when evaluated at the true values, then the null hypothesis is true; otherwise, it is false.

We can now replace the unknown quantities in the hypothesis measure with estimates. Let $(X_{1,1}, X_{2,1}, \ldots, X_{n_1,1})$ be the sample from the first distribution and $(X_{1,2}, X_{2,2}, \ldots, X_{n_2,2})$ the sample from the second distribution. The first subscript indicates the observation number, while the second subscript tells us which of the two distributions the observation belongs to. Assume also that the observations are independent across groups.

Both μ_1 and μ_2 are unknown, but we can use the sample averages of the observations from each distribution as estimates of μ_1 and μ_2, respectively:

$$\overline{X}_1 = \frac{1}{n_1} \cdot \left(X_{1,1} + X_{2,1} + \ldots + X_{n_1,1} \right)$$

$$\overline{X}_2 = \frac{1}{n_2} \cdot \left(X_{1,2} + X_{2,2} + \ldots + X_{n_2,2} \right)$$

We now choose a test statistic that resembles the one we used to test a hypothesis about a single mean value in Chapter 14. We thus divide the estimated hypothesis measure, $\overline{X}_1 - \overline{X}_2$, by the variance of the estimated hypothesis measure. Since the observations from the two groups are independent, the sample averages, $\bar{X}_1$ and $\bar{X}_2$, are also independent. The variance of the estimated hypothesis measure is therefore given by:

$$V(\bar{X}_1 - \bar{X}_2) = V(\bar{X}_1) + V(\bar{X}_2) = \frac{\sigma_1^2}{n_1} + \frac{\sigma_2^2}{n_2}$$

where σ_1^2 and σ_2^2 are the variances of the two distributions. If these are unknown, they must also be estimated. We can do this using the estimator for the variance from Chapter 12:

$$S_1^2 = \frac{1}{n_1 - 1} \sum_{i=1}^{n_1} (X_{i,1} - \bar{X}_1)^2$$

$$S_2^2 = \frac{1}{n_2 - 1} \sum_{i=1}^{n_2} (X_{i,2} - \bar{X}_2)^2$$

where S_1^2 is the estimator for σ_1^2, and S_2^2 is the estimator for σ_2^2.

We are now ready to define our test statistic:

$$Z = \frac{(\bar{X}_1 - \bar{X}_2)}{\sqrt{\dfrac{S_1^2}{n_1} + \dfrac{S_2^2}{n_2}}}$$

This test statistic approximately follows a standard normal distribution under the null hypothesis when we have large sample sizes, n_1 and n_2. p-values and critical values are therefore also found using the standard normal distribution.

15.1.2 Equal variances

In some situations it is reasonable to assume that the two unknown variances are equal: $\sigma_1^2 = \sigma_2^2 = \sigma^2$. In these cases, we can write the variance of the estimated hypothesis measure as:

$$V(\bar{X}_1 - \bar{X}_2) = \sigma^2 \cdot \left(\frac{1}{n_1} + \frac{1}{n_2} \right)$$

In this situation, we achieve a better estimate of σ^2, and therefore $V(\bar{X}_1 - \bar{X}_2)$, by using the so-called "pooled variance estimator":

$$S_p^2 = \frac{(n_1 - 1) \cdot S_1^2 + (n_2 - 1) \cdot S_2^2}{n_1 + n_2 - 2}$$

The test statistic then looks like this:

$$Z = \frac{(\bar{X}_1 - \bar{X}_2)}{\sqrt{S_p^2 \cdot \left(\dfrac{1}{n_1} + \dfrac{1}{n_2} \right)}}$$

but it has the same approximate distribution under H_0 as the test statistics in Section 15.1.1.

Example 15.2: Educational background – part 2

The consultancy company from Example 15.1 selects a simple random sample of 30 observations among the employees with apprenticeships and 50 observations among employees who went to technical college. From the sample, the company calculates the following two productivity averages: $\bar{X}_1 = 22.54$ and $\bar{X}_2 = 19.34$ (measured as value added in euros per hour worked) and the sample variances: $S_1^2 = 19.13$ and $S_2^2 = 22.25$. The company tests the following hypotheses:

$$H_0: \mu_1 = \mu_2$$

$$H_1: \mu_1 > \mu_2$$

The alternative hypothesis is therefore that people with an apprenticeship are more productive. The value of the test statistic, Z, can be calculated as:

$$Z = \frac{22.54 - 19.34}{\sqrt{\dfrac{19.13}{30} + \dfrac{22.25}{50}}} = 3.08$$

If the consultancy company believes that the two unknown variances are equal, then the value of the test statistic is instead given by:

$$Z = \frac{22.54 - 19.34}{\sqrt{\frac{(30 - 1) \cdot 19.13 + (50 - 1) \cdot 22.25}{30 + 50 - 2} \cdot \left(\frac{1}{30} + \frac{1}{50}\right)}} = 3.02$$

Because the alternative hypothesis is one-sided, and of the form $H_1 = \mu_1 > \mu_2$, only large values of Z will be considered as evidence against the null hypothesis. At a significance level of 5%, the critical value is therefore given by the 0.95-quantile from the standard normal distribution, which is 1.64. The consultancy company therefore rejects H_0 and concludes that employees with an apprenticeship are more productive.

15.1.3 Normally distributed observations with known variances

If the observations in the two samples are normally distributed with known variances, σ_1^2 and σ_2^2, then we can show that the test statistic:

$$Z = \frac{(\bar{X}_1 - \bar{X}_2)}{\sqrt{\frac{\sigma_1^2}{n_1} + \frac{\sigma_2^2}{n_2}}}$$

follows an exact standard normal distribution under the null hypothesis. This is true regardless of the sample sizes, and parallels the result in Section 14.3 when we tested a hypothesis about a single mean value.

15.1.4 Normally distributed observations with unknown variances

If the observations in the two samples are normally distributed, but this time with unknown variances, then we can show that the test statistic (now designated as "T"):

$$T = \frac{(\bar{X}_1 - \bar{X}_2)}{\sqrt{\frac{S_1^2}{n_1} + \frac{S_2^2}{n_2}}}$$

is approximately t-distributed with $n_1 + n_2 - 2$ degrees of freedom under the null hypothesis. If the variances, σ_1^2 and σ_2^2, are identical, then we use the pooled variance estimator instead, and the test statistic is then exactly t-distributed.

If the consultancy company from Example 15.2 believes that the observations in the sample are normally distributed, then it should use the 0.95-quantile from the t-distribution with $30 + 50 - 2 = 78$ degrees of freedom instead of the 0.95-quantile from the standard normal distribution. However, because the number of degrees of freedom is so large, the two quantiles are both equal to 1.64. The fact that the observations in the samples are normally distributed does not, therefore, change the consultancy company's conclusion in this case.

15.1.5 Bernoulli-distributed observations

The last special case to consider is a situation where the observations in the two samples are Bernoulli-distributed. This might be the case, for example, if we wish to test whether the proportion of a given type is the same in the two groups. Here the null hypothesis is: $H_0 : p_1 = p_2$, where p_1 and p_2 are the proportions of the given type in group 1 and group 2, respectively. Alternatively we might wish to test whether the probabilities, p_1 and p_2, of "heads" with two different (loaded) coins are the same.

If the sample size is large, then we can use the Z-test described above, since p_1 and p_2 are the mean values of two Bernoulli-distributed variables. When we are dealing with a single Bernoulli distribution, as in Section 14.5, we can calculate the variance directly from the mean value under the null hypothesis. However, in comparing two Bernoulli distributions, we do not know the mean values, p_1 and p_2, under the null hypothesis, only that they must be identical. Therefore, the variances must also be identical. We can therefore use the pooled variance estimator, which in this case looks like this:

$$S_p^2 = \overline{p}^p \cdot \left(1 - \overline{p}^p\right), \qquad \text{hvor } \overline{p}^p = \frac{n_1 \cdot \overline{p}_1 + n_2 \cdot \overline{p}_2}{n_1 + n_2}$$

where $\overline{p}_1$ and $\overline{p}_2$ are the two sample averages (the estimated proportions), and $\overline{p}^p$ is the average for the total sample. The test statistic therefore becomes:

$$Z = \frac{\overline{p}_1 - \overline{p}_2}{\sqrt{\overline{p}^p \cdot \left(1 - \overline{p}^p\right) \cdot \left(\dfrac{1}{n_1} + \dfrac{1}{n_2}\right)}}$$

which follows an approximate standard normal distribution under the null hypothesis.

Example 15.4: Exam

A business school wants to test whether the probability of passing an exam depends on the teacher who has taught the subject. In other words:

$$H_0 : p_1 = p_2$$

$$H_1 : p_1 \neq p_2$$

where p_1 is the probability of passing with teacher 1 and p_2 is the probability of passing with teacher 2. The school now selects a simple random sample of 25 and 36 students, respectively, from the two teachers' exams. It finds that the proportion of those selected who passed with teacher 1 was $7/25 = 0.28$, while for teacher 2 the proportion was $14/36 = 0.389$. The value of the test statistic is therefore:

$$Z = \frac{0.28 - 0.389}{\sqrt{0.344 \cdot \left(1 - 0.344\right) \cdot \left(\dfrac{1}{25} + \dfrac{1}{36}\right)}} = -0.88$$

since: $\quad \overline{p}^p = \dfrac{25 \cdot 0.28 + 36 \cdot 0.389}{25 + 36} = 0.344$

At a significance level of 5%, the critical values from the standard normal distribution are 1.96 and −1.96. The business school cannot therefore reject the null hypothesis that there is the same probability of passing with the two teachers.

15.1.6   Testing the difference between two mean values – an overview

Table 15.1 sums up the results from the previous sections.

Table 15.1: Test of two mean values with a simple random sample for each group, $H_0 : \mu_1 = \mu_2$

	Alternative hypotheses		
	$H_1 : \mu_1 \neq \mu_2$	$H_1 : \mu_1 > \mu_2$	$H_1 : \mu_1 < \mu_2$
Test statistic and distribution under H_0			
The general case: Large sample sizes (Sections 15.1.1 and 15.1.2)			
σ_1^2 and σ_2^2 known: $$Z = \frac{(\bar{X}_1 - \bar{X}_2)}{\sqrt{\sigma_1^2/n_1 + \sigma_2^2/n_2}} \sim {}^A N(0,1)$$			
σ_1^2 and σ_2^2 unknown: $$Z = \frac{(\bar{X}_1 - \bar{X}_2)}{\sqrt{S_1^2/n_1 + S_2^2/n_2}} \sim {}^A N(0,1)$$	p-value: $2 \cdot \Phi(-\lvert z\rvert)$	p-value: $1 - \Phi(z)$	p-value: $\Phi(z)$
σ_1^2 and σ_2^2 unknown but equal: $$Z = \frac{(\bar{X}_1 - \bar{X}_2)}{\sqrt{S_p^2 \cdot (1/n_1 + 1/n_2)}} \sim {}^A N(0,1)$$ where: $$S_p^2 = \frac{(n_1 - 1) \cdot S_1^2 + (n_2 - 1) \cdot S_2^2}{n_1 + n_2 - 2}$$	Critical values: $Z_{\alpha/2}$ and $Z_{1-\alpha/2}$	Critical value: $Z_{1-\alpha}$	Critical value: Z_{α}
Normally distributed observations (Sections 15.1.3 and 15.1.4)			
σ_1^2 and σ_2^2 known: $$Z = \frac{(\bar{X}_1 - \bar{X}_2)}{\sqrt{\sigma_1^2/n_1 + \sigma_2^2/n_2}} \sim N(0,1)$$	p-value: $2 \cdot \Phi(-\lvert z\rvert)$	p-value: $1 - \Phi(z)$	p-value: $\Phi(z)$
	Critical values: $Z_{\alpha/2}$ and $Z_{1-\alpha/2}$	Critical value: $Z_{1-\alpha}$	Critical value: Z_{α}

$\rightarrow$

σ_1^2 and σ_2^2 unknown:

$$T = \frac{(\bar{X}_1 - \bar{X}_2)}{\sqrt{S_1^2/n_1 + S_2^2/n_2}} \sim^A t(n_1 + n_2 - 2)$$

σ_1^2 and σ_2^2 unknown but equal:

$$T = \frac{(\bar{X}_1 - \bar{X}_2)}{\sqrt{S_p^2 \cdot (1/n_1 + 1/n_2)}} \sim t(n_1 + n_2 - 2)$$

where:

$$S_p^2 = \frac{(n_1 - 1) \cdot S_1^2 + (n_2 - 1) \cdot S_2^2}{n_1 + n_2 - 2}$$

p-value: $2 \cdot P(T \le -|t|)$	p-value: $P(T > t)$	p-value: $P(T < t)$
Critical values: $t_{\alpha/2}(n_1 + n_2 - 2)$ and $t_{1-\alpha/2}(n_1 + n_2 - 2)$	Critical value: $t_{1-\alpha}(n_1 + n_2 - 2)$	Critical value: $t_{\alpha}(n_1 + n_2 - 2)$

Test of proportion: $X_i \sim$ Ber(p) and large sample sizes (Section 15.1.5)

$$Z = \frac{\bar{p}_1 - \bar{p}_2}{\sqrt{\bar{p}^p \cdot (1 - \bar{p}^p) \cdot \left(\frac{1}{n_1} + \frac{1}{n_2}\right)}} \sim^A N(0,1)$$

where: $\bar{p}^p = \dfrac{n_1 \cdot \bar{p}_1 + n_2 \cdot \bar{p}_2}{n_1 + n_2}$

p-value: $2 \cdot \Phi(-|z|)$	p-value: $1 - \Phi(z)$	p-value: $\Phi(z)$
Critical values: $Z_{\alpha/2}$ and $Z_{1-\alpha/2}$	Critical value: $Z_{1-\alpha}$	Critical value: Z_{α}

Notes:
1. z and t are the observed values of the test statistic.
2. α is the significance level.
3. Z_α is the α-quantile from the standard normal distribution, and $t_\alpha(n_1 + n_2 - 2)$ is the α-quantile from the t-distribution with $n_1 + n_2 - 2$ degrees of freedom.

15.2 Testing differences between multiple mean values (variance analysis)

One way to examine differences between multiple distributions is to study whether their mean values are different. In this section, we will test whether the mean values in a series of distributions (groups) are the same. As above, we are interested in the distributions of X given $Y = y$ for different values of y. In this section, there are K different distributions, i.e. $y = 1, y = 2, \ldots, y = K$. The null hypothesis is:

$$H_0 : \mu_1 = \mu_2 = \ldots = \mu_K$$

H_1 : At least one of the mean values is not like the others

where μ_k is the mean value of the conditional distribution $f(x|y = k)$. Note that for the null hypothesis to be false only requires that one distribution's mean value is different from the other distributions' mean values.

The hypothesis measure we use to distinguish between the null- and the alternative hypothesis is given by:

$$\sum_{k=1}^{K} (\mu_k - \mu)^2$$

where μ is some average of the mean values for the K distributions. It could be either the simple average, $\mu = (1/K)\sum_{k=1}^{K}\mu_k$, or a weighted average, $\mu = \sum_{k=1}^{K} w_k \cdot \mu_k$, where the w_ks are positive weights that sum to one. In any case, when the true values are inserted, this hypothesis measure is 0 if all of the mean values are the same, whereas it is greater than 0 if one of the mean values is different from the others.

As previously, we use the sample averages to estimate the mean values. Let $X_{1,k}, X_{2,k}, \ldots, X_{n_k,k}$ be a simple random sample of n_k observations from distribution k. The estimate of the mean value, μ_k, for distribution k is therefore given by:

$$\overline{X}_k = \frac{1}{n_k} \cdot \left(X_{1,k} + X_{2,k} + \ldots + X_{n_k,k} \right)$$

Now, if we use the μ where the weights, w_k, are the relative sample sizes, n_k/n, the estimator for μ is just the simple average of all of the observations:

$$\overline{X} = \sum_{k=1}^{K} \frac{n_k}{n} \cdot \overline{X}_k = \sum_{k=1}^{K} \frac{n_k}{n} \cdot \frac{1}{n_k} \sum_{i=1}^{n_k} X_{i,k} = \frac{1}{n} \sum_{k=1}^{K} \sum_{i=1}^{n_k} X_{i,k}$$

where n is the total number of observations in the K samples, $n = n_1 + n_2 + \ldots + n_K$.

An estimator for the hypothesis measure is then:

$$\sum_{k=1}^{K} \left(\overline{X}_k - \overline{X} \right)^2 \cdot \frac{n_k}{n}$$

where we have weighted each group according to its share of the total sample size, n_k/n. This means that a deviation between $\overline{X}_k$ and $\overline{X}$ for a distribution k, from which we have a small sample, n_k, will have less influence than a deviation between $\overline{X}_k$ and $\overline{X}$ for a distribution from which we have a large sample.

For the test statistic to get a wellknown distribution, we must assume that the variances in the K distributions are equal:

$\sigma_1^2 = \dots = \sigma_K^2 = \sigma^2$. By dividing the estimated hypothesis measure above by an estimate of this variance, we arrive at the test statistic:

$$F = \frac{\sum_{k=1}^{K} \left(\overline{X}_k - \overline{X} \right)^2 \cdot \dfrac{n_k}{n}}{\dfrac{1}{n} \sum_{k=1}^{K} \sum_{i=1}^{n_k} \left(X_{i,k} - \overline{X}_k \right)^2} \cdot \frac{\dfrac{1}{K-1}}{\dfrac{1}{n-K}} = \frac{SSTR/(K-1)}{SSE/(n-K)}$$

where:

$$SSTR = \sum_{k=1}^{K} \left(\overline{X}_k - \overline{X} \right)^2 \cdot n_k$$

$$SSE = \sum_{k=1}^{K} \sum_{i=1}^{n_k} \left(X_{i,k} - \overline{X}_k \right)^2 = \sum_{k=1}^{K} \left(n_k - 1 \right) \cdot S_k^2$$

and S_k^2 is the sample variance in the kth sample. If the observations in the samples are normally distributed, then we can show that the test statistic is F-distributed with $(K-1, n-K)$ degrees of freedom under the null hypothesis.

As with the t-distribution and the χ^2-distribution, the F-distribution consists of a family of distributions. However, in contrast to the two other distributions, the F-distribution is characterised by two parameters, or two sets of degrees of freedom. The example shown in Figure 15.1 is the F-distribution with 5 and 9 degrees of freedom, written $F(5, 9)$. The most important quantiles for the F-distribution are shown in Tables 5 and 6 at the back of the book.

Figure 15.1:
F-distribution
with (5, 9)
degrees of
freedom

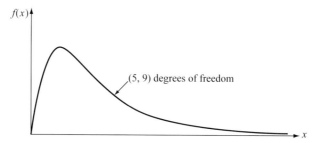

An alternative interpretation of the test statistics is as follows: *SSTR* is a measure of how much each group's average, $\overline{X}_k, k = 1,\dots,K$, differs from the total sample's average, $\overline{X}$. *SSE*, on the other hand, measures the variance within each sample. This means that if *SSTR* is large in relation to *SSE*, then this is an indication that there is a greater variance between samples than within the samples. This suggests that the mean values of the K distributions are not the same, and it must therefore be regarded as evidence against the null hypothesis. In fact, we can show that under the null hypothesis both the numerator and the denominator in the test statistic are estimators of the variance, σ^2, in the K distributions. Under H_1, however, it is only the denominator that is an estimator of σ^2, whereas the numerator grows with the sample size, n. The test statistic will therefore assume a large value (and lead to rejection of the null hypothesis) if the alternative hypothesis is true and if n is sufficiently large. This interpretation is the reason the analysis has traditionally been termed *variance analysis*.

Variance analysis

Purpose: Test of equal mean values in K normal distributions with the same variance, σ^2, using a simple random sample from each group.

Hypothesis:

$$H_0 : \mu_1 = \mu_2 = \ldots = \mu_K$$

$$H_1 : \text{At least one } \mu_k \text{ is not like the others,}$$

where $\mu_k, k = 1,\ldots,K$ are the unknown mean values in the K distributions.

Test statistic:

$$F = \frac{SSTR/(K-1)}{SSE/(n-K)} \sim F(K-1, n-K) \text{ under } H_0$$

where:

$$SSTR = \sum_{k=1}^{K} \left(\bar{X}_k - \bar{X} \right)^2 \cdot n_k$$

$$SSE = \sum_{k=1}^{K} \sum_{i=1}^{n_k} \left(X_{i,k} - \bar{X}_k \right)^2 = \sum_{k=1}^{K} (n_k - 1) \cdot S_k^2$$

and $\bar{X}_k$ is the sample average in the kth sample with n_k observations, and n is the size of the total sample.

$\rightarrow$

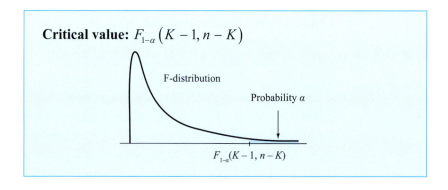

Critical value: $F_{1-\alpha}\left(K-1, n-K\right)$

F-distribution

Probability α

$F_{1-\alpha}(K-1, n-K)$

Example 15.5: Export markets

An exporter wants to compare average demand among customers in three of its major export markets. For this purpose, it has selected the sample shown in Table 15.2.

Table 15.2:
Sample results from three export markets

	Sample size	Sample average	Sample variance
Market 1	16	56.32	17.23
Market 2	12	64.12	10.11
Market 3	11	59.34	18.13
Total	39	59.57	

The exporter believes that it is reasonable to consider the three samples as simple random samples with normally distributed observations, all of which have the same variance, σ^2. He therefore decides to use the variance analysis from the box above to test his hypothesis. He calculates the values of *SSTR* and *SSE* as follows:

$$SSTR = \sum_{k=1}^{K}\left(\bar{X}_k - \bar{X}\right)^2 \cdot n_k$$

$$= \left(56.32 - 59.57\right)^2 \cdot 16 + \left(64.12 - 59.57\right)^2 \cdot 12$$

$$+ \left(59.34 - 59.57\right)^2 \cdot 11 = 418.01$$

$$SSE = \sum_{k=1}^{K}\left(n_k - 1\right) \cdot S_k^2 = (16 - 1) \cdot 17.23 + (12 - 1) \cdot 10.11$$

$$+ (11 - 1) \cdot 18.13 = 550.96$$

This results in the following value of the test statistic:

$$F = \frac{SSTR/(K-1)}{SSE/(n-K)} = \frac{418.01/(3-1)}{550.96/(39-3)} = 13.66$$

Under the null hypothesis, the test statistic is F-distributed with $(3-1, 39-3) = (2, 36)$ degrees of freedom. The 0.95-quantile of this distribution is 3.26, and therefore the null hypothesis can be rejected. The average demand is therefore not the same in the three markets.

15.3   Testing the effect of a treatment

Social scientists are often interested in how a treatment affects individuals. A treatment could be, for example, an employee attending a training course. Here, we could be interested in testing whether the course has a positive effect on the employee's subsequent productivity, measured by his or her salary.

For this purpose, we can use various estimation methods, depending on the type of data available. In this section, we will look at three different types of data. The first type is when we have observations on elements that have been treated and elements that have not been treated. The elements that have not been treated are also called the *control group*.

The second type of data is when we do not have a control group but we instead observe the same element twice over time, before the treatment and afterwards. The third type of data combines the first two types; we have a control group, which is also observed at the same points in time as the elements that receive treatment.

15.3.1   Treatment group and control group are observed once

When you only observe the treatment group and the control group once, the estimation and test of the effect of a treatment is done in the same manner as in Section 15.1.1. Let μ^{treat} be the mean value of X for those treated and μ^{con} the mean value of X for the control group. If the treatment group and the control group do not differ from each other except for the fact that the former has received the treatment, then $\mu^{treat} - \mu^{con}$ is the mean effect of the treatment. We therefore choose the hypotheses as:

$$H_0 : \mu^{treat} - \mu^{con} = 0$$

$$H_1 : \mu^{treat} - \mu^{con} \neq 0$$

The estimator, D, of the effect of the treatment is:

$$D = \bar{X}^{treat} - \bar{X}^{con}$$

where $\bar{X}^{treat}$ is the sample average in the treatment group, and $\bar{X}^{con}$ is the sample average in the control group. The test statistic then becomes:

$$Z = \frac{(\bar{X}^{treat} - \bar{X}^{con})}{\sqrt{\dfrac{\left(S^{treat}\right)^2}{n_{treat}} + \dfrac{\left(S^{con}\right)^2}{n_{con}}}}$$

where n_{treat} and n_{con} are the number of observations in the treatment group and control group, respectively, and $\left(S^{treat}\right)^2$ and $\left(S^{con}\right)^2$ are the sample variances for the two groups. The test statistic then follows an approximate standard normal distribution, exactly as in Section 15.1.1.

15.3.2 Treatment group is observed twice without a control group

In this subsection, we discuss how to test the effect of a treatment in cases where we only observe elements that have been treated. This is particularly relevant in a situation with a controlled experiment, such as a laboratory experiment.

Assume that the elements receive treatment between time t and $t + 1$, and let $X_{i,t}^{treat}$ be the observation of the ith selected element at time t, while $X_{i,t+1}^{treat}$ is the observation of the element at time $t + 1$. The data is thus of the type: $\left((X_{1,t}^{treat}, X_{1,t+1}^{treat}), (X_{2,t}^{treat}, X_{2,t+1}^{treat}), \ldots, (X_{n_{treat},t}^{treat}, X_{n_{treat},t+1}^{treat})\right)$. Assume also that the sample is a simple random sample. As such, the pairs $(X_{i,t}^{treat}, X_{i,t+1}^{treat})$ are independent of each other. Typically, however, the two observations in a pair are not independent. Since there are n_{treat} elements, which we observe twice, there are $2 \cdot n_{treat}$ observations in total. Data of this kind, where we observe the same elements several times, are called *panel data*.

We assume that the effect of the treatment for element i is equal to $X_{i,t+1}^{treat} - X_{i,t}^{treat}$. Since μ_t^{treat} and μ_{t+1}^{treat} are the mean values at time t and $t + 1$, respectively, for the population that has received treatment, the mean effect of the treatment is equal to $\mu_{t+1}^{treat} - \mu_t^{treat}$. This leads to the following two hypotheses:

$$H_0 : \mu_{t+1}^{treat} - \mu_t^{treat} = 0$$

$$H_1 : \mu_{t+1}^{treat} - \mu_t^{treat} \neq 0$$

We use the hypothesis measure $h(\mu_t^{treat}, \mu_{t+1}^{treat}) = \mu_{t+1}^{treat} - \mu_t^{treat}$, which is equal to the mean effect of the treatment. The estimated hypothesis measure, which is also the estimated effect, D, of the treatment is:

$$D = \bar{X}_2^{treat} - \bar{X}_1^{treat}$$

where $\bar{X}_1^{treat} = \dfrac{1}{n_{treat}} \displaystyle\sum_{i=1}^{n} X_{i,1}^{treat}$ is the sample average at time $t = 1$, and

$\bar{X}_2^{treat} = \dfrac{1}{n_{treat}} \displaystyle\sum_{i=1}^{n} X_{i,2}^{treat}$ is the sample average at time $t + 1 = 2$.

The test statistic is constructed in the same way as when testing a mean value, i.e.:

$$Z = \frac{\bar{X}_2^{treat} - \bar{X}_1^{treat}}{\sqrt{V\left(\bar{X}_2^{treat} - \bar{X}_1^{treat}\right)}}$$

Since the pairs $(X_{i,t}, X_{i,t+1})$ are independent, it is possible to rewrite the variance in the denominator of the test statistics as follows:

$$V\left(\bar{X}_2^{treat} - \bar{X}_1^{treat}\right) = V\left(\frac{1}{n_{treat}} \sum_{i=1}^{n_{treat}} X_{i,2}^{treat} - \frac{1}{n_{treat}} \sum_{i=1}^{n_{treat}} X_{i,1}^{treat}\right)$$

$$= V\left(\frac{1}{n_{treat}} \left(\sum_{i=1}^{n_{treat}} X_{i,2}^{treat} - \sum_{i=1}^{n_{treat}} X_{i,1}^{treat}\right)\right)$$

$$= \frac{1}{n_{treat}^2} \cdot V\left(\sum_{i=1}^{n_{treat}} \left(X_{i,2}^{treat} - X_{i,1}^{treat}\right)\right) = \frac{1}{n_{treat}} \cdot V\left(X_{i,2}^{treat} - X_{i,1}^{treat}\right)$$

Since $X_{i,1}^{treat}$ and $X_{i,2}^{treat}$ are not independent, the last expression is not equal to the sum of the variances of $X_{i,1}^{treat}$ and $X_{i,2}^{treat}$. However, we can estimate the last expression directly, as the sample consists of pairs $(X_{i,t}^{treat}, X_{i,t+1}^{treat})$. An estimator for the variance, $V\left(\bar{X}_2^{treat} - X_1^{treat}\right)$, is then:

$$\hat{V}\left(\bar{X}_2^{treat} - X_1^{treat}\right) = \frac{1}{n_{treat}} \cdot \left(\frac{1}{n_{treat} - 1} \sum_{i=1}^{n_{treat}} \left(\left(X_{i,2}^{treat} - X_{i,1}^{treat}\right) - \left(\bar{X}_2^{treat} - \bar{X}_1^{treat}\right)\right)^2\right)$$

As before, when the sample size is sufficiently large (e.g. a minimum of 30 observations), the test statistic follows an approximate standard normal distribution under the null hypothesis.

15.3.3 Treatment group and control group are observed twice

In the social sciences, where experiments are rarely conducted in a laboratory, particular care must be taken to ensure an adequate control group. The purpose of a control group is to take account of the effects of other factors that may affect the elements treated during the period t to $t+1$, apart from the impact of the treatment itself. If the control group and the treatment group are exposed to the same "other" factors, we can use the control group to remove the effect of these other factors.

The only reason that the control group changes mean value from t to $t+1$ is because of these other factors. The impact of these other factors is therefore $\mu_{t+1}^{con} - \mu_{t}^{con}$, where μ_{t}^{con} is the mean value at time t for the control group in the population. We assume that the impact on the treatment group of these other factors is the same as on the control group. In addition, the treatment group also receives the effect of the treatment. Under these assumptions, the effect, B, of the treatment is:

$$B = \left(\mu_{t+1}^{treat} - \mu_{t}^{treat} \right) - \left(\mu_{t+1}^{con} - \mu_{t}^{con} \right)$$

where μ_{t}^{treat} is the mean value at time t for the treatment group. The hypotheses are therefore:

$$H_0 : \left(\mu_{t+1}^{treat} - \mu_{t}^{treat} \right) - \left(\mu_{t+1}^{con} - \mu_{t}^{con} \right) = 0$$

$$H_1 : \left(\mu_{t+1}^{treat} - \mu_{t}^{treat} \right) - \left(\mu_{t+1}^{con} - \mu_{t}^{con} \right) \neq 0$$

We can estimate the hypothesis measure using:

$$D = \left(\bar{X}_{t+1}^{treat} - \bar{X}_{t}^{treat} \right) - \left(\bar{X}_{t+1}^{con} - \bar{X}_{t}^{con} \right).$$

Since this is equal to the difference between two differences, it is also called the "diff-in-diff" estimator. The test statistic takes the same form as before:

$$Z = \frac{\left(\bar{X}_{2}^{treat} - \bar{X}_{1}^{treat} \right) - \left(\bar{X}_{2}^{con} - \bar{X}_{1}^{con} \right)}{\sqrt{V\left(\left(\bar{X}_{2}^{treat} - \bar{X}_{1}^{treat} \right) - \left(\bar{X}_{2}^{con} - \bar{X}_{1}^{con} \right) \right)}}$$

Where $t+1 = 2$ and $t+1$.

We assume that the sample from the control group, $\left(\left(X_{1,1}^{con}, X_{1,2}^{con} \right), ..., \left(X_{n_{con},1}^{con}, X_{n_{con},2}^{con} \right) \right)$, consists of n_{con} paired observations, and that these pairs constitute a simple random sample. Similarly, we assume that the sample from the treatment group,

An insight into statistics for the social sciences

$$\left(\left(X_{1,1}^{treat}, X_{1,2}^{treat}\right),...,\left(X_{n_{treat},1}^{treat}, X_{n_{treat},2}^{treat}\right)\right),$$ consists of n_{treat} paired observations, which constitute a simple random sample. We also assume that the observations from the treated part of the population are statistically independent of the observations from the control group. Based on these assumptions, we can write the variance from the denominator in the above test statistics as:

$$V\left(\left(\bar{X}_2^{treat} - \bar{X}_1^{treat}\right) - \left(\bar{X}_2^{con} - \bar{X}_1^{con}\right)\right)$$

$$= \frac{1}{n_{treat}} \cdot V\left(X_{i,2}^{treat} - X_{i,1}^{treat}\right) + \frac{1}{n_{con}} \cdot V\left(X_{i,2}^{con} - X_{i,1}^{con}\right)$$

We can estimate the last two variance expressions directly, as the sample consists of pairs. Estimators for these two variances are:

$$\hat{V}\left(X_{i,2}^{treat} - X_{i,1}^{treat}\right) = \frac{1}{n_{treat}-1} \sum_{i=1}^{n_{treat}} \left(\left(X_{i,2}^{treat} - X_{i,1}^{treat}\right) - \left(\bar{X}_2^{treat} - \bar{X}_1^{treat}\right)\right)^2$$

$$\hat{V}\left(X_{i,2}^{con} - X_{i,1}^{con}\right) = \frac{1}{n_{con}-1} \sum_{i=1}^{n_{con}} \left(\left(X_{i,2}^{con} - X_{i,1}^{con}\right) - \left(\bar{X}_2^{con} - \bar{X}_1^{con}\right)\right)^2$$

When the samples are sufficiently large for both the group of treated subjects and the control group, the test statistic follows an approximate standard normal distribution under the null hypothesis.

Example 15.6: Job training

A study of 40 subjects assessed before and after a training course gave the result that the average hourly wage rate increased from $\bar{X}_1^{treat}$ = DKK 200 per hour to $\bar{X}_2^{treat}$ = DKK 220 per hour. For a control group of 30 subjects who were studied at the same time, the result was $\bar{X}_1^{con}$ = DKK 190 per hour and $\bar{X}_2^{con}$ = DKK 205 per hour. If we run the test without the use of the control group, as in Section 15.3.2, we get the following value for the test statistic:

$$\frac{220 - 200}{\sqrt{64}} = 2.5$$

where the denominator is the square root of the estimated variance. This implies that the null hypothesis is rejected. We conclude, therefore, that the training course has a statistically significant effect on wages.

If, however, we include the control group, as in Section 15.3.3, we get

$$\frac{(220 - 200) - (205 - 190)}{\sqrt{58}} = 0.66$$

where the denominator is again the square root of the estimated variance. In this case, the null hypothesis is accepted, and we conclude that the training course does not have a statistically significant effect on wages.

The reason for the two different conclusions may be that, without using a control group, we end up including the effects of other factors such as general wage increases due to inflation or an economic upswing, which have nothing to do with the training course.

15.4   Testing the difference between two variances

In the previous section, we tested whether two or more mean values were equal. We may also be interested in testing whether two variances are equal. This could be the case in a situation where we are considering using the pooled variance estimator but are unsure about the appropriateness of doing so. It could also be that we want to test whether the yield on two shares has the same variance.

For this purpose, as in Section 15.1, we need a simple random sample from each group. We also have to assume that the observations in these samples are normally distributed:

$$\left(X_{1,1}, X_{2,1}, \ldots, X_{n_1,1}\right), \text{ where } X_{i,1} \sim N\left(\mu_1, \sigma_1^2\right)$$

$$\left(X_{1,2}, X_{2,2}, \ldots, X_{n_2,2}\right), \text{ where } X_{i,2} \sim N\left(\mu_2, \sigma_2^2\right)$$

The hypotheses are:

$$H_0 : \sigma_1^2 = \sigma_2^2$$

$$H_1 : \sigma_1^2 \neq \sigma_2^2$$

To test these hypotheses, we will use the hypothesis measure σ_1^2/σ_2^2. If the null hypothesis is true, then this measure is equal to 1, otherwise it is different from 1. The estimated hypothesis measure – which in this case is also our test statistic – is obtained by replacing the variances with the sample variances:

$$F = \frac{S_1^2}{S_2^2}$$

where S_1^2 is the estimator for σ_1^2, and S_2^2 is the estimator for σ_2^2. It can now be shown that this test statistic is F-distributed with $(n_1 - 1, n_2 - 1)$ degrees of freedom under the null hypothesis. If the alternative hypothesis is two-sided, both high and low values of F compared to 1 will serve as evidence against the null hypothesis. If, on the other hand, the alternative hypothesis is one-sided, either high or low values of F will serve to reject H_0, depending on the nature of H_1. Table 15.3 summarises the procedure.

Table 15.3: Testing the difference between two variances with two independent simple random samples, $H_0 : \sigma_1^2 = \sigma_2^2$

	Alternative hypotheses		
	$H_1 : \sigma_1^2 \neq \sigma_2^2$	$H_1 : \sigma_1^2 > \sigma_2^2$	$H_1 : \sigma_1^2 < \sigma_2^2$
Test statistic and distribution under H_0			
Normally distributed observations			
$F = \dfrac{S_1^2}{S_2^2} \sim F(n_1 - 1, n_2 - 1)$	Critical values: $F_{\alpha/2}(n_1 - 1, n_2 - 1)$ and $F_{1-\alpha/2}(n_1 - 1, n_2 - 1)$	Critical value: $F_{1-\alpha}(n_1 - 1, n_2 - 1)$	Critical value: $F_{\alpha}(n_1 - 1, n_2 - 1)$

Notes:
1. α is the significance level.
2. $F_\alpha(n_1 - 1, n_2 - 1)$ is the α-quantile from the F-distribution with $(n_1 - 1, n_2 - 1)$ degrees of freedom.

In Example 15.2, the consultants used the pooled variance estimator. It would, therefore, be interesting to test whether the variances in the two distributions are actually the same. Based on the calculated sample variances, $S_1^2 = 19.13$ and $S_2^2 = 22.25$, we calculate the following value of the test statistic:

$$F = \frac{19.13}{22.25} = 0.86$$

If the alternative hypothesis is two-sided and the consultants use a 5% significance level, then they must use the 0.025-quantile and the 0.975-quantile from the F-distribution with (29, 49) degrees of freedom. These quantiles are 0.50 and 1.88, respectively. The consultancy company can therefore not reject the null hypothesis, and it can confidently use the pooled variance estimator.

15.5 Exercises

1. Review questions
   a) Briefly explain which test statistics can be used when you want to test a hypothesis about two mean values. Explain the reasoning behind the test statistics and specify their distributions under H_0.
   b) What do you understand by the pooled variance estimator? When is it used?
   c) Explain the reasoning behind the test statistic you would use when testing a hypothesis about two proportions. What are the assumptions required to use this? What is its distribution under the null hypothesis?
   d) What can variance analysis be used for? Explain how to interpret *SSTR* and *SSE* and the test statistic F. What distribution does F follow under H_0?
   e) Explain how to test a hypothesis about the effect of a treatment and explain the three different approaches presented in this chapter.
   f) Which test statistic can you use to test a hypothesis about two variances? What are the prerequisites for being able to use it and what is its distribution under H_0?

2. Assume that you have two simple random samples with 50 and 70 observations, respectively. The sample average in the first sample is $\bar{X}_1 = 12.95$, while in the second sample it is $\bar{X}_1 = 13.2$. You now want to test the null hypothesis $H_0 : \mu_1 = \mu_2$ against the alternative hypothesis $H_1 : \mu_1 \neq \mu_2$.
   a) Write up the appropriate test statistic if the variances are known: $\sigma_1^2 = \sigma_2^2 = 0.60$.
   b) What is the distribution of the test statistic under H_0 if the observations in the samples are normally distributed? What if they are not normally distributed?
   c) Calculate the value of the test statistic as well as the p-value.
   d) Can you reject H_0 at a 5% significance level? At a 10% significance level?

   Assume instead that the variances are unknown, but that the sample variances are calculated as $S_1^2 = 0.57$ and $S_2^2 = 0.63$.
   e) Write up the appropriate test statistic, assuming that the underlying variances are not equal.
   f) What distribution does this test statistic follow under H_0 if it is assumed that the observations in the samples are normally distributed?
   g) If the observations in the samples are not normally distributed, what distribution does the test statistic then follow?
   h) For each of the two cases in f) and g), find the critical values if you are testing at a 5% significance level, and compare these.
   i) Calculate the value of the test statistic as well as the p-value.
   j) At what significance level can we reject H_0?

3. A bank wants to compare the mean turnover among corporate customers in two of its branches. It selects two samples, one from each branch's clientèle. The results of the two samples are:

	n	$\bar{X}$ (tDKK)	S
Branch 1	25	1,267.7	210.8
Branch 2	30	1,443.4	278.0

   a) Define the null hypothesis and the alternative hypothesis.
   b) Explain which test statistic is useful for testing the hypothesis in question a).
   c) What is the distribution of this test statistic under the null hypothesis? Under what assumptions does this apply?
   d) Calculate the value of the test statistic as well as the p-value.

e) What are the critical values of the test statistic in a test with a 5% significance level? Can we reject H_0 at a 5% significance level?
The bank is considering using the pooled variance estimator when calculating the test statistic.

f) How can you test whether it is reasonable to use the pooled variance estimator?

g) Write up the null hypothesis and the alternative hypothesis for this test.

h) Find the relevant test statistic for the test in question g) and state its distribution under H_0.

i) Find the critical values when using a 5% and 10% significance level, respectively.

j) Complete the test of whether the bank can use the pooled variance estimator.

k) Answer questions b) to e) using the pooled variance estimator.

4. In 1997 and 2002, a research institute conducted two surveys on attitudes to alcohol advertising on TV. In 1997, 74% of respondents were against, while the figure in 2002 was 72%. The institute therefore concluded that resistance to this type of advertising is on the wane. The number of subjects interviewed was 957 in 1997 and 1,012 in 2002.

a) Under what circumstances is it reasonable to assume that the two samples are simple random samples and independent?

b) Which test can you use to determine whether the institute is correct in its conclusion?

c) Complete the test and determine under which conditions the conclusion can be accepted.

d) Based on your results, what would you conclude about the development from 1997 to 2002?

5. Over a long period, a share analyst has observed the annual dividend payments on (equally priced) shares for a group of companies in the pharmaceutical industry. She has collected observations from 10 companies over 5 years, a total of 50 observations. She has calculated the sample average as $\overline{X} = 11.43$ and the sample variance to $S^2 = 86.8$.

a) Discuss whether you can consider these observations a simple random sample. How can you interpret the population from which the sample is drawn?

The analyst believes that this is a simple random sample and wants to test whether the standard deviation, σ, on the yields is less than DKK 10.

b) What test statistic should she use, and what assumptions does she have to make?

c) Specify the null hypothesis and the alternative hypothesis.

d) Find the critical value for a test with a significance level of 5%.

e) Calculate the value of the test statistic and decide whether the analyst can accept her hypothesis.

The analyst has also observed dividend payments from a number of IT companies. Here, she has a total of 43 observations with a sample average of $\overline{X} = 14.47$ and a sample variance of $S^2 = 142.7$. She now wants to test whether the variances in the yields for the two types of shares are the same.

f) What test statistic should she use in that case, and what assumptions must she make?

g) Specify the null hypothesis and the alternative hypothesis.

h) Find the critical value for a test with a significance level of 10%.

i) Calculate the value of the test statistic and decide whether the null hypothesis should be rejected.

6. A study of the number of new appointments made in the past year by small Danish companies in Jutland, on Funen and on Sealand, resulted in the following:

	Sample size	Sample Average	Sample variance
Jutland	95	3.21	3.97
Funen	35	4.50	4.11
Sealand	108	2.44	4.35

An inquisitive person now wants to study whether the average number of new appointments in companies on Funen is the same as in the two other regions.

a) Which test can he use for this purpose?

b) Explain the preconditions for the test.

c) Specify the null hypothesis and the alternative hypothesis.

d) Find the critical value for a test with a significance level of 5%.

e) Calculate the value of the test statistic and decide whether the hypothesis can be accepted or must be rejected.

16 Testing relationships and distributions using qualitative data

In this chapter, we will test different properties of one or more discrete random variables. Discrete random variables often arise when working with qualitative data. They can be used to represent qualitative choices, for example, whether a person chooses public or private transport to get to work, or whether someone buys a diesel- or a petrol-driven car. We can test whether a discrete random variable is distributed in a certain way, and whether there exists a relationship between two discrete random variables.

Many tests relating to qualitative data are based on a basic test called an χ^2-test. The idea behind the χ^2-test is to compare the observed (empirical) distribution of the discrete random variables with a hypothetical distribution, i.e. one derived from a theory or a hypothesis.

In Section 16.1, we look at the construction of the χ^2-test. In Section 16.2, we use the test to analyse whether a discrete random variable follows a particular distribution. In Section 16.3, we introduce a test for independence between two random variables, and in Section 16.4 we test whether two distributions are identical (homogeneous).

16.1 The χ^2-test

In this section, we introduce the χ^2-test upon which all of the tests in this chapter are based. Assume that a random variable, X, can assume K possible values: $x_1, \ldots, x_K$. We also refer to these as K different *categories*. The probabilities for these different values (categories) are: $p_1, \ldots, p_K$, i.e. $P(X = x_k) = p_k$. We can use the χ^2-test to test hypotheses about these unknown probabilities.

When constructing a hypothesis test, the first task is to specify the null hypothesis and the alternative hypothesis. In this case, they are:

$$H_0 : p_1 = \pi_1, p_2 = \pi_2, \ldots, p_K = \pi_K$$

$$H_1 : \text{at least one } p_k \neq \pi_k, \quad k = 1, \ldots, K$$

where $\pi_1, \ldots, \pi_K$ are the hypothesised probabilities for the K possible outcomes. In this section, we simply use this null hypothesis without explaining where it comes from. In the following sections, we present various theories that give rise to specific probabilities, $\pi_1, \ldots, \pi_K$. In any case, the idea is to assess whether a theory is appropriate based on whether the probabilities that it predicts, $\pi_1, \ldots, \pi_K$, are consistent with the true, but unknown, probabilities, $p_1, \ldots, p_K$.

In order to distinguish between the null hypothesis and the alternative hypothesis, we use the following hypothesis measure:

$$\sum_{k=1}^{K} (p_k - \pi_k)^2$$

This is equal to 0 if the null hypothesis is true, whereas it is greater than 0 if it is false. To run the test, we must first replace the unknown values in the measure with estimates. In the present case, the unknown values are the probabilities, $p_1, \ldots, p_K$. In order to estimate these, we assume that we have a simple random sample, $(X_1, \ldots, X_n)$. Let Z_k be the number of observations in the sample with the value x_k. If we have n observations, and Z_k of them have the value x_k, then the estimate of the probability p_k is given by Z_k / n, (i.e. the proportion of observations in the sample with the value x_k). Estimates of the other probabilities can be calculated in the same way. Our sample thus allows us to construct estimates for all of the unknown values in the hypothesis measure.

If the test statistic is to have a distribution under the null hypothesis that is easy to approximate, we need to modify the estimated hypothesis measure slightly. More specifically, it can be shown that the test statistic has to look like this:

$$\chi^2 = \sum_{k=1}^{K} n \cdot \frac{\left(Z_k / n - \pi_k \right)^2}{\pi_k} = \sum_{k=1}^{K} \frac{\left(Z_k - n \cdot \pi_k \right)^2}{n \cdot \pi_k}$$

Using the last expression on the right-hand side above makes it easier to calculate the value of the test statistic, since Z_k is just the number of observations in the sample with the value x_k, while $n \cdot \pi_k$ is the expected number of observations with the value x_k in a sample with n elements according to the null hypothesis. The χ^2-test compares the observed frequency, Z_k, with the expected frequency under the null hypothesis,

$n \cdot \pi_k$. Table 16.1 gives a schematic overview of the elements needed to calculate the test statistic.

In order to use the χ^2-test, we have to know the distribution of the test statistic under the null hypothesis. If our sample is a simple random sample, we can approximate the test statistic's distribution with a χ^2-distribution. This is a good approximation if the sample size is large. The number of degrees of freedom in this distribution depends on the number of π_ks we can choose "freely". If there are K categories, then the number of degrees of freedom cannot exceed $K-1$. The explanation is that, since the π_ks must add up to one, then a maximum of $K-1$ probabilities can be chosen freely. The last probability must be equal to one minus the sum of the other $K-1$ probabilities. Of course, all the $K-1$ probabilities must still be between zero and one, and their sum cannot exceed one.

Table 16.1:
The χ^2-test:
Probabilities and frequencies

Category	Unknown probability	Probability under H_0	Observed frequency	Expected frequency under H_0
1	p_1	π_1	Z_1	$\pi_1 \cdot n$
2	p_2	π_2	Z_2	$\pi_2 \cdot n$
.	.	.	.	.
.	.	.	.	.
K	p_K	π_K	Z_K	$\pi_K \cdot n$
Sum:	1	1	n	n

In the next section, we look at different theories that lead to specific probabilities, $\pi_1,\ldots,\pi_K$, to be tested. In these cases, we also show how to determine the number of degrees of freedom for the distribution of the test statistic under H_0.

Since the hypothesis measure above is 0 when it is evaluated using the true values under the null hypothesis, only large values of the test statistic are considered as evidence against H_0. Therefore, if we want a 5% significance level, we must use the 0.95-quantile from the relevant χ^2-distribution.

16.2   Test of a distribution

Using the χ^2-test, we can find out whether a sample was selected from a given distribution. If we suspect a coin might be loaded, for example, we can examine this by testing whether the probability of each of the two outcomes is 1/2. This will give $K = 2$ categories, and the probabilities under the null hypothesis will then be: $\pi_1 = \pi_2 = 0.5$. More generally, any discrete distribution gives rise to certain probabilities, $\pi_1, ..., \pi_K$, and we can then use the χ^2-test to determine whether the observed sample is consistent with these probabilities, or whether we have to reject the presumed distribution. In this section, we consider various examples of such tests of a distribution.

Example 16.1: A discrete distribution – rolling the dice

A dice is rolled 60 times, resulting in the outcomes in Table 16.2. Can we accept, with a 5% significance level, that the dice is not loaded?

The null hypothesis and alternative hypothesis are:

H_0 : The dice is not loaded, i.e. $p_1 = 1/6, ..., p_6 = 1/6$

H_1 : The dice is loaded, i.e. at least one $p_k \neq 1/6$

Table 16.2:
60 rolls of the dice

	1s	2s	3s	4s	5s	6s	Total
Observed frequency	8	11	6	13	10	12	60

Note that if one of the probabilities is different from 1/6, then at least two of them will have to be different from 1/6, as the sum will always have to be 1.

In order to find the value of the test statistic, we must first calculate the expected number of outcomes under the null hypothesis. In a sample of 60 elements, the expected number of 1s is given by $60 \cdot 1/6 = 10$. The same is true for the other five outcomes. The value of the test statistic is therefore:

$$\chi^2 = \frac{(8-10)^2}{10} + \frac{(11-10)^2}{10} + \frac{(6-10)^2}{10} + \frac{(13-10)^2}{10}$$
$$+ \frac{(10-10)^2}{10} + \frac{(12-10)^2}{10} = 3.4$$

We find the critical value from the χ^2-distribution with: $6 - 1 = 5$ degrees of freedom. The reason that the number of degrees of freedom is equal to 5 is that we could "freely" choose five of the probabilities under H_0. The 0.95-quantile from the χ^2-distribution with 5 degrees of freedom is 11.1. We can therefore conclude that the null hypothesis cannot be rejected, and we accept that the dice is not loaded.

Example 16.2: A binomial distribution – part 1

Let the random variable X be the number of boys in a family with four children. If whether a boy or girl is conceived is entirely a matter of chance, then X is binomially distributed with the parameters $n = 4$ and $p = 0.5$. The probability that a family with four children will have no boys is:

$$P(X = 0) = \binom{4}{0} \cdot 0.5^0 \cdot 0.5^4 = 0.0625$$

Similarly, we can calculate the other probabilities for X as:

$$P(X = 1) = 0.25, \quad P(X = 2) = 0.375,$$
$$P(X = 3) = 0.25, \quad P(X = 4) = 0.0625$$

The null hypothesis and alternative hypothesis are then:

$H_0 : X \sim \text{Bin}(4, 0.5)$, i.e.
$\pi_0 = 0.0625, \ \pi_1 = 0.25, \ \pi_2 = 0.375, \ \pi_3 = 0.25, \ \pi_4 = 0.0625$

$H_1 : X$ is not Bin(4, 0.5), i.e.
at least one of the probabilities is not as under H_0

A simple random sample of 100 families with four children provided the results shown in Table 16.3:

Table 16.3:
Male children I

Number of male children (category)	Observed frequency	Probability under H_0	Expected frequency under H_0
0	8	0.0625	$100 \cdot 0.0625 = 6.25$
1	20	0.25	$100 \cdot 0.25 = 25$
2	28	0.375	$100 \cdot 0.375 = 37.5$
3	32	0.25	$100 \cdot 0.25 = 25$
4	12	0.0625	$100 \cdot 0.0625 = 6.25$
Total	100	1	100

Table 16.3 also shows the expected frequencies under the null hypothesis with a sample size of 100. We use these expected frequencies to find the value of the test statistic:

$$\chi^2 = \frac{(8 - 6{,}25)^2}{6.25} + \frac{(20 - 25)^2}{25} + \frac{(28 - 37.5)^2}{37.5} + \frac{(32 - 25)^2}{25} + \frac{(12 - 6.25)^2}{6.25} = 11.15$$

The distribution of the test statistic under the null hypothesis is approximately the χ^2-distribution with degrees of freedom equal to the number of categories minus one, i.e. $5 - 1 = 4$. With a 5% significance level, we must therefore use the 0.95-quantile of the χ^2-distribution with 4 degrees of freedom, which is 9.49. We can therefore reject H_0, that the number of boys in families with four children is binomially distributed with $n = 4$ and $p = 0.5$.

We do not always have to completely specify the distribution that we want to test. The choice of distribution can also be partly determined by the sample. For example, we might want to test whether the distribution is binomial, but we may be uncertain about the value of the parameter p. We can then use the sample to first arrive at an estimate of the parameter p, and then test whether the distribution can be a binomial distribution with this particular value of p. Example 16.3 illustrates this.

Example 16.3: A binomial distribution – part 2

Instead of testing whether the distribution of X in Example 12.2 is Bin(4, 1/2), we will now test whether $X \sim \text{Bin}(4, p)$, with a value of p determined by the estimate of p from the sample. In order to obtain an estimate of p, we use the fact that the mean value of a binomially distributed random variable, $X \sim \text{Bin}(m, p)$, is $E(X) = m, p$. Since the sample average, $\overline{X}$, is an estimate of the mean value, $E(X)$, an estimate of p is given by $\hat{p} = \overline{X}/m$. Thus, we use the sample to determine the binomial distribution (the value of p) that best matches the sample. Then, using the sample, we test whether X can be binomially distributed with this value of p.

The null hypothesis and alternative hypothesis are therefore:

$$H_0 : X \sim \text{Bin}(4, p)$$

$$H_1 : X \text{ is not } \text{Bin}(4, p)$$

For the sample from Example 16.2, the estimate of p is:

$$\hat{p} = \frac{0 \cdot 8 + 1 \cdot 20 + 2 \cdot 28 + 3 \cdot 32 + 4 \cdot 12}{100} \Big/ 4 = 0.55$$

Based on this, the probabilities of X under the null hypothesis are calculated to be:

$$P(X = 0) = \binom{4}{0} \cdot 0.55^0 \cdot 0.45^4 = 0.04$$

and:

$$P(X = 1) = 0.20, \quad P(X = 2) = 0.37,$$
$$P(X = 3) = 0.30, \quad P(X = 4) = 0.09$$

We can now revise Table 16.3 (from Example 16.2) with the new probabilities shown in Table 16.4.

Table 16.4:
Male children II

Number of male children (category)	Observed frequency	Probability under H_0	Expected frequency under H_0
0	8	0.04	$100 \cdot 0.04 = 4$
1	20	0.20	$100 \cdot 0.20 = 20$
2	28	0.37	$100 \cdot 0.37 = 37$
3	32	0.30	$100 \cdot 0.30 = 30$
4	12	0.09	$100 \cdot 0.09 = 9$
Total	100	1	100

The value of the test statistic can then be calculated as:

$$\chi^2 = \frac{(8-4)^2}{4} + \frac{(20-20)^2}{20} + \frac{(28-37)^2}{37}$$
$$+ \frac{(32-30)^2}{30} + \frac{(12-9)^2}{9} = 7.32$$

The number of degrees of freedom under the null hypothesis differs from that in Example 16.2, where p was determined by the number of categories minus one under H_0. In the present case, we lose an extra degree of freedom because p is estimated. The test statistic is therefore approximately χ^2-distributed with $K - 1 - 1 = 5 - 1 - 1 = 3$ degrees of freedom. With a 5% significance level, the critical value is 7.81. Therefore, we cannot reject the null hypothesis that the number of male children is binomially distributed.

It is also possible to test a discrete distribution with an infinite number of potential outcomes. If, for example, X is Poisson-distributed, then it can assume the values: 0,1,2,... Here, we cannot directly use the χ^2-test, as it only allows K possible outcomes. However, we can define a new random variable that has $K - 1$ outcomes in common with X, while the final outcome (the Kth outcome) is the collection of all of the outcomes of X that are not included in the first $K - 1$ possibilities. The procedure is illustrated in Example 16.4.

Example 16.4: Bankruptcies

We want to analyse whether the number of bankruptcies per month in a given industry is Poisson-distributed. Let the random variable X specify the number of bankruptcies in a given month. The hypotheses are then:

$$H_0 : X \sim \text{Poi}(\lambda)$$

$$H_1 : X \text{ is not } \text{Poi}(\lambda)$$

If X is Poisson-distributed, then the expected value of X is equal to $E(X) = \lambda$. We can, therefore, use the sample average, $\overline{X}$, to get an estimate of $E(X)$, and thereby λ. Observations from the industry over 250 months have provided the simple random sample shown in Table 16.5.

Table 16.5: Bankruptcies: observed frequencies

No. of bankruptcies (category)	Observed frequency
0	10
1	70
2	110
3	30
4	20
5	10
Total	250

The estimate of λ can then be calculated as:

$$\hat{\lambda} = \bar{X} = \frac{0 \cdot 10 + 1 \cdot 70 + 2 \cdot 110 + 3 \cdot 30 + 4 \cdot 20 + 5 \cdot 10}{250} = 2.04$$

We can now calculate the expected frequencies under the null hypothesis using the estimate of λ. The probability for $X = 0$ is:

$$P(X = 0) = \frac{\hat{\lambda}^0}{0!} \cdot e^{-\lambda} = \frac{2.04^0}{0!} \cdot e^{-2.04} = 0.13$$

Correspondingly, we get:

$$P(X = 1) = 0.27, \quad P(X = 2) = 0.27, \quad P(X = 3) = 0.18,$$
$$P(X = 4) = 0.09, \quad P(X = 5) = 0.04$$

The remaining probability, $P(X \geq 6)$, is then: $1 - 0.13 - 0.27 - 0.27 - 0.18 - 0.09 - 0.04 = 0.02$. As the realised sample does not have a higher outcome than the value 5, it is natural to create a category called "6 or higher". Under the null hypothesis, the probability of an outcome in this category is 0.02.

We can now draw up a table with the observed and expected frequencies (see Table 16.6).

Table 16.6:
Bankruptcies: frequencies and probabilities

Number of bankruptcies (category)	Observed frequency	Probability under H_0	Expected frequency under H_0
0	10	0.13	$250 \cdot 0.13 = 32.5$
1	70	0.27	$250 \cdot 0.27 = 67.5$
2	110	0.27	$250 \cdot 0.27 = 67.5$
3	30	0.18	$250 \cdot 0.18 = 45$
4	20	0.09	$250 \cdot 0.09 = 22.5$
5	10	0.04	$250 \cdot 0.04 = 10$
≥ 6	0	0.02	$250 \cdot 0.02 = 5$
Total	250	1	250

The value of the test statistic is:

$$\chi^2 = \frac{(10 - 32.5)^2}{32.5} + \frac{(70 - 67.5)^2}{67.5} + \frac{(110 - 67.5)^2}{67.5}$$

$$+ \frac{(30 - 45)^2}{45} + \frac{(20 - 22.5)^2}{22.5} + \frac{(10 - 10)^2}{10} + \frac{(0 - 5)^2}{5} = 52.7$$

As in the previous example, the number of degrees of freedom is: $K - 1 - 1$, since one of the parameters, λ, is estimated. With a 5% significance level, we must therefore use the 0.95-quantile from the χ^2-distribution with $7 - 1 - 1 = 5$ degrees of freedom. This is 11.1, and we can, therefore, reject the null hypothesis that the number of bankruptcies is Poisson-distributed.

The following box summarises the procedure for testing a distribution.

χ^2-test of a distribution

Purpose: To test whether a discrete random variable, X, with K outcomes (categories), follows a particular distribution.

Hypotheses:

$$H_0 : p_1 = \pi_1(\theta_1,...,\theta_d), p_2 = \pi_2(\theta_1,...,\theta_d),..., p_K = \pi_K(\theta_1,...,\theta_d)$$

$$H_1 : \text{at least one } p_k \neq \pi_k(\theta_1,...,\theta_d), k = 1,...,K$$

where $p_k, k = 1,...,K$ are the true but unknown probabilities, and $\pi_k(\theta_1,...,\theta_d), k = 1,...,K$, are the probabilities according to the null hypothesis, which can depend on d unknown parameters, $\theta_1,...,\theta_d$, in the assumed distribution for X.

Test statistic:

$$\chi^2 = \sum_{k=1}^{K} \frac{\left(Z_k - n \cdot \hat{\pi}_k\left(\widehat{\theta_1,...,\theta_d}\right)\right)^2}{n \cdot \hat{\pi}_k\left(\widehat{\theta_1,...,\theta_d}\right)} \sim^A \chi^2(K - 1 - d) \text{ under } H_0$$

where Z_k is the observed frequency of category k in a simple random sample of size n, and $\hat{\pi}_k(\theta_1,...,\theta_d)$ is the estimated probability for category k under H_0, found using estimates, $\theta_1,...,\theta_d$, of the d unknown parameters of the assumed distribution of X. $\rightarrow$

Critical value: $\chi^2_{1-\alpha}(K-1-d)$

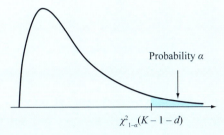

Examples:

1. $H_0: X \sim \text{Bin}(m, p)$

   - Categories: $X = 0, X = 1, \ldots, X = m \;\;\Rightarrow\;\; K = m + 1$

   - $\pi_k(p) = P(X = k) = \binom{m}{k} \cdot p^k \cdot (1 - p)^{m-k}$

   - Unknown parameter: $p \;\;\Rightarrow\;\; d = 1$

   - Estimate of $p : \hat{p} = \overline{X}/m$, where $\overline{X}$ is the sample average

2. $H_0: X \sim \text{Poi}(\lambda)$:

   - Categories: $X = 0, X = 1, \ldots, X = m - 1, X \geq m$, where m is sufficiently large $\Rightarrow\;\; K = m + 1$

   - $\pi_k(\lambda) = P(X = k) = \dfrac{\lambda^k}{k!} \cdot e^{-\lambda}$

   - Unknown parameter: $\lambda \;\;\Rightarrow\;\; d = 1$

   - Estimate of $\lambda : \hat{\lambda} = \overline{X}$, where $\overline{X}$ is the sample average

16.3　Testing a relationship between two discrete random variables

If two random variables are dependent, it means that we can use the information about the outcome of one random variable to predict the outcome of the other. If they are independent, then there is no connection between their outcomes. In Chapter 3, we presented the formal definition of independence. In this section, we will describe how we can use the χ^2-test to test whether two discrete random variables are independent.

Independence between two random variables, X and Y, means that the joint probability function, $f(x, y)$, is equal to the marginal probability function for X, $f_X(x)$, multiplied by the marginal probability function for Y, $f_Y(y)$. The null hypothesis and alternative hypothesis are therefore:

$$H_0 : \text{Independence, i.e. } f(x,y) = f_X(x) \cdot f_Y(y)$$
for all values of x and y

$$H_1 : \text{Dependence, i.e. } f(x,y) \neq f_X(x) \cdot f_Y(y)$$
for at least one value of x and y

The true unknown probabilities, p_k, are equal to $f(x,y)$, while the hypothetical probabilities, π_k, are equal to $f_X(x) \cdot f_Y(y)$. If X can assume c values, $x_1, x_2, \ldots, x_c$, and Y can assume r values, $y_1, y_2, \ldots, y_r$, then there is a total of $c \cdot r$ possible outcomes of (X,Y). There are, therefore, $K = c \cdot r$ different categories.

Since $f_X(x)$ and $f_Y(y)$ are unknown, we do not know in advance the probabilities under $H_0 : \pi_k = f_X(x) \cdot f_Y(y)$. However, based on the sample, we can reach an estimate for both $f_X(x)$ and $f_Y(y)$, and we can use these estimates to calculate the hypothetical probabilities, π_k, for the K categories. Example 16.5 illustrates this.

Example 16.5: Defective cars – part 1

A car manufacturer has two factories that produce a certain model. The producer would like to know whether there is a relationship between where a car is produced and whether it is defective. Let the random variable X be 0 if a randomly selected car is defective, and 1 if it is not, and let the random variable Y indicate with the values 1 and 2 whether the car is produced in factory 1 or 2. The manufacturer has observed the simple random sample of 300 cars shown in Table 16.7.

Table 16.7: Defective cars: observed frequencies

	$Y = 1$ (factory 1)	$Y = 2$ (factory 2)	Total
$X = 0$ (defective)	23	30	53
$X = 1$ (not defective)	68	179	247
Total	91	209	300

The observed number of the different combinations of X and Y corresponds to the Z_ks from Section 16.1. In this case, there are four categories with 23, 30, 68 and 179 observations, respectively.

Based on the sample, the probabilities under H_0, $\pi_k = f_X(x) \cdot f_Y(y)$, are calculated. The estimate of the marginal probability $f_X(x)$ is calculated by counting all of the observations in which $X = x$, and dividing this number by the total number of observations. For example, the estimate of $f_X(0)$ is given by $(23 + 30) / 300 = 0.177$. The estimates of the marginal probabilities, $\hat{f}_X(x)$ and $\hat{f}_Y(y)$, are calculated in this way in Table 16.8.

Table 16.8:
Defective cars: estimates of marginal probabilities

	$Y = 1$ (factory 1)	$Y = 2$ (factory 2)	$\hat{f}_X(x)$
$X = 0$ (defective)	23	30	53/300
$X = 1$ (not defective)	68	179	247/300
$\hat{f}_Y(y)$	91/300	209/300	

Based on the estimates of the marginal probabilities, we can calculate estimates of the probabilities under the null hypothesis: $\hat{\pi}_k = \hat{f}_X(x) \cdot \hat{f}_Y(y)$. As we are eventually going to use the expected number of observations in each cell, $n \cdot \hat{\pi}_k = n \cdot \hat{f}_X(x) \cdot \hat{f}_Y(y)$, rather than just the expected probabilities, these values are presented in Table 16.9.

Table 16.9:
Defective cars: expected frequencies

	$Y = 1$ (factory 1)	$Y = 2$ (factory 2)	Total
$X = 0$ (defective)	$300 \cdot \dfrac{53}{300} \cdot \dfrac{91}{300} = 16.077$	$300 \cdot \dfrac{53}{300} \cdot \dfrac{209}{300} = 36.923$	53
$X = 1$ (not defective)	$300 \cdot \dfrac{247}{300} \cdot \dfrac{91}{300} = 74.923$	$300 \cdot \dfrac{247}{300} \cdot \dfrac{209}{300} = 172.077$	247
Total	91	209	300

The value of the test statistic can now be calculated in the same manner as before, using the observed frequencies from Table 16.7 and the expected frequencies from Table 16.9:

$$\chi^2 = \frac{(23 - 16.077)^2}{16.077} + \frac{(30 - 36.923)^2}{36.923} + \frac{(68 - 74.923)^2}{74.923}$$
$$+ \frac{(179 - 172.077)^2}{172.077} = 5.197$$

In order to use the χ^2-test, we must find its distribution under the null hypothesis. As before, the χ^2-test is approximately χ^2-distributed with a number of degrees of freedom that corresponds to the number of probabilities that can be chosen freely, minus the number of estimated parameters. Since we have estimated $c-1$ marginal probabilities for X (we do not need to calculate the last marginal probability for X, since the sum of the probabilities is 1) and $r-1$ marginal probabilities for Y, then the number of estimated parameters is $d = (r-1) + (c-1)$. The number of degrees of freedom is:

$$\text{Degrees of freedom} = c \cdot r - 1 - d = c \cdot r - 1 - (r-1) - (c-1) = (c-1) \cdot (r-1)$$

In Example 16.5 there are $r = 2$ possible values of X and $c = 2$ possible values of Y. Therefore, the χ^2-test is approximately χ^2-distributed with $(2-1)\cdot(2-1) = 1$ degree of freedom. With a 5% significance level, the critical value is 3.84 (0.95-quantile), and we can therefore reject H_0, that X and Y are independent. There is thus a statistically significant relationship between where a car is produced and whether it is defective.

In rejecting H_0, we cannot directly see from the value of the test statistic which cells are causing the deviation from H_0. For each cell (category) in the table, we can calculate a value, r_{xy}, which can indicate for which cells (i.e. which values of X and Y) the null hypothesis is violated. This value is given by:

$$r_{xy} = \frac{\left(Z_{xy} - n \cdot \pi_{xy}\right)}{\sqrt{n \cdot \pi_{xy} \cdot \left(1 - f_X(x)\right) \cdot \left(1 - f_Y(y)\right)}}$$

where $n \cdot \pi_{xy} = n \cdot f_X(x) \cdot f_Y(y)$ is the expected frequency, and Z_{xy} is the observed number in the cell where $X = x$ and $Y = y$. The underlying rationale behind r_{xy} is that it is numerically large for a cell if the observed frequency deviates greatly from the expected frequency under the null hypothesis. Conversely, it is numerically small if they do not deviate from each other. It can be shown that r_{xy} follows an approximate standard normal distribution under the null hypothesis. Therefore, if r_{xy} is numerically bigger than 1.96, then the cell concerned does not correspond to the null hypothesis at a 5% significance level.

From the figures in Examples 16.5 and 16.6, we can calculate r_{01} for the cell where $X = 0$ and $Y = 1$:

$$r_{01} = \frac{(23 - 16.077)}{\sqrt{16.077 \cdot \left(1 - \frac{53}{300}\right) \cdot \left(1 - \frac{91}{300}\right)}} = 2.28$$

The remaining three cells all have the same numerical value of r_{xy}. In this case, therefore, there is no additional information to be gained by calculating r_{xy}.

χ^2-test for independence

Purpose: To test whether two discrete random variables, X and Y, with, respectively, r and c possible outcomes, are independent.

Hypotheses:

H_0: Independence: $f\left(x_i, y_j\right) = f_X\left(x_i\right) \cdot f_Y\left(y_j\right)$ for $i = 1,\ldots,r, j = 1,\ldots,c$

H_1: Dependence, i.e. $f\left(x_i, y_j\right) \neq f_X\left(x_i\right) \cdot f_Y\left(y_j\right)$ for at least one outcome $\left(x_i, y_j\right)$

where $f_X\left(x_i\right)$ is the marginal probability function for X, $f_Y\left(y_j\right)$ is the marginal probability function for Y, and $f\left(x_i, y_j\right)$ is the joint probability function.

Test statistic:

$$\chi^2 = \sum_{i=1}^{r} \sum_{j=1}^{c} \frac{\left(Z_{ij} - n \cdot \hat{f}_X\left(x_i\right) \cdot \hat{f}_Y\left(y_j\right)\right)^2}{n \cdot \hat{f}_X\left(x_i\right) \cdot \hat{f}_Y\left(y_j\right)} \sim^A \chi^2\left((r-1) \cdot (c-1)\right) \text{ under } H_0$$

where Z_{ij} is the observed frequency of the outcome $\left(x_i, y_j\right)$ in a simple random sample of size n, and $\hat{f}_X(x_i)$ and $\hat{f}_Y(y_j)$ are the estimated marginal probability functions for X and Y.

Critical value: $\chi^2_{1-\alpha}\left((r-1) \cdot (c-1)\right)$

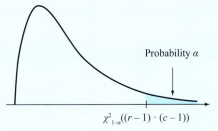

Probability α

$\chi^2_{1-\alpha}((r-1) \cdot (c-1))$

16.4 Test for homogeneity

We can also test whether a distribution of a random variable X is the same for different groups. We can define a group as all of the elements in a population that share a certain characteristic. The different characteristics in the population can be thought of as different values of a random variable, Y. A group can therefore be described as all of the elements where $Y = y$. When we compare the distribution of X across different groups defined by different values of Y, then it corresponds to comparing the conditional distributions of X given Y, $f_{X|Y}(x|y)$, for different values of y.

Example 16.8: Age distributions for men and women

Let us compare the age distribution among Danish men with the age distribution among Danish women. The population is everybody in the country. The random variable Y indicates whether a randomly selected person is a male ($Y = 1$) or a female ($Y = 2$). The second random variable, X, indicates the person's age in years. When we are to compare the distribution of X among men with the distribution of X among women, we have to compare the two conditional distributions: $f_{X|Y}(x|y = 1)$ and $f_{X|Y}(x|y = 2)$.

Homogeneity between the two groups, given by $Y = 1$ and $Y = 2$, implies that the two conditional distributions $f_{X|Y}(x|1)$ and $f_{X|Y}(x|2)$ must be the same for all values of x. This is exactly the same as requiring that X and Y are independent, since in this case $f_{X|Y}(x|y)$ does not depend on Y. That follows from the definition of independence in Chapter 4.

We can therefore test for the homogeneity of X between groups (defined by the values of Y) by testing whether X and Y are independent. The test procedure is therefore exactly the same as in Section 16.3.

16.5   Exercises

1. Review questions
   a) What type of tests can the χ^2-test be used for?
   b) Explain the basic principles behind the χ^2-test, including what the null hypothesis and alternative hypothesis are, and how the hypothesis measure used can distinguish between these hypotheses.
   c) Explain how the probabilities under the null hypothesis are found, when you want to test whether X is binomially distributed.
   d) What is the number of degrees of freedom in the distribution of the test statistic under H_0 in this case? What is the critical value?
   e) Explain how the χ^2-test can be used to test for independence between two random variables.
   f) What is the number of degrees of freedom in the distribution of the test statistic under H_0 in this case?
   g) Why is it that the test for homogeneity is the same as the test for independence?

2. In a study of car accidents on highways, the number of accidents observed on different days of the week are as follows:

Weekday	Number of accidents observed
Monday	112
Tuesday	87
Wednesday	121
Thursday	134
Friday	155
Saturday	97
Sunday	67

Based on this sample, we want to test the hypothesis that there is the same probability of accidents happening on different days of the week.
   a) Write up the null and alternative hypotheses.
   b) Calculate the expected frequencies under H_0.
   c) Specify the test statistic and calculate its value in this case.
   d) What is the critical value at a 5% significance level?
   e) Can the null hypothesis be rejected?

3. A factory owner suspects that the number of times a week that production stops due to machine error follows a Poisson-distribution. Over the past year, he has assembled the following 50 weekly observations:

Number of stoppages	Observed frequency
0	11
1	19
2	12
3	7
≥ 4	1
Total	50

a) Write up the null and alternative hypotheses.
b) Find the expected frequencies under H_0.
c) Set up the test statistic and specify its distribution under the null hypothesis.
d) Calculate the value of the test statistic and decide whether the owner's theory should be rejected.

4. A study of 200 couples' daily smoking habits gave the following results:

	Wife does not smoke	Wife smokes 1–20 cigarettes	Wife smokes >20 cigarettes
Husband does not smoke	57	33	11
Husband smokes 1–20 cigarettes	21	38	8
Husband smokes >20 cigarettes	6	14	12

You now want to use this data to examine whether spouses' smoking habits are independent.
a) Specify the appropriate null and alternative hypotheses.
b) Write up the test statistic and specify its distribution under the null hypothesis.

c) What is the critical value of the test statistic at a 5% significance level?
d) Calculate the expected frequencies under H_0.
e) Find the value of the test statistic and use this to determine whether the null hypothesis should be rejected.
f) Explain how the test in this case can also be seen as a test of homogeneity between groups.

5. A sports fan watching Wimbledon notes how two players serve. His observations are summarised in the following table:

	1st serve in	Fault on first serve, 2nd serve in	Double fault (fault on both 1st and 2nd serve)
Player A	63	28	8
Player B	43	32	2

The fan now wants to work out whether the distribution of serves is the same for both players.
a) Formulate the hypothesis that the fan wants to test.
b) Which test statistic can he use, and what is its distribution under the null hypothesis?
c) Calculate the expected frequencies under H_0.
d) Finally, calculate the value of the test statistic and decide whether the null hypothesis can be rejected at a 5% significance level.

17 Simple linear regression

In this chapter, we introduce one of the most common methods of modelling relationships between random variables: *regression analysis.* We can also use regression analysis to predict the outcome of a random variable by using information from the outcomes of other random variables.

In regression analysis, we specify the expected value of a random variable as a function of one or more other random variables. If, for example, X is the price of a product, and Y is the demand for the product, then the regression of Y on X gives us the expected demand for the product at different prices, i.e. at different values of X. In this chapter, we focus on simple linear regression, which means that the expected value of Y is a linear function of only one random variable, X. Explaining the expected value of Y with more than one random variable is called multiple regression, and we will look at this in Chapter 18.

In Section 17.1, we look at the general idea behind regression analysis. In Section 17.2, we focus on the case of simple linear regression, and in Section 17.3, we show how a sample can be used to calculate an estimate of a simple linear regression. In Section 17.4, we discuss different ways of analysing whether the linear regression is correctly specified. We can also test hypotheses about the regression function, as we show in Section 17.5. Finally, Section 17.6 deals with regression as a tool for making predictions.

17.1 Regression

The relationship between two random variables, X and Y, is described by their joint probability distribution, $f(x,y)$. On this basis, we can deduce how the value of one random variable is related to the distribution of the other random variable. In the following, we will focus on the relationship between a given value of X and the distribution of Y. This is described by the conditional distribution, $f_{Y|X}(y|x)$, as defined in Chapter 4. This gives us the probability distribution for Y, given that X has the value x.

17.1.1   The regression function

Perhaps the most basic type of information about the relationship between X and Y is whether they are statistically independent. We know from Chapter 4 that if X and Y are independent, then $f_{Y|X}(y|x) = f_Y(y)$, which means that X contains no information about Y. Regardless of which value X assumes, the distribution of Y is the same: $f_Y(y)$. If, on the other hand, X and Y are dependent, then the conditional distribution for Y, $f_{Y|X}(y|x)$, is different for different values of X. The value of X therefore gives us information about the distribution of Y.

Regression analysis focuses on the conditional mean, $E(Y|X = x)$, which is a descriptive measure for the conditional distribution, $f_{Y|X}(y|x)$. As we have shown previously, it is easier to interpret a descriptive measure than the entire distribution. The conditional mean is a function of x and is also called the *regression function* of Y on X. This function is defined formally for discrete and continuous random variables in the following box.

The regression function, $E(Y|X = x)$:

For a ***discrete random variable***, Y, the conditional mean of Y given $X = x$ is:

$$E(Y|X = x) = \sum_{i=1}^{N} y_i \cdot f_{Y|X}(y_i|x)$$

where $y_1, \ldots, y_N$ are the N possible values of Y, and $f_{Y|X}(y|x)$ is the conditional probability function defined in Chapter 4.

For a ***continuous random variable***, Y, the conditional mean of Y given $X = x$ is:

$$E(Y|X = x) = \int_{-\infty}^{\infty} y \cdot f_{Y|X}(y|x) \, dy$$

where $f_{Y|X}(y|x)$ is the conditional probability density function defined in Chapter 4.

The function $E(Y|X = x)$ is a function of x, and is called the regression function of Y on X.

The conditional means are calculated in the same way as the ordinary means in Chapter 5. The only difference is that the probability function (or the probability density function) has been replaced with the conditional probability function (or the conditional probability density function).

When we regress Y on X, X is called the *explanatory variable,* while Y is the *explained variable.* Other designations are sometimes used, for example X may be called the *independent variable* and Y the *dependent variable.*

Example 17.1: A regression function – part 1

Two discrete random variables, X and Y, have the joint probabilities shown in Table 17.1.

Table 17.1:
Joint and marginal probabilities for X and Y

	$X = 1$	$X = 2$	Marginal probability of Y: $f_Y(y)$
$Y = 0$	0.3	0.1	0.4
$Y = 1$	0.2	0.4	0.6
Marginal probability of X: $f_X(x)$	0.5	0.5	

In Table 17.1, the marginal probabilities for Y and X are also indicated. The conditional probabilities for Y given X are therefore calculated using the following formula from Chapter 4:

$$f_{Y|X}(y|x) = \frac{f(x, y)}{f_X(x)}$$

The result is summarised in Table 17.2.

Table 17.2:
Conditional probabilities for Y given X = x

$f_{Y|X}(y|1)$			$f_{Y|X}(y|2)$	
$Y = 0$	$\dfrac{0.3}{0.5} = 0.6$		$Y = 0$	$\dfrac{0.1}{0.5} = 0.2$
$Y = 1$	$\dfrac{0.2}{0.5} = 0.4$		$Y = 1$	$\dfrac{0.4}{0.5} = 0.8$

Hence, the mean value of Y, given $X = 1$, and the mean value of Y, given $X = 2$, can be calculated as:

$$E(Y|X = 1) = 0 \cdot f_{Y|X}\left(0|1\right) + 1 \cdot f_{Y|X}\left(1|1\right) = 0 \cdot 0.6 + 1 \cdot 0.4 = 0.4$$

$$E(Y|X = 2) = 0 \cdot f_{Y|X}\left(0|2\right) + 1 \cdot f_{Y|X}\left(1|2\right) = 0 \cdot 0.2 + 1 \cdot 0.8 = 0.8$$

The regression function of Y on X is then:

$$E(Y|X = x) = \begin{cases} 0.4 & \text{if} \quad x{=}1 \\ 0.8 & \text{if} \quad x{=}2 \end{cases}$$

Note that $E(Y|X = x)$ is a function of x. To emphasise this, let $h(x) = E(Y|X = x)$, and thus:

$$h(x) = \begin{cases} 0.4 & \text{if} \quad x{=}1 \\ 0.8 & \text{if} \quad x{=}2 \end{cases}$$

In Example 17.1, where X can only assume two different values, 1 and 2, we have two values for the regression function: $E(Y|X = 1)$ and $E(Y|X = 2)$. One interpretation of this is that there are two groups in the population, one of which is characterised by $X = 1$, while the other is characterised by $X = 2$. The mean values of Y for the two groups are $E(Y|X = 1)$ and $E(Y|X = 2)$, respectively.

Regression is, however, more generally applicable than to cases with only two possible values of X. If X can assume all sorts of values, then the regression function will provide the conditional mean value of Y for any of these values.

17.1.2   Predicting Y using the regression function

If we know the value of X, then we can use the regression function to predict the value of Y. The prediction is given by the conditional mean of Y, given the known value x of X, i.e. $E(Y|X = x)$.

It is important to remember that the regression of Y on X only gives us the relationship between x and the conditional mean of Y. The actual value of Y for a given x is rarely equal to the conditional mean. In the context of prediction using the regression function, the difference between the actual value of Y and the conditional mean of Y is called the *prediction error*:

$$U = Y - E(Y|X = x)$$

Because the expectation of Y given $X = x$ is $E(Y|X = x)$, the regression function is correct on average when used to predict Y; i.e. we will not expect it to make a systematic prediction error on Y. Therefore, the conditional mean value of the prediction error is equal to zero: $E(U|X = x) = 0$. Since $E(U|X = x) = 0$ for all values of x, then the mean value of U is also equal to zero, $E(U) = 0$.

If, in Example 17.1, we know that $X = 1$, then our prediction of Y is given by:

$$E(Y|X = 1) = 0.4$$

This prediction will never hit the mark, as Y is either 0 or 1. The prediction error is therefore:

$$U = \begin{cases} 0.4 - 0 = 0.4 & \text{if } Y=0 \\ 0.4 - 1 = -0.6 & \text{if } Y=1 \end{cases}$$

The expected value of the prediction error, U, given $X = 1$, is:

$$E(U|X = 1) = -0.4 \cdot f_{Y|X}(0|1) + 0.6 \cdot f_{Y|X}(0|2) = -0.4 \cdot 0.6 + 0.6 \cdot 0.4 = 0$$

Similarly, we can show that the prediction error also has the expected value 0, if $X = 2$.

If we use a method other than the regression function to predict Y, we typically get a different prediction error. We can then check which method is "best", provided that we define what is meant by the term "best". If by "best" we mean a prediction that will on average be correct, $E(U|X = x) = 0$, then the regression function, $E(Y|X = x)$, meets this criterion. If by "best" we mean a prediction that has the smallest variance of the prediction error, $V(U|X = x)$, then the regression function will also comply with this.[23] When we use the regression function to make predictions, it has both of these desirable properties.

We might be tempted to think that if we can predict Y with X, then X also causes Y. However, this need not be the case. If, for example, we specify the regression function of the amount of crime (Y) on the size of the police force (X) in different areas, then there is typically a positive relationship: the more police, the more crime. A causal interpretation of this relationship (i.e. that more police causes more crime) would suggest that to reduce crime, we need fewer police. However, another explanation could be that the police force is increased in an area where there is more crime. According to this explanation, crime causes the size of the police force. We cannot assess whether it is one or the other – or neither – of these explanations that is true, solely by means of the regression function. This is closely related to our discussion of spurious relationships in Chapter 3.

17.2 Simple linear regression

In practice, we often start by assuming that the conditional mean, $E(Y|X = x)$, is linear in the value of x. This means that if we have x on the first axis and the conditional mean of Y given $X = x$ on the second axis in a coordinate system, then the points will lie on a straight line. In Example 17.1, X can only assume two values, and so there is a linear relationship between x and $E(Y|X = x)$, since it is always possible to connect two points with a straight line. Had X been able to assume a third value, $X = 3$, then the relationship would not necessarily have been linear. If, for example, $E(Y|X = 3) = 0.5$, then the three points are no longer on a straight line, as illustrated in Figure 17.1a. If, however, $E(Y|X = 3) = 1.2$, then the relationship is linear. This is shown in Figure 17.1b.

---

23   The conditional variance, $V(Y|X = x)$, is like the conditional mean, $E(Y|X = x)$, defined with the help of the conditional probability (density) function, $f_{Y|X}(y|x)$. Formally, for a discrete random variable, Y, the conditional variance is given by:

$$V(Y|X = x) = \sum_{i=1}^{N} (y_i - E(Y|X = x))^2 \cdot f_{Y|X}(y_i|x)$$

where y_i are the possible values of Y. If Y is continuous, then the definition is:

$$V(Y|X = x) = \int_{-\infty}^{\infty} (y - E(Y|X = x))^2 \cdot f_{Y|X}(y|x)\, dy$$

Figure 17.1:
a) non-linear
and b) linear
relationship
between x and
$E(Y\mid X = x)$

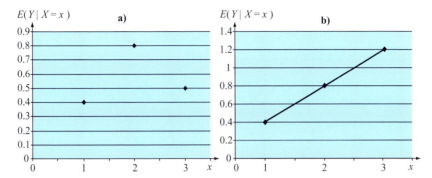

If the relationship between x and $E(Y|X = x)$ is linear, and there is only one explanatory variable, X, then we use the term *simple linear regression*. The box below contains the precise definition:

Simple linear regression of Y on X:

$$E(Y|X = x) = \beta_0 + \beta_1 \cdot x$$

where β_0 and β_1 are constant *coefficients,* called the *intercept coefficient* and *the slope coefficient,* respectively.

The simple linear regression of Y on X can also be written as:

$$Y = \beta_0 + \beta_1 \cdot X + U \text{ , where } E(U|X = x) = 0$$

Example 17.3: Blue Bull

A marketing agency has found out that the expected weekly demand, Y, for the soft drink Blue Bull is a linear function of the price, x:

$$E(Y|X = x) = 3{,}000 - 200 \cdot x$$

where Y is measured in the number of bottles, and the price, x, in DKK per bottle. If the price of Blue Bull is DKK 10 per bottle, then the expected demand is $3{,}000 - 200 \cdot 10 = 1{,}000$ bottles. On the other hand, if the price is DKK 11 per bottle, then the expected demand will fall to $3{,}000 - 200 \cdot 11 = 800$ bottles.

However, the actual demand is not necessarily the same as the expected demand. As previously discussed, the interpretation of an expected value is that if we imagine repeating the experiment an infinite number of times, then sales would average 800 bottles per week at a price of DKK 11 per bottle.

It can be shown that it is possible to calculate the coefficients, β_0 and β_1, from the variance of X and the covariance between X and Y. The formulas are given in the following box.

Calculation of coefficients in a simple linear regression:
In a simple linear regression, $E(Y|X = x) = \beta_0 + \beta_1 \cdot x$, the coefficients, β_0 and β_1, are given by:

$$\beta_1 = \frac{Cov(X,Y)}{V(X)} \quad \text{and} \quad \beta_0 = E(Y) - \beta_1 \cdot E(X)$$

The formulas help us interpret the simple linear regression. If X and Y are not correlated, then $Cov(X,Y) = 0$, and therefore $\beta_1 = 0$. The regression function in this case becomes $E(Y|X = x) = \beta_0 = E(Y)$, and therefore does not depend on the value of x. In other words, when X and Y are uncorrelated, we cannot use information about X to predict the expected value of Y. This is also the case if X and Y are independent, because independence implies that X and Y are uncorrelated. When we cannot use information about X to predict the mean value of Y, then our best guess about the conditional mean of Y given $X = x$ is the unconditional mean, $E(Y)$.

As can be seen in the formula for β_1, the sign on β_1 is determined by $Cov(X,Y)$, as $V(X)$ is always positive. If X and Y are positively correlated, then β_1 also has a positive sign. This means that the mean value of Y given $X = x$ is increasing in x. In Example 17.3, $\beta_1 = -200$, i.e. it is negative. This means that the price and the demand are negatively correlated, which intuitively fits with the assumption that higher prices reduce demand.

We can also interpret the regression in terms of the effect on the expected value of Y of a small change in x. Assume that we increase x by one unit. This implies that the expected value of Y changes as follows:

$$\Delta_{simple} = E(Y|X = x + 1) - E(Y|X = x)$$
$$= [\beta_0 + \beta_1 \cdot (x + 1)] - [\beta_0 + \beta_1 \cdot x] = \beta_1$$

where Δ_{simple} is the change in the expected value of Y when x is increased by one unit. The coefficient β_1 in the simple linear regression can thus be interpreted as the change in the expected value of Y when we increase the value of X by one. In Example 17.3, an increase of DKK 1 in the price of Blue Bull would therefore result in a decrease in expected demand by 200 bottles.

17.3　Estimation of the simple linear regression function

In practice, we do not know the coefficients, β_0 and β_1, from the linear regression of Y on X. In this section, we show how we can use a simple random sample to obtain estimates of β_0 and β_1, and therefore an estimate of the linear regression function.

17.3.1　The analogy principle of estimation

The formulas for β_0 and β_1 in the box in Section 17.2 build on the descriptive measures $E(Y)$, $E(X)$, $V(X)$ and $Cov(X,Y)$. As we have already seen in Chapters 10 and 12, estimates of these values can be obtained from a simple random sample. Each observation in the sample is a pair, consisting of an observation of X and an observation of Y. The sample is therefore: $((X_1,Y_1),(X_2,Y_2),...,(X_n,Y_n))$. In Chapter 10, we showed that estimators of $E(X)$ and $E(Y)$ are given by the sample averages:

$$\bar{X} = \frac{1}{n}\sum_{i=1}^{n}X_i \text{ and } \bar{Y} = \frac{1}{n}\sum_{i=1}^{n}Y_i$$

Similarly, in Chapter 12 we showed that estimators of $V(X)$ and $Cov(X,Y)$ are given by the sample variance and covariance:

$$S_X^2 = \frac{1}{n-1}\sum_{i=1}^{n}(X_i - \bar{X})^2 \text{ and}$$

$$\widehat{Cov}(X,Y) = \frac{1}{n-1}\sum_{i=1}^{n}(X_i - \bar{X})\cdot(Y_i - \bar{Y})$$

We can now use the analogy principle of estimation and replace all of the unknown quantities in the formulas for β_0 and β_1 with their sample counterparts. The estimators for β_0 and β_1 therefore become:

Estimators for β_0 and β_1:

$$\hat{\beta}_1 = \frac{\widehat{Cov}(X,Y)}{S_X^2} = \frac{\sum_{i=1}^{n}(X_i - \bar{X}) \cdot (Y_i - \bar{Y})}{\sum_{i=1}^{n}(X_i - \bar{X})^2} \quad \text{and}$$

$$\hat{\beta}_0 = \bar{Y} - \hat{\beta}_1 \cdot \bar{X}$$

The estimator for the simple linear regression is then:

$$\hat{E}(Y|X = x) = \hat{\beta}_0 + \hat{\beta}_1 \cdot x$$

Example 17.4: Red wine and income – part 1

A market survey selects a simple random sample of a person's monthly consumption of red wine, Y, measured in litres, and that person's monthly income, X, measured in DKK thousand per month. The realised sample with $n = 10$ observations is shown in Table 17.3.

Table 17.3:
Realised sample (income and consumption)

x_i (income)	y_i (consumption)
22.2	5.04
12.1	2.96
14.3	3.08
8.1	3.58
17.6	5.52
10.8	2.73
7	3.78
10.1	3.87
9.8	2.70
12.3	4.70

Based on the sample, we can compute the following estimates of $E(Y)$, $E(X)$, $V(X)$ and $Cov(X,Y)$:

$$\bar{X} = 12.43 \quad \text{and} \quad \bar{Y} = 3.797$$
$$S_X^2 = 21.0 \quad \text{and} \quad \widehat{Cov}(X,Y) = 2.82$$

Thus, the estimates of β_0 and β_1 are:

$$\hat{\beta}_1 = \frac{\widehat{Cov(X,Y)}}{S_X^2} = \frac{2.82}{21.0} = 0.134$$

$$\hat{\beta}_0 = \bar{Y} - \hat{\beta}_1 \cdot \bar{X} = 3.797 - 0.134 \cdot 12.43 = 2.131$$

and the estimate of the linear regression function thus becomes:

$$\hat{E}(Y|X = x) = \hat{\beta}_0 + \hat{\beta}_1 \cdot x = 2.131 + 0.134 \cdot x$$

There is, therefore, a positive correlation between income and expected consumption. An increase in income of DKK 1,000 per month leads to an expected change in red wine consumption of 0.134 litres.

Note that we cannot conclude that the relationship is causal. It may be that people drink more red wine because they have a higher income. However, it may also be that the desire to drink more red wine motivates them to earn more.

17.3.2   Ordinary least squares

The estimators $\hat{\beta}_0$ and $\hat{\beta}_1$ are often called the *ordinary least squares (OLS) estimators*. The reason for this name is that the way in which $\hat{\beta}_0$ and $\hat{\beta}_1$ are calculated can also be seen as an attempt to find a straight line, $b_0 + b_1 \cdot x$, that lies as close as possible to the observed values of Y in the sample. As a measure of the distance between the line and the observations of Y in the sample, we use the sum of the vertical distances squared. This sum is:

$$\sum_{i=1}^{n}\left(Y_i - \left(b_0 + b_1 \cdot X_i\right)\right)^2$$

This is illustrated in Figure 17.2 for a sample with eight observations (the black dots).

Figure 17.2:
Ordinary least
squares (OLS)

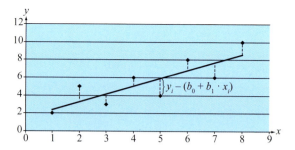

It can be shown that the values of b_0 and b_1, which ensure that the above sum of squares is as small as possible, are exactly the same as the estimators $\hat{\beta}_0$ and $\hat{\beta}_1$ from the previous section. In other words, the estimators $\hat{\beta}_0$ and $\hat{\beta}_1$ ensure that the sum of the squared differences between each observation of Y and the estimated regression function are as small as possible. Hence the name "ordinary least squares".

17.3.3   Properties of OLS estimators

As with the other estimators we have studied, we would like to know the distribution of the OLS estimators, $\hat{\beta}_0$ and $\hat{\beta}_1$, in order to evaluate their properties. In this section, we will posit some assumptions under which we can derive their distribution.

In Chapter 10, we examined various properties that we would like estimators to possess. An estimator of β_1 is unbiased if its expected value is equal to β_1. Ideally, an estimator should also be consistent. This means that if the sample size is very large, then there is a probability close to 1 that the estimator is close to the true value, β_1. The following box contains a collection of assumptions under which $\hat{\beta}_0$ and $\hat{\beta}_1$ possess these properties.

Properties of OLS estimators in simple linear regression:

Assumptions:
1. Simple linear regression: $E(Y|X = x) = \beta_0 + \beta_1 \cdot x$
2. Simple random sample: $((X_1, Y_1), (X_2, Y_2), ..., (X_n, Y_n))$
3. $V(Y|X = x) = \sigma^2$, i.e. the variance of Y does not depend on x
4. Given that $X = x$, then Y is normally distributed.

Under the assumptions:
- 1 and 2: $\hat{\beta}_0$ and $\hat{\beta}_1$ are unbiased and consistent estimators of β_0 and β_1, respectively. Assuming that the variance of Y exists.

- 1, 2 and 3: $\hat{\beta}_0$ and $\hat{\beta}_1$ are approximately normally distributed:

$$\hat{\beta}_0 \sim^A N(\beta_0, \sigma^2_{\hat{\beta}_0}) \text{ and } \hat{\beta}_1 \sim^A N(\beta_1, \sigma^2_{\hat{\beta}_1})$$

where $\sigma^2_{\hat{\beta}_0}$ is the variance of $\hat{\beta}_0$ and $\sigma^2_{\hat{\beta}_1}$ the variance of $\hat{\beta}_1$

- 1, 2, 3 and 4: $\hat{\beta}_0$ and $\hat{\beta}_1$ are exactly normally distributed:

$$\hat{\beta}_0 \sim N(\beta_0, \sigma^2_{\hat{\beta}_0}) \text{ and } \hat{\beta}_1 \sim N(\beta_1, \sigma^2_{\hat{\beta}_1})$$

where $\sigma^2_{\hat{\beta}_0}$ is the variance of $\hat{\beta}_0$ and $\sigma^2_{\hat{\beta}_1}$ the variance of $\hat{\beta}_1$.

The first assumption ensures that we have the right specification of the regression function. The second assumption implies that, for example, (X_1, Y_1) and (X_2, Y_2) are independent. This means that X_1 is independent of both X_2 and Y_2, and similarly for Y_1. The assumption does not mean that X_1 is independent of Y_1. If it were, there would be no point in making the regression of Y on X. The third assumption says that the conditional variance of Y does not depend on the value of X. The property that the conditional variance of Y given X does not depend on X is called *homoscedasticity*. The opposite property, that the conditional variance of Y given X does depend on X, is called *heteroscedasticity*.

In order to make use of the result that $\hat{\beta}_0$ and $\hat{\beta}_1$ are normally distributed, we need estimates of the variances of $\hat{\beta}_0$ and $\hat{\beta}_1$ as well as an estimate of the variance, σ^2, of Y. The formulas for calculating these estimates are shown in the next box.

Estimate of σ^2, $\sigma^2_{\hat{\beta}_0}$ and $\sigma^2_{\hat{\beta}_1}$ in simple linear regression:

$$S^2_{\sigma^2} = \frac{1}{n-2}\sum_{i=1}^{n}\left(Y_i - (\hat{\beta}_0 + \hat{\beta}_1 \cdot X_i)\right)^2$$

$$S^2_{\hat{\beta}_0} = S^2_{\sigma^2} \cdot \left(\frac{1}{n} + \frac{\overline{X}^2}{\sum_{i=1}^{n}\left(X_i - \overline{X}\right)^2}\right)$$

$$S^2_{\hat{\beta}_1} = \frac{1}{n-1} \cdot \frac{S^2_{\sigma^2}}{S^2_X} = \frac{S^2_{\sigma^2}}{\sum_{i=1}^{n}\left(X_i - \overline{X}\right)^2}$$

We call the square roots of $S^2_{\hat{\beta}_0}$ and $S^2_{\hat{\beta}_1}$ the standard errors of $\hat{\beta}_0$ and $\hat{\beta}_1$ respectively.

17.3.4 Non-random explanatory variable

We can also use the OLS estimators in some cases where we do not have a simple random sample (assumption 2 in the box above), for example, in situations where we can control the explanatory variable, X. In such situations, X is not random, as we determine it in advance. For instance, those who produce a product are often able to set its price. A similar situation occurs in laboratory studies, where we can control the size of the dose that a subject ingests. In such cases, where the explanatory variable is not random, we say that X is fixed.

When X is fixed, we replace assumption 2 about a simple random sample with an assumption 2', which only says that the Ys are uncorrelated.[24] The other three assumptions from the box above remain essentially unchanged. Formally, we can no longer use the terms conditional expectation and conditional variance given $X = x$, since X is no longer random but is determined by us. Therefore, we replace assumption 1 of the conditional expectation $E\left(Y|X = x\right)$ with a new assumption

---

24 This is a weaker assumption than the assumption of simple random sampling which implies that the different Y_i are independent. If X is stochastic, assumption 2) from section 17.3.3 also places restrictions on X. This is not the case with the new assumption 2') because X is now fixed, i.e. defined by us. In order for the approximative distribution of $\hat{\beta}_0$ and $\hat{\beta}_1$ in the following box to be correct, certain restrictions have to be placed on X. Using the same values of X if repeating the experiment is a simple and sufficient restriction.

1' about the unconditional expectation, $E(Y)$. Correspondingly, we replace assumption 3 about the conditional variance $V(Y|X = x)$ with a new assumption 3' about the unconditional variance, $V(Y)$. However, the interpretations of these two assumptions are the same as previously for all practical purposes. The following box summarises the results when X is fixed.

Properties of OLS estimators in simple linear regression with fixed X:

Assumptions:
1'. Simple linear regression: $E(Y) = \beta_0 + \beta_1 \cdot x$
2'. The Ys are uncorrelated i.e. $Cov(Y_i, Y_j) = 0$ for all values of i and j, where $i \neq j$
3'. $V(Y) = \sigma^2$ where σ^2 does not depend on x
4'. Y is normally distributed.

Under the assumptions:
- 1' and 2': $\hat{\beta}_0$ and $\hat{\beta}_1$ are unbiased and consistent estimators of β_0 and β_1, respectively

- 1', 2' and 3': $\hat{\beta}_0$ and $\hat{\beta}_1$ are approximately normally distributed:

$$\hat{\beta}_0 \sim^A N(\beta_0, \sigma^2_{\hat{\beta}_0}) \text{ and } \hat{\beta}_1 \sim^A N(\beta_1, \sigma^2_{\hat{\beta}_1})$$

where $\sigma^2_{\hat{\beta}_0}$ is the variance of $\hat{\beta}_0$, and $\sigma^2_{\hat{\beta}_1}$ the variance of $\hat{\beta}_1$

- 1', 2', 3' and 4': $\hat{\beta}_0$ and $\hat{\beta}_1$ are exactly normally distributed.

Estimates of $\sigma^2_{\hat{\beta}_0}$ and $\sigma^2_{\hat{\beta}_1}$ can be calculated the same way as with a random X.

17.4   Specification test of the simple linear regression

Before using the estimated regression function to interpret a relationship between Y and X, we must make sure that the regression model is reasonable, i.e. the assumptions in the model are not violated. In the next subsections, we will show different graphical methods for working out whether the assumptions are met.

For the simple linear regression model, we identified four assumptions in the box in Section 17.3.3 that allow us to determine the properties of the OLS estimator. We can get a good idea of whether the assumptions hold by looking at different types of graphs. For this, we will need the following values:

Estimated dependent variable:

$$\hat{Y}_i = \hat{E}(Y|X = x_i) = \hat{\beta}_0 + \hat{\beta}_1 \cdot x_i, \ i = 1,\ldots,n$$

Residual:

$$\hat{U}_i = Y_i - \hat{Y}, \ i = 1,\ldots,n$$

For each observation, (x_i, y_i), in the realised sample, we can compute $\hat{y}_i$ and $\hat{u}_i$ from the formulas above. $\hat{y}_i$ is an estimate of the conditional expectation of Y, given the specific value of X for the ith observation in the sample. The realised residual, $\hat{u}_i$, is the difference between this conditional expectation and the actual observation, y_i, in the sample, i.e. the vertical distance between the estimated regression function and the ith observation of Y (see Figure 17.3).

Example 17.5: Red wine and income – part 2

In Example 17.4, we found the following values of the estimators: $\hat{\beta}_1 = 0.134$ and $\hat{\beta}_0 = 2.131$. The estimated values of the dependent variable are then given by: $\hat{y}_i = 2.131 + 0.134 \cdot x_i$. In table 17.4, $\hat{y}_i$ and $\hat{u}_i$ are calculated for the ten observations in the sample:

Table 17.4: Estimated dependent variables, $\hat{y}_i$ and residuals, $\hat{u}_i$

x_i (income)	y_i (consumption)	$\hat{y}_i$	$\hat{u}_i$
22.2	5.04	5.11	-0.07
12.1	2.96	3.75	-0.79
14.3	3.08	4.05	-0.97
8.1	3.58	3.22	0.36
17.6	5.52	4.49	1.03
10.8	2.73	3.58	-0.85
7	3.78	3.07	0.71
10.1	3.87	3.48	0.39
9.8	2.70	3.44	-0.74
12.3	4.70	3.78	0.92

If we ignore the rounding errors, then the sum of the residuals is zero. This is a general property of OLS estimators.

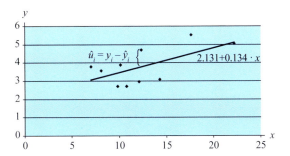

We can perform formal statistical tests about the four assumptions from the previous section. However, describing these tests would be beyond the scope of this book. Many statistical software programmes do, however, automatically calculate these tests. We can also use the statistical software to plot all the graphs we describe below, and it is astonishing how much insight into a problem can be gained by looking at the different plots. So even if we are testing the assumptions formally, we should always look carefully at the plots as well. Below, we consider each assumption in turn.

17.4.1   Assumption 1: Functional form

In order to examine whether the conditional mean of Y is linear in x, we can plot the estimated residuals, $\hat{u}_i$, against $\hat{y}_i$ in a co-ordinate system with $\hat{y}_i$ on the horizontal axis. We can also plot the residuals, $\hat{u}_i$, against x_i. These plots are called *residual plots*. If assumption 1 is correct, the residuals should be distributed around the horizontal axis 1 without any particular pattern. Figure 17.4 shows a situation where the linear regression function is (probably) correct. In Figure 17.4a, y_i is plotted against x_i, while Figure 17.4b shows the residual plot. Note that the residuals seem to be randomly distributed around the horizontal axis.

Figure 17.4:
Correct
functional form

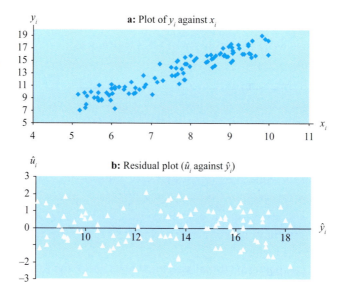

a: Plot of y_i against x_i

b: Residual plot ($\hat{u}_i$ against $\hat{y}_i$)

On the other hand, in Figure 17.5, we have a situation where the linear regression function is (probably) incorrect. In part a of the figure, y_i is plotted against x_i and we can see that the relationship is curved (convex). This is even clearer in the residual plot in part b. Here, we can see that the residuals are positive for low and high values of $\hat{y}_i$, whereas the residuals are negative for medium values of $\hat{y}_i$. There is therefore a tendency for the estimated conditional mean, $\hat{E}(Y|X = x)$, to be systematically wrong, which means that the chosen linear form for the conditional mean is probably incorrect. Instead, it looks as if that there could be a quadratic (x^2) relationship between x and the expected value of Y.

Figure 17.5:
Incorrect
functional form

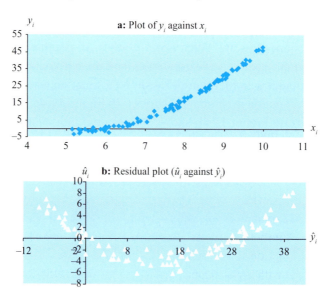

a: Plot of y_i against x_i

b: Residual plot ($\hat{u}_i$ against $\hat{y}_i$)

17.4.2　Assumption 2: Simple random sample

The assumption that we have a simple random sample may be cast into doubt if, for instance, we have collected the sample over time. An example might be a sample of house prices, in which the first observation ($i = 1$) is for the year 1980, the next observation ($i = 2$) is for the year 1981, and so on, up to, say, ($i = 21$) for 2000. A sample collected in this way is called a *time series*. Since there is often a connection between what happened last year and what happens this year, it will make the observations dependent. In other words, last year's house prices contain information about house prices this year. In this case, the sample is no longer a simple random sample, because that would require that the observations were independent.

If we have a sample of observations over time (a time series), we can plot the residuals, $\hat{u}_i$, against time, i. If it is a simple random sample, the residuals should be randomly distributed around the horizontal axis.

However, there may also be other reasons why the sample is not a simple random one. If, in Example 17.4, we had collected the sample by asking ten customers in the local wine shop about their income and their consumption of wine, this would hardly constitute a simple random sample from the whole population. We would probably expect that customers in the store would drink wine on average more than other people in their income bracket. In other words, Y for these individuals would have a tendency to be larger than the conditional mean value of Y for people with the same income. It can be shown that the OLS estimator in this case is not even consistent, which means that the results are not credible. In this case, the cause is *selection bias*, which means that the probability of being included in the sample depends on the explained variable, Y. We described a similar situation in Chapter 9.

Note that the probability of being in the sample could also depend on the explanatory variable, X, for example income. However, the fact that the selection depends on the explanatory variable does not cause a problem for the consistency of the OLS estimator.

17.4.3　Assumption 3: Homoscedasticity

The assumption of homoscedasticity means that the variance of Y must be the same regardless of the value of X. Heteroscedasticity can arise, for example, when we are studying consumption of a product, and income is the explanatory variable. People with higher incomes, X, have greater opportunity to consume than those with lower incomes. As a result, their consumption is not only higher but often also varies more than that of people with a low income. The variation around the conditional mean value, i.e. the variation in Y given $X = x$, is thus higher for large values of X.

To get an idea of whether the assumption of homoscedasticity holds true, we can look at the squared residuals, $\hat{U}_i^2$. These provide an indication of the variance of U given X, and therefore of the variance of Y given X.[25] We can plot the squared residuals against the explanatory variable. If the assumption of homoscedasticity is correct, the spread of the squared residuals should be the same for different values of the explanatory variable. Figure 17.6 illustrates a situation where the variance of Y given X depends on x (or the size of Y). In part a of the figure, y_i is plotted against x_i and shows that the y_is are more dispersed for high values of x_i. This impression is confirmed in part b, where the squared residuals, $\hat{u}_i^2$, are plotted against $\hat{y}_i$ and in part c, where the squared residuals $\hat{u}_i^2$ are plotted against x_i. In both cases, the variation increases for higher values of $\hat{y}$ and x_i respectively.

Figure 17.6:
Heteroscedasticity

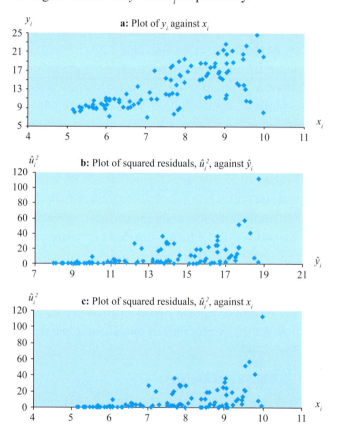

25   By substituting for Y, the conditional variance of Y given X can be written as:

$$V(Y|X = x) = V(\beta_0 + \beta_1 \cdot X + U|X = x)$$

In this expression, X can be considered as a constant, as we condition on X being equal to x. Hence, $\beta_0 + \beta_1 \cdot X$ can be considered as a constant in the second expression, leaving U as the only random variable. It then follows that $V(Y|X = x) = V(U|X = x)$ according to the calculation rules for variances from Chapter 5.

17.4.4 Assumption 4: Normally distributed observations

It is also useful to know whether assumption 4 about normally distributed observations is satisfied, because it implies that we can derive the distributions for $\hat{\beta}_0$ and $\hat{\beta}_1$ even when the sample is small. As we will show in section 17.5, these distributions can be used when we wish to test hypotheses about the size of the coefficients. In order to test assumption 4, we will in this section show two graphical techniques that can be used to compare an estimated distribution with a hypothesised distribution (in this case, the normal distribution).

The framework for the graphical techniques is as follows. Suppose we want to compare an estimated cumulative distribution function $\hat{F}_U(u)$ with a hypothesised cumulative distribution function $F_U^0(u)$. The estimated cumulative distribution function $\hat{F}_U(u)$ could be the empirical distribution function introduced in Section 12.4, while the hypothesised cumulative distribution function $F_U^0(u)$ is chosen by us. It could, for example, be the standard normal cumulative distribution function, which is denoted by $\Phi(u)$. A straightforward comparison of $\hat{F}_U(u)$ and $F_U^0(u)$ is to draw a graph for each of them in the same diagram with u on the horizontal axis, and $\hat{F}_U(u)$ and $F_U^0(u)$ on the vertical axis. If the graphs fall on top of each other, then this indicates that the two distributions are similar. If there are large differences between the two distributions, these will also be easy to detect in such a diagram. If the differences are not too big, for example if the differences occur only for very small or large values of u, they may be hard to see in such a diagram. It is for that reason that we now introduce two alternative graphical techniques.

The first of the graphical techniques is called a (p,p)-plot. In a (p,p)-plot, we pick a value for u, e.g. u_1, and then we mark a point in a co-ordinate system with $F_U^0(u_1)$ as the first co-ordinate (the horizontal axis) and $\hat{F}_U(u_1)$ as the second co-ordinate (the vertical axis). In other words, the point in the co-ordinate system becomes $(F_U^0(u_1), \hat{F}_U(u_1))$. Note that the value of u_1 itself is not used on either the horizontal or the vertical axis. The idea behind this exercise is that if $\hat{F}_U(u)$ and $F_U^0(u)$ are identical, then the point $(F_U^0(u_1), \hat{F}_U(u_1))$ should lie on the 45-degree line. Therefore, we can check whether $\hat{F}_U(u)$ and $F_U^0(u)$ are identical by picking a number of different values for u, marking the corresponding points $(F_U^0(u), \hat{F}_U(u))$ in the co-ordinate system, and checking whether they all lie on the 45-degree line. The plot of $(F_U^0(u), \hat{F}_U(u))$ for all the different values of u is called a (p,p)-plot, or a probability plot. The name (p,p) refers to the fact that both the first and second co-ordinates are (cumulative) probabilities.

The main advantage of the (p,p)-plot, compared to a simple diagram with the graphs of $F_U^0(u)$ and $\hat{F}_U(u)$, is that it is much easier to check whether a graph lies on top of the 45-degree line than it is to check whether two graphs of two non-linear functions lie on top of each other. Furthermore, as the possible values of a cumulative distribution function lie between 0 and 1, it is only necessary to draw the 45-degree line and the (p,p)-plot between the two points (0,0) and (1,1), whereas the graphs of $F_U^0(u)$ and $\hat{F}_U(u)$ must be drawn for all possible values of u (i.e. potentially all values between $-\infty$ and ∞).

Now we use the (p,p)-plot described above to check whether assumption 4 seems to hold. That is, we need to check if Y is normally distributed for each value of X. This is a daunting task since X may take on many different values and, thus, we need to make a (p,p)-plot for each possible value of X. We can, however, simplify the problem a bit, since assumption 1 gives us the mean of Y for each value of X and assumption 3 says that the variance of Y does not depend on X. These two assumptions can be used to transform the problem of checking normality of Y for each value of X into the problem of checking whether U is normally distributed. The reason is that if $Y \sim N(\beta_0 + \beta_1 x, \sigma^2)$, then $U = Y - (\beta_0 + \beta_1 x) \sim N(0, \sigma^2)$, and while the distribution of Y depends on x, the distribution of U does not depend on x. Therefore, we merely need to check if U is normally distributed.

To check whether U is normally distributed, we need an estimator of the distribution of U. Since we can calculate the residuals $\hat{U}$, we can calculate the empirical distribution function of the residuals, $\hat{F}_U(u)$. This is given by:

$$\hat{F}_U(u) = \frac{number\ of\ \hat{U}_i s\ with\ value \leq u}{n}$$

We can then compare this empirical distribution function to the normal distribution with mean value equal to 0 and variance σ^2, i.e. $F_U^0(u) = \Phi\left((u-0)/\sqrt{\sigma^2}\right)$, where we can use the sample variance of the residuals, $S_{\sigma^2}^2$, instead of σ^2. Thus, we get the (p,p)-plot by plotting:

$$\left(\Phi\left(\frac{u}{\sqrt{S_{\sigma^2}^2}} \right), \cdot \hat{F}_U(u) \right)$$

for all values of u (in the sample). If the residuals are normally distributed, then the resulting graph will be a straight 45-degree line between the points (0, 0) and (1, 1). In practice, the points will never lie exactly on a straight line, but the relevant question is also whether there is evidence of systematic deviations from the 45-degree line, which would indicate a lack of normality. The next example illustrates how to construct the (p,p)-plot in practice.

The spreadsheet below contains a sample of 30 observations of a stochastic variable, X. In column B, we have the sorted observations, and in column C the empirical distribution function, $\hat{F}_X(x)$. We wish to examine whether X is normally distributed. We should therefore compare the empirical distribution function for X to $F_X^0(x) = \Phi\left((x - \bar{X}) / S\right)$, where $\bar{X}$ and S are, respectively the average and standard deviation from the sample, since the true mean and standard deviation are unknown. In column E, the probabilities, $\Phi((x - \bar{X})/S)$, are calculated for the values of x in the sample. The graph shows $\hat{F}_X(x)$ plotted against $\Phi((x - \bar{X})/S)$ for the 30 observations in the sample.

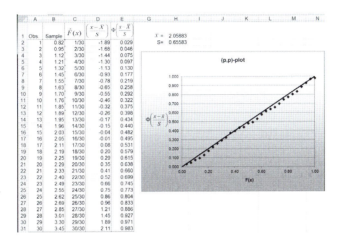

	A	B	C	D	E
	Obs	Sample	$\hat{F}(x)$	$\left(\frac{x-\bar{X}}{S}\right)$	$\Phi\left(\frac{x-\bar{X}}{S}\right)$
1					
2	1	0.82	1/30	-1.89	0.029
3	2	0.95	2/30	-1.68	0.046
4	3	1.12	3/30	-1.44	0.075
5	4	1.21	4/30	-1.30	0.097
6	5	1.32	5/30	-1.13	0.130
7	6	1.45	6/30	-0.93	0.177
8	7	1.55	7/30	-0.78	0.219
9	8	1.63	8/30	-0.65	0.258
10	9	1.70	9/30	-0.55	0.292
11	10	1.76	10/30	-0.46	0.322
12	11	1.85	11/30	-0.32	0.375
13	12	1.89	12/30	-0.26	0.398
14	13	1.95	13/30	-0.17	0.434
15	14	1.96	14/30	-0.15	0.440
16	15	2.03	15/30	-0.04	0.482
17	16	2.05	16/30	-0.01	0.495
18	17	2.11	17/30	0.08	0.531
19	18	2.19	18/30	0.20	0.579
20	19	2.25	19/30	0.29	0.615
21	20	2.29	20/30	0.35	0.638
22	21	2.33	21/30	0.41	0.660
23	22	2.40	22/30	0.52	0.699
24	23	2.49	23/30	0.66	0.745
25	24	2.55	24/30	0.75	0.773
26	25	2.62	25/30	0.86	0.804
27	26	2.69	26/30	0.96	0.833
28	27	2.85	27/30	1.21	0.886
29	28	3.01	28/30	1.45	0.927
30	29	3.30	29/30	1.89	0.971
31	30	3.45	30/30	2.11	0.983

$\bar{X} = 2.05883$
$S = 0.65583$

In the graph above, the points lie approximately on a straight line between (0,0) and (1,1), and it therefore seems reasonable to assume that the observations are normally distributed.

Figure 17.7 shows another sample. Note that in this case the points deviate from the straight line at the ends. This distribution is therefore unlikely to be a normal distribution.

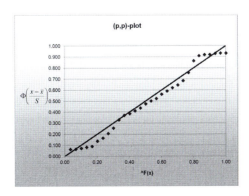

The second graphical technique is called a (q,q)-plot. The basic idea is that if two distributions are identical, then they also have the same quantiles (see Section 5.3 for the definition of a quantile). In the (p,p)-plot, we plotted probabilities of an estimated distribution against the probabilities of a hypothesised distribution. In the (q,q)-plot, we plot the quantiles of an estimated distribution against the quantiles of a hypothesised distribution.

Specifically, the (q,q)-plot is constructed as follows. Let q_p^0 be the p-quantile of the hypothesised cumulative distribution function, $F_U^0(u)$, and let $\hat{q}_p$ be the p-quantile of the estimated cumulative distribution function $\hat{F}_U(u)$. For example, consider the p_1-quantile. Then mark the point with $q_{p_1}^0$ as the first coordinate (the horizontal axis) and $\hat{q}_{p_1}$ as the second coordinate (the vertical axis). If the two distributions are identical, then the point $(q_{p_1}^0, \hat{q}_{p_1})$ should be located on the 45-degree line. Therefore, we can check if $\hat{F}_U(u)$ and $F_U^0(u)$ are identical by picking a number of different values for p, mark the corresponding points $(q_p^0, \hat{q}_p)$ in the coordinate system, and check whether they all lie on the 45-degree line. The plot of $(q_p^0, \hat{q}_p)$ for all values of p is called a (q,q)-plot or a quantile plot.

Typically, we choose the quantiles to be plotted in a (q,q)-plot as follows: the smallest observation in the sample is an estimator for the $(1 - 0.5)/n$-quantile, while the second smallest observation is an estimator for the $(2 - 0.5)/n$-quantile, and so on. If there are ten observations in the sample, the smallest observation is, therefore, an estimator for the 0.05-quantile (since $(1 - 0.5)/10 = 0.05$), the second smallest an estimator for the 0.15-quantile, and so on, up to the largest observation, which is an estimator for the 0.95-quantile. Thus, we simply plot the observations from our sample on the horizontal axis in the diagram.

On the vertical axis, we plot the corresponding theoretical quantiles from the hypothesised distribution, e.g. the normal distribution. Here, we know that the following linear relationship exists between a normally distributed variable, X, and a standard normal variable, Z:

$$Z = \frac{X - \mu}{\sigma}$$

where μ is the mean value of X, and σ is the standard deviation of X. So, instead of examining whether the theoretical quantiles for X form a straight line (the 45-degree line) with the estimated quantiles, we might as well check whether the theoretical quantiles for Z form a straight line (although not necessarily the 45-degree line) with the estimated quantiles. Accordingly, we plot the corresponding theoretical quantiles

An insight into statistics for the social sciences

for Z on the vertical axis. These can be found using Table 2 at the back of the book.

Example 17.7: (q, q)-plot

The sample used in Example 17.6 contained 30 observations. The smallest observation is used as an estimator for $(1 - 0.5) / 30 = 1/60 =$ the 0.0167-quantile, while the second smallest is used as an estimator for $(2 - 0.5) / 30 = 1/20 =$ the 0.05-quantile, and so on. In the spreadsheet below, we have inserted the corresponding percentiles from the standard normal distribution. We have also plotted the 30 empirical quantiles, i.e. the sample observations, against the 30 theoretical quantiles. The resulting picture confirms the conclusion from Example 17.6.

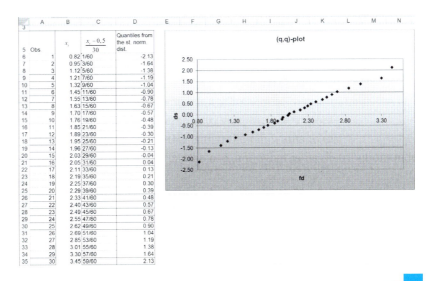

	A	B	C	D
		x_i	$\dfrac{x_i - 0.5}{30}$	Quantiles from the st. norm. dist.
5	Obs			
6	1	0.82	1/60	-2.13
7	2	0.95	3/60	-1.64
8	3	1.12	5/60	-1.38
9	4	1.21	7/60	-1.19
10	5	1.32	9/60	-1.04
11	6	1.45	11/60	-0.90
12	7	1.55	13/60	-0.78
13	8	1.63	15/60	-0.67
14	9	1.70	17/60	-0.57
15	10	1.76	19/60	-0.48
16	11	1.85	21/60	-0.39
17	12	1.89	23/60	-0.30
18	13	1.95	25/60	-0.21
19	14	1.96	27/60	-0.13
20	15	2.03	29/60	-0.04
21	16	2.05	31/60	0.04
22	17	2.11	33/60	0.13
23	18	2.19	35/60	0.21
24	19	2.25	37/60	0.30
25	20	2.29	39/60	0.39
26	21	2.33	41/60	0.48
27	22	2.40	43/60	0.57
28	23	2.49	45/60	0.67
29	24	2.55	47/60	0.78
30	25	2.62	49/60	0.90
31	26	2.69	51/60	1.04
32	27	2.85	53/60	1.19
33	28	3.01	55/60	1.38
34	29	3.30	57/60	1.64
35	30	3.45	59/60	2.13

17.5 Hypothesis testing and confidence intervals

If we believe that the regression model's assumptions have been complied with, we can move on to test the hypotheses that may have motivated the regression analysis in the first place. In this section, we describe how to test hypotheses about the slope coefficient, β_1, in the regression function.

To test whether the explanatory variable has an effect on the expected value of the explained variable, we test whether the slope coefficient is equal to 0 or different from 0. More generally, however, we would like to test whether the slope coefficient is equal to a certain value, β_1^0, or different from this value. The superscript "0" indicates that this is the value of the coefficient under the null hypothesis.

We can follow the same approach as we did in Chapter 14 when testing a hypothesis about a mean value. We therefore start by specifying the null- and alternative hypotheses, which in this case are:

$$H_0 : \beta_1 = \beta_1^0$$

$$H_1 : \beta_1 \neq \beta_1^0$$

The next step is to draft a hypothesis measure that discriminates between the null hypothesis and the alternative hypothesis when we insert the true value. Here, we use the same hypothesis measure as when testing a mean value, namely, $h(\beta_1) = \beta_1 - \beta_1^0$. If the true value satisfies the null hypothesis, then this hypothesis measure is equal to 0, otherwise it is different from 0.

The last step is to construct the test statistic based on the hypothesis measure. First we replace unknown quantities with estimates. The only unknown quantity in this case is β_1, which we can replace with the OLS estimator, $\hat{\beta}_1$. To ensure that the test statistic has a distribution that is easy to work with, we choose a test statistic similar to the one used when testing a mean value. We divide the hypothesis measure by the estimated standard error of $\hat{\beta}_1$. This is just the square root of $S_{\hat{\beta}_1}^2$, for which we gave the formula in Section 17.2. The box below summarises the test.

Test of the slope coefficient, β_1, in the simple linear regression:

$$H_0 : \beta_1 = \beta_1^0$$

$$H_1 : \beta_1 \neq \beta_1^0$$

Test statistic: $T = \dfrac{\hat{\beta}_1 - \beta_1^0}{\sqrt{S_{\hat{\beta}_1}^2}}$

Under the assumptions 1, 2 and 3, $T \sim^A N(0,1)$ is under H_0.

Under the assumptions 1, 2, 3 and 4, $T \sim t(n-2)$ under H_0.

An insight into statistics for the social sciences

In Example 17.4, we calculated an estimate of the regression of a person's consumption of red wine, Y, on the person's income, X. We found that the relationship was positive. One question is whether the relationship found is also statistically significant or whether it can simply be ascribed to the natural variation inherent in a sample. We will therefore now test whether the relationship is statistically significant at a 5% significance level.

The null- and alternative hypotheses are: $H_0 : \beta_1 = 0$ and $H_1 : \beta_1 \neq 0$. To compute the test statistic, we first find $S^2_{\hat{\beta}_1}$. According to the box in Section 17.3.3, this is given by:

$$S^2_{\hat{\beta}_1} = \frac{S^2_{\sigma^2}}{(n-1) \cdot S^2_X}$$

We already know from Example 17.4 that $S_X^2 = 21{,}0$. Thus, we just need to calculate $S^2_{\sigma^2}$:

$$S^2_{\sigma^2} = \frac{1}{n-2}\sum_{i=1}^{n}\left(y_i - (\hat{\beta}_0 + \hat{\beta}_1 \cdot x_i)\right)^2 = \frac{1}{n-2}\sum_{i=1}^{n}\hat{u}_i^2 = \frac{5.533}{10-2} = 0.6916$$

Therefore:

$$S^2_{\hat{\beta}_1} = \frac{S^2_{\sigma^2}}{(n-1)\cdot S^2_X} = \frac{0.6916}{(10-1)\cdot 21.0} = 0.00366$$

The value of the test statistic is then:

$$T = \frac{\hat{\beta}_1 - \beta_1^0}{\sqrt{S^2_{\hat{\beta}_1}}} = \frac{0.134 - 0}{\sqrt{0.00366}} = 2.21$$

We then find the critical values from the standard normal distribution. With $\alpha = 0.05$ these are: -1.96 and 1.96. Since T is greater than 1.96, we reject the null hypothesis and accept that there is a relationship between expected red wine consumption and income. Note that if we had chosen, instead, to use the critical values from the t-distribution with $n - 2 = 10 - 2 = 8$ degrees of freedom, we would not have rejected H_0 at a 5% significance level.

Using exactly the same procedure as in the hypothesis test for the slope coefficient described above, we can test a hypothesis about the intercept, β_0.

We can also set up confidence intervals for the unknown coefficients, β_0 and β_1, using the same techniques as in Chapter 13. The box below shows the formulas involved:

Confidence interval for a coefficient in the linear regression function:

Under the assumptions 1, 2 and 3, the approximate $(1 - \alpha)$-confidence interval for β_k ($k = 0$ or $k = 1$) is:

$$\left[\hat{\beta}_k - Z_{1-\alpha/2} \cdot \sqrt{S_{\hat{\beta}_k}^2} \;,\; \hat{\beta}_k + Z_{1-\alpha/2} \cdot \sqrt{S_{\hat{\beta}_k}^2}\right]$$

where $Z_{1-\alpha/2}$ is the $(1 - \alpha/2)$-quantile from the standard normal distribution.

Under the assumptions 1, 2, 3 and 4, the exact $(1 - \alpha)$-confidence interval for β_k ($k = 0$ or $k = 1$) is:

$$\left[\hat{\beta}_k - t_{1-\alpha/2}(n - 2) \cdot \sqrt{S_{\hat{\beta}_k}^2} \;,\; \hat{\beta}_k + t_{1-\alpha/2}(n - 2) \cdot \sqrt{S_{\hat{\beta}_k}^2}\right]$$

where $t_{1-\alpha/2}(n - 2)$ is the $(1 - \alpha/2)$-quantile from the t-distribution with $n - 2$ degrees of freedom.

17.6   The uncertainty of predictions in simple linear regression

We can use the estimated regression function to predict Y, or the expected value of Y given a particular value of our explanatory variable. In Example 17.3, we showed how to use the regression function to predict the expected demand for the Blue Bull soft drink at a given price, x. This would be useful if we wanted to work out what price would generate the greatest profit for the company producing Blue Bull.

In Example 17.3, we knew that the regression function was $E(Y|X = x) = 3{,}000 - 200 \cdot x$, where Y was the demand, and x the price. Using this, we can predict:

a.   The expected demand at a given price, x^*: $E(Y|X = x^*)$
b.   The actual demand at a given price, x^*: $Y = E(Y|X = x^*) + U$

The asterisk on x indicates that this is a value we choose. Our prediction of the expected demand is $E(Y|X = x^*) = 3,000 - 200 \cdot x^*$. Because the regression function is known, this prediction is without uncertainty. The prediction of the actual demand, Y, is also $E(Y|X = x^*) = 3,000 - 200 \cdot x^*$, as we do not know U, but we do know that U has expected value $E\left(U\middle|X = x^*\right)$ equal to 0. In our prediction of the actual demand, Y, U is thus the prediction error.

In practice, we do not know the regression function but, as we saw above, we are often able to estimate it. We can then use this estimate to predict the expected value of Y given our chosen value x^* of X. By inserting into the estimated regression function, we get:

$$\hat{Y} = \hat{E}(Y|X = x^*) = \hat{\beta}_0 + \hat{\beta}_1 \cdot x^*$$

This is our prediction of the expected value of Y given x^*, i.e. point a) above. It is also our prediction of the actual value of Y given x^*, i.e. point b) above.

Since we only have an estimate of the regression function, both our prediction of the expected value of Y given x^* and the prediction of Y given x^* are affected by sample uncertainty. In the following two subsections, we show how to determine the magnitude of this uncertainty in the two situations.

17.6.1   Uncertainty of the prediction of the expected value of Y

The uncertainty in the estimate of the expected value of Y given X stems exclusively from the uncertainty in the estimates of the unknown parameters: β_0 and β_1.

The prediction of the estimated value of Y given $X = x^*$ in the simple linear regression model is:

$$\hat{Y} = \hat{E}(Y|X = x^*) = \hat{\beta}_0 + \hat{\beta}_1 \cdot x^*$$

The uncertainty of this estimator is shown in the box below.

Uncertainty of the prediction of the expected value of Y given $X=x^*$ in the simple linear regression model:

Prediction: $\hat{Y} = \hat{E}(Y|X = x^*) = \hat{\beta}_0 + \hat{\beta}_1 \cdot x^*$

Prediction error: $W^* = E(Y|X = x^*) - \hat{E}(Y|X = x^*)$

Variance of the prediction error:

$$V\left(W^*\right) = \sigma^2 \cdot \left(\frac{1}{n} + \frac{(x^* - \bar{X})^2}{\sum\limits_{i=1}^{n}(X_i - \bar{X})^2} \right)$$

Here, the prediction error is called W^* to indicate that it is the difference between the true expected value and the estimated expected value, whereas U is the difference between the actual value and the expected value. We can arrive at an estimate of $V(W^*)$ by substituting σ^2 with $S_{\sigma^2}^2$.

From the box, it follows that the uncertainty of the prediction (the variance of W^*) is greater if x^* is far from the average, $\bar{x}$, in the sample than if x^* is near $\bar{x}$. The intuition behind this is that the data (the sample) we have used to estimate the regression function is found around the sample mean, and therefore we have more information about Y given X if it is in the vicinity of the sample average of X. In addition, we can see that the uncertainty decreases if we are able to increase the sample size, n. If the sample size is very (infinitely) large, then the uncertainty disappears completely.

As with other estimates, we can provide a confidence interval for the unknown value – here, the conditional mean $E\left(Y|X = x^*\right)$. It looks like this:

Confidence interval for the conditional mean of Y given $X = x^*$ in the simple linear regression model:

Under the assumptions 1, 2 and 3, the approximate $(1 - \alpha)$-confidence interval for $E\left(Y \middle| X = x^*\right)$ is:

$$\left[\hat{E}(Y|X = x^*) - Z_{1-\alpha/2} \cdot \sqrt{\hat{V}(W^*)} \, , \right.$$

$$\left. \hat{E}(Y|X = x^*) + Z_{1-\alpha/2} \cdot \sqrt{\hat{V}(W^*)} \right]$$

where $Z_{1-\alpha/2}$ is the $(1 - \alpha/2)$-quantile from the standard normal distribution.

Under the assumptions 1, 2, 3 and 4, the exact $(1 - \alpha)$-confidence interval for $E\left(Y \middle| X = x^*\right)$ is:

$$\left[\hat{E}(Y|X = x^*) - t_{1-\alpha/2}(n-2) \cdot \sqrt{\hat{V}(W^*)} \, , \right.$$

$$\left. \hat{E}(Y|X = x^*) + t_{1-\alpha/2}(n-2) \cdot \sqrt{\hat{V}(W^*)} \right]$$

where $t_{1-\alpha/2}(n-2)$ is the $(1 - \alpha/2)$-quantile from the t-distribution with $n-2$ degrees of freedom.

17.6.2 Uncertainty of the prediction of the value of Y

The uncertainty of the prediction of Y given X stems both from the uncertainty of the estimates of the unknown parameters β_0 and β_1, and from the uncertainty due to Y's distribution around its expected value.

The prediction of Y given $X = x^*$ in the simple linear regression model is:

$$\hat{Y} = \hat{E}(Y|X = x^*) = \hat{\beta}_0 + \hat{\beta}_1 \cdot x^*$$

where the asterisk on x again indicates that we have chosen this value. This prediction is equal to the prediction of the expected value of Y from the previous section. The uncertainty of this prediction (estimator) is shown in the box below.

Uncertainty of the prediction of the value of Y given $X = x^*$ in the simple linear regression model:

Prediction: $\hat{Y} = \hat{E}(Y|X = x^*) = \hat{\beta}_0 + \hat{\beta}_1 \cdot x^*$

Prediction error: $U^* = Y - \hat{E}(Y|X = x^*)$

The variance of the prediction error is:

$$V\left(U^*\right) = \sigma^2 \cdot \left(1 + \frac{1}{n} + \frac{(x^* - \bar{X})^2}{\sum_{i=1}^{n}(x_i - \bar{X})^2} \right) = \sigma^2 + V\left(W^*\right)$$

Compared to Section 17.6.1, σ^2 has been added to the variance of the prediction error. This is because we are predicting Y, not just the expected value of Y. The prediction error, U^*, is therefore a sum of two errors: (a) the error from Section 17.6.1, which is due to the use of the estimated regression function to predict the expected value of Y, and (b) the error from Section 17.1.2, which is because we predict Y with its expected value. This latter prediction error has the variance σ^2, and this explains the difference between $V(U^*)$ and $V(W^*)$. We can arrive at an estimate of $V(U^*)$ by substituting σ^2 with $S^2_{\sigma^2}$.

Even when the sample size is very large, the uncertainty does not disappear completely in this case. The uncertainty we remove by using a large sample size is the uncertainty that comes from the unknown regression function, i.e. the prediction error from Section 17.6.1. The uncertainty caused by the fact that Y is not equal to but distributed around its conditional mean, $E\left(Y|X = x\right)$, is unavoidable.

We can also calculate a confidence interval for Y, as in the box below.

Confidence interval for Y given $X = x^*$ in the simple linear regression model:

Under the assumptions 1, 2 and 3, the approximate $(1 - \alpha)$-confidence interval for $E(Y|X = x^*)$ is:

$$\left[\hat{E}(Y|X = x^*) - Z_{1-\alpha/2} \cdot \sqrt{\hat{V}(U^*)} \, , \right.$$

$$\left. \hat{E}(Y|X = x^*) + Z_{1-\alpha/2} \cdot \sqrt{\hat{V}(U^*)} \right]$$

where $Z_{1-\alpha/2}$ is the $(1 - \alpha/2)$-quantile from the standard normal distribution.

Under the assumptions 1, 2, 3 and 4, the exact $(1 - \alpha)$-confidence interval for $E(Y|X = x^*)$ is:

$$\left[\hat{E}(Y|X = x^*) - t_{1-\alpha/2}(n - 2) \cdot \sqrt{\hat{V}(U^*)} \, , \right.$$

$$\left. \hat{E}(Y|X = x^*) + t_{1-\alpha/2}(n - 2) \cdot \sqrt{\hat{V}(U^*)} \right]$$

where $t_{1-\alpha/2}(n - 2)$ is the $(1 - \alpha/2)$-quantile from the t-distribution with $n - 2$ degrees of freedom.

17.7   Exercises

1. Review questions
   a) What is a regression function?
   b) Explain how the regression function can be used to predict the value of a random variable, Y.
   c) What is the prediction error?
   d) Explain what simple linear regression is, and provide an interpretation of the coefficient, β_1.
   e) Explain how you would obtain an estimate of the regression function. What is the interpretation of the ordinary least squares (OLS) method?
   f) What are the properties of the estimators? Under what assumptions?
   g) Account for the assumptions underlying the simple linear regression model, and explain how you can check them graphically.

h) Which test statistic is used to test hypotheses about the coefficients in the regression function? Which distribution does it have
under H_0?

i) Account for the two types of prediction that can be made by using the estimated regression function. Which of the two predictions is associated with the greatest uncertainty? Why?

2. Based on a simple random sample, a local authority has estimated
the expected distance, Y (measured in km), between home and work
as a function of a person's income, X (measured in DKK 100,000).
The relationship is estimated to be $\hat{E}(Y|X = x) = 12 + 3 \cdot x$.

a) How much does the expected distance to work change if income
rises by DKK 100,000?

b) Test the hypothesis that a person's income has no influence on
the expected distance between home and work, based on an esti-
mated variance of $\hat{\beta}_1$ (the coefficient of x) of $S_{\hat{\beta}_1}^2 = 2,1$.

c) Can you conclude that higher income causes a longer distance
to work?

3. In a study of demand for 20-second commercials, Y, a television
station had a marketing agency estimate the following relationship
with the price (measured in DKK 1,000), P, of a 20-second com-
mercial block.

$$\hat{E}(Y|P = p) = 800 - 50 \cdot p$$

The relationship is estimated with OLS on a simple random sample
of $n = 20$ observations. The average price, $\bar{p}$, in the sample is 10
and $S_{\sigma^2}^2 = 121$. Furthermore,

$$\sum_{i=1}^{20}(p_i - \bar{p})^2 \text{ also} = 80$$

a) Interpret the estimated regression function.

b) What is the prediction of the expected demand if you choose the
prices $p = 5$ and $p = 10$, respectively?

c) What is the prediction of the actual demand at these prices?

d) Compare and discuss your answers to questions b) and c).

e) What is the uncertainty of the prediction of the expected demand
at the prices $p = 5$ and $p = 10$, respectively?

f) In question e), why is there a difference in the uncertainty when
the price is 5 and 10, respectively?

g) What is the uncertainty of the prediction of the actual demand at the prices p = 5 and p = 10, respectively?

h) Why is there a difference in the answers to questions e) and g) in the case where the price is 10?

i) Construct a 0.95-confidence interval for the regression function when the price is 10.

4. In a residential neighbourhood, house prices (in DKK millions), Y, have been collated and the number of square metres, X, in the last eight houses sold have been calculated. The realised sample is provided in the following table:

House price, y_i	Square metres, x_i
1.4	135
1.8	160
2.1	210
1.7	175
1.9	180
1.2	140
1.8	180
1.6	155

a) Discuss the reasonableness of assuming that the sample is a simple random sample.

b) Calculate the OLS estimate of the regression function.

c) Check whether the underlying assumptions hold.

d) Test whether house size has a statistically significant relationship with the expected price at a 5% significance level.

e) Predict the expected price of a 180-m² house.

f) Construct a 0.90 confidence interval for the regression function.

18 Multiple linear regression

In this chapter, we extend the regression analysis from Chapter 17 to multiple linear regression. In multiple linear regression, you explain the expected value of the dependent variable, Y, with more than one random variable. This allows us to analyse the relationship between two random variables, Y and X, while keeping the effects of other random variables constant.

In Section 18.1, we introduce the multiple linear regression model and discuss how it is interpreted, compared to the simple linear regression model. We look at the estimation of the multiple linear regression function in Section 18.2. As we did with simple linear regression, we also look at specification tests (Section 18.3), hypothesis testing (Section 18.4) and predictions (Section 18.5). In Section 18.6, we consider alternative non-linear versions of a regression function. In Section 18.7, we discuss the consequences of not being able to observe a potentially relevant random variable in the regression. Finally, Section 18.8 returns to Chapter 3's discussion of spurious relationships.

18.1 The multiple linear regression model

As its title suggests, multiple linear regression is an extension of simple linear regression, which has only one explanatory variable, to the case with multiple explanatory variables. Let $X_1, X_2, ..., X_K$ be K different random variables. The multiple linear regression model is given by:

$$E(Y|X_1 = x_1, X_2 = x_2, ..., X_K = x_K)$$
$$= \beta_0 + \beta_1 \cdot x_1 + \beta_2 \cdot x_2 + ... + \beta_K \cdot x_K$$

where $\beta_0, \beta_1, \beta_2, ..., \beta_K$ are coefficients. We can also write the multiple linear regression model as:

$$Y = \beta_0 + \beta_1 \cdot X_1 + \beta_2 \cdot X_2 + ... + \beta_K \cdot X_K + U$$

$$\text{where } E(U \mid X_1 = x_1, X_2 = x_2,..., X_K = x_K) = 0$$

The prediction error U is interpreted in the same way as in the case of simple linear regression in Chapter 17.

As with the simple linear regression model, we can formulate $\beta_0, \beta_1,..., \beta_K$ in terms of the population variances and covariances of the Y and the Xs. However, since these expressions are rather complicated, we will skip them. What is far more important in this context is the interpretation of the multiple linear regression model.

Example 18.1: Blue Bull – part 1

In Example 17.3, we looked at the expected demand for the soft drink Blue Bull as a function of its price. We can now extend this model of the demand for Blue Bull so that it also takes into account a competing soft drink, Caco Laco. Let Y_{BB} be the demand for Blue Bull, while we let X_{BB} be the price of Blue Bull and X_{CL} the price of Caco Laco. Furthermore, assume that the expected demand for Blue Bull as a function of the price of Blue Bull and the price of Caco Laco is:

$$E\left(Y_{BB} \mid X_{BB} = x_{BB}, X_{CL} = x_{CL}\right) = 2,500 - 250 \cdot x_{BB} + 100 \cdot x_{CL}$$

where Y_{BB} is measured in number of bottles and the prices are measured in DKK per bottle. If the price of Blue Bull is DKK $x_{BB} = 10$ per bottle and the price of Caco Laco is also DKK $x_{CL} = 10$ per bottle, then the expected demand for Blue Bull is equal to $2,500 - 250 \cdot 10 + 100 \cdot 10 = 1,000$ bottles. This is the same value as in Example 17.3, where the price of Blue Bull was also DKK 10 per bottle.

However, we can now work out the expected demand for Blue Bull at different prices than DKK 10 of the competing product Caco Laco. If the price of Caco Laco is raised to DKK 11 per bottle, then the expected demand for Blue Bull becomes: $2,500 - 250 \cdot 10 + 100 \cdot 11 = 1,100$ bottles. A price increase of DKK 1 per bottle of Caco Laco therefore increases the expected demand for Blue Bull by 100 bottles.

An interpretation of the multiple linear regression model can be obtained by calculating the effect on the expected value of Y of a small change in one of the explanatory variables. To be able to compare with the simple linear regression model, let us consider the following two regression functions:

(i) $E(Y|X_1 = x_1) = \beta_0 + \beta_1 \cdot x_1$

(ii) $E(Y|X_1 = x_1, X_2 = x_2) = \gamma_0 + \gamma_1 \cdot x_1 + \gamma_2 \cdot x_2$

We label the coefficients in (ii) γ to distinguish them from the βs in (i). In (i), the expected value of Y is conditional on x_1, whereas in (ii) the expected value of Y is conditional on both x_1 and x_2. In Section 17.2, we found that the effect on the expected value of Y of increasing x_1 by one unit is $\Delta_{simple} = \beta_1$ in the simple linear regression model. In a similar way, we can work out the effect on the expected value of Y of increasing x_1 by one unit in the multiple linear regression model in (ii):

$$\Delta_{multiple,x_1} = E(Y|X_1 = x_1 + 1, X_2 = x_2) - E(Y|X_1 = x_1, X_2 = x_2)$$
$$= [\gamma_0 + \gamma_1 \cdot (x_1 + 1) + \gamma_2 \cdot x_2] - [\gamma_0 + \gamma_1 \cdot x_1 + \gamma_2 \cdot x_2] = \gamma_1$$

where $\Delta_{multiple,x_1}$ is the change in the expected value of Y if x_1 is increased by one unit.[26]

The interpretation of β_1 is that it represents the change in the expected value of Y of increasing x_1 by one unit. The interpretation of γ_1 is slightly different: it is the change in the expected value of Y of increasing x_1 by one unit, given that x_2 is unchanged. The difference in the interpretation is therefore that x_2 is kept unchanged in (ii), whereas in (i), x_2 is not necessarily unchanged when we increase x_1 by one unit. In other words, we have not conditioned on the value of x_2 in the simple linear regression model in (i).

Example 18.2: Blue Bull – part 2

We can compare the effects of a higher price of Blue Bull in examples 17.3 and 18.1. If we only condition on the price of Blue Bull and not the price of Caco Laco, as in Example 17.3, then the relationship is:

$$E(Y_{BB}|X_{BB} = x_{BB}) = 3{,}000 - 200 \cdot x_{BB}$$

If the price of Blue Bull is DKK 11 per bottle instead of DKK 10, then expected demand falls from 1,000 to 800 bottles, i.e. $\Delta_{simple} = -200$.

If we also condition on the price of Caco Laco, as in Example 18.1, then the relationship is:

---

26   We can make similar calculations for any x in the multiple linear regression model. For example, if we increase x_2 and keep x_1 constant, we get $\Delta_{multiple,x_2} = \gamma_2$.

$$E\left(Y_{BB}\middle|X_{BB} = x_{BB}, X_{CL} = x_{CL}\right) = 2{,}500 - 250 \cdot x_{BB} + 100 \cdot x_{CL}$$

If the price of Caco Laco is DKK 10 per bottle, then the expected demand for Blue Bull drops from 1,000 to 750 bottles when the price of Blue Bull increases from DKK 10 to 11 per bottle, i.e. $\Delta_{multiple, x_{BB}} = -250$.

The fall in the estimated demand therefore differs according to which of the two regression models we use. This is not an error. The explanation is that the first result is achieved without assuming anything about the price of Caco Laco, whereas the price of Caco Laco is maintained at a certain level (DKK 10) in the calculation of the second result. In other words, the second result uses more information, as it includes the price of Caco Laco. However, this does not mean that the first result is uninteresting. The first result implicitly takes into account the fact that the price of Caco Laco is typically not unchanged when the price of Blue Bull goes up. Instead, it may also go up and imply that the demand for Blue Bull drops less than when the price of Caco Laco is kept constant. The relationship between the price of Caco Laco and the price of Blue Bull can be measured by the correlation between X_{BB} and X_{CL}.

As Example 18.2 shows, we must be precise in how we interpret the regression model. The right interpretation is that everything that is not included in the model (i.e. variables that we have not conditioned on) can vary freely. To describe this, we say "all other things *not* being equal".

We can also interpret the difference between the simple and multiple linear regression models by considering a population. Assume that there are only two different values of x_1 in the population. In a simple linear regression, we compare the average value of y for the two parts of the population that have different values of x_1. However the portion of the population that has the first value of x_1 consists of various subgroups that have different values of x_2. Similarly, the other portion of the population (the one with the second value of x_1) also consists of various subgroups with different values of x_2. In multiple linear regression, we compare the average value of y for those subgroups of the population that also have the same value of x_2. In other words, in simple and multiple linear regression, we compare different groups of elements.

18.2   Estimation of the multiple linear regression model

In practice, we can use a simple random sample, $(X_{i,1},...,X_{i,K},Y_i)$, $i = 1,...,n$, to construct an estimate of the unknown coefficients in the multiple linear regression model. The method that we used to work out the estimates in the simple linear model can also be used with multiple linear regression.

The ordinary least squares (OLS) estimator minimises the sum of the squared vertical distances between the observations and the regression line. In other words, $\hat{\beta}_0, \hat{\beta}_1,...,\hat{\beta}_K$ are those choices of $b_0, b_1,...,b_K$ that make the squared sum:

$$\sum_{i=1}^{n}\left(y_i - (b_0 + b_1 \cdot x_{i,1} + ... + b_K \cdot x_{i,K})\right)^2$$

as small as possible.

We can derive explicit expressions for $\hat{\beta}_0, \hat{\beta}_1,...,\hat{\beta}_K$, but these are relatively complicated. Most statistics and spreadsheet software includes built-in formulae for the OLS estimators. Such programmes are also able to calculate estimates on the variances, $\sigma^2_{\hat{\beta}_0}, \sigma^2_{\hat{\beta}_1},...,\sigma^2_{\hat{\beta}_K}$, of $\hat{\beta}_0, \hat{\beta}_1,...,\hat{\beta}_K$.

We denote the estimators with the symbols $S^2_{\hat{\beta}_0}, S^2_{\hat{\beta}_1},...,S^2_{\hat{\beta}_K}$. The square roots of $S^2_{\hat{\beta}_0}, S^2_{\hat{\beta}_1},...,S^2_{\hat{\beta}_K}$ are called the *standard errors* of $\hat{\beta}_0, \hat{\beta}_1,...,\hat{\beta}_K$. The properties for the OLS estimators in the multiple linear regression model are summed up in the box below.

Properties of OLS estimators in multiple linear regression

Assumptions:
1. Multiple linear regression model:

$$E(Y|X_1 = x_1, X_2 = x_2,..., X_K = x_K) = \beta_0 + \beta_1 \cdot x_1 + \beta_2 \cdot x_2 + ... + \beta_K \cdot x_K$$

2. Simple random sample:

$$\left((X_{1,1}, X_{1,2},..., X_{1,K}, Y_1), (X_{2,1}, X_{2,2},..., X_{2,K}, Y_2),...,(X_{n,1}, X_{n,2},..., X_{n,K}, Y_n)\right)$$

3. The variance of Y does not depend on $X_1, X_2,..., X_K$:

$$V(Y|X_1 = x_1, X_2 = x_2,..., X_K = x_K) = \sigma^2$$

4. Given $X_1 = x_1, X_2 = x_2,..., X_K = x_K$, Y is normally distributed.

Under the assumptions:
- 1 and 2, $\hat{\beta}_0, \hat{\beta}_1,..., \hat{\beta}_K$ are unbiased and consistent estimators of $\beta_0, \beta_1,..., \beta_K$
- 1, 2 and 3, $\hat{\beta}_0, \hat{\beta}_1,..., \hat{\beta}_K$ are approximately normally distributed:

$$\hat{\beta}_0 \sim^A N(\beta_0, \sigma^2_{\hat{\beta}_0}), \hat{\beta}_1 \sim^A N(\beta_1, \sigma^2_{\hat{\beta}_1}),..., \hat{\beta}_K \sim^A N(\beta_K, \sigma^2_{\hat{\beta}_K})$$

  where $\sigma^2_{\hat{\beta}_0}, \sigma^2_{\hat{\beta}_1},..., \sigma^2_{\hat{\beta}_K}$ are the variances of $\hat{\beta}_0, \hat{\beta}_1,..., \hat{\beta}_K$
- 1, 2, 3 and 4, $\hat{\beta}_0, \hat{\beta}_1,..., \hat{\beta}_K$ are exactly normally distributed.

The properties for the OLS estimators in the multiple linear regression model are more or less the same as in the simple linear model. However, the estimator for σ^2 is slightly different. The formula is now:

$$S^2_{\sigma^2} = \frac{1}{n-(K+1)} \sum_{i=1}^{n} \left(Y_i - (\hat{\beta}_0 + \hat{\beta}_1 \cdot X_{i,1} + \hat{\beta}_2 \cdot X_{i,2} + ... + \hat{\beta}_K \cdot X_{i,K})\right)^2$$

The difference is that in the simple linear regression model, we estimate two unknown coefficients, β_0 and β_1, whereas in the multiple linear regression model we estimate $K + 1$ coefficients, $\hat{\beta}_0, \hat{\beta}_1,..., \hat{\beta}_K$. We therefore divide by $n - (K + 1)$ instead of $n - 2$.

Example 18.3: Blue Bull – part 3

In reality, the manufacturer of Blue Bull does not know the value of the coefficients in the regression model from Example 18.1. The manufac-

turer is therefore interested in estimating the coefficients in the following regression model:

$$E(Y_{BB}|X_{BB} = x_{BB}, X_{CL} = x_{cl}) = \beta_0 + \beta_{BB} \cdot x_{BB} + \beta_{CL} \cdot x_{CL}$$

This model is assumed to satisfy assumptions 1, 3 and 4 in the box
above.

For the estimation, the manufacturer has selected a simple random
sample (assumption 2) of 12 observations: (1578, 8.7, 10.9), (681, 11.9,
10.1), (1283, 9.6, 11.7), (1328, 9.0, 9.4), (483, 11.7, 10.7), (826, 11.9,
12.0), (874, 10.2, 12.0), (1069, 10.1, 9.7), (1688, 8.2, 10.2), (1012, 8.3,
9.4), (817, 11.2, 11.3) and (907, 10.1, 9.9), where the first number in
each parenthesis is the demand for Blue Bull and the following two
figures are, respectively, the price of Blue Bull and Caco Laco.

Based on these observations, the manufacturer computes the esti-
mates of the three coefficients to be $\hat{\beta}_0 = 2{,}654$, $\hat{\beta}_{BB} = -245$ and
$\hat{\beta}_{CL} = 81$. The standard errors of these estimators are $S_{\hat{\beta}_0} = 707$,
$S_{\hat{\beta}_{BB}} = 50$ and $S_{\hat{\beta}_{CL}} = 70$.

18.3   Specification tests in the multiple linear regression model

As with the simple linear regression model, it is possible to examine
the underlying assumptions of the model from the box in Section 18.2.
In this section, we discuss briefly how to check the assumptions using
graphical methods. The graphical methods are essentially the same as
for simple linear regression, and therefore we will only point out the
few differences and otherwise refer the reader to Section 17.4.

We examine assumption 1, about the functional form, with a resid-
ual plot where we have $\hat{y}_i$ on the horizontal axis and $\hat{u}_i$ on the vertical
axis. The only difference between this and the simple linear regression
model is in the calculation of $\hat{y}_i$. In the multiple linear regression model, we calculate $\hat{y}_i$ as follows:

$$\hat{y}_i = \hat{\beta}_0 + \hat{\beta}_1 \cdot x_{i,1} + \dots + \hat{\beta}_K \cdot x_{i,K}$$

while the residuals, as previously, are calculated as:

$$\hat{u}_i = y_i - \hat{y}_i$$

If assumption 1 is to be satisfied, there must not be a systematic variation around the horizontal axis (exactly as in Chapter 17).

We can analyse assumption 2 about the simple random sample in cases where the sample is collected over time. As we did in Chapter 17, we can then plot the residuals with the time of observation on the horizontal axis. If the observations are independent, then the residuals ought to be randomly distributed around this axis.

Assumption 3 about homoscedasticity means that the variance of Y (or U) must not be a function of one or more of the explanatory variables, X. To work out whether this assumption is satisfied, we therefore plot the squared residuals against each of the explanatory variables and against $\hat{y}_i$.

Assumption 4 about normality can be studied with a (p, p)-plot or a (q, q)-plot, as shown in Chapter 17. Both cases require the empirical distribution function of the residuals. We calculate this in the same way as in Section 17.4.4, with the simple linear regression model.

18.4 Hypothesis testing and confidence intervals with multiple linear regression

In the multiple linear regression model, it is possible to test many different types of hypotheses. For example, we can test whether an explanatory variable has any relation to the dependent variable, Y, or whether multiple explanatory variables have the same relationship to the dependent variable, Y. In the next subsections, we look at these situations, all of which are characterised by the fact that we are testing a hypothesis about one or more coefficients.

18.4.1 Testing a hypothesis about a single coefficient

If we want to test whether an explanatory variable is related to the expected value of the explained variable, then this corresponds to testing whether the coefficient to the explanatory variable is equal to 0. More generally, we would like to test whether, say, the coefficient, β_k, to the kth explanatory variable, x_k, is equal to a certain value, β_k^0. The superscript "0" indicates that this is the value of the coefficient under the null hypothesis.

We adopt the same approach as in Section 17.5, where we tested a coefficient in the simple linear regression model. The hypotheses are:

$$H_0 : \beta_k = \beta_k^0$$

$$H_1 : \beta_k \neq \beta_k^0$$

As our hypothesis measure, we use $h(\beta_k) = \beta_k - \beta_k^0$, where we estimate β_k with the OLS estimator, $\hat{\beta}_k$. To arrive at a test statistic with a distribution that is easy to use, we divide the hypothesis measure by the square root of its variance, the estimate of which is $S_{\hat{\beta}_k}^2$. The box below summarises the test.

Test of a coefficient in the multiple linear regression model

$$H_0 : \beta_k = \beta_k^0$$

$$H_1 : \beta_k \neq \beta_k^0$$

Test statistic: $T = \dfrac{\hat{\beta}_k - \beta_k^0}{\sqrt{S_{\hat{\beta}_k}^2}}$

Under assumptions 1, 2 and 3, $T \sim^A N(0,1)$ under H_0.

Under assumptions 1, 2, 3 and 4, $T \sim t(n - K - 1)$ under H_0.

Example 18.4: Blue Bull – part 4

The manufacturer of Blue Bull wants to test whether the price of Caco Laco plays a role in the expected demand for Blue Bull. The hypotheses to be tested are therefore:

$$H_0 : \beta_{CL} = 0$$

$$H_1 : \beta_{CL} \neq 0$$

Based on the estimates from Example 18.3, the manufacturer calculates the value of the test statistic as:

$$T = \frac{81 - 0}{70} = 1.16$$

The critical value from the standard normal distribution in a test at a 5% significance level is 1.96. The manufacturer therefore concludes that the price of Caco Laco plays no statistically significant role.

Using the same techniques as in Chapter 13, we can also construct confidence intervals for the unknown coefficients, $\beta_0, \beta_1, \beta_2, ..., \beta_K$. The formulae for these are shown in the box below.

Confidence intervals for a coefficient in the multiple linear regression model

Under assumptions 1, 2 and 3, the approximate $(1 - \alpha)$-confidence interval for β_k is:

$$\left[\hat{\beta}_k - Z_{1-\alpha/2} \cdot \sqrt{S_{\hat{\beta}_k}^2} \ , \ \hat{\beta}_k + Z_{1-\alpha/2} \cdot \sqrt{S_{\hat{\beta}_k}^2} \right]$$

where $Z_{1-\alpha/2}$ is the $(1 - \alpha/2)$-quantile from the standard normal distribution.

Under assumptions 1, 2, 3 and 4, the exact $(1 - \alpha)$-confidence interval for β_k is:

$$\left[\hat{\beta}_k - t_{1-\alpha/2}(n - K - 1) \cdot \sqrt{S_{\hat{\beta}_k}^2} \ , \ \hat{\beta}_k + t_{1-\alpha/2}(n - K - 1) \cdot \sqrt{S_{\hat{\beta}_k}^2} \right]$$

where $t_{1-\alpha/2}(n - K - 1)$ is the $(1 - \alpha/2)$-quantile from the t-distribution with $n - K - 1$ degrees of freedom.

18.4.2 Testing the joint significance of all of the explanatory variables

In this subsection, we test whether any of the explanatory variables are related to the expected value of Y. This gives us the following hypotheses:

$$H_0 : \beta_1 = 0, \beta_2 = 0, ..., \beta_K = 0$$

$$H_1 : \text{at least one } \beta_k \neq 0 \, , \, k = 1, ..., K$$

Note that the intercept coefficient, β_0, is not included. If $\beta_1 = 0, \beta_2 = 0, ..., \beta_K = 0$, then β_0 is equal to the mean value, $E(Y)$.

In this case, we can derive inspiration for a hypothesis measure that distinguishes between the null- and the alternative hypotheses by considering the following two regression models, which arise from the null hypothesis and the alternative hypothesis, respectively:

$$Y = \beta_0 + U_r \qquad\qquad\qquad \text{(the restricted model)}$$

$$Y = \beta_0 + \beta_1 \cdot X_1 + ... + \beta_K \cdot X_K + U_u \qquad \text{(the unrestricted model)}$$

Here, the subscripts r and u on U indicate that U_r belongs to the model that arises from the null hypothesis (also called the restricted model), while U_u belongs to the model that arises from alternative hypothesis (also called the unrestricted model). If the null hypothesis is true, then the variance of U_r and U_u will be the same, as the two models would then be identical. If the alternative hypothesis is true, however, then we can show that the variance of U_r must be greater than the variance of U_u. Intuitively, this is because a part of Y's variance is then explained by some of the Xs in the unrestricted model, and thus there is less variance left in U_u. In the restricted model, however, there are no Xs, which is why U_r necessarily has the same variance as Y. We also sometimes call the variance of U the unexplained part of the variance of Y. Under the alternative hypothesis, the unexplained part of Y's variance is greater in the restricted model than in the unrestricted model.

The hypothesis measure describes the difference between the variance in the restricted and the unrestricted model. Let σ_r^2 be the variance of U_r, and σ_u^2 the variance of U_u. The hypothesis measure is then:

$$h(\sigma_r^2, \sigma_u^2) = \sigma_r^2 - \sigma_u^2$$

Using the true values of the variances, this measure is equal to 0 when the null hypothesis is true, but greater than 0 when the alternative hypothesis is true.

As we have previously seen, it is best to construct a test statistic in such a way that it has a distribution that is easy to work with. Firstly, we replace the unknown parameter values with estimators. Let $\hat{\sigma}_r^2$ be the following estimator for σ_r^2:

$$\hat{\sigma}_r^2 = \frac{1}{n-1}\sum_{i=1}^{n}\left(\ddot{u}i - \hat{\beta}_0\right)^2 = \frac{1}{n-1} \cdot$$

where $RSSR = \sum_{i=1}^{n}\left(Y_i - \hat{\beta}_0\right)^2$ is the sum of the squared residuals from an OLS estimation of the restricted model. Similarly, we let $\hat{\sigma}_u^2$ be the following estimator for σ_u^2:

$$\hat{\sigma}_u^2 = \frac{1}{n - (K + 1)}\sum_{i=1}^{n}\left(Y_i - \left(\hat{\beta}_0 + \hat{\beta}_1 \cdot X_{i,1} + \dots + \hat{\beta}_K \cdot X_{i,K}\right)\right)^2$$

$$= \frac{1}{n - (K + 1)} \cdot USSR$$

where $USSR = \sum_{i=1}^{n}\left(Y_i - \left(\hat{\beta}_0 + \hat{\beta}_1 \cdot X_{i,1} + \dots + \hat{\beta}_K \cdot X_{i,K}\right)\right)^2$ is the sum of the squared residuals from an OLS estimation of the unrestricted model.

It can then be shown that the test statistic:

$$\chi^2 = n \cdot \frac{\hat{\sigma}_r^2 - \hat{\sigma}_u^2}{\hat{\sigma}_u^2}$$

is approximately χ^2-distributed with K degrees of freedom under the null hypothesis. For small values of χ^2, we accept the null hypothesis, while for large values we reject the null hypothesis. Note that the number of degrees of freedom is given by the difference between the number of restrictions under the null hypothesis, which is K, and the number of restrictions under the alternative hypothesis, which is 0.

However, we often use a slightly modified test statistic. This is derived under the assumption that Y is normally distributed. In this case, it is possible to derive the exact distribution for the following test statistic:

$$F = \frac{\left(\frac{n - 1}{n - (K + 1)} \cdot \hat{\sigma}_r^2 - \hat{\sigma}_u^2\right)\Big/ K}{\hat{\sigma}_u^2 \big/ (n - (K + 1))}$$

When the null hypothesis is true, then this test statistic is F-distributed with $(K, n - K - 1)$ degrees of freedom. We can also write this test statistic as follows:

$$F = \frac{(RSSR - USSR)/K}{USSR/(n - K - 1)}$$

It is typically this version of the test statistic that is used in practice. Moreover, we also often use this test statistic, even though Y is not normally distributed. In this case, the test statistic is only approximately

F-distributed with $(K, n - K - 1)$ degrees of freedom under the null hypothesis. As above, we accept the null hypothesis for small values of the test statistic and reject it for large values.

The above division by K in the numerator and by $(n - K - 1)$ in the denominator, can be interpreted as divisions by the number of degrees of freedom. When calculating the denominator, we estimate $K + 1$ parameters, $\beta_0, ..., \beta_K$. The number of degrees of freedom is therefore the number of observations, n, minus the number of estimated parameters, $K + 1$. In the numerator, there are $n - 1$ degrees of freedom associated with $RSSR$, as we are in this case estimating one parameter, β_0. From this we substract $USSR$, which is associated with $n - (K + 1)$ degrees of freedom, as we are here estimating $K + 1$ parameters, $\beta_0, ..., \beta_K$. As $USSR$ is deducted from $RSSR$, there are a total of $n - 1 - (n - K - 1) = K$ degrees of freedom. This is also equal to the number of extra restrictions imposed by the null hypothesis compared to the alternative hypothesis – namely, that the K parameters $\beta_1, ..., \beta_K$ are equal to 0.

Example 18.5: Blue Bull – part 5

Encouraged by finding that the price of Caco Laco does not affect the demand for Blue Bull, the manufacturer now wants to examine whether price plays any role at all. He therefore tests the following hypotheses:

$$H_0 : \beta_{BB} = \beta_{CL} = 0$$

$$H_1 : \beta_{BB} \neq 0 \text{ or } \beta_{CL} \neq 0$$

Based on the sample from Example 18.3, the manufacturer calculates $RSSR = 1,433,284$ and $USSR = 379,409$. The value of the test statistic is therefore:

$$F = \frac{(1,433,284 - 379,409)/2}{379,409/(12 - 2 - 1)} = 12.5$$

The critical value from the F-distribution with $(2, 9)$ degrees of freedom is 4.26. The manufacturer therefore concludes that at least one of the coefficients in the regression model is statistically significant.

18.4.3   Testing other hypotheses in the multiple linear regression model

In Section 18.4.2, we tested a null hypothesis in which there were K restrictions on the model. This led to a test statistic, which was a function of the squared residuals from the restricted model and the squared residuals from the unrestricted model. This approach can also be used in conjunction with a number of other hypotheses.

An example would be to test whether some of the coefficients assume certain values. For example, we might be interested in testing the following hypotheses about the first q coefficients:

$$H_0 : \beta_1 = \beta_1^0, \beta_2 = \beta_2^0, ..., \beta_q = \beta_q^0$$

$$H_1 : \text{at least one } \beta_k \neq \beta_k^0, \ k = 1, ..., q$$

where β_k^0 is the value of the coefficient of x_q under the null hypothesis. In the section above, $q = K$ and $\beta_k^0 = 0$ for $k = 1, ..., K$.

We use the same hypothesis measure and test statistic as above. The regression model, which arises from the alternative hypothesis, is the regression of Y on $X_1, ..., X_K$. Based on an OLS estimation of this regression, we can calculate the unrestricted sum of squared residuals ($USSR$).

We can write the regression model, which follows from the null hypothesis, as:

$$Y = \beta_0 + \beta_1^0 \cdot X_1 + \beta_2^0 \cdot X_2 + ... + \beta_q^0 \cdot X_q + \beta_{q+1} \cdot X_{q+1}$$
$$+ ... + \beta_K \cdot X_K + U_u$$

Here, it is only the coefficients, $\beta_0, \beta_{q+1}, ..., \beta_K$, that are unknown and have to be estimated. For this purpose, we can use the following trick. If we define the random variable Z to be:

$$Z = \beta_1^0 \cdot X_1 + \beta_2^0 \cdot X_2 + ... + \beta_q^0 \cdot X_q$$

and subtract this from both sides of the equality sign in the previous equation, we get:

$$Y - Z = \beta_0 + \beta_{q+1} \cdot X_{q+1} + ... + \beta_K \cdot X_K + U_r$$

If we then define a new random variable given by:

$$Y^* = Y - Z = Y - (\beta_1^0 \cdot X_1 + \beta_2^0 \cdot X_2 + ... + \beta_q^0 \cdot X_q)$$

then we can estimate the coefficients, $\beta_0, \beta_{q+1}, ..., \beta_K$, with an OLS estimation of the regression of Y^* on $X_{q+1}, ..., X_K$. The sum of the squared residuals from this estimation is equal to $RSSR$.

Once we have found $USSR$ and $RSSR$, we can calculate the test statistic. As in Section 18.4.2, there are $n - (K + 1)$ degrees of freedom associated with $USSR$. There are, however, $n - (K + 1 - q)$ degrees of freedom associated with the $RSSR$, as we here estimate $(K + 1 - q)$ parameters. The test statistic then looks like this:

$$F = \frac{(RSSR - USSR)/q}{USSR/(n - K - 1)}$$

As in the previous section, we can interpret q as the number of extra restrictions that the null hypothesis imposes compared to the alternative hypothesis. The test statistic is approximately F-distributed with $(q, n - K - 1)$ degrees of freedom under the null hypothesis.

This structure of the test statistic, in which we compare the sum of the squared residuals from the OLS estimation of, respectively, the restricted and the unrestricted model, has general application.

As one last example, suppose that we want to test whether the sum of the coefficients β_1 and β_2 is equal to a given value, β_{1+2}^0. The hypotheses are thus:

$$H_0 : \beta_1 + \beta_2 = \beta_{1+2}^0$$

$$H_1 : \beta_1 + \beta_2 \neq \beta_{1+2}^0$$

The restricted model can here be written as follows:

$$Y = \beta_0 + \beta_1 \cdot X_1 + (\beta_{1+2}^0 - \beta_1) \cdot X_2 + \beta_3 \cdot X_3 + ... + \beta_K \cdot X_K + U_r$$

Or as:

$$Y - \beta_{1+2}^0 \cdot X_2 = \beta_0 + \beta_1 \cdot (X_1 - X_2) + \beta_3 \cdot X_3 + ... + \beta_K \cdot X_K + U_r$$

We can then define two new random variables:

$$Y^* = Y - \beta_{1+2}^0 \cdot X_2 \text{ and } X_1^* = X_1 - X_2$$

The restricted regression model can therefore also be written as:

$$Y^* = \beta_0 + \beta_1 \cdot X_1^* + \beta_3 \cdot X_3 + ... + \beta_K \cdot X_K + U_r$$

The sum of the squared residuals from the OLS estimation of this model is then equal to *RSSR*. *USSR* is found, as previously, by the OLS estimation of the unrestricted model.

The test statistic is:

$$F = \frac{(RSSR - USSR)/1}{USSR/(n - K - 1)}$$

Note that, because the null hypothesis only imposes one additional restriction, we only divide by 1 in the numerator. The number of restrictions is not, therefore, determined by how many variables are involved in the null hypothesis (in this case two), but by the number of restrictions in which they are involved.

18.5   Predictions in the multiple linear regression model

Predictions based on the multiple linear regression model are calculated in the same way as for the simple linear regression model. The calculation of the uncertainty is more complicated, but the interpretation is unchanged.

When predicting the mean value of Y, conditional on a number of explanatory variables, $X_1, ..., X_K$, we have to select values for these explanatory variables. Let these values be $x_1^*, ..., x_K^*$. The prediction is then represented by:

$$\hat{Y}^* = \hat{\beta}_0 + \hat{\beta}_1 \cdot x_1^* + ... + \hat{\beta}_K \cdot x_K^*$$

This prediction is used, as in simple linear regression, to predict both the value of Y and the conditional mean of Y.

We can then calculate the uncertainty in this prediction. However, since the expression of this uncertainty is complicated, we will omit it here.

18.6   Non-linear regression models

In many cases, it is sufficient to consider a linear regression model. Sometimes, however, theory tells us explicitly that the regression function should be non-linear. At other times, the graphic tests in sections 17.4.1 and 18.3 will reveal that the regression function is likely to be non-linear. In this section, we look more closely at different types of non-linear regression model. However, it is still possible, with some adjustment, to estimate some of these using the OLS method.

Below are four examples of non-linear regression models:

i) $\quad E(Y|X_1 = x_1, X_2 = x_2) = \beta_0 + \beta_1 \cdot x_1 + \beta_2 \cdot x_2 + \beta_3 \cdot x_1 \cdot x_2$

ii) $\quad E(Y|X_1 = x_1) = \beta_0 + \beta_1 \cdot x_1 + \beta_2 \cdot (x_1)^2$

iii) $\quad E(Y|X_1 = x_1) = \beta_0 + (x_1)^{\beta_1}$

iv) $\quad E(\ln(Y)|X_1 = x_1) = \beta_0 + \beta_1 \cdot \ln(x_1)$

The first regression model is non-linear in the explanatory variables because it includes the product $x_1 \cdot x_2$. The next regression model is non-linear because the explanatory variable is squared. In both i) and ii), however, the coefficients enter linearly on the right-hand side. In the third regression model, on the other hand, both the explanatory variable and one of the coefficients enter non-linearly, because of the term $(x_1)^{\beta_1}$. Finally, in the fourth regression model, both the explanatory variable and the dependent variable enter in a non-linear way because we use the logarithm of both of them. However, the coefficients enter linearly in this case, as in the first two cases.

Below, we show how to estimate regression models using the OLS method, even when they are non-linear in the variables, as long as they are linear in the coefficients.

18.6.1 Estimation of a non-linear regression model with OLS

In many cases, we can rewrite a non-linear regression model as a linear regression model. Consider the following simple model:

$$E(Y|X_1 = x_1) = \beta_0 + \beta_1 \cdot g(x_1)$$

where $g(\ )$ is a known non-linear function. Since the function $g(\ )$ is known, we can define a new explanatory variable as:

$$z_1 = g(x_1)$$

By inserting this in the first expression, we get:

$$E(Y|X_1 = x_1) = \beta_0 + \beta_1 \cdot g(x_1) = \beta_0 + \beta_1 \cdot z_1 = E(Y|Z_1 = z_1)$$

The regression of Y on Z_1, in which $Z_1 = g(X_1)$, is then a simple linear regression model. As such, the expressions for the coefficients, as we saw in Section 17.2, are given by:

$$\beta_1 = \frac{Cov(Z_1, Y)}{V(Z_1)} \text{ and } \beta_0 = E(Y) - \beta_1 \cdot E(Z_1)$$

Example 18.6: Squared explanatory variable

A regression model is given by:

$$E(Y|X = x) = \beta_0 + \beta_1 \cdot x^2$$

This model is non-linear in x. However, if we define a new variable, $z = x^2$, then the regression model:

$$E(Y|Z = z) = \beta_0 + \beta_1 \cdot z$$

is linear in z. With a random sample, we can therefore calculate the estimates of β_0 and β_1 using the least squares method. This gives the following estimate of $E(Y|Z = z)$:

$$\hat{E}(Y|Z = z) = \hat{\beta}_0 + \hat{\beta}_1 \cdot z$$

which is the same as:

$$\hat{E}(Y|X = x) = \hat{\beta}_0 + \hat{\beta}_1 \cdot x^2$$

since $z = x^2$. It is therefore possible to obtain an estimate of the non-linear regression function of x by estimating the regression model using z.

This trick of reformulating a non-linear regression model to a linear regression model only works if there is a reformulation, $z = g(x)$, that does not involve unknown parameters, and where the regression model is linear in z. If, for example, $E(Y|X = x) = \beta_0 + x^{\beta_1}$ as in case iii) above, then z must be equal to x^{β_1} for $E(Y|Z = z)$ to be linear in z. However, since we do not know β_1, the function $g(\ )$ is not known in advance. Therefore, we cannot calculate z, or reformulate the regression model as a linear function of z. Thus we cannot use the OLS method in this case.[27]

We can also use the OLS method in cases where the dependent variable, Y, is transformed by a known function. Example iv) above has $\ln(Y)$ as the dependent variable. Here, we can define a new variable, $Y^* = \ln(Y)$, and a new explanatory variable, $z = \ln(x)$. We can then make the simple linear regression of Y^* on Z in order to estimate the two coefficients β_0 and β_1.

18.6.2 Linear regression as an approximation of non-linear regression

Although the correct regression model is non-linear, we can still – with the correct interpretation – benefit from using a linear regression model.

In the simple linear regression model, the prediction error is given by:

$$ U \;=\; Y - E(Y|X = x) \;=\; Y - (\beta_0 \,+\, \beta_1 \cdot x) $$

In Section 17.6, we used the variance of the prediction error, $V(U)$, as a measure of the uncertainty (the quality) of a prediction. The best predictor of Y, as a function of x, is the function that gives us the smallest variance, $V(U)$.

Now suppose that the regression $E\big(Y\big|X = x\big)$ is non-linear. If you were to choose a linear model to approximate the true non-linear regression, then the best choice would be to use the linear regression model, since this choice would minimise the variance of the prediction error.

18.6.3 Interaction terms between explanatory variables

In practice, it is possible that the effect of an explanatory variable will depend on the size of another explanatory variable. For example, the effect of watering the garden can be greater if it has been dry for a long time than if it has rained continuously for the last week. When two explanatory variables affect each other, we say that there is interaction between the two variables. In this section, we look more closely at the most commonly used model for interaction between two variables.

In example i) at the beginning of this section, we had the following regression function:

---

27   A non-linear version of the least squares method exists, which we can use to calculate estimates of β_1 and β_2 in such cases.

$$E(Y|X_1 = x_1, X_2 = x_2) = \beta_0 + \beta_1 \cdot x_1 + \beta_2 \cdot x_2 + \beta_3 \cdot x_1 \cdot x_2$$

Here, the terms $x_1 \cdot x_2$ is called an interaction term. The effect of the interaction term can be seen when we measure the effect on the expected value of Y by increasing x_1 by one unit, given that x_2 is constant. This effect is:

$$\begin{aligned}
\Delta_{interaction, x_1} &= E(Y|X_1 = x_1 + 1, X_2 = x_2) - E(Y|X_1 = x_1, X_2 = x_2) \\
&= [\beta_0 + \beta_1 \cdot (x_1 + 1) + \beta_2 \cdot x_2 + \beta_3 \cdot (x_1 + 1) \cdot x_2] - \\
&\quad [\beta_0 + \beta_1 \cdot x_1 + \beta_2 \cdot x_2 + \beta_3 \cdot x_1 \cdot x_2] = \beta_1 + \beta_3 \cdot x_2
\end{aligned}$$

This effect, $\Delta_{interaction, x_1} = \beta_1 + \beta_3 \cdot x_2$, can be compared with the effect of increasing x_1 in the "regular" multiple linear regression model without the interaction terms. Here, the effect is just β_1. In the model with an interaction term, the effect of increasing x_1 by one unit, given that x_2 is constant, depends on the value of x_2. If, for example, Y is the consumption of heat in a house, x_1 the indoor temperature, and x_2 the outdoor temperature, then an interaction term could take into account that when the indoor temperature, x_1, increases by one degree, the increase in heat consumption is less when the outdoor temperature, x_2, is high instead of low.

Regression models with interaction terms are useful when we want to determine whether various groups in a population are identical. If there are two groups in the population, then we can define a random variable – also called a *dummy variable* – that assumes the value 0 for one group and the value 1 for the other. Example 18.7 illustrates the use of a dummy variable in a regression model with interaction terms.

Example 18.7: Wage discrimination

A consultancy company wants to study whether or not there is wage discrimination against women who have had the same training as men. Let X_1 be a dummy variable defined by:

$$X_1 = \begin{cases} 0 & \text{if woman} \\ 1 & \text{if man} \end{cases}$$

Since salary depends on experience, we also include a random variable, X_2, which is an individual's experience measured in years. The salary, Y, is measured in DKK 1,000 p.a.

The consultant estimates a regression model with interaction terms and gets the following result:

$$E(Y|X_1 = x_1, X_2 = x_2) = 200 - 10 \cdot x_1 + 4 \cdot x_2 + 3 \cdot x_1 \cdot x_2$$

For women, the regression of wages on experience is given by:

$$E(Y|X_1 = 0, X_2 = x_2) = 200 - 10 \cdot 0 + 4 \cdot x_2 + 3 \cdot 0 \cdot x_2 = 200 + 4 \cdot x_2$$

and for men:

$$E(Y|X_1 = 1, X_2 = x_2) = 200 - 10 \cdot 1 + 4 \cdot x_2 + 3 \cdot 1 \cdot x_2 = 190 + 7 \cdot x_2$$

Figure 18.1:
Saleries for
men and
women

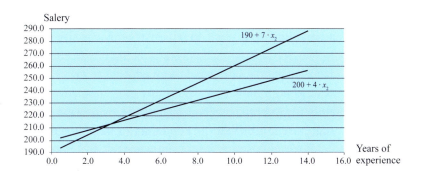

The regression functions for women and men are therefore different. A man without experience ($x_2 = 0$) has an expected salary that is DKK 10,000 lower than for a woman without experience. On the other hand, men's expected income rises more with experience than women's income. After four years of experience, men's expected income is DKK 218,000, whereas for women it is DKK 216,000.

We can also directly calculate the difference between men and women, which is: $\Delta_{interaction, x_1} = -10 + 4 \cdot x_2$. The difference is therefore negative if the experience totals fewer than 2.5 years (i.e. the expected income is lowest for a man in this case), whereas it is positive for experience greater than 2.5 years. If we interpret the result (that $\Delta_{interaction, x_1}$ is different from 0) as discrimination, then wage discrimination between the two genders depends on their experience.

In order to estimate the coefficients in a regression model with interaction terms, we can use the same trick as above, where we defined new variables. Here, we can define a new random variable $Z = X_1 \cdot X_2$. This gives us:

$$E(Y|X_1 = x_1, X_2 = x_2, Z = z) = \beta_0 + \beta_1 \cdot x_1 + \beta_2 \cdot x_2 + \beta_3 \cdot z$$

By the regression of Y on X_1, X_2 and Z, we can estimate the coefficients using the least squares method as previously.

18.7   Omitted variables

One major problem in real-life situations is the existence of explanatory variables that we would like to include in the regression, but which we cannot observe and therefore cannot include. For example, we may be interested in analysing whether education has an effect on wages. In doing this, we would like to condition on (i.e. control for) a person's innate ability, so that we do not mistakenly classify a positive relationship between education and wages as being due to education if it is actually because people who have more education were born with abilities that lead to both higher pay and more education. However, it is often very difficult to obtain a good observable measure for innate abilities, and therefore it is difficult to condition on these in a regression model.

We can illustrate the consequences of this problem more formally by considering the three variables Y, X_1 and X_2, where Y could be wages, X_1 education and X_2 ability. Suppose we are interested in regressing Y on X_1 and X_2 in order to interpret the effect of X_1 on Y when X_2 has been controlled for. If, however, we have not observed X_2, then we can only regress Y on X_1. In this context, we call the variable X_2 an *omitted variable*.

As previously discussed in this chapter, there are differences between the interpretation of the regression of Y on X_1 and X_2, and the regression of Y on X_1. In this section, we will illustrate this difference by showing what happens if we interpret the effect of X_1 on Y in the regression of Y on X_1 as if we had actually regressed Y on both X_1 and X_2.

We can infer the effect of an omitted variable by considering the regression of Y on X_1 and X_2:

$$E(Y|X_1 = x_1, X_2 = x_2) = \beta_0 + \beta_1 \cdot x_1 + \beta_2 \cdot x_2$$

If, instead, we regress Y on only X_1, then it can be shown that:

$$E(Y|X_1 = x_1) = \beta_0 + \beta_1 \cdot x_1 + \beta_2 \cdot E(X_2|X_1 = x_1)$$

The term $E(X_2|X_1 = x_1)$ corresponds to the regression of X_2 on X_1. Let us assume that this regression is a simple linear regression given by: $E(X_2|X_1 = x_1) = \alpha_0 + \alpha_1 \cdot x_1$. Then by inserting this in the above expression, we get:

$$E(Y|X_1 = x_1) = \beta_0 + \beta_1 \cdot x_1 + \beta_2 \cdot (\alpha_0 + \alpha_1 \cdot x_1)$$
$$= (\beta_0 + \beta_2 \cdot \alpha_0) + (\beta_1 + \beta_2 \cdot \alpha_1) \cdot x_1 = \beta_0^* + \beta_1^* \cdot x_1$$

where $\beta_0^* = \beta_0 + \beta_2 \cdot \alpha_0$ and $\beta_1^* = \beta_1 + \beta_2 \cdot \alpha_1$. If our goal is to find β_1 when we regress Y on X_1, then we do not achieve this. Instead, we get β_1 plus $\beta_2 \cdot \alpha_1$. The value $\beta_2 \cdot \alpha_1$ is called the *omitted variable bias*, because it shows up in the coefficient, β_1^*, to x_1 when we omit x_2. We can see that this omitted variable bias depends both on the relationship between X_1 and X_2 (as given by α_1) and by the importance of X_2 in the original regression model (as given by β_2).

The interpretation of the coefficient to x_1 in the regression of Y on X_1 depends on how we regard the other variables (here x_2). If we are only interested in the regression of Y on X_1 without controlling for x_2, then the regression of Y on X_1 delivers the right result. However, if we are interested in interpreting the coefficient to x_1 in the regression of Y on X_1 as if we have controlled for other effects (here x_2), then the regression of Y on X_1 does not deliver the right result unless α_1 is 0 or β_2 is 0. In other words, if X_1 is uncorrelated with X_2, which means that α_1 is equal to 0, then it does not matter that we have omitted X_2. Neither does it matter if the omitted variable does not belong in the regression of Y on X_1 and X_2, which means that β_2 is equal to 0.

18.8   Spurious relationships in regression analysis

Back in Chapter 3, we discussed different interpretations of the apparent relationships that we find when using statistical analyses. In practice, a major problem is to assess whether a relationship is real or spurious. In order to give meaning to the concepts "real" and "spurious", we have to think of causal relationships – namely, whether one variable causes the other, or both are caused by a third variable.

The main conclusion of our discussion in Chapter 3 was that a spurious relationship is one in which two random variables are statistically dependent but statistically independent when we condition on a third random variable. This third variable could be the one that actually causes the two other variables, for example, innate ability causing both higher wages and more education.

Statistical dependence is defined by means of probabilities. Since statistical independence means that the random variables are uncorrelated, we can use multiple regression analysis as a practical approach to check whether a relationship is real or spurious. For example, if we regress Y on X_1 and find that X_1 is statistically related to the conditional mean of Y, how can we figure out whether this relationship is real or spurious? If we suspect that a third variable, X_2, is the underlying cause for the relationship between Y and X_1, then we can try to regress Y on both X_1 and X_2. If the relationship between Y and X_1 is spurious, then the coefficient of X_1 will equal 0 in this regression.

We can improve our understanding of this by using the results from Section 18.7 on omitted variable bias. Here, we found that the coefficient of X_1 in the regression of Y on X_1 was given by $\beta_1^* = \beta_1 + \beta_2 \cdot \alpha_1$, where β_2 is the effect of X_2 in the regression of Y on X_1 and X_2, and α_1 is the effect of X_1 in the regression of X_2 on X_1. If the relationship between Y and X_1 is spurious, then β_1 is equal to 0. However, this does not mean that the coefficient of X_1 in the regression of Y on X_1 will be zero, since this coefficient is equal to $\beta_1^* = \beta_1 + \beta_2 \cdot \alpha_1$. With $\beta_1 = 0$ it is therefore equal to $\beta_1^* = \beta_2 \cdot \alpha_1$. The spurious relationship between Y and X_1 therefore manifests itself as an omitted variable bias, when we do not control for the underlying variable, X_2, that gives rise to the spurious relationship. With multiple linear regression, it is relatively easy to include a series of variables in order to check for a potential spurious relationship.

18.9   Exercises

1. Review questions
    a) Explain what multiple linear regression is, and provide an inter-
       pretation of the coefficients.
    b) What are the properties of the estimators? Under what assump-
       tions?
    c) Account for the difference between simple linear and multiple
       linear regression, including the difference in the interpretation of
       the coefficients.
    d) Account for the assumptions underlying the multiple linear re-
       gression model, and explain how we can check them graphically.
    e) Which test statistics would you use to test hypotheses about the
       coefficients in the regression function? What are their distribu-
       tions under H_0?
    f) Explain how, in some cases, even non-linear regression models
       can be estimated using the least squares method.
    g) Explain what is meant by an omitted variable bias.
    h) Explain how to check if a relationship is spurious by use of mul-
       tiple linear regression.

2. The expected salary, Y (DKK 1,000) depends on the length of an individual's education, X_1 (years), and experience, X_2 (years). The relationship is:

$$E(Y|X_1 = x_1, X_2 = x_2) = 90 + 8 \cdot x_1 + 3 \cdot x_2$$

a) Sketch the regression function for subjects with 9 and 18 years of education, respectively.
b) Interpret the coefficients to x_1 and x_2.

3. A regression of Y on X_1 gives:

$$E(Y|X_1 = x_1) = 25 + 4 \cdot x_1$$

and the regression of Y on X_1 and X_2 gives:

$$E(Y|X_1 = x_1, X_2 = x_2) = 23 + 7 \cdot x_2$$

a) Interpret the coefficients in the two regression functions.
b) What can explain that a regression of Y on X_1 depends on X_1, whereas a regression of Y on both X_1 and X_2 does not depend on X_1?

Probability tables

Table 1. The standard normal distribution: cumulative probabilities

Table 2. The standard normal distribution: quantiles

Table 3. The t-distribution: quantiles

Table 4. The χ^2-distribution: quantiles

Table 5. The F-distribution: 0.95 quantiles

Table 6. The F-distribution: 0.975 quantiles

Table 1. The standard normal distribution: cumulative probabilities

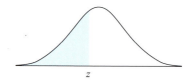

z	0	1	2	3	4	5	6	7	8	9
-3.0	0.0013	0.0013	0.0013	0.0012	0.0012	0.0011	0.0011	0.0011	0.0010	0.0010
-2.9	0.0019	0.0018	0.0018	0.0017	0.0016	0.0016	0.0015	0.0015	0.0014	0.0014
-2.8	0.0026	0.0025	0.0024	0.0023	0.0023	0.0022	0.0021	0.0021	0.0020	0.0019
-2.7	0.0035	0.0034	0.0033	0.0032	0.0031	0.0030	0.0029	0.0028	0.0027	0.0026
-2.6	0.0047	0.0045	0.0044	0.0043	0.0041	0.0040	0.0039	0.0038	0.0037	0.0036
-2.5	0.0062	0.0060	0.0059	0.0057	0.0055	0.0054	0.0052	0.0051	0.0049	0.0048
-2.4	0.0082	0.0080	0.0078	0.0075	0.0073	0.0071	0.0069	0.0068	0.0066	0.0064
-2.3	0.0107	0.0104	0.0102	0.0099	0.0096	0.0094	0.0091	0.0089	0.0087	0.0084
-2.2	0.0139	0.0136	0.0132	0.0129	0.0125	0.0122	0.0119	0.0116	0.0113	0.0110
-2.1	0.0179	0.0174	0.0170	0.0166	0.0162	0.0158	0.0154	0.0150	0.0146	0.0143
-2.0	0.0228	0.0222	0.0217	0.0212	0.0207	0.0202	0.0197	0.0192	0.0188	0.0183
-1.9	0.0287	0.0281	0.0274	0.0268	0.0262	0.0256	0.0250	0.0244	0.0239	0.0233
-1.8	0.0359	0.0351	0.0344	0.0336	0.0329	0.0322	0.0314	0.0307	0.0301	0.0294
-1.7	0.0446	0.0436	0.0427	0.0418	0.0409	0.0401	0.0392	0.0384	0.0375	0.0367
-1.6	0.0548	0.0537	0.0526	0.0516	0.0505	0.0495	0.0485	0.0475	0.0465	0.0455
-1.5	0.0668	0.0655	0.0643	0.0630	0.0618	0.0606	0.0594	0.0582	0.0571	0.0559
-1.4	0.0808	0.0793	0.0778	0.0764	0.0749	0.0735	0.0721	0.0708	0.0694	0.0681
-1.3	0.0968	0.0951	0.0934	0.0918	0.0901	0.0885	0.0869	0.0853	0.0838	0.0823
-1.2	0.1151	0.1131	0.1112	0.1093	0.1075	0.1056	0.1038	0.1020	0.1003	0.0985
-1.1	0.1357	0.1335	0.1314	0.1292	0.1271	0.1251	0.1230	0.1210	0.1190	0.1170
-1.0	0.1587	0.1562	0.1539	0.1515	0.1492	0.1469	0.1446	0.1423	0.1401	0.1379
-0.9	0.1841	0.1814	0.1788	0.1762	0.1736	0.1711	0.1685	0.1660	0.1635	0.1611
-0.8	0.2119	0.2090	0.2061	0.2033	0.2005	0.1977	0.1949	0.1922	0.1894	0.1867
-0.7	0.2420	0.2389	0.2358	0.2327	0.2296	0.2266	0.2236	0.2206	0.2177	0.2148
-0.6	0.2743	0.2709	0.2676	0.2643	0.2611	0.2578	0.2546	0.2514	0.2483	0.2451
-0.5	0.3085	0.3050	0.3015	0.2981	0.2946	0.2912	0.2877	0.2843	0.2810	0.2776
-0.4	0.3446	0.3409	0.3372	0.3336	0.3300	0.3264	0.3228	0.3192	0.3156	0.3121
-0.3	0.3821	0.3783	0.3745	0.3707	0.3669	0.3632	0.3594	0.3557	0.3520	0.3483
-0.2	0.4207	0.4168	0.4129	0.4090	0.4052	0.4013	0.3974	0.3936	0.3897	0.3859
-0.1	0.4602	0.4562	0.4522	0.4483	0.4443	0.4404	0.4364	0.4325	0.4286	0.4247
-0.0	0.5000	0.4960	0.4920	0.4880	0.4840	0.4801	0.4761	0.4721	0.4681	0.4641

z	0	1	2	3	4	5	6	7	8	9
0.0	0.5000	0.5040	0.5080	0.5120	0.5160	0.5199	0.5239	0.5279	0.5319	0.5359
0.1	0.5398	0.5438	0.5478	0.5517	0.5557	0.5596	0.5636	0.5675	0.5714	0.5753
0.2	0.5793	0.5832	0.5871	0.5910	0.5948	0.5987	0.6026	0.6064	0.6103	0.6141
0.3	0.6179	0.6217	0.6255	0.6293	0.6331	0.6368	0.6406	0.6443	0.6480	0.6517
0.4	0.6554	0.6591	0.6628	0.6664	0.6700	0.6736	0.6772	0.6808	0.6844	0.6879
0.5	0.6915	0.6950	0.6985	0.7019	0.7054	0.7088	0.7123	0.7157	0.7190	0.7224
0.6	0.7257	0.7291	0.7324	0.7357	0.7389	0.7422	0.7454	0.7486	0.7517	0.7549
0.7	0.7580	0.7611	0.7642	0.7673	0.7704	0.7734	0.7764	0.7794	0.7823	0.7852
0.8	0.7881	0.7910	0.7939	0.7967	0.7995	0.8023	0.8051	0.8078	0.8106	0.8133
0.9	0.8159	0.8186	0.8212	0.8238	0.8264	0.8289	0.8315	0.8340	0.8365	0.8389
1.0	0.8413	0.8438	0.8461	0.8485	0.8508	0.8531	0.8554	0.8577	0.8599	0.8621
1.1	0.8643	0.8665	0.8686	0.8708	0.8729	0.8749	0.8770	0.8790	0.8810	0.8830
1.2	0.8849	0.8869	0.8888	0.8907	0.8925	0.8944	0.8962	0.8980	0.8997	0.9015
1.3	0.9032	0.9049	0.9066	0.9082	0.9099	0.9115	0.9131	0.9147	0.9162	0.9177
1.4	0.9192	0.9207	0.9222	0.9236	0.9251	0.9265	0.9279	0.9292	0.9306	0.9319
1.5	0.9332	0.9345	0.9357	0.9370	0.9382	0.9394	0.9406	0.9418	0.9429	0.9441
1.6	0.9452	0.9463	0.9474	0.9484	0.9495	0.9505	0.9515	0.9525	0.9535	0.9545
1.7	0.9554	0.9564	0.9573	0.9582	0.9591	0.9599	0.9608	0.9616	0.9625	0.9633
1.8	0.9641	0.9649	0.9656	0.9664	0.9671	0.9678	0.9686	0.9693	0.9699	0.9706
1.9	0.9713	0.9719	0.9726	0.9732	0.9738	0.9744	0.9750	0.9756	0.9761	0.9767
2.0	0.9772	0.9778	0.9783	0.9788	0.9793	0.9798	0.9803	0.9808	0.9812	0.9817
2.1	0.9821	0.9826	0.9830	0.9834	0.9838	0.9842	0.9846	0.9850	0.9854	0.9857
2.2	0.9861	0.9864	0.9868	0.9871	0.9875	0.9878	0.9881	0.9884	0.9887	0.9890
2.3	0.9893	0.9896	0.9898	0.9901	0.9904	0.9906	0.9909	0.9911	0.9913	0.9916
2.4	0.9918	0.9920	0.9922	0.9925	0.9927	0.9929	0.9931	0.9932	0.9934	0.9936
2.5	0.9938	0.9940	0.9941	0.9943	0.9945	0.9946	0.9948	0.9949	0.9951	0.9952
2.6	0.9953	0.9955	0.9956	0.9957	0.9959	0.9960	0.9961	0.9962	0.9963	0.9964
2.7	0.9965	0.9966	0.9967	0.9968	0.9969	0.9970	0.9971	0.9972	0.9973	0.9974
2.8	0.9974	0.9975	0.9976	0.9977	0.9977	0.9978	0.9979	0.9979	0.9980	0.9981
2.9	0.9981	0.9982	0.9982	0.9983	0.9984	0.9984	0.9985	0.9985	0.9986	0.9986
3.0	0.9987	0.9987	0.9987	0.9988	0.9988	0.9989	0.9989	0.9989	0.9990	0.9990

Note:
The table shows the probability $P(Z \leq z)$, defined as the shaded area in the figure. For example, to find $P(Z \leq 2.31)$, the "1" column is matched with the "2.3" row to give the result $P(Z \leq 2.31) = 0.9896$.

Table 2. The standard normal distribution: quantiles

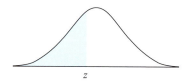

$P(Z \leq z)$	z
0.001	-3.0902
0.005	-2.5758
0.010	-2.3263
0.020	-2.0537
0.025	-1.9600
0.030	-1.8808
0.040	-1.7507
0.050	-1.6449
0.100	-1.2816
0.150	-1.0364
0.200	-0.8416
0.250	-0.6745
0.300	-0.5244
0.350	-0.3853
0.400	-0.2533
0.450	-0.1257
0.500	0
0.550	0.1257
0.600	0.2533
0.650	0.3853
0.700	0.5244
0.750	0.6745
0.800	0.8416
0.850	1.0364
0.900	1.2816
0.950	1.6449
0.960	1.7507
0.970	1.8808
0.975	1.9600
0.980	2.0537
0.990	2.3263
0.995	2.5758
0.999	3.0902

Table 3. The *t*-distribution: quantiles

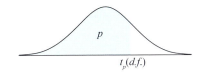

Degrees of freedom (d.f.)	p								
	0.60	0.70	0.80	0.85	0.90	0.95	0.975	0.990	0.995
1	0.325	0.727	1.376	1.963	3.078	6.314	12.706	31.821	63.657
2	0.289	0.617	1.061	1.386	1.886	2.920	4.303	6.965	9.925
3	0.277	0.584	0.978	1.250	1.638	2.353	3.182	4.541	5.841
4	0.271	0.569	0.941	1.190	1.533	2.132	2.776	3.747	4.604
5	0.267	0.559	0.920	1.156	1.476	2.015	2.571	3.365	4.032
6	0.265	0.553	0.906	1.134	1.440	1.943	2.447	3.143	3.707
7	0.263	0.549	0.896	1.119	1.415	1.895	2.365	2.998	3.499
8	0.262	0.546	0.889	1.108	1.397	1.860	2.306	2.896	3.355
9	0.261	0.543	0.883	1.100	1.383	1.833	2.262	2.821	3.250
10	0.260	0.542	0.879	1.093	1.372	1.812	2.228	2.764	3.169
11	0.260	0.540	0.876	1.088	1.363	1.796	2.201	2.718	3.106
12	0.259	0.539	0.873	1.083	1.356	1.782	2.179	2.681	3.055
13	0.259	0.538	0.870	1.079	1.350	1.771	2.160	2.650	3.012
14	0.258	0.537	0.868	1.076	1.345	1.761	2.145	2.624	2.977
15	0.258	0.536	0.866	1.074	1.341	1.753	2.131	2.602	2.947
16	0.258	0.535	0.865	1.071	1.337	1.746	2.120	2.583	2.921
17	0.257	0.534	0.863	1.069	1.333	1.740	2.110	2.567	2.898
18	0.257	0.534	0.862	1.067	1.330	1.734	2.101	2.552	2.878
19	0.257	0.533	0.861	1.066	1.328	1.729	2.093	2.539	2.861
20	0.257	0.533	0.860	1.064	1.325	1.725	2.086	2.528	2.845
21	0.257	0.532	0.859	1.063	1.323	1.721	2.080	2.518	2.831
22	0.256	0.532	0.858	1.061	1.321	1.717	2.074	2.508	2.819
23	0.256	0.532	0.858	1.060	1.319	1.714	2.069	2.500	2.807
24	0.256	0.531	0.857	1.059	1.318	1.711	2.064	2.492	2.797
25	0.256	0.531	0.856	1.058	1.316	1.708	2.060	2.485	2.787
26	0.256	0.531	0.856	1.058	1.315	1.706	2.056	2.479	2.779
27	0.256	0.531	0.855	1.057	1.314	1.703	2.052	2.473	2.771
28	0.256	0.530	0.855	1.056	1.313	1.701	2.048	2.467	2.763
29	0.256	0.530	0.854	1.055	1.311	1.699	2.045	2.462	2.756
30	0.256	0.530	0.854	1.055	1.310	1.697	2.042	2.457	2.750
40	0.255	0.529	0.851	1.050	1.303	1.684	2.021	2.423	2.704
50	0.255	0.528	0.849	1.047	1.299	1.676	2.009	2.403	2.678
∞	0.253	0.524	0.842	1.036	1.282	1.645	1.960	2.326	2.576

Notes:
1) The table shows the quantiles $t_p(d.f.)$. For example, to find the 0.7 quantile in the *t*-distribution with 5 degrees of freedom, $t_{0.7}(5)$, the "5" row is matched with the "0.70" column to give the result $t_{0.7}(5) = 0.559$.
2) The *t*-distribution is symmetric; thus, $t_{1-p}(d.f.) = -t_p(d.f.)$.

Table 4. The χ^2-distribution: quantiles

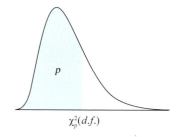

$\chi^2_p(d.f.)$

Degreees of freedom (d.f.)	p												
	0.01	0.025	0.05	0.10	0.20	0.30	0.50	0.70	0.80	0.90	0.95	0.975	0.99
1	0.000	0.001	0.004	0.016	0.064	0.148	0.455	1.074	1.642	2.706	3.841	5.024	6.635
2	0.020	0.051	0.103	0.211	0.446	0.713	1.386	2.408	3.219	4.605	5.991	7.378	9.210
3	0.115	0.216	0.352	0.584	1.005	1.424	2.366	3.665	4.642	6.251	7.815	9.348	11.345
4	0.297	0.484	0.711	1.064	1.649	2.195	3.357	4.878	5.989	7.779	9.488	11.143	13.277
5	0.554	0.831	1.145	1.610	2.343	3.000	4.351	6.064	7.289	9.236	11.070	12.833	15.086
6	0.872	1.237	1.635	2.204	3.070	3.828	5.348	7.231	8.558	10.645	12.592	14.449	16.812
7	1.239	1.690	2.167	2.833	3.822	4.671	6.346	8.383	9.803	12.017	14.067	16.013	18.475
8	1.646	2.180	2.733	3.490	4.594	5.527	7.344	9.524	11.030	13.362	15.507	17.535	20.090
9	2.088	2.700	3.325	4.168	5.380	6.393	8.343	10.656	12.242	14.684	16.919	19.023	21.666
10	2.558	3.247	3.940	4.865	6.179	7.267	9.342	11.781	13.442	15.987	18.307	20.483	23.209
11	3.053	3.816	4.575	5.578	6.989	8.148	10.341	12.899	14.631	17.275	19.675	21.920	24.725
12	3.571	4.404	5.226	6.304	7.807	9.034	11.340	14.011	15.812	18.549	21.026	23.337	26.217
13	4.107	5.009	5.892	7.042	8.634	9.926	12.340	15.119	16.985	19.812	22.362	24.736	27.688
14	4.660	5.629	6.571	7.790	9.467	10.821	13.339	16.222	18.151	21.064	23.685	26.119	29.141
15	5.229	6.262	7.261	8.547	10.307	11.721	14.339	17.322	19.311	22.307	24.996	27.488	30.578
16	5.812	6.908	7.962	9.312	11.152	12.624	15.338	18.418	20.465	23.542	26.296	28.845	32.000
17	6.408	7.564	8.672	10.085	12.002	13.531	16.338	19.511	21.615	24.769	27.587	30.191	33.409
18	7.015	8.231	9.390	10.865	12.857	14.440	17.338	20.601	22.760	25.989	28.869	31.526	34.805
19	7.633	8.907	10.117	11.651	13.716	15.352	18.338	21.689	23.900	27.204	30.144	32.852	36.191
20	8.260	9.591	10.851	12.443	14.578	16.266	19.337	22.775	25.038	28.412	31.410	34.170	37.566
21	8.897	10.283	11.591	13.240	15.445	17.182	20.337	23.858	26.171	29.615	32.671	35.479	38.932
22	9.542	10.982	12.338	14.041	16.314	18.101	21.337	24.939	27.301	30.813	33.924	36.781	40.289
23	10.196	11.689	13.091	14.848	17.187	19.021	22.337	26.018	28.429	32.007	35.172	38.076	41.638
24	10.856	12.401	13.848	15.659	18.062	19.943	23.337	27.096	29.553	33.196	36.415	39.364	42.980
25	11.524	13.120	14.611	16.473	18.940	20.867	24.337	28.172	30.675	34.382	37.652	40.646	44.314
26	12.198	13.844	15.379	17.292	19.820	21.792	25.336	29.246	31.795	35.563	38.885	41.923	45.642
27	12.879	14.573	16.151	18.114	20.703	22.719	26.336	30.319	32.912	36.741	40.113	43.195	46.963
28	13.565	15.308	16.928	18.939	21.588	23.647	27.336	31.391	34.027	37.916	41.337	44.461	48.278
29	14.256	16.047	17.708	19.768	22.475	24.577	28.336	32.461	35.139	39.087	42.557	45.722	49.588
30	14.953	16.791	18.493	20.599	23.364	25.508	29.336	33.530	36.250	40.256	43.773	46.979	50.892
40	22.164	24.433	26.509	29.051	32.345	34.872	39.335	44.165	47.269	51.805	55.758	59.342	63.691
50	29.707	32.357	34.764	37.689	41.449	44.313	49.335	54.723	58.164	63.167	67.505	71.420	76.154
60	37.485	40.482	43.188	46.459	50.641	53.809	59.335	65.227	68.972	74.397	79.082	83.298	88.379

Note:
The table shows the quantiles $\chi^2_p(d.f.)$. For example, to find the 0.2 quantile in the χ^2-distribution with 3 degrees of freedom, $\chi^2_{0.2}(3)$, the "3" row is matched with the "0.20" column to give the result $\chi^2_{0.2}(3) = 1.005$.

An insight into statistics for the social sciences

Table 5. The *F*-distribution: 0.95 quantiles

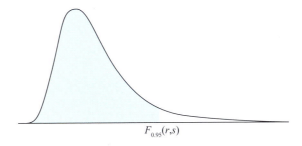

$$F_{0.95}(r,s)$$

d.f., s	d.f., r												
	1	2	3	4	5	6	8	10	12	15	20	24	30
1	161.45	199.50	215.71	224.58	230.16	233.99	238.88	241.88	243.91	245.95	248.01	249.05	250.10
2	18.51	19.00	19.16	19.25	19.30	19.33	19.37	19.40	19.41	19.43	19.45	19.45	19.46
3	10.13	9.55	9.28	9.12	9.01	8.94	8.85	8.79	8.74	8.70	8.66	8.64	8.62
4	7.71	6.94	6.59	6.39	6.26	6.16	6.04	5.96	5.91	5.86	5.80	5.77	5.75
5	6.61	5.79	5.41	5.19	5.05	4.95	4.82	4.74	4.68	4.62	4.56	4.53	4.50
6	5.99	5.14	4.76	4.53	4.39	4.28	4.15	4.06	4.00	3.94	3.87	3.84	3.81
7	5.59	4.74	4.35	4.12	3.97	3.87	3.73	3.64	3.57	3.51	3.44	3.41	3.38
8	5.32	4.46	4.07	3.84	3.69	3.58	3.44	3.35	3.28	3.22	3.15	3.12	3.08
9	5.12	4.26	3.86	3.63	3.48	3.37	3.23	3.14	3.07	3.01	2.94	2.90	2.86
10	4.96	4.10	3.71	3.48	3.33	3.22	3.07	2.98	2.91	2.85	2.77	2.74	2.70
11	4.84	3.98	3.59	3.36	3.20	3.09	2.95	2.85	2.79	2.72	2.65	2.61	2.57
12	4.75	3.89	3.49	3.26	3.11	3.00	2.85	2.75	2.69	2.62	2.54	2.51	2.47
13	4.67	3.81	3.41	3.18	3.03	2.92	2.77	2.67	2.60	2.53	2.46	2.42	2.38
14	4.60	3.74	3.34	3.11	2.96	2.85	2.70	2.60	2.53	2.46	2.39	2.35	2.31
15	4.54	3.68	3.29	3.06	2.90	2.79	2.64	2.54	2.48	2.40	2.33	2.29	2.25
16	4.49	3.63	3.24	3.01	2.85	2.74	2.59	2.49	2.42	2.35	2.28	2.24	2.19
17	4.45	3.59	3.20	2.96	2.81	2.70	2.55	2.45	2.38	2.31	2.23	2.19	2.15
18	4.41	3.55	3.16	2.93	2.77	2.66	2.51	2.41	2.34	2.27	2.19	2.15	2.11
19	4.38	3.52	3.13	2.90	2.74	2.63	2.48	2.38	2.31	2.23	2.16	2.11	2.07
20	4.35	3.49	3.10	2.87	2.71	2.60	2.45	2.35	2.28	2.20	2.12	2.08	2.04
21	4.32	3.47	3.07	2.84	2.68	2.57	2.42	2.32	2.25	2.18	2.10	2.05	2.01
22	4.30	3.44	3.05	2.82	2.66	2.55	2.40	2.30	2.23	2.15	2.07	2.03	1.98
23	4.28	3.42	3.03	2.80	2.64	2.53	2.37	2.27	2.20	2.13	2.05	2.01	1.96
24	4.26	3.40	3.01	2.78	2.62	2.51	2.36	2.25	2.18	2.11	2.03	1.98	1.94
25	4.24	3.39	2.99	2.76	2.60	2.49	2.34	2.24	2.16	2.09	2.01	1.96	1.92
30	4.17	3.32	2.92	2.69	2.53	2.42	2.27	2.16	2.09	2.01	1.93	1.89	1.84
40	4.08	3.23	2.84	2.61	2.45	2.34	2.18	2.08	2.00	1.92	1.84	1.79	1.74
60	4.00	3.15	2.76	2.53	2.37	2.25	2.10	1.99	1.92	1.84	1.75	1.70	1.65

Notes:
1) The table shows the 0.95 quantiles in the *F*-distribution with (r, s) degrees of freedom. For example, to find the 0.95 quantile in the *F*-distribution with $(4,3)$ degrees of freedom, the "3" row is matched with the "4" column to give the result $F_{0.95}(4,3) = 9.12$.
2) The 0.05 quantile in the *F*-distribution with (s, r) degrees of freedom are $F_{0.05}(s,r) = \dfrac{1}{F_{0.95}(r,s)}$. For example, the 0.05 quantile in the *F*-distribution with $(6,5)$ degrees of freedom are $F_{0.05}(6,5) = \dfrac{1}{F_{0.95}(5,6)} = \dfrac{1}{4.39} = 0.23$.

Table 6. The F-distribution: 0.975 quantiles

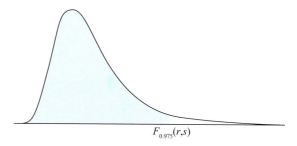

$F_{0.975}(r,s)$

d.f., s	d.f., r												
	1	2	3	4	5	6	8	10	12	15	20	24	30
1	647.79	799.50	864.16	899.58	921.85	937.11	956.66	968.63	976.71	984.87	993.10	997.25	1001.41
2	38.51	39.00	39.17	39.25	39.30	39.33	39.37	39.40	39.41	39.43	39.45	39.46	39.46
3	17.44	16.04	15.44	15.10	14.88	14.73	14.54	14.42	14.34	14.25	14.17	14.12	14.08
4	12.22	10.65	9.98	9.60	9.36	9.20	8.98	8.84	8.75	8.66	8.56	8.51	8.46
5	10.01	8.43	7.76	7.39	7.15	6.98	6.76	6.62	6.52	6.43	6.33	6.28	6.23
6	8.81	7.26	6.60	6.23	5.99	5.82	5.60	5.46	5.37	5.27	5.17	5.12	5.07
7	8.07	6.54	5.89	5.52	5.29	5.12	4.90	4.76	4.67	4.57	4.47	4.41	4.36
8	7.57	6.06	5.42	5.05	4.82	4.65	4.43	4.30	4.20	4.10	4.00	3.95	3.89
9	7.21	5.71	5.08	4.72	4.48	4.32	4.10	3.96	3.87	3.77	3.67	3.61	3.56
10	6.94	5.46	4.83	4.47	4.24	4.07	3.85	3.72	3.62	3.52	3.42	3.37	3.31
11	6.72	5.26	4.63	4.28	4.04	3.88	3.66	3.53	3.43	3.33	3.23	3.17	3.12
12	6.55	5.10	4.47	4.12	3.89	3.73	3.51	3.37	3.28	3.18	3.07	3.02	2.96
13	6.41	4.97	4.35	4.00	3.77	3.60	3.39	3.25	3.15	3.05	2.95	2.89	2.84
14	6.30	4.86	4.24	3.89	3.66	3.50	3.29	3.15	3.05	2.95	2.84	2.79	2.73
15	6.20	4.77	4.15	3.80	3.58	3.41	3.20	3.06	2.96	2.86	2.76	2.70	2.64
16	6.12	4.69	4.08	3.73	3.50	3.34	3.12	2.99	2.89	2.79	2.68	2.63	2.57
17	6.04	4.62	4.01	3.66	3.44	3.28	3.06	2.92	2.82	2.72	2.62	2.56	2.50
18	5.98	4.56	3.95	3.61	3.38	3.22	3.01	2.87	2.77	2.67	2.56	2.50	2.44
19	5.92	4.51	3.90	3.56	3.33	3.17	2.96	2.82	2.72	2.62	2.51	2.45	2.39
20	5.87	4.46	3.86	3.51	3.29	3.13	2.91	2.77	2.68	2.57	2.46	2.41	2.35
21	5.83	4.42	3.82	3.48	3.25	3.09	2.87	2.73	2.64	2.53	2.42	2.37	2.31
22	5.79	4.38	3.78	3.44	3.22	3.05	2.84	2.70	2.60	2.50	2.39	2.33	2.27
23	5.75	4.35	3.75	3.41	3.18	3.02	2.81	2.67	2.57	2.47	2.36	2.30	2.24
24	5.72	4.32	3.72	3.38	3.15	2.99	2.78	2.64	2.54	2.44	2.33	2.27	2.21
25	5.69	4.29	3.69	3.35	3.13	2.97	2.75	2.61	2.51	2.41	2.30	2.24	2.18
30	5.57	4.18	3.59	3.25	3.03	2.87	2.65	2.51	2.41	2.31	2.20	2.14	2.07
40	5.42	4.05	3.46	3.13	2.90	2.74	2.53	2.39	2.29	2.18	2.07	2.01	1.94
60	5.29	3.93	3.34	3.01	2.79	2.63	2.41	2.27	2.17	2.06	1.94	1.88	1.82

Notes:

1) The table shows 0.975 quantiles in the F-distribution with (r, s) degrees of freedom (d.f.). For example, to find the 0.975 quantile in the F-distribution with (4,3) degrees of freedom, the "3" row is matched with the "4" column to give the result $F_{0.975}(4,3) = 15.10$.

2) The 0.025 quantile in the F-distribution with (s, r) degrees of freedom are $F_{0.025}(s,r) = \dfrac{1}{F_{0.975}(r,s)}$. For example, the

0.025 quantile in the F-distribution with (6,5) degrees of freedom are $F_{0.025}(6,5) = \dfrac{1}{F_{0.975}(5,6)} = \dfrac{1}{5.99} = 0.17$.

An insight into statistics for the social sciences

Index

standard error 408, 435
standardisation 156
standard normal distribution 155
state distribution 172
statistics 21
stochastic process 168
stochastic process, incident 169
stochastic process, discrete
    time 168
stochastic process, contin-
    uous time 168
stochastic process, realisa-
    tion 168
stratified sample averages 249
stratification 210, 245
stratification without re-
    placement 258
stratum sample size 254
super population 50

T
target population 206
test statistic 315, 324
t-distribution 285
time series 413
treatment 349
type-I error 312
type-II error 312

U
unbiased 236
uncertainty 17, 19
union of events 57
unrestricted model 441

V
validity 211
variable, dependent 397
variable, explained 397
variable, explanatory 397
variable, independent 397
variable, random 77, 169
variance 40, 108, 115
variance analysis 361
variance, continuous ran-
    dom variable 118
variance, discrete stochas-
    tic variable 115
variance, rules for calculat-
    ing 117, 118
variance, sum of random
    variables 131

W
waiting-time distribution 174
Wiener process 190